Transnational
Russian Studies

Transnational Modern Languages

Transnational Modern Languages promotes a model of Modern Languages not as the inquiry into separate national traditions, but as the study of languages, cultures and their interactions. The series aims to demonstrate the value – practical and commercial, as well as academic and cultural – of modern language study when conceived as transnational cultural enquiry.

The texts in the series are specifically targeted at a student audience. They address how work on the transnational and the transcultural broadens the confines of Modern Languages; opens an extensive range of objects of research to analysis; deploys a complex set of methodologies; and can be accomplished through the exposition of clearly articulated examples.

The series is anchored by *Transnational Modern Languages: A Handbook*, ed. Jenny Burns (Warwick) and Derek Duncan (St. Andrews), which sets out the theoretical and conceptual scope of the series, the type of research on which it is based and the kinds of questions that it asks. Following on from the *Handbook*, the series includes a text for the study of the following Modern Languages:

Transnational French Studies, ed. Charles Forsdick (Liverpool) and Claire Launchbury (Leeds)

Transnational German Studies, ed. Rebecca Braun (Lancaster) and Ben Schofield (KCL)

Transnational Spanish Studies, ed. Catherine Davies (IMLR) and Rory O'Bryen (Cambridge)

Transnational Italian Studies, ed. Charles Burdett (Durham), Loredana Polezzi (Cardiff) and Marco Santello (Leeds)

Transnational Portuguese Studies, ed. Hilary Owen (Manchester/Oxford) and Claire Williams (Oxford)

Transnational Russian Studies, ed. Andy Byford (Durham), Connor Doak (Bristol) and Stephen Hutchings (Manchester)

Transnational Russian Studies

edited by
Andy Byford, Connor Doak,
and Stephen Hutchings

LIVERPOOL UNIVERSITY PRESS

First published 2020 by
Liverpool University Press
4 Cambridge Street
Liverpool
L69 7ZU

British Library Cataloguing-in-Publication data
A British Library CIP record is available

ISBN 978-1-78962-087-0 (HB)
ISBN 978-1-78962-088-7 (PB)

Typeset by Carnegie Book Production, Lancaster
Printed in the UK by CPI Group (UK) Ltd, Croydon CR0 4YY

Contents

Part II.   Beyond and Between Languages

Part III.   Cultures Crossing Borders

Part IV. Russia Going Global

Figures and Tables

The cover image is a reproduction of Nadezhda Udal'tsova's painting *Still Life* [Natiurmort], oil on canvas, 67 cm x 89 cm (1914–15). It is reproduced with the permission of The State Russian Museum, St Petersburg.

Acknowledgements

This book forms part of the Transnational Modern Languages series by Liverpool University Press, edited by Charles Burdett, Jenny Burns, Derek Duncan, and Loredana Polezzi. During the preparation of this volume, we met regularly with the series editors, as well as the editors of the other volumes. These meetings provided an opportunity for an energizing dialogue across modern languages, which helped shape this book.

Funding in support of this project came from the UK's Arts and Humanities Research Council (AHRC). The volume was produced in the context of the Cross-Language Dynamics: Reshaping Community programme of research, one of the four multi-institutional consortia contributing to the AHRC's Open World Research Initiative (OWRI; 2016–20; grant number: AH/N004647/1), the aim of which is to promote the distinctive value of modern languages research and to help regenerate the study of modern languages in the UK. Preparations for the volume included the symposium 'Transnational Russian Studies', which took place in Durham on 14–16 September 2017. Our thanks go to all those who took part in and contributed to this event both intellectually and organizationally.

Our administrative assistant, Oliver Taslic, provided logistical support with the final stages of compiling the manuscript. The University of Bristol generously provided additional funding to support his work. We would also like to thank the staff at Liverpool University Press, especially Anthony Cond and Chloe Johnson, for commissioning this book, guiding it through review, and for helping with the production. Finally, our thanks also go to the two anonymous scholars who reviewed the manuscript on behalf of the press for their generous remarks and valuable suggestions for improvement.

Contributors

Marijeta Bozovic is Assistant Professor of Slavic Languages and Literatures, affiliated with Film and Media Studies and Women's, Gender, and Sexuality Studies at Yale University. A specialist in twentieth- and twenty-first-century Russian and East European cultures with broad comparative interests, she is the author of *Nabokov's Canon: From Onegin to Ada* (Northwestern University Press, 2016) and co-editor of *Watersheds: Poetics and Politics of the Danube River* (Academic Studies Press, 2016, with Matthew D. Miller) and *Nabokov Upside Down* (Northwestern University Press, 2017, with Brian Boyd). She is currently working on her second monograph, *Avant-Garde Post-: Radical Poetics after the Soviet Union*.

Andy Byford is Professor of Russian at Durham University. He has published on the history of Russian humanities scholarship, human sciences, and professions, as well as on the contemporary Russian-speaking diaspora in the UK. He is the author of *Literary Scholarship in Late Imperial Russia: Rituals of Academic Institutionalization* (Legenda, 2007) and *Science of the Child in Late Imperial and Early Soviet Russia* (Oxford University Press, 2020).

Philip Ross Bullock is Professor of Russian Literature and Music at the University of Oxford, and Fellow and Tutor in Russian at Wadham College. He has published widely on various aspects of Russian culture from the eighteenth century to the present and has a particular interest in the reception of Russian culture abroad. His most recent book is *Pyotr Tchaikovsky* (Reaktion, 2016).

Julie Curtis is Professor of Russian Literature and Fellow of Wolfson College, University of Oxford. Much of her published research has concerned writers of the early Stalin years, especially Mikhail Bulgakov and Evgenii Zamiatin. She also teaches a specialist option on Russian drama and has in recent years been pursuing research into Russian-language drama in the Putin era, including the ways in which it has developed in Ukraine and Belarus as well as Russia since the year 2000. Her research into contemporary Russian drama is funded by the AHRC under two of its OWRI projects, based in Oxford and in Manchester. She is the editor of the volume *New Drama in Russian: Performance, Politics and Protest* (Bloomsbury, 2020).

Amelia M. Glaser is Associate Professor of Russian and Comparative Literature at the University of California, San Diego, where she teaches courses in Russian literature, Jewish literature, literary theory, and translation studies. She is the author of *Jews and Ukrainians in Russia's Literary Borderlands* (Northwestern University Press, 2012) and the editor of *Stories of Khmelnytsky: Competing Literary Legacies of the 1648 Ukrainian Cossack Uprising* (Stanford University Press, 2015). She is also the co-editor of *Comintern Aesthetics* (University of Toronto Press, 2020, with Steven S. Lee). She is currently working on a study of internationalist Yiddish poetry in the 1930s.

Connor Doak is Lecturer in Russian at the University of Bristol. He works primarily on nineteenth- and twentieth-century Russian literature and culture, with a special interest in gender and sexuality and their representation in literary texts. He is currently working on a monograph exploring how the poet Vladimir Maiakovskii uses verse to negotiate the shifting terrain of masculinity in revolutionary Russia and the early Soviet period. He has also published on fatherhood in Chekhov's stories and how queer theory can elucidate Dostoevskii's novels.

Tatiana Filimonova is Assistant Professor in Russian Studies at the College of Wooster, Ohio. Her research focuses on contemporary Russian literature and its interactions with political, social, and ideological changes in Russian society after the fall of the Soviet Union. She has published on Eurasianism in contemporary Russian fiction, including in the prose of Vladimir Sorokin, and Pavel Krusanov. She has also examined contemporary Russian and Siberian identity in documentary film and the prose of Mikhail Tarkovskii.

Michael Gorham is Professor of Russian Studies at the University of Florida. He is the author of two award-winning books on language culture and politics: *After Newspeak: Language Culture and Politics in Russia from Gorbachev to Putin* (Cornell University Press, 2014) and *Speaking in Soviet Tongues: Language Culture and the Politics of Voice in Revolutionary Russia*

(Northern Illinois University Press, 2003). He has recently published two co-edited works, *Digital Russia: The Language, Culture, and Politics of New Media Communication* (Routledge, 2014, with Ingunn Lunde and Martin Paulsen) and a special issue of *Zeitschrift für Slavische Philologie* (72:2–73:1, 2017) dedicated to 'The Culture and Politics of Verbal Prohibition in Putin's Russia', as well as articles devoted to the political and rhetorical impact of trolls, hackers, blogging bureaucrats, tweeting presidents, dictators on Instagram, and the institutional forces attempting to reign them in.

Stephen Hutchings is Professor of Russian Studies at the University of Manchester. He has published widely on Russian literature, culture, media, and film. His most recent books are *Nation, Ethnicity and Race on Russian Television: Mediating Post-Soviet Difference* (Routledge, 2015, with Vera Tolz) and *Projecting Russia in a Mediatized World: Recursive Nationhood* (Routledge, forthcoming). Stephen is Associate Editor of *Russian Journal of Communication* and he is currently Principal Investigator on two large grant projects: 'Reframing Russia for the Global Mediasphere' and 'Cross-Language Dynamics: Reshaping Community'.

Jeanne-Marie Jackson is Assistant Professor of World Anglophone Literature at Johns Hopkins University, having received her PhD in Comparative Literature from Yale. Her first book is *South African Literature's Russian Soul: Narrative Forms of Global Isolation* (Bloomsbury, 2015). Her second, *The African Novel of Ideas*, is forthcoming with Princeton University Press.

Cathy McAteer is the postdoctoral research fellow on the project 'The Dark Side of Translation: 20th and 21st Century Translation from Russian as a Political Phenomenon in the UK, Ireland, and the USA' at the University of Exeter. She holds a PhD in Russian from the University of Bristol, where she has also taught Russian-English translation for the MA Translation Studies programme. Her main research interests are in the field of classic Russian literature in English translation during the twentieth century, using archival material to shed new light on historical commissions.

Olga Maiorova is Associate Professor of Russian Literature and History at the University of Michigan. She specializes in the intersections between literature, intellectual history, and representations of nationality, especially in the context of Imperial Russia. She is the author of *From the Shadow of Empire: Defining the Russian Nation through Cultural Mythology, 1855–1870* (University of Wisconsin Press, 2010) and numerous articles on Russian literature and cultural history. She has edited several books, including

Dostoevsky in Context (Cambridge University Press, 2016, with Deborah Martinsen) and a two-volume edition in Russian of previously unpublished works by the writer Nikolai Leskov (with Kseniia Bogaevskaia and Lia Rosenblium). She is currently writing a monograph on literary and visual representations of Central Asia in Imperial Russia.

Stephen M. Norris is the Walter E. Havighurst Professor of Russian History and the Director of the Havighurst Center for Russian and Post-Soviet Studies at Miami University (Oxford, Ohio). He is the author of two books on Russian cultural history, *A War of Images: Russian Popular Prints, Wartime Culture, and National Identity, 1812–1945* (Northern Illinois University Press, 2006) and *Blockbuster History in the New Russia: Movies, Memory, Patriotism* (Indiana University Press, 2012). He has edited or co-edited five volumes, including *The City in Russian Culture* (Routledge, 2018, with Pavel Lyssakov) and *Museums of Communism: New Memory Sites in Central and Eastern Europe* (Indiana University Press, forthcoming). At present he is researching and writing a biography of Boris Efimov, the Soviet political caricaturist.

Vitaly Nuriev is Leading Researcher at the Federal Research Center 'Computer Science and Control', Russian Academy of Sciences. His primary research interests lie in literary translation. He has published on various aspects of literary and machine translation, corpus linguistics, and theories of knowledge creation. His current focus is on the role and influence of literary translation in contemporary Russia. He also translates from French and English. In 2017, his translation of Neil Gaiman's *The Ocean at the End of the Lane* was nominated for the Iasnaia Poliana Prize.

Dušan Radunović is Associate Professor in the School of Modern Languages and Cultures, Durham University, where he teaches Russian cinema, visual studies, and social and cultural history. His publications include a monograph on Mikhail Bakhtin (in Serbian), the co-edited volume *Language, Ideology, and the Human: New Interventions* (Routledge, 2012, with Sanja Bahun), and a forthcoming monograph on the genesis of the concept of form in the Russian humanities of the late imperial and early Soviet years. As part of the AHRC-funded cross-institutional project 'Cross-Language Dynamics: Reshaping Community', he investigates manifestations of transnationalism on the Soviet and post-Soviet screen. In addition to this, he works on 1920s' Georgian cinema in its intersection with early-Soviet art practices and the politics of national emancipation.

Ellen Rutten is Professor of Literature and Chair of the Department of Russian and Slavic Studies at the University of Amsterdam. Her research interests include post-Soviet and global contemporary literature, art, design, and social media. She is the author of *Unattainable Bride Russia: Gendering Nation, State, and Intelligentsia in Russian Intellectual Culture* (Northwestern University Press, 2010) and *Sincerity after Communism: A Cultural History* (Yale University Press, 2017), among other publications. She leads the research project 'Sublime Imperfections: Creative Interventions in Post-1989 Europe' (University of Amsterdam, 2015–20) and is editor-in-chief of the journal *Russian Literature*.

Lara Ryazanova-Clarke is Professor of Russian and Sociolinguistics and Director of the Princess Dashkova Russian Research Centre at the University of Edinburgh. Her main publications include *The Russian Language Today* (Routledge, 1999, with Terence Wade), *The Russian Language Outside the Nation*, *The Vernaculars of Communism: Language, Ideology and Power in the Soviet Union and Eastern Europe* (Routledge, 2014, with Petre Petrov), the two-volume *French and Russian in Imperial Russia* (Edinburgh University Press, 2015, with Derek Offord, Vladislav Rjéoutski, and Gesine Argent), and a special issue of *International Journal of Bilingualism and Bilingual Education* on the 'Commodification of Russian' (2017, with Sebastian Muth). She is Series Editor of the Russian Language and Society book series at Edinburgh University Press.

Vlad Strukov is Associate Professor in Film and Digital Culture at the University of Leeds. His work explores theories of empire and nationhood, global journalism and grass-roots media, consumption and celebrity by considering the Russian Federation and the Russian-speaking world as his case study. Recent publications include *Contemporary Russian Cinema: Symbols of a New Era* (Edinburgh University Press, 2016), *Russian Culture in the Era of Globalisation* (Routledge, 2018), *Memory and Securitization in Contemporary Europe* (Palgrave, 2018), and *Popular Geopolitics: Plotting an Evolving Interdiscipline* (Routledge, 2018). He is also an independent art and film curator. He makes regular appearances in international media such as Al Jazeera, American Public Radio, BBC, and RBK.

Galin Tihanov is the George Steiner Professor of Comparative Literature at Queen Mary University of London. He has held visiting appointments at Yale University, St Gallen University, the University of Sao Paulo, Peking University, Seoul National University, and the Higher School of Economics in

Moscow. He has published widely on German, Russian, and East European cultural and intellectual history; his current research is on world literature, cosmopolitanism, and exile. His latest book is *The Birth and Death of Literary Theory: Regimes of Relevance in Russia and Beyond* (Stanford University Press, 2019). He is currently writing *Cosmopolitanism: A Very Short Introduction* for Oxford University Press.

Vera Tolz is Sir William Mather Professor of Russian Studies at the University of Manchester. She has published widely on various aspects of Russian nationalism, identity politics, and the relationship between intellectuals and the state in the imperial and Soviet periods. Her most recent books are *Nation, Ethnicity and Race on Russian Television: Mediating Post-Soviet Difference* (Routledge, 2015, with Stephen Hutchings), and *'Russia's Own Orient': The Politics of Identity and Oriental Studies in the Late Imperial and Early Soviet Periods* (Oxford University Press, 2011). She is currently involved in 'Reframing Russia for the Global Mediasphere', a collaborative research project on the broadcasting and audience engagement strategies of RT (formerly Russia Today).

Sergey Tyulenev is Associate Professor and Director of the MA in Translation Studies at the School of Modern Languages and Cultures, Durham University. He has published widely on linguistic, cultural, and social aspects of translation, translation historiography, and the epistemology of translation studies. His publications include *Applying Luhmann to Translation Studies* (Routledge, 2012), *Translation and the Westernization of Eighteenth-Century Russia: Translation and Society* (Frank & Timme, 2012), and *Translation in the Public Sphere* (Palgrave, 2018).

Introduction

Transnationalizing Russian Studies

Andy Byford, Connor Doak, and Stephen Hutchings

Framing Russian Studies

What does it mean to embark on a degree in Russian?[1] At one level, the answer is obvious: Russianists should aspire to proficiency in the Russian language as well as a deep understanding of Russian culture and society. On further inspection, though, this answer throws up a whole new set of questions. The term 'Russian' is not as self-explanatory as it may first seem. The Russian Federation – like the Soviet Union and the Russian Empire before it – is a multi-ethnic country with over 100 minority languages and cultures, dozens of which have official status in specific republics within Russia. Russian communities and cultural producers are to be found across the world, in locales as diverse as Riga, Tel Aviv, and Brighton Beach. That which we call Russian culture is co-produced and reproduced, consumed and reinvented across the globe, in different languages of the world and by agents with or without connections to Russia itself.

---

[1] As befits a volume on the transnational, we recognize that there is some significant variation of academic cultures and structures across different countries, including those that would form part of the Anglophone world. While Russianists in, say, the UK, the USA, and Australia will largely acquire the same set of knowledge and skills on a degree, they will not necessarily do so within the same kind of institutional framework. We cannot in the discussion that follows do justice to all the different institutional configurations in our field. Our analysis often starts from the British context, as all three editors, as well as the press, are UK-based. However, we try to acknowledge the differences with other contexts where appropriate, particularly the USA, which is the largest centre for Russian studies outside Russia.

1

Russians themselves have two different words for 'Russian' – *russkii* and *rossiiskii*. *Russkii* is the term used to refer to the Russian language [russkii iazyk].[2] It refers also to the East Slavic ethnocultural group associated with that language. It is similarly the term used to designate literature in that language [russkaia literatura]. *Rossiiskii*, by contrast, means, roughly, 'pertaining to the Russian Federation'. It is the word found in the names of federal institutions and documents; citizens talk of carrying a *rossiiskii*, not a *russkii* passport. The associated term *rossiiane*, used to refer to citizens of the Russian Federation, is a more inclusive, civic designation that encompasses the full diversity of ethnic groups within the world's largest country, all of whom have their own languages, from the Chechens in the Caucasus to the Buryats in southern Siberia and the Yakuts in the far north, to name but a few.[3] Also worthy of mention is a third term, *russkoiazychnyi*, 'Russophone'. This label unites speakers of the Russian language, irrespective of citizenship and nationality, whether they reside in the former Soviet republics (many of which – such as Kazakhstan or Latvia – maintain substantial Russian-speaking communities) or further afield, in all the corners of the globe that the Russian (or indeed Russian-speaking) diaspora has reached. Finally, much of the culture that was produced in the Russian language during the Soviet era (1917–91) tends to be labelled 'Soviet' rather than 'Russian'. This is especially true for certain domains of cultural production, such as, for example, cinema.

Clearly, therefore, students of Russian cannot afford a static and unitary conception of Russia as a discrete nation with a singular language, culture, and history. As we shall argue in this introduction, it is vital for anyone who identifies with Russian studies, whether as scholar or student, to engage in a systematic and critical reflection of the various ways in which 'Russia' and 'Russian culture' have been historically framed and defined. What we see as particularly important here is the avoidance of potential methodological

---

[2] The first published Russian grammar, produced by the eighteenth-century polymath Mikhail Lomonosov, was, however, titled *Rossiiskaia gramatika* (1755), the term *rossiiskii* signalling that this was a grammar of the language of the Russian imperium, which was not ethno-dialectically uniform.

[3] In the sixteenth century, though, when the term *rossiane* first appeared, it referred to a both ethnically and territorially blurred larger body of Eastern Slavic peoples, in the context of the incorporation into Muscovy of lands on its western fringes which used to be part of Kievan Rus. It was only in the 1990s, under Boris El'tsin, that the term *rossiane* acquired its current meaning of citizens of a multi-ethnic Russian Federation, although related usage had arisen earlier, in the Russian post-1917 emigration, when it was used to imagine a new, still multi-ethnic, Russian state that would replace the Soviet Union (see Grishchenko 2012).

blind spots associated with so-called 'methodological nationalism' (Wimmer & Glick Schiller 2002, 2003). To counter such pitfalls, we propose a transnational approach to Russian studies. This, crucially, does not mean applying some general theory of the transnational to all things 'Russian'. Rather, what we are seeking to stimulate in the remaining sections of this introduction is an interrogation of how the distinctive history of nation-making, empire-building, and diasporization that has shaped our field's object of study also shapes how Russian studies is 'done'. The key consequence of this is that Russian studies must forge *its own* path out of such methodological impasses. This, we argue at the end of this introduction, also includes using the unique resources and expertise developed within Russian studies itself to account for what 'the transnational' might look like from a 'Russian' vantage point. It means taking seriously the fact that the 'object' that Russian studies engages with is also always, inevitably, a subject in its own right.

Russian studies has never been blindly 'nationalist', and certainly not simplistically so. The history of the Russian state and society makes it difficult to conceptualize things 'Russian' in conventionally national terms. Programmes in Russian have, in fact, historically been more inclined than programmes in some other languages to extend beyond the national paradigm otherwise typical of modern languages and to instead conceive of Russian studies as closer to a form of area studies, a discipline rooted in a broadly imperial paradigm.[4] This has led not only to greater readiness among Russianists to teach culture that is not strictly speaking 'Russian' (e.g. cinema produced in non-Russian parts of the former Soviet Union) but also to go beyond the study of cultural production per se and incorporate into Russian studies programmes approaches that are less typical of modern languages. Indeed, Russian programmes have not only followed other modern languages in moving away from an exclusive focus on language and literature to one that embraces the study of film, theatre, visual culture, and the media but they are also often more open to incorporating elements from history, politics, sociology, international relations, or anthropology.[5]

---

[4] This, of course, is the case also with some other languages, such as Arabic or Spanish.

[5] In France, programmes in 'la civilization russe' offer a not dissimilar framework that is open to a wide variety of disciplinary approaches to the study of Russian culture and society. Whatever the country, different institutions will offer differently inflected programmes, depending on the research specialization of the faculty (although staff will, of course, invariably teach topics outside their research interests). While disciplinary versatility is often to the field's advantage, the diversity of methodologies and approaches can also at times make it challenging for both researchers and students to maintain a common sense of purpose and a shared disciplinary language.

Historically, the study of Russian has in fact been embedded in a variety of frameworks and these have often coexisted, intermixed, and overlapped. The oldest framework, dating back to the nineteenth century, positions the study of Russian language and culture in the context of the study of the wider group of Slavonic languages, alongside the parallel Romance and Germanic groups. This framework, rooted in Indo-European philology, has during the twentieth century and especially in the context of the Cold War been juxtaposed with an alternative, geopolitical, one, where the study of Russian is envisaged as part of the study of the Soviet-dominated, and for the most part Slavic, eastern Europe on the other side of the Iron Curtain. In other words, the study of Russian came thereby to be positioned comfortably and conveniently across both a philological and an area studies framework, insofar as these happened to broadly coincide. This framework has thrived under the 'Russian and Slavonic studies' or 'Russian and East European studies' labels. Since the collapse of the Soviet Union, this framework often also includes the term 'Eurasian' as a way of incorporating research on non-Slavic, 'Asian' parts of the former Soviet area. Needless to say, these terms remain politically problematic in that in different ways they perpetuate and naturalize notions of Russian hegemony in eastern Europe and former Soviet Eurasia. On the other hand, they also show that 'Russian studies' has always been embedded in a transnational, and this often means tacitly imperial, dimension. Within these larger frameworks, the study of specifically Russian language and culture has existed both as a programme in its own right and as a contributor to a more interdisciplinary (but generally social and political science-dominated) study of said geopolitical area.

At the same time, however, over the course of the twentieth century, the Indo-European framework, which embeds languages, as well as their study, within larger language families, gave way to a very different, broadly 'national', principle of organizing the study of modern languages. According to this principle, which rose to prominence from the First World War onwards, each language acquires a *nation-like* autonomous status within an overarching 'international' of modern languages. This new framework, however, has led to the gradual marginalization of 'smaller' languages, with some, such as Czech, Polish, or Serbo-Croat, increasingly taught only as subsidiary subjects, often withering away as 'non-viable'. By contrast, this framework rewarded a set of 'larger' languages with relatively stable institutional (i.e. departmental) autonomy. Within this framework, which came to dominate modern languages during the twentieth century and survives to the present day, the study of Russian language and culture came to be modelled as essentially equivalent in form and status to the study of French, German, Spanish, and Italian language and culture, which are seen as representing the 'core' modern languages. Within this select group, Russian is, in terms of student and staff numbers, invariably one of the smaller units. However, it also tends to position itself as a rather more unusual and exotic member, often looking to punch above its weight, and is bolstered in this by Russia's enduring geopolitical and cultural significance on the world stage.

Most recently, though, the normally separate, parallel programmes of study in the respective 'core' languages are being steadily driven closer together and urged to integrate at a deeper level. Efforts to maximize administrative efficiency have at most UK universities led to the disappearance of autonomous language departments as such, prompting harmonization across different language programmes and their ever-greater integration within an overarching modern languages structure.[6] Such a shift is also being promoted and justified on pedagogical grounds, with a push from some quarters for modern languages to 'move with the times' and break out of the mould that structures the study of each language and culture as a separate programme. Academics in modern languages are now increasingly encouraged to create courses that enable students to study languages, cultures, and societies not in isolation but as part of a dynamic, multilingual, and transcultural, global whole. The latter approach remains, however, in tension with the continuing need for modern languages to build, maintain, and strengthen expertise in a *specific* language, culture, community, and geopolitical area. This tension can emerge especially at the level of implementation, since courses that cut across different languages and promote a global vision of culture can sometimes be introduced not as supplements to but at the expense of courses that offer a more detailed and in-depth – indeed 'thick', as developed by Geertz (1973) – understanding of one particular language, culture, and society.

So how does one go about trying to reconcile these seemingly opposing demands? The Transnational Modern Languages (TML) series, of which this volume is a part, intends to resolve precisely some of the above dilemmas (see Burns & Duncan forthcoming). The TML project posits that language, society, and culture are not isomorphic – that is, they do not neatly coincide – but form complex constellations in which it is not straightforward to predict where the boundaries defining a given language or culture might lie, who

---

[6] In the USA, individual languages have tended to retain their departmental identity and autonomy, although smaller departments are sometimes fused into a joint unit, as has notably happened to German and Russian at some institutions.

might be laying these boundaries, how, and why.[7] What the transnational approach to the study of languages and cultures emphasizes instead is that language and culture must be conceptualized as flows of signification across boundaries. However, what one must continue to bear in mind is that, in the modern era, the boundaries of language and culture (not least as objects studied by modern languages), are still dominantly constructed in broadly 'national' terms, meaning that it remains essential to take into account the dynamics of nation construction and deconstruction, historically and politically contingent as they might be, when studying the life of languages and cultures, as well as the life of communities that are defined as bearers of particular languages and cultures.

Thus, on the one hand, the transnational approach resists eliding, sidelining, or ignoring ongoing 'boundary-work' (see Gieryn 1983) on which the existence of languages and cultures depends, but instead historicizes and deconstructs the social construction of languages and cultures. On the other, it shows that the *study* of languages and cultures should not itself reproduce these boundaries and merely repeat this same boundary-work; rather, as modes of signification, as means of encoding and decoding meaning, languages and cultures are never to be studied as matching the socially constructed boundaries hardwiring languages and cultures to communities that are being identified with them precisely through said boundary-work. In other words, the transnational approach seeks to account, simultaneously, for two equally important parallel processes on which language and culture as phenomena depend – the ongoing complex and diverse construction of 'the national' through particular forms of boundary-making that goes on around languages and cultures, and the continuous parallel processes of crossing or transgressing, relativizing or reconfiguring, breaching or transcending the boundaries thus constructed.

The transnational thereby helps us to navigate between the Scylla of essentialism (e.g. in the case of Russian studies, the fetishization of Russianness as

---

[7] Our own understanding of the transnational more generally draws on scholarship in a number of fields, including the social anthropologist Ulf Hannerz's influential *Transnational Connections* (1996), Steven Vertovec's *Transnationalism* (2009), and Sanjeev Khagram and Peggy Levitt's edited volume *Transnational Studies Reader* (2008). An ongoing 'transnational turn' has been under way in historical studies since the 1990s. See, *inter alia*, Tyrrell (2007), Iriye (2013), Saunier (2013). Thus far, the term 'transnational' has been embraced more eagerly in the social sciences and in history than in, say, literary studies, where the concept of 'world literature' has taken root, for example in the work of Casanova (2004) and Damrosch (2003). However, Paul Jay's *Global Matters: The Transnational Turn in Literary Studies* (2010) makes the case specifically for the 'transnational', as does John Burt Foster Jr.'s *Transnational Tolstoy* (2013), the latter specifically in a Russian context.

a fixed identity) and the Charybdis of globalism (such as postulates that the linguistic and cultural specificity of things 'Russian' are sheer ephemera in a highly globalized world). Thus, it is critical to the transnational approach not only to aim to avert tacit essentializations of nationally circumscribed cultures, but also to avoid falling victim to the complementary risk of turning all cultural flows into a single all-subsuming global process. In this the TML project follows Ulf Hannerz's understanding of the term 'transnational' as 'more humble' than the term 'global', as an often 'more adequate label for phenomena which can be of quite variable scale and distribution, even when they do share the characteristic of not being contained within a state' (1996: 6). In fact, as Ian Tyrrell has argued, the 'transnational' is paradoxically 'broader' (as well as, in Hannerz's terms, 'humbler') than the 'deterministic and unidirectional juggernaut of globalisation' (2007).

While the 'transnational' must be contrasted with the 'global', it must also be distinguished from the 'international'. While the term 'international' emphasizes the role of *states* as corporate actors, 'In the transnational arena, the actors may [...] be individuals, groups, movements, business enterprises', and so forth (Hannerz 1996: 6). As John Burt Foster puts it: 'If "inter" assumed orderly, almost diplomatic processes of give-and-take among well-defined units, "trans" poses a less regulated, even unpredictably creative surge of forces across borders that no longer seem as firmly established' (2013: 2). Yet, as Hannerz himself points out, 'there is a certain irony in the tendency of the term transnational to draw attention to what it negates – that is, to the continued significance of the national' (1996: 6). This is inherent in the ambiguities of the Latin prefix *trans-* itself, which designates not just a movement across, but also a gesturing beyond.

When applied specifically to the study of modern languages, the transnational approach is to be seen as a response to a major reproach addressed at modern languages as a field – namely, the criticism that the way we approach our subject area almost inevitably leads to the pitfalls of what has been described as 'methodological nationalism' – an epistemological stance which *naturalizes* the division of humanity in broadly 'national' terms (Wimmer & Glick Schiller 2002, 2003). Crucially, this critique must be understood as fundamentally epistemological in kind – a critique of the *underlying assumptions of scholarship*, not an empirical claim about the relevance or irrelevance of nations in the contemporary globalized world.[8]

---

[8] Of course, 'methodological nationalism' is hardly a problem only for modern languages. It is endemic in much of the humanities and social sciences. For this reason, a search for alternative models, global and transnational, has been sweeping across the various disciplines in recent years, not least in history, where Werner and

This is not, of course, to say that scholars should not respond to major, transformative historical developments and align their paradigms and approaches accordingly. However, the vicissitudes of history are not automatically the best guides to the organization of knowledge production. For example, even as the neoliberal triumphalism of the 1990s–2000s prompted scholars to start foregrounding the significance of global interactions over and above national dynamics, the rise of right-wing populism during the 2010s is forcing the pendulum to swing the other way. Of course, the global dynamics of twenty-first-century forms of neonationalism, which directly interconnect Donald Trump's populism in the USA, Vladimir Putin's 'traditional values' agenda, Viktor Orbán's premiership in Hungary, Pauline Hanson's One Nation Party in Australia, and the 'Brexiteers' in the UK, are prompting the development of new frameworks of analysis and interpretation which seek to explain and interpret precisely the transnational dimensions of the phenomenon in question (de Cleen & Galanopoulos 2016; Zúquete 2015). New frames of analysis, not least those rooted in the concept of the transnational, are also needed to understand Russia's contemporary political and cultural positioning in the wider world, including its strategies of nation-building both at home and among Russophone communities beyond its borders.

When it comes to the more specific question of what needs to be done for Russian studies, in particular, to avoid the epistemological error of 'methodological nationalism', the matter is not simply one of countering some supposed insulation of the study of Russian language, culture, and society from explorations of wider, transnational, political, and cultural dynamics.[9] Rather more

Zimmerman's (2006) concept of *histoire croisée* has been an influential tool for transnationalizing, and deconstructing, claims to national specificity. At the same time, one must also be wary of a rather different, implicit methodological nationalism that tends to affect the social sciences in particular, and notably the field of international relations, in which theories of 'soft power', for instance, were until recently based almost exclusively on the US model.

[9] Indeed, Russian studies as a field has, in fact, always been open to a transnational perspective and a number of recent works have made this quite explicit. As studies that have influenced us, we would highlight Edith W. Clowes's *Russia on the Edge* (2011), which analyses how Russian identity is constructed at the periphery, in contact with other cultures, as well as John Burt Foster Jr.'s *Transnational Tolstoy* (2013), which shows how a canonical Russian writer is himself a product of transnational forces and how his work has travelled to and influenced writers and societies across the globe. More recently still, Kevin M. F. Platt's *Global Russian Cultures* (2018) has drawn attention to the multiple meanings of Russian identity and culture in a globalized world, where 'Russianness' is made not only in the Russian Federation, but by Russophone communities around the globe. *Russian Culture in the Era of Globalisation* (2018), edited by Sarah Hudspith and Vlad Strukov, decouples

problematic in Russian studies, in fact, has been a distinctive kind of Russian (or Soviet) *exceptionalism*, which can be found even in some of the best scholarship on Russia. Exceptionalism informs a great deal of Russia's intellectual and political history, from the messianism found in Dostoevskii's late work to Vladimir Putin's view of Russia's unique national destiny on the world stage. Needless to say, these kinds of essentialized notions of Russianness have long fallen out of favour in academia, but an implicit, quieter, exceptionalism continues to exist in Russian studies, in teaching as well as research. Resorting to it often helps specialists in the subject brand Russian studies as distinctive in the increasingly competitive marketplace of higher education, but whether this is always warranted intellectually is less certain. This is not, of course, to deny either specificity or uniqueness to things 'Russian' (or, say, 'Soviet'). It is certainly not to say that identifying some historically or culturally distinctive structure, pattern, or empirical manifestation as specifically 'Russian' (or 'Soviet') is to automatically fall foul of the sin of 'exceptionalism'. Rather, the issue is one of avoiding making this exceptionalism *methodological*; in other words, of studying things 'Russian' (or 'Soviet') as exceptional by default. It is a question of recognizing that the identity of things labelled 'Russian', specifically as that which Russian studies studies, is an ever-shifting construct with multiple, competing meanings, in flux across space and time, produced by variously positioned agents with a myriad different claims and agendas.

'Russia' as Epistemic Frame

Indeed, in this context, 'Russia' and 'Russian culture' need to be considered not just objects of study but also *epistemic frames*[10] which are of critical importance to scholars who situate their work in the domain of knowledge production dubbed Russian studies. To speak of Russia and Russian culture as 'frames' refers to their function as tacit, taken for granted, axiomatic constructs (whether academic, political, or merely commonsensical); as,

---

globalization from Westernization, arguing that Russia in the twenty-first century has developed its own vision of globality that increasingly comes into conflict with Western notions of globalization. Hudspith and Strukov highlight how producers of Russian culture – from 'high' culture like opera and ballet to popular culture such as television and YouTube videos – are enmeshed in a global system of cultural exchange and a global game of politics and power.

[10] Epistemic frames have been understood as that which governs ways of knowing, deciding what is worth knowing, and adding to the collective body of knowledge and understanding of a given community of practice (Shaffer 2006). Piaget and Garcia (1983) introduced the term *cadre épistemique* as deriving from a particular social and historical context in which knowledge develops.

in Bourdieu's terms, 'structures of vision and division' (1998: 53–56) that delimit, shape, underpin, and then remain embedded in the architecture of whatever meanings are attributed to culture understood as pertaining to Russia. As frames, they carry the imaginaries (i.e. internalized social representations) (e.g. see Taylor 2003) that position Russian culture in, and tie it to, a particular geo-historical time-space, an embodied community or network of subcommunities, a society marked by certain assumed patterns of self-reproduction; a specific set of symbolic codes (especially language); and an evolving canon of cultural artefacts and producers. As knowledge-producing professionals, Russian studies scholars are responsible for constructing Russia and Russian culture as frames both for their own professional community and for those outside it. At the same time, they are continuously confronted with the construction of these frames by others – academics in their own or other fields, other kinds of intellectuals and specialists, and lay individuals, including both those who might be claiming Russian culture as 'theirs' and those who might be particularly keen to Other it (positively or negatively).

If Russia and Russian culture are to be understood as epistemic constructs, then transnationalizing Russia and Russian culture is itself an epistemic project – an interrogation and deconstruction of epistemic boundary-work involved in constructions of 'Russia' and 'Russian culture'. This is why what we are ultimately claiming to be doing in this collected volume is transnationalizing *Russian studies*, a domain of knowledge production. And if this is so, then what we mean by 'transnationalizing' cannot be dependent on and tied to some narrow definition of the nation, for 'nation' itself is a framing concept, directing the framing of Russia and Russian culture down particular lines. This also applies to other, competing, framing concepts of relevance, such as 'empire'; indeed, the latter too must, in the context of the project of transnationalizing, be understood as an epistemic frame that in a very specific way governs how 'Russia' is to be studied and known.

There is, of course, a reason why the term 'transnationalizing', which contains the term 'nation' at its morphological and semantic core, is an appropriate one to use here. The TML project targets a very particular *politics of framing* – a politics that has a certain vector – namely, the demarcation and construction of *a* culture along broadly national lines. The 'nationalization' of culture is both a political and an epistemic vector which has dominated the entirety of the humanities since the end of the eighteenth century. However, this nationalizing vector does not, in fact, in any way predetermine the exact ways in which a specific 'nation' is imagined or demarcated; in other words, the ways in which Russia and Russian culture (as opposed to some other, say French or German, culture) might actually be framed. As we shall see in the brief discussion that follows, the framing of Russian culture by scholars and non-scholars is complex and multiple – made up of many different kinds of frames, which are often juxtaposed and intertwined even when seemingly contradictory.

The framing of Russian culture as a national culture usually assumes that this culture should be rooted in a particular, historic, and above all linguistically demarcated ethnic group, construed as a biologically existing people, extending genealogically through time, occupying a certain space, and, over time, developing statehood, thereby evolving from a mere tribe into a fully fledged nation. And, indeed, the origins of Russian culture are conventionally traced to a branch of East Slavic tribes who are said to have inhabited territories in the east of the European continent and eventually formed the core population of two premodern state formations, Kievan Rus (from the ninth to the thirteenth century) and, after the latter's demise, Muscovy or the Grand Duchy of Moscow (from the thirteenth to the sixteenth century). Significantly, however, such framings of the ethnic, territorial, and statehood origins of Russian culture have hardly required either ethnocultural purity or territorial integrity and coherence. Rather, the framing of Russia and Russian culture here usually emphasizes the vagueness, expansiveness, and in-betweenness of people, territory, and culture. Even the Russians' Slavic origins are readily accepted as culturally indeterminate – traversed and shaped by a multitude of other cultural influences (Iranian, Turkic, Finno-Ugric, Nordic) during the centuries-long great migrations from late antiquity to the early Middle Ages.[11]

This indeterminacy of origins is there also in the imaginary of the formation of the first Russian state itself, with the legendary establishment of Kievan Rus in the ninth century by Scandinavian invaders from the north and then its extensive politico-cultural shaping by the neighbouring Greek-dominated Byzantine Empire in the south, not to speak of continuous military, political, and economic engagements with numerous surrounding culturally varied ethnic groups to both east and west along highly porous and shifting boundaries. Similarly, the eventual transfer of the centre of Russian statehood to Moscow during the Mongol Yoke (thirteenth to fifteenth century) is invariably accepted as arising just as strongly from Muscovy's comfortable embeddedness in the political culture of the Asian empire of the Khans as from its self-promotion as an emerging new centre of eastern Christendom.

Certainly, ideologies of Russian 'nationhood' assume that such indeterminacy of cultural and political roots does not necessarily prevent the 'Russian people' from remaining self-identical despite or, paradoxically,

---

[11] A useful general introduction to Russian history underpinning the discussion that follows can be found in Riasanovsky and Steinberg (2016).

precisely because of the whirlwind of extrinsic influences in which they have been historically caught up. What has been arguably less important here is the self-identity of 'Russians' as a biological mass. Indeed, Russia's late-nineteenth-century physical anthropologists posited a 'mixed racial type' as the prevailing one in the empire, although they were methodologically committed to dissociating the concept of race from either ethnic culture or nationhood (Mogilner 2013). Moreover, some have defined Russia precisely as a synthesizer of cultures: Andrew Wachtel points to one current of Russian national identity that emphasizes the country's supposed 'spongelike ability to absorb the best that other peoples had to offer as the basis for a universal, inclusive national culture' (1999: 52). Dostoevskii's Pushkin Speech of 1880 is a case in point: the novelist lauds the poet as a distinctively 'Russian spirit' *precisely because* he could 'exemplify [...] the genius of another people' (Dostoevsky 1994: 1292).[12] Such cultural syncretism, Wachtel suggests, gives translation a privileged role in Russia, not only in the establishment of a national and imperial culture in the nineteenth century, but also in the maintenance of a Soviet identity and culture in the twentieth. The Soviet Union had a vibrant culture of translation between Russia and its smaller national and regional languages, underpinned by a schizophrenic nationalities policy that supported smaller languages and cultures so long as they did not challenge the state's political ideology or threaten the hegemonic status of Russian. Wachtel concludes that 'the entire Soviet cultural project represents merely an extension of the universalizing translation project that had already been felt intuitively as Russia's mission in the nineteenth century' (1999: 72).

The commitment to a supposedly syncretic notion of Russianness could be coupled not only with political utopianism, but also with religious messianism. Dostoevskii concluded his Pushkin Speech by prophesizing that Russia's ultimate destiny was 'to utter the ultimate word of great, general harmony, ultimate brotherly accord of all tribes through the law of Christ's Gospel!' (Dostoevsky 1994: 1294).[13] These words echo a more general positing of 'Russianness' as something fundamentally spiritual; something that, to paraphrase Tiutchev,

[12] The speech was delivered on 5 June 1880 at the unveiling of a new Pushkin monument. Dostoevskii praised Pushkin as the epitome of the synthesizing impulse that he saw in Russian culture, lauding his 'capacity to respond to the whole world' and suggesting that this very breadth made him peculiarly Russian. For Dostoevskii, Pushkin epitomized Russia's national destiny more broadly. An English translation of the full speech is available in Dostoevsky (1994: 1281–95).

[13] Russia is not unique in universalizing its national idea. France's claim to be the world's standard-bearer for liberty in its specifically Western interpretation is another example. Arguably, national identity and the universalizing impulse are inextricably tied.

exists principally as an article of faith.[14] The core of this spiritual self-identity tends, moreover, to be rooted in a fantasy of Russia's and the Russian people's 'chosen-ness', which is imagined, of course, in a broadly religious key, as chosenness essentially by God, and this first for great suffering but ultimately for salvation. That said, even the narratives that construct the distinctiveness of the Russian people's spiritual identity still thrive, in fact, on the latter's indeterminacy – on motifs of dualism and schism, on the problematization of vertical structures and central religious institutions, and the constant harking back to horizontal, anarchic, alternative, hidden, secretive forms of spirituality.

The identification of Russia with Orthodoxy has been mythologized as resulting from an historic choice – the famous ninth-century 'baptism of Rus'. This then led both to an *appropriation* of Orthodoxy by Russia (the development of specifically 'Russian Orthodoxy') and to an *assimilation* of Russians into it, notably through the coupling of ethnic and religious identity, so that the 'Russian people' [russkie] became an 'Orthodox people' [pravoslavnye]. Yet Orthodox culture was never an ethnic culture, but the culture of an imperial *civilization*. Initially, this was the imaginary of an eastern Christian civilization that it was Moscow's ambition to embody in the guise of the 'Third Rome' (as famously proclaimed by monk Filofei in the sixteenth century), with Russia being construed as the de facto imperial successor to fallen Byzantium. This ideology served as the basis for the self-construction of Russian statehood in the shape of an imperial tsardom during the sixteenth and seventeenth centuries. The idea of the uniqueness of Russia's historical path as a social, cultural, and political formation acquired in this context a civilizational rather than ethnic form.[15] Moreover, both faith and ethnicity were ultimately subordinated to a distinctive form of state power that was assumed to lie at the centre of Russia's historic identity. In the nineteenth century, this was turned into an official ideology of Russian autocracy in the motto 'Orthodoxy, Autocracy, Nationality'.[16]

---

[14] The metaphysical poet Fedor Tiutchev (1803–73) penned an influential epigram in 1866 depicting Russia as a mysterious force only understood by faith: 'Умом Россию не понять, / Аршином общим не измерить: / У ней особенная стать – / В Россию можно только верить' [Russia cannot be understood with the mind, / No common yardstick can measure her. / Russia stands along, unique: / One can only have faith in Russia] (Tiutchev 2003: 165).

[15] The notion of a 'Third Rome' has persisted in underpinning the uniqueness of things Russian in later, Soviet, but also more recent ideological formations. See Poe (2001).

[16] The motto Pravoslavie, samoderzhavie, narodnost' was invented by Count Sergei Uvarov and embraced by Tsar Nicholas I during the second quarter of the nineteenth century.

Much of the work of transnationalizing Russia to date has been directed precisely towards breaking down this entrenched epistemic frame of Russia as civilizationally unique and exceptional, usually by placing it in a comparative framework and by challenging narratives of Russia's or the USSR's inherent difference or supposed insulation from the rest of the world (e.g. Clark 2011). Dominating this discussion has been the question of Russia's ambivalent participation in *modernity*, here understood as a set of sociocultural norms and attitudes, practices and imaginaries that arose in post-Renaissance Europe in the context of the industrial, scientific, philosophical, and political revolutions that have shaped the modern world between the seventeenth and twentieth centuries (e.g. Hoffmann 2011; David-Fox 2015). Critical to placing Russia in the context of modernity, however, has been the framing of Russian culture not so much as the culture of some chosen historic people, but as the culture of a *successful empire* (the longest-lasting land empire, in fact) – an entity forged through territorial expansion and the conquest of *other* peoples (the *inorodtsy*). When framed as a culture of imperial civilization, Russian culture becomes ethnically plural and fuzzy – it is the culture '*of* Russia' [rossiiskaia] rather than 'Russian' [russkaia]. This *modern* version of Russian culture as the culture of an imperial civilization refers, of course, not to the theocratic roots of the Third Rome, but to Peter the Great's early-eighteenth-century reforging of Russia into a military empire on the European model – a form in which the Russian state persisted until the collapse of autocracy in 1917. This is an empire oriented, at least in principle, not towards the past (tracing imperial Christendom backwards) but the future – explicitly identifying with the form of European modernity that asserted itself through the might of the state, especially in militarily led great power expansion, and then (inevitably) conflict with equivalent imperial rivals on the international stage. Peter's European vision has, indeed, been historically victorious, but it has also reproduced the pattern of framing Russian culture as fundamentally split – here in terms of its ambivalent relationship to modernity; a split symbolized by yet another move of the state's capital from Moscow to St Petersburg in the early eighteenth century.

The development of Russia as a powerful imperial state is understood, however, to have occurred largely at the expense of another key development of modernity – namely, the appearance of the nation state as modernity's normative polity. This is usually presented as the historic failure of the Russians to develop a cohesive identity as 'one nation', growing instead, during the eighteenth century in particular, into an imperfectly formed, fractured nation, split in a fundamental way between a tiny, but powerful, Europeanized elite and an enslaved, illiterate, brutally exploited, and effectively 'colonized' peasant mass (Etkind 2011). To counter this, certain segments of the elite, namely the Slavophiles, who in the middle of the nineteenth century blamed this split in the nation primarily on Westernization, constructed an alternative, romantic ideal of a homogenous 'one nation', defined by a mystical, premodern, and thus nominally ethnic (broadly Slavic), but in reality highly nationalist form of utopian communitarianism that was explicitly dissociated from modern (Western) state forms – in effect, a nationalism without the nation state.

At the same time, though, the modern, or rather Petrine, framing of Russian culture as a culture of an imperial civilization, over the course of the nineteenth century, allowed its shape and form to emphasize neither ethnic purity nor national homogeneity. Instead, it came to develop a far more complex dynamic of civilization-building and colonial negotiation as critical to the identity of Russia and Russian culture as the dominant culture of an empire. This dynamic has, as a result, entailed pendulum-like shifts between policies of imperialist Russification, on the one hand, and the pragmatic tolerance of or even support and admiration for the 'lesser' cultures of the various imperial subjects. Crucially, though, 'Russification' usually implied the imposition on others of an *imperial*, rather than strictly ethnic, culture. The ethnic culture of the Russian people themselves became, in turn, 'folklore'. At the same time, in the context of what was a diffuse and imprecise system of both ethnic and territorial differentiation under the tsars, the denominational label 'Orthodox' [pravoslavnyi], rather than the ethnic 'Russian', became a particularly common form of self-identification among the empire's ethnic Russian subjects, namely the peasantry (many of whom would have been serfs until 1861), and this specifically as this group's way of distinguishing itself from others within the empire.

The downfall of the tsarist empire and the formation of the Soviet Union introduced a radically new political inflection to the meanings of Russian culture as dominant culture of what was now constructed as an unprecedented entity – a supposedly highly progressive kind of 'free union of free nations'. The USSR was developed as something of a 'post-empire' – a radically new type of state, expressly built to overcome both bourgeois nationalism and capitalist imperialism, yet in which, paradoxically, both neo-colonial approaches and active nation-building reached new levels (Slezkine 1994; Hirsch 2005). Crucially, the Bolshevik regime invested far more attention and effort than its predecessor in politically, administratively, and culturally constructing, systematizing, and controlling the Union's multinational structure (in both ethnic and territorial terms) under the umbrella of a larger, ideologically framed, supranational 'Soviet' cultural identity. Within it, 'Russian culture' blurred with 'Soviet culture', in part as a purportedly neutral interconnector and pragmatic medium, but also as the presumed most advanced culture within the Union – the locomotive of the multinational Union's speedy progress towards communism (see, for example, Tyulenev & Nuriev in this volume).

What arose as a new, Soviet, civilization came, in fact, to be construed, in line with Marxist theory, as the only true spearhead of history – a civilization ready to take the mantle of modernity over from old Europe by diverging from and overtaking the (bourgeois and fascist) West. This was therefore a modern, future-oriented version of the Third Rome, with the USSR at the helm of a Communist, rather than Christian, International. For sure, within the Soviet Union a rich variety of specifically Russian nationalisms proliferated (see Brudny 1998) which reframed the meanings of Russian identity and culture rather differently from what its role was officially meant to be (as merely the 'form' in which a *Soviet* culture would manifest itself). However, the shapes taken by the late-twentieth- and early-twenty-first-century Russian nationalisms both before and since the collapse of the USSR have generally continued to construct Russia in both ethnically and territorially indeterminate ways, ranging from the narrowly folkloric 'village Russia' to an expansive Russia as de facto 'Eurasia', with a range of different imaginaries of Russian statehood, usually of a quasi-imperial kind, somewhere in-between (compare also with Tolz, Maiorova, and Filimonova in this volume).

Irrespective of the historic indeterminacy of where Russia actually lies, of where it begins and ends, of where its centre and where its periphery might be, of who counts as its people(s) and how they should be identified, of what this state is called and where its capital might be – all of the frames sketched above imply a (topological) 'inside' within which Russian culture develops or is developed and to which it therefore properly belongs. At the same time, however, there is also a highly important set of frames constructing Russian culture as something that flourishes *beyond or outside* Russia itself. Firstly, Russian culture has in significant ways been situated in *exilic or diasporic cultural production*, which boomed especially in the the post-1917 émigré culture of the so-called 'Russia Abroad' (Raeff 1990), and then continued in new forms in the late-Soviet and post-Soviet migration waves, right up to the present day. Included in this frame one might at times even find writings by emigrants or their descendants which, while strongly thematizing a 'Russian' predicament (within or beyond Russian borders), are not necessarily written in Russian, but in English, French, German, or Hebrew, or else deliberately work with a linguistic hybrid of one kind or another. Secondly, and this principally from the Second World War to the late 1980s, Russian culture was also recognized internationally as the *culture of a world superpower*, responsible for leading the spread of communism in competition with the increasingly global English-language culture of the USSR's superpower rival – the USA. And thirdly, Russian culture has also been prominently framed as a *branded cultural export or import* with universalist pretentions and the status of one of the great world cultures. Here Russian culture became a major contributor to the canons of *world* literature, cinema, theatre, ballet, music, and art, and thus a confident participant in all manner of cosmopolitan cultural mixes, even while retaining and foregrounding its own distinctive 'brand' features.

Finally, from the early twenty-first century, partly through the consequences of the break-up of the former Soviet 'empire' and partly through the exceptional degree of mobility and intercultural interaction and hybridization that characterizes today's globalized world, Russian culture has been developed not simply as a culture beyond Russia itself or as part of a universalist 'world culture', but also as a 'global culture' in the sense of transcending the above-described inside-outside binary, not least by explicitly relativizing the relevance of nation state borders in determining the boundaries of both Russia and Russian culture.

The projections of Russian culture as 'global culture' are themselves diverse, however. At one end of the spectrum is the Russian state's own construct of the 'Russian World' [Russkii Mir; RM]. Though global, RM is imagined as 'anchored' in the Russian Federation itself, as a powerful player on the international stage but also as what Rogers Brubaker (2011) calls a 'nationalizing state'. Indeed, the concept of RM is not only being promoted globally, outside Russia (e.g. through the operations of the Russian World Foundation, the Russian government's soft power organization), but also inside it through the development of an explicitly ethnically inflected (*russkii* rather than *rossiiskii*) nation-building frame which has since the mid-2010s been imposed across an otherwise multi-ethnic territory through new laws and policies introduced to gradually erode Russia's existing, federally organized, multiculturalism. Secondly, RM is imagined as being held together across the globe by a network of so-called 'compatriots' [sootechestvenniki] – a concept that is distinct from that of expatriates since it does not entail citizenship of the Russian Federation. Compatriots are understood to exist in all parts of the world and include both the so-called 'beached diaspora' (Laitin 1998) of Russians who after the dissolution of the USSR ended up citizens of a non-Russian former Soviet republic and Russophone migrants from any migrant wave. A compatriot is, in principle, anyone who openly identifies with and actively supports the maintenance of Russian language and culture abroad. Compatriotism is, however, at least tacitly, also expected to translate into a form of loyalty to the Russian Federation itself, which is why compatriots are supported through a network of official organizations and included in this way in Russia's global soft power projects. And, finally, RM is also often understood to be rooted in a distinct set of civilizational values (sometimes dubbed 'Eurasian'), which imply competition with rival civilizations (Western, Islamic, Chinese). Russia itself is here imaged as one of the major 'poles' of a so-called 'multipolar world' – the successor to the hegemonic US-dominated 'unipolar world' that followed immediately after the fall of communism.

There is, however, an alternative conception of the 'Russian World' that similarly understands Russian culture as anchored in a specific national language, history, and traditions, which then disperses across and exists in the global world in a variety of ways, but does not imply the idea of a 'Russian civilization' in competition or conflict with other world civilizations. This other construction of the 'Russian World' is still fundamentally patriotic, but its patriotism is that typical of a Russian intelligentsia traditionally wary of state power.[17] It is, in fact, an expression of cultural patriotism that explicitly avoids direct association with the state and envisages Russian culture going global not as a cultural projection of Russian statehood but, quite the contrary, as this culture actively *freeing itself* from the state. Ultimately, as a construct of 'global Russianness', this understanding of the 'Russian World' assembles not 'compatriots', but those whom Kwame Anthony Appiah (1997) has called 'cosmopolitan patriots'.[18]

Finally, at the other end of the spectrum is a radically constructivist framing of 'Russian culture' as a 'global culture'. Here, Russian culture is posited as something that lacks any kind of secure core, that is not guaranteed by a singular people, state, language, history, or civilization, that is not unitary, let alone exceptional, but fundamentally *diffracted* into a multiplicity of competing projects and claims, articulations and imaginaries, whatever inflection (romantic, patriotic, ludic, ironic, cosmopolitan) is attributed within these diffractions to a 'Russian' identity (see especially Platt 2018). In this liberal frame, which permits, for instance, the possibility of 'Russian literature' being written by 'non-Russians', the 'Russian World' can take forms,

---

[17] Svetlana Aleksievich, winner of the 2015 Nobel Prize in Literature, referred to 'Russia's great culture' in this way in her Nobel Lecture, titled 'On the Battle Lost' (2015).

[18] This alternative conception of the 'Russian World' as expressive of a 'global Russianness' that needs to be contrasted with the 'Russian World' as an ideological project of the Russian state was discussed by Lara Ryazanova-Clarke in the paper 'Znai nashikh: The Russophone World in the UK', which she presented at the 'Transnational Russian Studies' symposium in Durham on 14–16 September 2017.

exist in places, belong to people, and be articulated in languages that would normally have been constructed as external to this 'world', or even be labelled its Other (as in the burgeoning of 'Russian-American' writing, for example). This frame of 'global Russian cultures' (emphatically in the plural) is first and foremost an intellectual project – a reflection of a particular scholarly perspective of our time, and one that emanates from outside Russia itself. However, this does not mean that this is a purely academic frame. Insofar as the 'Russian World' is by definition an ideological construct, the idea of 'global Russian cultures' cannot avoid being ideological itself. For this frame does not posit the 'Russian World' simply as an object of study; it also represents an explicit polemical challenge both to the neo-nationalist ideology of the current Russian state and to essentializations of Russianness that are inherent in alternative non- or anti-state conceptions of the 'Russian World'. What 'global Russian culture' offers instead is a radical alternative, based on the total opening up of the question of the ownership of and belonging to that which we are to label 'Russian culture'.

The Transnational in Reverse Perspective

The above is, of course, just a provisional sketch of the broad range of divergent frames within which Russian language, culture, and society can be and have been placed, in the past as well as the present. As this brief outline suggests, Russian studies cannot afford to be reduced to the study of phenomena circumscribed by some predetermined set of historic borders, confined to a single overarching linguistic code, or referred to some homogenous cultural community, however broadly and flexibly any of these are defined. More importantly, though, our purpose here has been to reinforce the point that it is fundamental for Russian studies to actively engage in the deconstruction of the boundary-work involved in the delimitation of things 'Russian' and also to show that transnationalizing Russia and Russian culture is itself, as an epistemological project, not a simple and narrow task.

However, what still remains to be done, we believe, is to invert the terms of the analysis and to ask what it might mean epistemologically to view the transnational from a *Russian* vantage point. Indeed, as specialists in Russian studies, all the contributors to this volume lay claim, at least implicitly, not only to knowledge *about* Russia but also to knowledge that enables one to see and reconceptualize the world from distinctively Russian perspectives (bearing in mind, of course, everything said above about the plurality and contingency of what 'Russian' means here). Indeed, part of the responsibility of Russian studies as a field of expertise is to re-present, analyse, and interpret *views 'from within'*. Taking examples from this very volume, Russianists will seek to account for Russia's own imperializing version of nationhood (Tolz; Maiorova); or Russians' literary articulations of homosexuality (Doak); or the disruptions, restrictions, and innovations of competing Russian-language media operations (Gorham; Strukov; Hutchings). This, moreover, entails not just presenting the 'Russian perspective' but at the same time adding something new to conceptualizations of empire, nation, sexuality, or media politics more generally. Indeed, incorporating this view 'from within' with a view 'from without' is critical to completing the epistemological turn that we are advocating under the banner of transnationalizing the study of Russia and Russian culture.[19]

The paradox entailed in the double movement that we are proposing here is captured in the notion of 'reverse perspective' [obratnaia perspektiva], which was developed by the early-twentieth-century Russian religious thinker Pavel Florenskii to account for the 'distorted' imagery of Russian religious icons, which appear to flout the laws of linear perspective. Rather than lines converging and objects diminishing in size as they recede from a predetermined imagined viewer, the lines of iconic objects become convergent the closer they are to the actual viewer placed before the icon, while background figures may be larger than those in the foreground. Far from being naively ignorant of linear perspective, icon painters saw perspective as artificially generating a mere illusion, constructed from the fixed vantage point of a notional, constructed observer. They strove, by contrast, to thrust the actual observer into the heart of a reality in which objects and figures have *their own* presence: 'Forms should be apprehended according to their own life; they should be represented through themselves, according to the way they have been apprehended, and not in the foreshortenings of a perspective laid out beforehand' (Florensky 2006: 218). Crucially, what reverse perspective does is to turn the viewer of the icon, paradoxically, into both scrutinizer and scrutinized. Moreover, reverse perspective is conceptualized as a means of immersing the viewer in a reality that is explicitly distinguished from a merely illusory image, a deliberate construct of a reality, ultimately an abstraction of life.

The paradox of reverse perspective may also be re-expressed in the terms that the young Mikhail Bakhtin used to conceptualize aesthetic creation. In his early writings, Bakhtin (1990) rejected what he called 'theoreticism', which he condemned for its tendency to create abstractions from unique human

---

[19] This, of course, applies to modern languages more generally. As expressed by French studies scholar Neil Kenny, modern languages as a discipline involves 'the study of languages and of their associated cultures and societies from simultaneously the inside and the outside' (cit. Wells 2017).

experiences. In its place he proposed what he described as an 'ethical' under-standing of aesthetic creation. He equated aesthetic creativity to an act of love in which 'the author' starts off by entering the life of 'the hero', apprehending it from within and taking care to preserve intact its irreducible particularity. 'The author', however, then had to exit that life and apprehend it lovingly from without in order to 'complete' [zavershit'] it and give it meaning.[20] In aesthetic creation, the other's life is thereby, according to Bakhtin, lovingly co-experienced from within, but in order to turn it into a meaningful whole, the authorial self must eventually return to its position of 'outsidedness' [vnenakhodimost']. Thus, in Bakhtin's account, the fundamental difference of 'the other' must be neither fetishized nor reduced to an instance of an abstract generality. Instead, it is to be 'completed from without', whilst retaining a singularity experienced in its totality 'from within'.

We are here extending the 'ethical' reframing that Bakhtin develops with reference to aesthetic creation, in which an author gives meaning to that which s/he creates, to the epistemological task that lies before specialists in Russian studies. Our task requires us not only to apprehend, understand, and give meaning to things 'Russian', but also to communicate that meaning, as specialists, to others. This 'ethical' move is certainly not to re-introduce, by the back door, a form of Russian exceptionalism that we have argued against and are determined to avoid. Rather, it is to recognize that, just as the 'Russian' in 'Russian studies' is not restricted to the Russian 'nation' but covers a plurality of meanings and contexts, so we need to build from our Russian studies work a multi-layered, multi-dimensional, multi-perspectival picture *of the transnational itself.*

Translated into practical terms, we are bound, therefore, to adopt multiple methodological variants on the transnational paradigm. Thus, some of our contributors work comparatively, juxtaposing the Russian with the non-Russian

---

[20] Confusingly, though not uncharacteristically for Bakhtin, the same ethical privileging of the non-reductive act of communication between one free, uniquely embodied consciousness and another is, in his later work, associated with the opposite notion of 'unfinalizability' or 'unfinalizedness' [nezavershennost']. He sees the great novels of Dostoevskii as the ultimate expression of this phenomenon. It is possible that the latter formulation, which is the one that Connor Doak applies in his chapter in the present volume, reflects Bakhtin's tacit, coded battle against the constraints on freedom imposed by Stalinism in its most repressive phase. Whatever the explanation, Bakhtin is consistent in pursuing a lifelong resistance to schematic abstraction, in his belief in the power of the aesthetics of verbal creativity to confront it, and in the ethical importance of incarnating the realm of truth in the concrete event of being with and for the other. For a fuller discussion of Bakhtin's intellectual development, see Morson and Emerson (1989).

(Jackson; Bozovic). Others operate cross-culturally, tracing movement across Russian and non-Russian space-time configurations, both within a broadly defined post/imperial space (Glaser; Tyulenev & Nuriev; Radunović) and beyond it (Bullock; McAteer; Norris). Others still apply what might be termed a transcultural approach, testing universal theories out on Russian cases (Tihanov; Rutten). This process can be represented as a spectrum that extends from an emphasis on the particular to a privileging of the general, with most chapters in this volume shuttling to and fro along it.

It is no coincidence that we have chosen two theorists deeply immersed in the Russian philosophical tradition to illuminate our approach to a transnational framework for which we claim general applicability; this is a case of our 'object of study' acquiring subjectivity and 'speaking back' to us, even as we frame it from without. Nor is it coincidental that both Bakhtin and Florenskii abhorred abstraction and struggled within their different idioms to formulate ways of thinking about universal meaning which managed to conserve the particularity of the embodied individual. Both Florenskii and Bakhtin (in his early phase) linked embodiment in this sense to the mystery of Christ: the Son of God, whose divinity remained undiminished by the acquisition of an irreducibly particular, suffering human form. Seen through this prism, but shorn of its theological baggage, the term 'transnational' also designates our search to derive 'universal' yet 'embodied' meaning from our object of study – an 'object', though, that is simultaneously a speaking 'subject'.

Structure of the Book

In presenting the results of this search, we have divided our book into four parts. The first, 'Nation, Empire, and Beyond', presents some of the ways in which the multi-ethnic space once claimed by the Russian Empire and the Soviet Union can be explored as a geopolitical or geocultural frame within which a variety of national, imperial, and postcolonial entanglements are enacted as part of the region's ongoing cultural politics. Vera Tolz opens this section with a critique of discourses past and present which have used Russia's multinationality as a way of exceptionalizing Russian policies and practices *vis-à-vis* colonial subjects. She connects this to Russia's ongoing negotiations of its ambivalent relationship with the West. The latter has persistently served as a mirror, but one in which Russia, paradoxically, keeps seeking the image of the Other. Amelia Glaser's chapter follows this by examining the intersection of nineteenth-century Russian, Ukrainian, and Yiddish literary imaginations, focusing, through the figure of the 'marketplace', on the nefarious inter-cultural 'horse-trading' that went on in the Russian Empire's multilingual western borderlands. Olga Maiorova in turn explores the engagement of a group of Russian Tolstoians with local communities in early-twentieth-century Central Asia (Turkestan). She uses this case to demonstrate the reciprocal nature of cross-cultural transfer in the area, calling for a re-evaluation of our understanding of 'Russification' in the area through the prism of rather more complex forms of cultural exchange that went on in the empire's eastern peripheries.

Dušan Radunović then shifts our attention onto the importance of symbolic appropriations of *space* as a key part of empire- and nation-building, both during the Soviet era and since then. His chapter looks at the deconstruction of the crucial political bond between territory and nation, specifically in cinematic works produced during the 2000s in Georgia and Kazakhstan. Radunović argues that the films he analyses (by Mikheil Kalatozishvili and Giorgi Ovashvili) deploy the visual symbolism of space as a metaphor for the distinctive experience of the transnational in which the people of post-Soviet Eurasia are caught up – an experience that runs counter to the obsessive nation-building preoccupations of the post-Soviet states themselves, and that needs to be located primarily in the domain of personal affect. This first section of the book concludes with Tatiana Filimonova's analysis of Vladimir Sorokin's 2013 novel *Telluria*, a satirical reworking of Eurasian geopolitics in a dystopian post-post-national world, which is as whimsical as it is unmistakably rooted in Russo-Soviet history, or rather, the ideological phantasms that stem from it.

The second part, titled 'Beyond and Between Languages' foregrounds the crucial role that *language* plays in circumscribing culture, and especially literature, in national terms, while simultaneously serving, paradoxically, as both the means of and the obstacle to transnational, interlingual, and cross-cultural communication. Galin Tihanov opens this section by examining the Russian formalist Viktor Shklovskii's interest in 'world literature'. Shklovskii understood the term not as a canon of foreign classics to be incorporated into a universalist treasure trove of 'Soviet culture' (as Maksim Gor'kii, for example, had conceived it), but as a framework that confirms the concept of 'literariness' as something above and beyond language; and hence something 'portable' beyond the work's original language. Marijeta Bozovic's chapter brings this crucial question into the present by reminding us of the influence that Vladimir Nabokov, 'Russian émigré' turned model 'world writer', has had on contemporary figurations of 'world literature'. For Nabokov, too, 'world literature' ceases to be a canon, and is instead reconceptualized as a form of *reading* – namely, the reading of great works of literature as a means of imbibing the greatness of literature as such. However, as Bozovic argues, both Nabokov and the 'world writers' who echo his work (namely, the South African J. M. Coetzee and the Iranian Azar Nafisi) appear to suggest, perhaps pessimistically, that this kind of reading of world literature – reading figured in the novels of all three writers as a form of pedagogical seduction – commonly ends in communicative failure. Cathy McAteer switches our attention to the focus of *producing* – rather than reading – 'world literature' in her study of how Russian literary greats were transposed onto British soil, specifically in the context of the mid-twentieth-century Penguin Classics series. McAteer delves into the archives of the publisher Penguin Books to reveal the editorial conceptions and translation practices underpinning this series as it relates specifically to the publication of Russian classics. She shows how the various personal, institutional, and commercial factors that lay behind the commissioning of translations shaped the way in which Russian works reached the British public at the height of the Cold War.

The crucial role that translation plays not only in channelling cultural flows across state borders but also in controlling such flows within a single country is explored by Sergey Tyulenev and Vitaly Nuriev in a chapter that charts the development of a distinctive translation system within the multinational and multilingual USSR. Their analysis demonstrates how important it was for the Soviet regime to use translation as a means of politically integrating cultural production within the Union while at the same time fostering the policy of supporting the many languages and literatures of the Union's officially recognized nationalities. Tyulenev and Nuriev stress the pivotal yet ambiguous position in this system of the Russian language, from and into which the bulk of Soviet translation was carried out. The exploration of the vital, yet also problematic, role of Russian as lingua franca of this region, even after the collapse of the USSR, continues in Julie Curtis's examination of New Drama – a transnational avant-garde theatre movement which arose in the late 1990s in the triangle between Russia, Ukraine, and Belarus. Based on documentary techniques and focused on controversial sociopolitical topics of the day shared across all three countries, New Drama embraced Russian as its unquestioned linguistic medium during the 2000s. However, since the flaring up of armed conflict between Russia and Ukraine in 2015, the transnational character of the movement has come under severe strain, as has its Russophonism. Since then, the choice of national language and the way it is deployed now tops the list of concerns for many of the playwrights involved. Such a choice has come to serve as a key means of expressing not just a political but also a moral stance, something critical to New Drama as an aesthetic form.

Part three, titled 'Cultures Crossing Borders', focuses on the life and cultural transpositions of things 'Russian' in the global arena. Philip Bullock examines the complex transnational histories of performances of Russian operas based on major literary classics across the tsarist, Soviet, and post-Soviet eras. He challenges naive framings of 'Russian opera', 'Russian music', and 'Russian literature' as reflections of either a national consciousness or mythic otherness. Generalizing his findings concerning opera, Bullock argues that an analysis of how Russian culture is *performed* (in a wider, figurative sense as well) on the global stage (where 'the globe' would also encompass Russia or the USSR), enables one to see that much of what goes by 'Russian' needs to be understood as, in fact, inherently transnational. Stephen Norris's analysis of responses to Fedor Bondarchuk's 2013 film *Stalingrad* from both Russian and international audiences and film critics follows Bullock's lead, but adds a further point – namely, that 'the nation', as both abstract concept and concrete reality, is itself a fundamentally transnational phenomenon; or, more specifically, that what a given nation *means* is necessarily forged in a transnational arena. Indeed, Norris's analysis of the trials and tribulations of Bondarchuk's blockbuster shows how the transnational nature of twenty-first-century film production and consumption is directly shaping contemporary Russian patriotic culture. Norris highlights Russian patriotism's intimate entanglement with American patriotism, showing how Russian patriotic cinema can simultaneously shadow and copy Hollywood, dialogue with, and outdo it, while at the same time declaring itself, and in some respects genuinely being, against it.

While the Great Patriotic War has been a particularly important locus of Russia's patriotic self-construction under Putin, the same can be said of Russia's positioning in relation to a very different topic – that of gender and sexuality, especially as it relates to representations of queerness. As Connor Doak argues in his chapter, both Russia's and the West's narratives of gender and sexuality are invariably forged in transnational encounters with the Other. In order to de-reify the grand narrative that pits a traditionalist/homophobic Russia against the gay-friendly/decadent West as two civilizations with values diametrically at odds with one another, Doak offers a reading of two pieces of post-Soviet fiction (by Viktoria Tokareva and Margarita Meklina) whose plots revolve precisely around transnational encounters on the physical and symbolic border between Russia and the West, heterosexuality and homosexuality. As his analysis shows, when the question of the relationship between gender/sexuality and nation/civilization is examined through a literary lens, the answers become rather more ambiguous, with these narratives' authors, protagonists, and readers ending up rightly disoriented as to what is 'queer' and what is not.

The way in which 'Russia' encounters the wider world is of course never simply a matter of Russian-branded culture being projected onto the global stage. The transnational flow of things Russian implies that these are then not only appropriated and reinterpreted, but also, crucially, *re-performed in another's voice*, sometimes in seemingly unexpected ways and places.

Jeanne-Marie Jackson analyses how the 'Russian novel of ideas', exemplified by the works of Tolstoi and Dostoevskii, has informed the way certain novelists from southern Africa – namely, the Cape Town-based Imraan Coovadia and the Edinburgh-based émigré Zimbabwean Tendai Huchu – frame their own authorial, as well as their protagonists', searches for particular forms of 'salvation'. As emerges from Jackson's analysis, the great Russian writers' nineteenth-century confrontations with the problem of God and individual freedom, at a time when capitalist modernity came knocking hard on Russia's doors, resonate with some of the metaphysical dilemmas faced by contemporary transnational individuals ensnared by the global interconnectedness of everything in a universe in which truth seems to have become redundant. Jackson's discussion thereby inevitably opens up the question of how universal and how culturally and historically specific is humanity's search for greater meaning. Ellen Rutten's chapter asks a similar question, but in the context of aesthetics: can seemingly universal aesthetic concepts, such as, for instance, 'imperfection', be culturally appropriated (i.e. 'nationalized') – for example, by trying to develop an aesthetics of 'Russian imperfections'? Through an analysis of aesthetic claims about 'imperfection' made on such culturally diverse platforms as Russian online dating sites and scholarly interpretations of late-Soviet avant-garde art, Rutten shows that something like the 'aesthetics of imperfection' cannot be understood as either universal or culturally specific (say 'Russian'). While all aesthetics of imperfection are situated in specific 'thickenings' of social beliefs, cultural practices, and linguistic forms (meaning that there is nothing universal about the notion), these 'thickenings' will invariably be both translocal and transcultural (i.e. dependent for their meanings on the material and symbolic links that they form with other such 'cultural thickenings' even when the latter are situated in seemingly completely different sociocultural contexts).

The final section of the book, 'Russia Going Global', discusses Russia's positioning in the contemporary globalized world, examining both the ways in which this world has transformed Russia and the ways in which it is transformed by it. The period under consideration is the era of Vladimir Putin, whose positioning of Russia in the global community is premised on the idea that the latter must be transformed into a 'multipolar world', by which Putin means breaking the Western or, more specifically, American domination of some of the key instruments of globalization, including, especially, the internet. Michael Gorham's chapter focuses on this very issue, discussing the Kremlin's rhetoric around the idea of the so-called 'sovereign internet', which has so far served as a way to legitimize the imposition of state security controls over the use of information and communication technologies (ICTs) on Russian soil, even while cynically exploiting the laxity of such controls elsewhere in the world. Gorham exposes the hybrid and seemingly contra-dictory nature of Russian state rhetoric on ICTs, but he interprets it as stemming from pragmatic opportunism and the need to target a variety of audiences, both in Russia and in the larger global community. The coexistence of multiple, mixed messages is not unique to contemporary Russian state rhetoric, and is revealed as an inherent characteristic of the global mediascape more generally. A closely related finding emerges out of Stephen Hutchings's analysis of the multipronged operations of Russia's main international broad-caster, RT. Hutchings shows how in the global media environment, in which RT is reputedly promulgating 'Russia's position', there is, in fact, no discernible 'anchor' for such a position. Indeed, one should not look for it either in the ideologies, strategies, and policies of the Kremlin or in RT's own institutional structures and professional agendas. As a result, 'Russia's position', if it can be called this, becomes, in RT's articulation, exceedingly difficult to pin down. Yet, as Hutchings argues, the protean character of RT programming and online output is not the outcome of some overarching Machiavellian strategy, but the effect of rather random and reactive tactics of survival in the unpre-dictable ecosystem of the twenty-first-century globalized media.

The peculiar nature of this environment is further explored in Vlad Strukov's discussion of Meduza – a quality online media outlet with offices in Latvia, but whose commentary and news (both original and aggregated) are directed at Russian audiences concerned primarily with Russia-related politics. Crucially, though, as Strukov argues, Meduza avoids a clear identifi-cation with any given geographical location, nation state, language, financial base, diasporic community, political group, or ideological position. Instead it generates a distinctive cultural environment through a dynamic of inter-active engagement with online material by an audience whose online activity is in its totality 'Russia-oriented', but geographically, ideologically, politically, and economically 'unanchored'. While Strukov's findings are based on an analysis of larger patterns of online media activity of a particular kind of 'Russo-centric' but ultimately deterritorialized form of 'global Russianness', Lara Ryazanova-Clarke is interested in how the latter is produced in the discourse of individuals who self-identify as Russian but reside outside Russia. Her chapter provides a sociolinguistic analysis of how Russians living in the UK negotiate their conflicting allegiances to homeland, host country, and diasporic community. By dissecting the discourse of her subjects' interview self-presentations, Ryazanova-Clarke reveals that each individual construction of 'global Russianness' is, in a Bakhtinian sense, multi-voiced: each interview acts as a stage on which a variety of ideological positions, from the patriotic to the cosmopolitan, come together to interweave dialogically each interviewee's distinctive narrative of transnational belonging or, indeed, non-belonging.

The Transnational as Transgressional

Ryazanova-Clarke's finding is a fitting conclusion for a volume which calls for an embodied, dialogic approach to the study of humanity. This approach is central to the way we understand and deploy the concept of 'the transnational'. In the latter, the prefix *trans-* combines the senses of 'between' and 'beyond' – of both 'crossing' and 'surpassing' the constructed boundaries that divide humanity in broadly 'national' terms. However, what is also entailed in the notion of 'the transnational', in both of the above senses, is an act of *transgression* – a 'violation' of the normative order of things which takes place at the point of 'stepping across' boundaries. A 'transgression' implies, crucially, that the boundary that is being crossed is neither accepted nor done away with. Thus, the transnational as transgressional implies neither simply the study of cultural flows across 'national' boundaries nor some utopian transcendence, even disappearance, of these boundaries as such. Instead, the transnational implies *working through* such boundaries, remembering at every step of the way both the perils and the potentials that they harbour.

Indeed, here we must caution against the hubristic notion of a linear teleology running from the tyranny of empires, through the flawed, nativist democracy of nations to the global harmony of the post-national. As Rana Dasgupta implies, in its readiness to denigrate and negate the past, such a narrative risks compromising the future:

> Empires were not democratic, but were built to be inclusive of all those who came under their rule. It is not the same with nations, which are founded on the fundamental distinction between who is in and who is out – and therefore harbour a tendency toward ethnic purification. This makes them much more unstable than empires, for that tendency can always be stoked by nativist demagogues [...] In the previous century it was decided with amazing alacrity that empires belonged to the past, and the future to nation states. (2018)

As should be clear from the above summary of the volume's structure, a number of the chapters that follow (Tolz; Maiorova; Radunović, Filimonova; Curtis; Tyulenev & Nuriev) demonstrate how the Russian experience, imperial and post-imperial, offers both corroborations of, and challenges to, Dasgupta's position. But what of language? Again, several chapters in our volume demonstrate the instructive potential of the Russian experience. For example, the transnational Meduza news portal (Strukov), the London-based Russian-speaking diaspora (Ryazanova-Clark), and 'New Drama' in the former Soviet area (Curtis) illustrate contexts in which language can work through and beyond its associations with nation and empire in order to detach itself from them and reassert a post-imperial unifying function.

Indeed, the transnational reframing of our Russian cases directly questions the axiom 'monolingualism = bad / multilingualism = good' that seems to be a present article of faith among self-respecting modern linguists. Just as the multilingual is often the monolingual multiplied, so the monolingual (single-languaged) does not equate to the univocal (single-voiced), but can, under certain conditions, be capacious and inclusive (Denman 2017). This subversive conviction is shared by Bernard Avishai in relation to the role that the linguistic sensibility shared by Hebrew speakers in Tel Aviv could play in creating a truly inclusive Israeli state:

> The latter Hebrew is self-ironising, playfully anglicised – erotic, brassy, metaphorical, mischievous. This is the Hebrew every with-it Israeli knows and every democratic Israeli unknowingly counts on [...] The Hebrew of Tel Aviv is spacious enough for Arabs to absorb its nuances and yet remain Arabs, at least in the hybridised way minorities everywhere adapt to a majority's language and the culture it subtends. (2018)

Avishai's understanding of what it means to 'know' a language is broader than the mastery of vast lexical inventories, grammatical paradigms, rules of syntax, and oral/aural communication skills to which learners aspire in modern languages classes. It includes the multiple idiolects, attitudinal tones, speech genres, and stylistic registers through which ideas, thoughts, ideologies, and entire world views acquire flesh. As Valentin Voloshinov put it, language is not a function of the fixed, abstract systems we associate with the 'French', 'Russian', and 'Spanish' of language textbooks. Rather:

> The speaker's focus of attention is brought about in line with the particular, concrete utterance he is making [...] For him the center of gravity lies [...] in that new and concrete meaning it acquires in the particular context [...] What is important for the speaker about a linguistic form is not that it is a stable and self-equivalent signal but that it is an always changeable and adaptable sign. (Voloshinov 1973: 67–68)

There are lessons here for the way modern languages are taught, suggesting that (a) the separation of 'language acquisition and skills' from the study of literary, cultural, and historical 'content' is both suspect and false, and (b) that the teaching of modern languages, sociolinguistics, ethnolinguistics, and critical discourse analysis should go hand in hand, pointing towards new interdisciplinary allegiances. The discussion of the inseparability of language from the thoughts and ideas that it notionally 'encases' brings us full circle to the principle of Russian culture as an embodied community or linguistically defined network of subcommunities in a particular geo-historical chronotope – the concept, another of Bakhtin's (1981) richly productive neologisms, of time in-corporated (i.e. em-bodied) into space, and of space lived through time. This principle defines not just Russian studies, or even modern languages, but all of the humanities.

Moreover, if the humanities involves the study of shifting configurations of the relationship between language, chronotope, and intersubjectivity, the corollary is that each component of that trio is dependent upon the other two. We assert our humanity *as* intersubjectively connected communities, *in* language, *through* time-space. Such a formulation does not reduce all meaning to the function of the abstract, thinking subject. The notion of embodiment relates not just to that subject's corporeality. It also describes his/her situated-ness within a particular chronotope lived in communion with others through language. Moreover, even in the solipsistic form of individual consciousness, language is by definition intersubjective since, as 'inner speech' (to give it Voloshinov's formulation), consciousness is inherently social. The humanities we are describing have at their heart language in its widest definition, one whose understanding requires the specialist knowledge of modern linguists working in close collaboration with, and providing concrete, spatiotemporal context to, sociolinguists and discourse analysts drawn from multiple disciplinary arenas – literary, political, anthropological, and other. Indeed, as Mary Louise Pratt explains, epistemologically, reality can only be known *through* language and each actual language will generate its own distinctive version of that reality; hence the importance of 'knowing languages and of knowing the world through languages' (2003: 112).

Our intervention comes at a point when both the humanities and the social sciences are increasingly in thrall to methodologies designed to process ever larger quantities of 'big data'. However, the very idea of installing 'data' at the centre of the humanities is inimical to its mission. Bakhtin differentiates the exact and the human sciences by distinguishing the former's focus on lifeless 'things' (for which we can read 'data') from the latter's interest in speaking 'subjects':

In opposition to the subject there is [for the exact sciences] only a voiceless thing. Any object of knowledge (including man) can be perceived and cognized as a thing. But a subject as such cannot be perceived and studied as a thing, for as a subject it cannot, while remaining a subject, become voiceless, and, consequently, cognition of it can only be dialogic. (1986: 160–61)

A not dissimilar emphasis is to be found in Patricia Clavin's definition of the transnational itself. For Clavin, transnationalism is 'first and foremost about people: the social spaces they inhabit, the networks they form and the ideas they exchange' (2005: 422). Missing from Clavin's account is language: for without language, these ideas cannot be expressed nor exchanged, nor these spaces made social. It is the latter perspective that modern languages as a domain of study provides, giving, through the study of language and culture, access to human beings in the fullness of their spatiotemporally lived, intersubjective existence. With this key omission made good, we come close to identifying an intellectual agenda in which the transnational is something to be embraced even as it is transcended and transformed into something else: the transnational as *trans-national*. Here we draw on debates around the emerging concept of 'translocality', characterized by Greiner and Sakdapolrap as 'a "transgressing" of locally bounded, fixed understandings of place [which] at the same time emphasises the importance of places as nodes where flows that transcend spatial scales converge' (2013: 377). Wherever such a 'transgressing' ends up, it will bear the heavy responsibility of serving as a staging post for an as yet inchoate, but radical, rethinking of the humanities, and of the still precarious place of modern languages within it, including more specific areas of research, teaching, and expertise, such as Russian studies.

Works Cited

Aleksievich, Svetlana. 2015. 'On the Battle Lost'. Nobel Lecture <https://www.nobelprize.org/prizes/literature/2015/alexievich/25408-nobel-lecture-2015/> [accessed 23 August 2018].

Appiah, Kwame Anthony. 1997. 'Cosmopolitan Patriots', *Critical Inquiry*, 23(3): 617–39.

Avishai, Bernard. 2018. 'The Fight to Determine the Very Essence of Israel', *Guardian*, 20 May <https://www.theguardian.com/commentisfree/2018/may/20/the-fight-to-define-the-very-essence-of-israel?CMP=Share_iOSApp_Other> [accessed 20 July 2018].

Bakhtin, Mikhail. 1981. 'Forms of Time and of the Chronotope in the Novel' in M. Holquist and C. Emerson (eds), *The Dialogic Imagination: Four Essays by M.M. Bakhtin* (Austin, TX: University of Texas Press), 84–258.

——. 1986. 'Towards a Methodology for the Human Sciences' in M. M. Bakhtin, *Speech Genres and Other Late Essays*, ed. Caryl Emerson and Michael Holquist (Austin, TX: University of Texas Press), 159–70.

——. 1990. *Art and Answerability: Early Philosophical Essays*, ed. Michael Holquist and Vadim Liapunov (Austin, TX: University of Texas Press).

Bourdieu, Pierre. 1998. *Practical Reason: On the Theory of Action* (Stanford, CA: Stanford University Press).

Brubaker, Rogers. 2011. 'Nationalizing States Revisited: Projects and Processes of Nationalization in Post-Soviet States', *Ethnic and Racial Studies*, 34(11): 1785–814.

Brudny, Yitzhak M. 1998. *Reinventing Russia: Russian Nationalism and the Soviet State, 1953–1991* (Cambridge, MA: Harvard University Press).

Burns, Jenny, and Derek Duncan (eds). Forthcoming. *Transnational Modern Languages: A Handbook* (Liverpool: Liverpool University Press).

Casanova, Pascale. 2004. *The World Republic of Letters*, trans. M. B. DeBevoise (Cambridge, MA: Harvard University Press).

Clark, Katerina. 2011. *Moscow, the Fourth Rome: Stalinism, Cosmopolitanism, and the Evolution of Soviet Culture, 1931–1941* (Cambridge, MA: Harvard University Press).

Clavin, Patricia. 2005. 'Defining Transnationalism', *Contemporary European History*, 14(4): 421–39.

Clowes, Edith W. 2011. *Russia on the Edge: Imagined Geographies and Post-Soviet Identity* (Ithaca, NY: Cornell University Press).

Damrosch, David. 2003. *What Is World Literature?* (Princeton, NJ and Oxford: Princeton University Press).

Dasgupta, Rana. 2018. 'The Demise of the Nation State', *Guardian*, 5 April <https://www.theguardian.com/news/2018/apr/05/demise-of-the-nation-state-rana-dasgupta> [accessed 20 July 2018].

David-Fox, Michael. 2015. *Crossing Borders: Modernity, Ideology, and Culture in Russia and the Soviet Union* (Pittsburgh, PA: University of Pittsburgh Press).

De Cleen, Benjamin, and Antonin Galanopoulos. 2016. 'Populism, Nationalism and Transnationalism', Open Democracy, 25 October <https://www.opendemocracy.net/can-europe-make-it/antonis-galanopoulos-benjamin-de-cleen/you-can-use-populism-to-send-migrants-back> [accessed 17 August 2018].

Denman, Feargus. 2017. 'Our Languages, Our Language Ideologies, and Russian Language in Ireland: Monolingualism in the Midst of Cultural and Linguistic Diversity' (unpublished PhD thesis, Trinity College Dublin).

Dostoevsky, Fyodor. 1994. *A Writer's Diary Volume 2: 1877–1881*, trans. and ed. Kenneth Lantz (Evanston, IL: Northwestern University Press).

Etkind, Alexander. 2011. *Internal Colonization: Russia's Imperial Experience* (Cambridge: Polity Press).

Florensky, Pavel. 2006. *Beyond Vision: Essays on the Perception of Art* (London: Reaktion Books).

Foster, John Burt, Jr. 2013. *Transnational Tolstoy: Between the West and the World* (New York and London: Bloomsbury Academic).

Geertz, Clifford. 1973. 'Thick Description: Toward an Interpretive Theory of Culture' in Clifford Geertz, *The Interpretation of Cultures: Selected Essays* (New York: Basic Books), 3–30.

Gieryn, Thomas F. 1983. 'Boundary-Work and the Demarcation of Science from Non-Science: Strains and Interests in Professional Ideologies of Scientists', *American Sociological Review*, 48(6): 781–95.

Greiner, Clemens, and Patrick Sakdapolrap. 2013. 'Translocality: Concepts, Applications and Emerging Research Perspectives', *Geography Compass*, 7(5): 373–84.

Grishchenko, Aleksandr I. 2012. 'K noveishei istorii slova *rossiiane*', *Russkii iazyk v nauchnom osveshchenii*, 1: 119–39.

Hannerz, Ulf. 1996. *Transnational Connections: Cultures, People, Places* (London: Routledge).

Hirsch, Francine. 2005. *Empire of Nations: Ethnographic Knowledge and the Making of the Soviet Union* (Ithaca, NY: Cornell University Press).

Hoffmann, David L. 2011. *Cultivating the Masses: Modern State Practices and Soviet Socialism, 1914–1939* (Ithaca, NY: Cornell University Press).

Hudspith, Sarah, and Vlad Strukov (eds). 2018. *Russian Culture in the Era of Globalisation* (London: Routledge).

Iriye, Akira. 2013. *Global and Transnational History: The Past, Present, and Future* (Basingstoke, UK and New York: Palgrave Macmillan).

Jay, Paul. 2010. *Global Matters: The Transnational Turn in Literary Studies* (Ithaca, NY: Cornell University Press).

Khagram, Sanjeev, and Peggy Levitt (eds). 2008. *The Transnational Studies Reader: Intersections & Innovations* (New York: Routledge).

Laitin, David D. 1998. *Identity in Formation: The Russian-Speaking Populations in the Near Abroad* (Ithaca, NY: Cornell University Press).

Mogilner, Marina. 2013. *Homo Imperii: A History of Physical Anthropology in Russia* (Lincoln, NE: University of Nebraska).

Morson, Gary Saul, and Caryl Emerson. 1989. 'Introduction' in *Rethinking Bakhtin: Extensions and Challenges*, ed. Gary Saul Morson and Caryl Emerson (Evanston, IL: Northwestern University Press), 1–49.

Piaget, Jean, and Rolando Garcia. 1983. *Psychogenèse et histoire des sciences* (Paris: Flammarion).

Platt, Kevin M. F. 2018. *Global Russian Cultures* (Madison, WI: Wisconsin University Press).

Poe, Marshall. 2001. 'Moscow, the Third Rome: The Origins and Transformations of a "Pivotal Moment"', *Jahrbücher für Geschichte Osteuropas*, 49(3): 412–29.

Pratt, Mary Louise. 2003. 'Building a New Public Idea about Language', *Profession* (MLA Association): 110–19 <https://livelongday.files.wordpress.com/2011/08/prattnewpublicidea.pdf> [accessed 19 July 2018].

Raeff, Marc. 1990. *Russia Abroad: A Cultural History of the Russian Emigration, 1919–1939* (Oxford: Oxford University Press).

Riasanovsky, Nicholas, and Mark Steinberg. 2016. *A History of Russia* (Oxford: Oxford University Press).

Saunier, Pierre-Yves. 2013. *Transnational History* (Basingstoke, UK and New York: Palgrave Macmillan).

Shaffer, David W. 2006. 'Epistemic Frames for Epistemic Games', *Computers & Education*, 46(3): 223–34.

Slezkine, Yuri. 1994. 'The USSR as a Communal Apartment, or How a Socialist State Promoted Ethnic Particularism', *Slavic Review*, 53(2): 414–52.

Taylor, Charles. 2003. *Modern Social Imaginaries* (Durham, NC: Duke University Press).

Tiutchev, F. I. 2003. *Polnoe sobranie sochinenii. Tom vtoroi: Stikhotvoreniia 1850–1873* (Moscow: Klassika).

Tyrrell, Ian. 2007. 'What Is Transnational History?' (blog post) <https://iantyrrell. wordpress.com/what-is-transnational-history/> [accessed 9 August 2018].

Vertovec, Steven. 2009. *Transnationalism* (London and New York: Routledge).

Voloshinov, Valentin. 1973. *Marxism and the Philosophy of Language*, trans. L. Matejka and I. Titunik (Cambridge, MA: Harvard University Press).

Wachtel, Andrew. 1999. 'Translation, Imperialism, and National Self-Definition in Russia', *Public Culture*, 11(1): 49–73.

Wells, Naomi. 2017. 'British Academy Plenary Round Table: Does Modern Languages Have a Disciplinary Identity?' (blog post) <http://projects.alc. manchester.ac.uk/cross-language-dynamics/british-academy-plenary-round-table-does-modern-languages-have-a-disciplinary-identity/> [accessed 19 July 2018].

Werner, Michael, and Bénédicte Zimmerman. 2006. 'Beyond Comparison: *Histoire Croisée* and the Problem of Reflexivity', *History and Theory*, 45(1): 30–50.

Wimmer, Andreas, and Nina Glick Schiller. 2002. 'Methodological Nationalism and Beyond: Nation-State Building, Migration and the Social Sciences', *Global Networks*, 2(4): 301–34.

——. 2003. 'Methodological Nationalism, the Social Sciences, and the Study of Migration: An Essay in Historical Epistemology', *The International Migration Review*, 37(2): 576–610.

Zúquete, José Pedro. 2015. 'The New Frontlines of Right-Wing Nationalism', *Journal of Political Ideologies*, 20(1): 69–85.

Part I

Nation, Empire, and Beyond

1

Transnational, Multinational, or Imperial?

The Paradoxes of Russia's (Post)coloniality

Vera Tolz

Ever since the nation emerged as a particularly powerful way of imagining a political community in the late eighteenth century, the notion of a discrete national tradition has been unable to withstand close scrutiny. Cultural, political, and economic flows across 'national' borders and the importance of the external Other for any definition of the national self ensure that there is always a strong transnational dimension at the very heart of forging the nation. In the case of Russia, the long history of a geographically contiguous imperial state, in which peoples with different cultures, languages, and religions have been living side by side, makes the myth of a clearly defined national community all the more ephemeral. Elaborating on this point, Nancy Condee argues against understanding Russia's 'imagined community' as a 'nation', for this can only hinder 'our understanding of Russia's discursive formations'. Instead, she urges scholars to employ analytical strategies that would help capturing Russia's 'imperial peculiarity' (Condee 2009: 10–11). Indeed, for example, what we normally call 'Russian culture' has been constituted through complex interactions between different traditions of the peoples of the multi-ethnic state, which was either imperial and colonial in nature in the tsarist period or had a quasi-imperial dimension in the Soviet era. Events of the post-Soviet period, such as the wars in Chechnya in 1994–96 and 1999–2009 or Russia's annexation of Crimea in 2014, can be productively seen as examples of an imperial situation. However, for over a century, Russians themselves have been using a different terminology to define their 'imagined community', such as a 'multi-people nation' [mnogonarodnaia natsiia], 'the multinational Soviet people' [mnogonatsional'nyi sovetskii narod], and 'the multinational people of the Russian Federation' [mnogonatsional'nyi narod Rossiiskoi Federatsii].

Are such references to multi-nationality, which implies a unique transnational and transcultural connectivity, mere euphemisms for talking about the dynamics typically pertaining to empire? Even if many external observers of Russia would be inclined to answer this question in the affirmative, the fact that, historically, particularly during the Soviet period, and today, Russians themselves are often reluctant to use the lens of imperialism to analyse Russia's culture, history, and politics, requires explanation. What are the origins of this reluctance and what does it tell us about how the relationship between the national, transnational, and imperial is perceived in the Russian context?

Explanations of Russia's unwillingness, particularly after the collapse of the Soviet Union in 1991, to interrogate its imperial history critically range from suggestions that Russia's role as imperial and colonial power has been 'obscured by its geographical contiguity with its colonies and by the sheer awfulness of its own twentieth-century history' (Lovell 2001: 516) to the simple claim that 'old imperial habits die hard' (Chernetsky 2003: 34). This chapter shifts the focus from 'objective' factors in shaping how Russia interprets its history to the subjective factor of perception, particularly to how Russians perceive the policies and intentions of their main Other: 'the West'. It is the West, rather than their own country, that Russians often imagine as pursuing aggressive and expansionist colonial policies. This chapter shows that, as early as in the first half of the nineteenth century, Russian thinkers articulated a set of ideas that we might now call 'postcolonial' (though that term, of course, did not exist at the time). From the start, the aim of this intellectual trend was not to interrogate Russia's own policies and practices, but to condemn Western colonialism, while claiming Russia to be one of its victims. Alternative frameworks and terminology were then invented to define and explain Russia's own empire-building. This approach, in which Russia's 'postcolonial' critique of the West tends to hinder scrutiny of Russia's own imperial past, has endured through the twentieth century to this day. As we will see, it still influences not only the framing of Russian identity in public discourses, but also scholarly interpretations of Russian history and culture.

The Origins of Russia's Postcolonial Thought

It was the Slavophiles who, in the 1840s, first used colonialism as the frame for their assessment of Russia's international and domestic situation. Paradoxically, in their writings, Russia appears to be not a European imperial state, as it was represented in official discourse of the time, but Europe's colony and a prime target of its cultural imperialism. A leading Slavophile thinker of the day, Aleksei Khomiakov, spoke about the existence in his country of two societal spheres – the external material sphere, where the borrowing of European technological innovations could be of value, and the internal sphere or, in Khomiakov's terminology, 'internal life' [vnutrenniaia zhizn'], which should maintain authentic roots and be protected from domination by an alien culture. Khomiakov's discussion anticipates ideas that would appear in the work of postcolonial theorists such as Partha Chatterjee some 150 years later (Chatterjee 1993). According to Khomiakov, in the case of Russia, Peter the Great's reforms allowed indigenous 'internal life' to become contaminated by western European influences. Despite the fact that there were different ways of making sense of the world and arriving at the 'truth', the Russian elites began to see one 'arbitrary approach' [proizvol'naia teoriia] – European Enlightenment thought – as normative and universal, the author complained. As a result, Russia became 'a colony' [koloniia] of those whom Khomiakov called 'European eclectics' [evropeiskie eklektiki]. Paradoxically, these colonizers were not foreign invaders who used military force to conquer Russia but the country's own elites, who internalized European ideas that were at odds with Russia's indigenous tradition and practices. These elites, Khomiakov claimed, started behaving like real colonizers, acting in their own country as if they 'had been thrown into a land of savages'. 'Like any colony anywhere in the world, we acquired a conquering character [kharakter zavoevatel'nyi]', he concluded. This was the 'conquest' of Russia's ordinary people [narod], largely the peasantry, by the country's elites whose own minds had been conquered by European culture (Khomiakov 1900: 92–93).

As Gerasimov et al. have argued, in the absence of any actual political subjugation of Russia by the 'West', the Slavophiles identified a colonial situation as above all 'an acute epistemological problem' (2013: 102). Ideas and theories imported from Europe were thus perceived as a particularly destructive tool of colonization. Similarly to future postcolonial theorists who emphasized the centrality of culture to European colonial projects (Dirks 2001), the Slavophiles saw Europe's cultural domination of the rest of the world as leading to a more profound (and ultimately negative) transformation of the impacted societies than could have been achieved through military and political means. In different forms, this interpretation was echoed by a range of nineteenth-century Russian authors (Peterson 2000).

Throughout the nineteenth century, representations of Western, particularly British, colonialism as brutally exploitative and destructive encouraged claims about the comparatively benign nature of Russia's imperial expansion (Tolz 2010: 275–86). For example, the concept of the 'natural borders' [estestvennye granitsy] of the Eurasian plain predetermining the Russian state's borders facilitated the late imperial historian Vasilii Kliuchevskii's conclusion that Russian empire-building was an act of self-colonization. In this interpretation, self-colonization meant the establishment of Russian rule over territories which had been predestined to be Russian, rather than the imposition of colonial control over culturally different communities or polities (Kliuchevskii 1987: 49–53). Significantly, while similarly self-serving justifications for colonial policies were typical for European empires of the time (Cooper 2005: 172), Russian intellectuals' attack on Europe's 'epistemological imperialism' was novel. It facilitated Russians' self-perception as subalterns and allowed them to imagine their own colonial enterprise as different.

The critique of Europe's cultural imperialism first acquired prominence among European intellectuals at the turn of the twentieth century (i.e. half a century after its articulation in Russia). For example, starting in the 1880s, European scholars, particularly those whose research focused on non-European languages and cultures, began to challenge dominant assumptions about the superiority of the European civilization and perceptions of European experiences as normative (Marchand 2009). In this period, Russian intellectuals again appeared at the forefront of the attack on Eurocentrism, which included a strong critique of European imperialism (Tolz 2011). This was especially the case with so-called 'Eurasianists' who claimed the existence on the territory of the Russian Empire of a unique civilization, which was neither European nor Asian. Anticipating later postcolonial critique of the dominant premises of Western scholarship, they attacked the methodologies of European scientific disciplines from anthropology to linguistics for assuming the universality of the European episteme and postulated European scholarship's complicity in colonial exploitation (Gerasimov et al. 2013: 104–05).

In the writings of the Eurasianists, the paradoxes of Russia's anti-Eurocentric critique fully crystallized. This critique reflected a peculiar dynamic of two conflicting interpretations of Russia. The first related to the representation of Russia's imperial policies as a positive example of managing ethnic diversity. In this interpretation, Russians appeared as founders of a superior type of polity. As one of the leading Eurasianists, Petr Savitskii, put it: 'Eurasia is the sphere of certain equality and fraternization of nations, which has no analogies in relations among nationalities within colonial empires. The Eurasian culture can be understood as a common product and common property of the peoples of Eurasia' (cit. Gerasimov et al. 2013: 107). The Eurasianists rejected any references to Russian imperialism and instead defined their 'imagined community' of Russia-Eurasia as a multi-people nation [mnogonarodnaia natsiia]. Simultaneously, echoing the Slavophiles, they represented Russia as a subaltern society whose indigenous cultural tradition had been distorted by European influences which were colonial in nature. Ultimately, this discourse of Russia's dual identity and the accompanying reimagination of Russia as a distinct Eurasian civilization were aimed at justifying the maintenance of the territorial integrity of the (former) Russian Empire.

This group of Eurasianists were émigrés who had fled Russia in the wake of the 1917 revolution. However, some academics who stayed in the country after the revolution also offered a particularly radical critique of established European paradigms of knowledge production in the 1920s. Some of their arguments bear a striking resemblance to (post-)Saidian postcolonial studies. For example, the controversial linguist and orientologist Nikolai Marr aimed to demonstrate that the colonial assumptions and racist prejudices of Indo-European philology led directly to the marginalization of languages and cultures without an established literary culture and to the unfounded prioritization of the so-called 'Aryans' in history (Tolz 2011: 125–27; Brandist 2017). In Marr's words, Indo-European philology was 'built on the oppression of the peoples of the East by the murderous colonial policies of European nations' (1934: 1).

A similarly sweeping criticism of Western scholarship was articulated by Marr's colleague, Sergei Ol'denburg. Criticizing his own discipline of oriental studies for 'rendering the East voiceless', Ol'denburg attacked European scholars for being influenced by the misplaced perception of profound difference between the East and the West. 'In the history of juxtaposing the East and the West, imperialistic tendencies always played a key role', he concluded. In a similar vein to what Edward Said would argue in his *Orientalism* (1978), Ol'denburg suggested that the very existence of the term 'oriental studies' [vostokovedenie] was a reflection of these attitudes, as there was no comparable discipline of 'occidental studies' [zapadovedenie] (Tolz 2011: 98). Yet, like the Eurasianists, these academics largely exempted Russia's own scholarship about the East from their critique. They claimed that the Russian tradition of producing knowledge about the 'Orient' was different from that of the European West. In their account, the Russians' experience of living in a multi-ethnic state with a large Asian population allowed them to embrace an inclusive transnationalism, while rejecting an exclusionary colonial viewpoint, and thereby to challenge the East-West dichotomy which framed European scholarship (Tolz 2011).

Such arguments fit, to some extent, the ideological environment of the 1920s, when the early Bolshevik government was claiming to be building a new type of multi-ethnic society on anti-imperial premises and leading the liberation of the peoples of the 'East' from Western colonial exploitation. In its condemnation of imperialism and colonialism, the early Bolshevik regime went further than former imperial scholars, unequivocally extending its critique to tsarist Russia. In official Bolshevik discourse of the time, tsarist imperial policies were not spared condemnation, and Lenin even singled out the Russians as a people particularly responsible for the colonial oppression of minorities (Martin 2001). The most influential pro-Bolshevik historian of the time, Mikhail Pokrovskii, explicitly mocked the idea of seeing Russia as 'a colony of western European capital' [koloniia dlia zapadnoevropeiskogo kapitala]; according to him, this view had enjoyed popularity particularly in the first decade of the twentieth century. Instead, Pokrovskii saw pre-revolutionary Russia as one of 'the greatest *colonial states* in the world' (Pokrovskii 1925, vol. 5–6: 89; emphasis in the original). He suggested that the contiguous nature of the Russian imperial state prevented many Russians from seeing Siberia, Central Asia, and the Caucasus as colonies, because they wrongly identified only Europe's overseas domains as such (Pokrovskii 1925). Never before or after in the Russian intellectual tradition was Russia so strongly criticized as a brutal colonial power as by the early Bolshevik leaders, particularly Lenin, and by pro-Bolshevik academics of the Pokrovskii school.

However, the public promotion of such ideas and their impact was limited and short-lived. In the 1930s, the revisionist agenda of the early twentieth century was replaced by new state-sponsored narratives that resurrected some of the crudest representations of Russian imperial policies of the tsarist era as either entirely beneficial for the conquered societies or a lesser evil than western European colonialism. This period also reproduced Orientalizing clichés about non-European societies and religions (Tillett 1969). In this context, the Russian people were reimagined as 'the elder brother' in the family of the Soviet nations (Martin 2001). This ideological shift resulted in Pokrovskii's posthumous fall from favour (Enteen 1978). But even during Pokrovskii's life, his closeness to the Bolshevik regime and the ideological crudeness of his writings discouraged leading humanities scholars, most of whom were critical of the Bolshevik regime, from engaging seriously with his arguments.

It is also significant that Pokrovskii's work unwittingly reinforced the very stereotypes and modes of Othering that he attempted to challenge. In fact, his broad conceptual framework was less 'postcolonial' than those of scholars such as Marr and Ol'denburg. Pokrovskii's main concern was not with the peoples and societies conquered by the empire, but with the situation in 'Russia proper'. The overarching argument of Pokrovskii's work is that the negative influences emanating from the peripheries of the empire were crucial for perpetuating the backwardness of Russian autocracy. In Pokrovskii's view, geographical distance and separation by water protected Britain and France from the corrupting influences of the 'primitive' cultures of the colonized. In contrast, the geography of the contiguous Russian imperial state allowed the 'primitive [pervobytnye] customs and norms' of its colonies to 'penetrate deeply into the centre' of the metropole (Pokrovskii 1925, vol. 5–6: 90–92).

In sum, the discussion of European and Russian colonialism in the Russian and Soviet intellectual traditions from the nineteenth century onwards combined original insights into the role of culture in colonial conquests and the questioning of European epistemology as normative, with self-serving arguments about the benign nature of Russia's territorial expansion and the supposed transnationalism of its culture. Representations of Russia as a brutal colonial power were short-lived and compromised by their simplistic framing and the complex relationship of their main proponents with the highly repressive political regime, which since the 1930s reappropriated positive interpretations of Russian imperial expansion anyway. Most Russians were little prepared, therefore, to hear claims, which suddenly began to be articulated in the late 1980s, during Mikhail Gorbachev's *glasnost'*, that the USSR was, in fact, an illegitimate empire after all.

Current Interpretations

In post-Soviet Russia, the tendency to contrast Russia's apparent ability to embrace multi-nationality with the West's destructive colonialism have persisted, informing official discourse (Putin 2012). Against this backdrop, public intellectuals, as well as some scholars, have been creatively engaging with both earlier Russian thought and Western postcolonial scholarship to interpret Russia's historical and current experiences. Contemporary authors who consider how the concept of (post)coloniality could be made relevant to understanding Russia's past and present do not constitute a single homogenous group, insofar as they put the ideas of Russian thinkers of the past, as well as those of contemporary postcolonial scholars, to very different uses. Some current interpretations of Russia's (post)coloniality are intellectual projects; others, however, have a clear political agenda.

Politicized claims about Russia's (post)coloniality have been formulated in the context of the currently growing anti-Western sentiments in Russia and the proliferation of conspiratorial explanations of both historical and current events. Thus prominent public intellectuals with access to mass media have been promoting the view that, following the collapse of the Soviet regime in 1991, the West has turned Russia into what the publicist Dmitrii Galkovskii has called a 'crypto-colony' [kriptokoloniia], a term used to describe a country that is formally independent but is in reality economically, politically, and culturally dependent on the West (Galkovskii 2011). What this means in the case of Russia is spelled out in the work of another public intellectual, Nikolai Starikov:

> In 1991, we were turned into a colony. El'tsin's government and the oligarchs were a typical colonial administration. A typical colonial

regime, which Anglo-Saxons [historically] have been imposing around the world, was established in Russia. They [the Anglo-Saxons] arrive in a country and buy off the local elites for beads [...] With the help of these corrupt elites, they then start pumping resources out of the country. We have had this regime since 1991. Under Putin, our country began moving towards sovereignty. However, the colonial regime is not completely overthrown. (Starikov 2012)

Such representations of Russia as a colony typically combine elements of Russia's own intellectual tradition, dating back to the Slavophiles and the Eurasianists, with contemporary Western scholarly concepts, though the latter are often not acknowledged. Galkovskii (2011), for example, insists that he is the sole inventor of the concept of crypto-colonialism. However, this concept, with a similar definition if not the same analytical application, was introduced a decade before Galkovskii by the Harvard anthropologist Michael Herzfeld. Herzfeld has used this concept to analyse the politics of culture in societies where Western colonialism works in disguise (i.e. societies that 'acquire their political independence at the expense of massive economic dependence'). In Herzfeld's account, these societies are in practice 'tributary nation-states' (2002: 900–01). Where Herzfeld uses the concept of crypto-colonialism to deconstruct political discourses and cultural practices in a wide range of societies, from Thailand to Greece, Galkovskii and Starikov deploy it to legitimize the current Russian government's confrontational stance towards the West.

An explicit rereading of Western postcolonial scholarship through the prism of the Slavophile critique of the relationship between Russia and the West is offered in the 2006 publication of the first ever Russian translation of Said's *Orientalism*. The author of the afterword to this edition, nationalist intellectual Konstantin Krylov, suggests that the main target of the Western technique of Orientalizing its Other is, in fact, Russia. Today, in Krylov's view, Russia is subjected to a greater degree of Orientalization than the Middle East, which has lately apparently been 'protected by political correctness'. But Western media and politicians are not held back by any restraints when they tell 'medieval fairy tales' about Russia. In the past, the West 'deprived peoples of the East of their own voice'; today it is the Russians who are not allowed 'to speak for themselves' (Krylov 2006: 635). Krylov thus makes direct use of the foundational text of postcolonial theory to articulate his version of the well-established argument about Russia's subaltern identity.

The perception that a peculiar amalgam of imperial (European) and subaltern identities makes Russia's historical experience of state-building unique is reflected in some current scholarship by academics of Russian origin working in foreign academic institutions, who offer a creative adaptation of postcolonial theory to the Russian case. We will now turn to the discussion of two representative works of this kind.

Alexander Etkind's use of postcolonial theory to develop the concept of Russia's 'internal colonization' can arguably be seen as a continuation of the search for Russia's subaltern identity. Etkind (2002, 2011) uses a wide range of analytical frameworks, from Said's Orientalism to Michael Hechter's notion of 'internal colonization' (developed on the case of the colonization of Britain's Celtic periphery by the English), to argue that, historically, in the case of Russia, the main Orientalized subaltern Other was, in fact, the Russian peasant. In drawing this conclusion, Etkind also relies, without explicitly interrogating it, on the Slavophiles' idea about the post-Petrine elites' colonization of their own people. While noting that Russia's internal colonization was accompanied by an external imperial expansion and that the two were closely intertwined, his account neglects to consider this external expansion in any depth. Etkind uses comparisons with Western European colonial experiences only to emphasize Russia's difference. In his words, 'The main vector of Russian colonization was directed not outwards, but inwards, inside the metropole [...] not towards Turkey, Poland or even Siberia, but into Tula, Pomor'e and Orenburg villages' (Etkind 2002: 275). 'The empire', he says, 'was colonizing its own Russian population. The scale of this task can only be compared to the British colonization of India' (Etkind 2002: 281). A wealth of telling examples are cited in support of this argument.

Advancing a single argument in a radical form is invariably fraught with the danger of overstating the case. Etkind's claim about the vector of Russian colonization is surprising in relation to the period he discusses. From the eighteenth century onwards, the Russian imperial state conquered huge new territories through directing its foreign policy both eastwards and westwards. This included Russia's participation in the partitions of Poland, and its conquest of Crimea as a result of a war with the Ottoman Empire and of the Caucasus through wars with the Ottomans and Persia. Other imperial acquisitions included Central Asia and the Kazakh steppe, the Amur region in the Far East, and Bessarabia in the West.

Some Western scholars have pointed out that the assumption of Russia's specificity can constitute an obstacle to scholars' engagement with postcolonial theory (Moore 2001; Khalid 2007). Etkind's work suggests that the emphasis on Russia's specificity can also facilitate this engagement. His creative adaptation of postcolonial theory is based on his strong claim about the uniqueness of the Russian case. But this claim is difficult to sustain. Recent scholarship which puts Russia in a proper comparative context shows that similarities between Russian and Western experiences of empire-building and empire maintenance are stronger than used to be assumed (Sahadeo 2010). In fact, Russian imperial actors of the time tended to compare their own policies with the policies of the British in India, not in the context of dealing with Russian peasants, but in relation to their actions in Central Asia (Morrison 2008).

Moreover, European states such as Britain and France both transformed and eradicated local cultures, practices, and traditions, particularly of the peasantry, as part of their domestic nation-building in the nineteenth century, using methods which were comparable to those analysed by Etkind in the Russian case (Hechter 1975; Baycroft 2008). Othering on the basis not of skin colour, but social origin, which the concept of internal colonization foregrounds, was also not specific to Russia. In Victorian Britain, for example, biological explanations were utilized to claim the inferiority of the working classes (Malik 1996: 91–98), in what appears to be a direct parallel to the Russian playwright Griboedov's suggestion that the elites and the peasants in Russia might have originated 'from different tribes' (cit. Etkind 2002: 274).

The concept of internal colonization is also applied by some scholars to contemporary Russia. Thus, in his book on Russia's postcolonial identity, the Tartu-based Russian scholar Viatcheslav Morozov echoes the Slavophiles' and Eurasianists' assumption that Russia 'has been colonized while remaining a sovereign state'. For Morozov, in the post-Soviet context, this feature of Russia is reflected in what he sees as the colonization of the country by its own elites 'on behalf of the global capitalist core' (2015: 32). These elites have only managed to achieve Russia's integration into the global economic and political mainstream as a 'semi-peripheral nation', given that the country has not been able to overcome its dependency on the West, both economic and cultural. Alluding to Homi Bhabha's (1984) concept of 'colonial mimicry', Morozov suggests that the subaltern status of today's Russia is reflected in the country's inability to articulate its own internationally convincing narratives. It is the resentment of this status that encourages its leadership's neo-imperial ambitions. From this account, Putin's Russia emerges as a distinctive type of 'subaltern empire', whose elites' actions are best understood if compared to the Indian elites' response to the British cultural domination.

Conclusion

There is, in fact, a lot to be said for Morozov's argument that the complex relationship between subaltern and imperial identities is important for our understanding of Russia's historical and current developments. As this chapter has argued, the Russian elites' perception of their country's subaltern character has hampered their ability critically to interrogate the nature of

Russian (and Soviet) state-building policies. Russia's troubled interaction with the 'West' often prompts its elites to adopt a defensive stance. Such a stance provides the context in which claims about the trans- and multi-nationality of Russia's statehood and culture, which is different from Western colonialism, are articulated, and in which the Bolshevik government could, for example, simultaneously engage in regaining the territory of the collapsed tsarist empire and attempt to act as the world's leader of decolonization, without acknowledging the contradiction or paradox that this entailed.

A systematic analysis of the relationship between subaltern and imperial identities in the case of Russia is likely to enrich and take forward postcolonial studies. For this undertaking to be successful, however, two pitfalls, which for too long have been influencing our thinking about the issue, should be avoided. First is the tendency to claim the uniqueness of the Russian case, representing Russian experiences as exceptional. While contemporary postcolonial studies as a field of scholarly enquiry has a strong transnational dimension in its rejection of national boundaries as a viable frame for exploring issues that have been central for maintaining colonial power, Russia's (post)coloniality is all too often evoked to construct imaginings of Russia's unique tradition. The notion of uniqueness falls apart, however, once a comparative approach is adopted, which reveals specific adaptations within the Russian context of wider transnational trends. The latter tend to be the result both of the circulation of ideas and actors across state and national borders and of structural similarities between state practices. The second pitfall is the tendency to use the narratives and concepts of the historical actors we are studying as our own tools of analysis. The Slavophiles and the Eurasianists offered striking insights into the relationship between culture and power, yet they were, above all, politically engaged thinkers whose interpretations of Russia's (post) coloniality reveal much about the intellectual and political environment of their time, but they are hardly objective or reliable guides to the policies and practices that we are striving to understand.

Works Cited

Baycroft, Timothy. 2008. *France: Inventing the Nation* (London: Arnold).

Bhabha, Homi. 1984. 'Of Mimicry and Man: The Ambivalence of Colonial Discourse', *Discipleship*, 28: 125–33.

Brandist, Craig. 2017. 'Marxism, Early Soviet Oriental Studies and the Problem of 'Power/Knowledge', *International Politics* <https://link.springer.com/article/1 0.1057%2Fs41311-017-0099-8> [accessed 18 July 2018].

Chatterjee, Partha. 1993. *The Nation and its Fragments: Colonial and Postcolonial Histories* (Princeton, NJ: Princeton University Press).

Chernetsky, Vitaly. 2003. 'Postcolonialism, Russia and Ukraine', *Ulbandus*, 7(1): 32–62.

Condee, Nancy. 2009. *The Imperial Trace: Recent Russian Cinema* (Oxford: Oxford University Press).

Cooper, Frederick. 2005. *Colonialism in Question: Theory, Knowledge, History* (Berkeley, CA: University of California Press).

Dirks, Nicholas. 2001. *Castes of Mind: Colonialism and the Making of Modern India* (Princeton, NJ: Princeton University Press).

Enteen, George. 1978. *The Soviet Scholar-Bureaucrat: M. N. Pokrovskii and the Society of Marxist Historians* (University Park, PA: Pennsylvania State University Press).

Etkind, Aleksandr. 2002. 'Bremia britogo cheloveka, ili Vnutrenniia kolonizatsiia Rossii', *Ab Imperio*, 1: 265–98.

——. 2011. *Internal Colonization: Russia's Imperial Experience* (Cambridge: Polity Press).

Galkovskii, Dmitrii. 2011. 'O kriptokolonii' <http://galkovsky.livejournal.com/183226.html> [accessed 2 August 2017].

Gerasimov, Ilya, Sergey Glebov, and Marina Mogilner. 2013. 'The Postimperial Meets the Postcolonial: Russian Historical Experience and the Postcolonial Moment', *Ab Imperio*, 2: 97–135.

Hechter, Michael. 1975. *Internal Colonialism: The Celtic Fringe in British National Development* (Berkeley, CA: University of California Press).

Herzfeld, Michael. 2002. 'The Absent Presence: Discourses of Crypto-Colonialism', *The South Atlantic Quarterly*, 101(4): 899–926.

Khalid, Adeeb. 2007. 'Introduction: Locating the (Post-)colonial in Soviet History', *Central Asian Survey*, 26(4): 465–73.

Khomiakov, Aleksei. 1900. 'O vosmozhnosti Russkoi khodozhestvennoi shkoly, 1847' in Aleksei Khomiakov, *Polnoe sobranie sochinenii*, vol. 1 (Moscow: Universitetskaia tipografiia), 73–101.

Kliuchevskii, Vasilii. 1987. 'Kurs russkoi istorii. Chast' I, Lektsiia II, 1904' in Vasilii Kliuchevskii, *Sochineniia v deviati tomakh*, vol. 1 (Moscow: Mysl'): 49–62.

Krylov, Konstantin. 2006. 'Itogi Saida: Zhizn' i kniga' in Edvard V. Said, *Orientalizm. Zapadnye kontseptsii Vostoka* (St Petersburg: Russkii mir), 598–635.

Lovell, Stephen. 2001. 'Review of *Imperial Knowledge: Russian Literature and Colonialism* by Ewa M. Thompson', *Slavonic and East European Review*, 79(3): 515–17.

Malik, Kenan. 1996. *The Meaning of Race: Race, History and Culture in Western Society* (New York: New York University Press).

Marchand, Suzanne L. 2009. *German Orientalism in the Age of Empire: Religion, Race and Scholarship* (New York: Cambridge University Press).

Marr, Nikolai. 1934. 'O iafeticheskoi teorii' in Nikolai Marr, *Izbrannye raboty*, vol. 3 (Moscow and Leningrad: Gosudarstvennoe sotsialno-ekonomicheskoie izdatel'stvo), 1–28.

Martin, Terry. 2001. *The Affirmative Action Empire: Nations and Nationalism in the USSR* (Ithaca, NY: Cornell University Press).

Moore, David Chioni. 2001. 'Is the Post- in Postcolonial the Post- in Post-Soviet? Toward a Global Postcolonial Critique', *Papers of the Modern Languages Association of America*, 116(1): 111–28.

Morozov, Viatcheslav, 2015. *Russia's Postcolonial Identity: A Subaltern Empire in a Eurocentric World* (London: Palgrave Macmillan).

Morrison, Alexander. 2008. *Russian Rule in Samarkand 1868–1910: A Comparison with British India* (Oxford: Oxford University Press).

Peterson, Dale E. 2000. *Up from Bondage: The Literatures of Russian and African American Soul* (Durham, NC: Duke University Press).

Pokrovskii, Mikhail. 1925. 'K voprosu ob osobennostiakh istoricheskogo razvitiia Rossii', *Pod znamenem marksizma*, vol. 4, 123–41 and vol. 5–6, 89–109.

Putin, Vladimir. 2012. 'Rossiia: Natsional'nyi vopros', *Nezavisimaia gazeta*, 23 January, 1.

Sahadeo, Jeff. 2010. 'Visions of Empire: Russia's Place in an Imperial World', *Kritika: Explorations in Russian and Eurasian History*, 11(2): 381–409.

Said, Edward W. 1978. *Orientalism* (New York: Pantheon Books).

Starikov, Nikolai. 2012. 'Rossiia – koloniia Zapada' <http://poznavatelnoe.tv/starikov_russia_koloniya> [accessed 2 August 2017].

Tillett, Lowell R. 1969. *The Great Friendship: Soviet Historians on the Non-Russian Nationalities* (Chapel Hill, NC: University of North Carolina Press).

Tolz, Vera. 2010. 'Rossiiskie vostokovedy i obshcheevropeiskie tendentsii v razmyshleniiakh ob imperiiakh kontsa XIX–nachala XX veka' in Martin Aust, Ricarda Vulpius, and Aleksei Miller (eds), *Imperium inter pares: rol' transferov v istorii Rossiiskoi imperii 1700–1917* (Moscow: NLO), 266–307.

——. 2011. *'Russia's Own Orient': The Politics of Identity and Oriental Studies in the Late Imperial and Early Soviet Periods* (Oxford: Oxford University Press).

2

Gogol''s Other Coat

Transnationalism in Russia's Literary Borderlands

Amelia M. Glaser

'We all emerged from under Gogol''s overcoat', Dostoevskii purportedly declared of Russian realism. If the 'we all' of Dostoevskii's oft-cited homage to Gogol' implies a linguistically Russian literary discourse inspired by Gogol''s short story 'The Overcoat' [Shinel', 1842], then a return to Gogol' as the founder of a national canon prompts us to modify our approach to the Russian literary tradition as such. A transnational understanding of the tsarist empire requires us to take Russia's literary history beyond the Russian language in order to scrutinize more closely its ethnic and linguistic entanglements. Such a perspective enables greater appreciation of the literary traditions of groups that would later build independent nation states, while simultaneously renewing our approach to the empire that influenced them. For an internally transnational reading of Russian literature it is worth training our focus on Russia's vast border regions. The Pale of Settlement – the western region of the Russian Empire where Jews were confined to live between, roughly, 1791 and 1917 – offers a case study in literary dialogues between coexisting groups – in this case between Russians, Ukrainians, and Jews (see map in Fig. 2.1). These groups did not always live in harmony, but the stories they wrote demonstrate an awareness of cultural, economic, and personal intersections within their Ukrainian contact zone.[1]

The Pale of Settlement, like other parts of the Russian Empire's vast border region, presented a tangible challenge to the imperial centre, precisely for its multitude of national minorities, with their range of languages, religious

---

[1] For two approaches to the 'contact zone' see Pratt (1992: 1–12), Bakhtin (1983: 34–50, esp. 45), as well as Glaser (2012), which includes a more extensive analysis of the authors and texts discussed in this article.

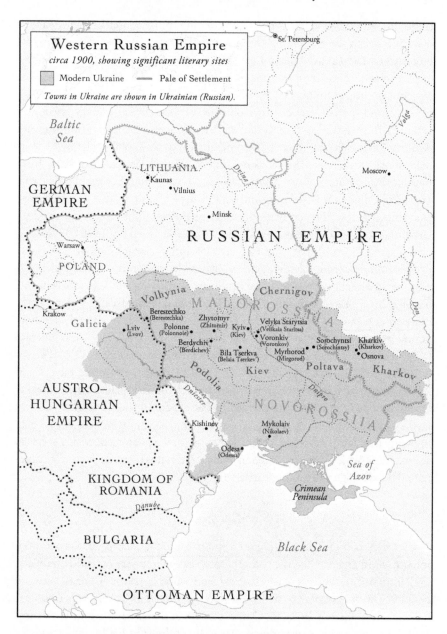

Fig. 2.1. Map of the western Russian Empire, *c.* 1900.
Map by Beehive Mapping (Glaser 2012; xii).

traditions, and cultural narratives. I am treating transnational literary relations here as a prism for examining the points of intersection that make up world literature as a whole, and the multiple literatures of the tsarist empire as a subset of that whole. These intersections allow us better to scrutinize the ways that national traditions influenced, resisted, and struggled with one another. With this in mind, I shall propose that one such transnational literary encounter emerged from under one of Gogol''s many literary garments. This was not Akakii Akakievich's overcoat, but the devilish 'red cloak' of Gogol''s first widely read short story, 'The Fair at Sorochintsy' [Sorochinskaia iarmarka], from *Evenings on a Village Farm Near Dikanka* [Vechera na khutore bliz Dikanki, 1831]. Published in St Petersburg and containing a Ukrainian glossary, this story has echoed across the centuries not only in Russian, but also in the modern Ukrainian and Yiddish literary traditions that flourished not far from Gogol''s birthplace in Sorochintsy. 'The Fair at Sorochintsy' established an imagined, peripheral folk centre for literature in Russia's borderlands – a Ukrainian fair that was in direct dialogue with the Petersburg core. I shall focus in this chapter on what I have elsewhere called Gogol''s 'commercial landscape' – the literary markets and fairs of the Ukrainian borderlands – which re-emerges in short fiction by, among others, the Ukrainian writer Hryhorii Kvitka-Osnov'ianenko (1778–1843) and the Yiddish writer Sholem Aleichem (1859–1916) (Glaser 2012: 24–56). The markets and fairs of tsarist Ukraine, attracting buyers and sellers from surrounding regions, were among the few places where diverse ethnic groups interacted. The literature that describes these commercial sites is, then, a literature of transnational encounter. The examples below – tales of uncanny transformations, of a coat, a portrait, and a goat, respectively – reveal the extent to which imperial Russian commercial sites inspired stories of transnational exchange within the Russian Empire.

The Coat

A few years before Gogol' depicted a multi-ethnic landscape in Sorochintsy, Johann Wolfgang von Goethe had generated his own theory of world literature, or *Weltliteratur*, which envisions it as a network, 'a traffic in ideas between peoples, a literary market to which the nations bring their intellectual treasures for exchange' (Strich 1971: 13; Damrosch 2003: 3).[2] With his fair, the ethnically Ukrainian Gogol' was doing just that: presenting his literary goods as products – fresh from his own backyard, in a language the Petersburg readers

---

[2] Goethe was corresponding with Eckermann about conceptions of *Weltliteratur* in the 1820s, in the decade leading up to his death in 1832. It is unlikely that Gogol' would have seen these notes before publishing his *Dikanka* cycles.

would understand. St Petersburg was then the centre of Russia's literary economy – a nineteenth-century Russian analogue to Pascale Casanova's Parisian 'World Republic of Letters', the geography of which 'is based on the opposition between a capital, on the one hand, and peripheral dependencies whose relationship to this centre is defined by their aesthetic distance from it' (Casanova 2004: 12). Gogol''s commercial landscape, as a peripheral challenge to the centre, is consecrated on the Petersburg publishing market, even as it reinforces early-nineteenth-century anxieties about the empire's borders. If, as Benedict Anderson has observed, premodern states 'were defined by their centres, borders were porous and indistinct, and sovereignties faded imperceptibly into one another' (1983: 19), modern empires strove for consolidated lands. By the time of the 1830–31 Polish uprising, the tsarist government was acutely aware of the risks of its multi-ethnic borderlands. The Ukrainian territories – called 'Little Russia' in contrast to the 'Greater Russia' of Eurasia – overlapped with the Jewish Pale of Settlement, much of which Catherine II had annexed from Poland in the eighteenth century. The markets and fairs in this region, where Jews, Ukrainians, Russians, and Poles (among other groups) met and exchanged goods, not only presented a geographical, cultural, and political counterpoint to the Russian imperial core of St Petersburg; their porousness also made them politically dangerous.

Gogol''s 'Fair at Sorochintsy' boasts a wealth of ethnic types, including Ukrainians, Russians, Jews, Poles, and Gypsies:

> a gypsy and peasant smacked hands violently after a bargain, crying out from pain, a drunken Jew slapped a woman on the backside; argumentative fishwives bandied abuse and crayfish [...] a Russian strokes his long, goatish beard with one hand. (2001: I 80)

The multiple ethnicities in Gogol''s commercial landscape sharpen the sense of a literary periphery. Gogol''s fictionalized provincial market presents the writer's birthplace – the village of Sorochintsy – as a literary home, even for his Russian readership. Gogol' had conjured folk practices and phrases via correspondence with his mother. He had drawn epigraphs from Ivan Kotliarevs'kyi's Ukrainian Virgilic travesty, *Eneida*, and his father's amateur Ukrainian plays (Kotliarevs'kyi 1989; Hohol'-Ianovskii 1918). For the Russophone Gogol', this Ukrainian flavour was not a liability, but an asset. As Edyta Bojanowska has observed, 'The cradle and treasury of Slavdom in Gogol's view, Ukraine could reorient Russia toward its Slavic roots and thus serve as an antidote to excessive Westernization, so inimical to an incipient national culture' (2007: 371). Ukrainian words, texts, and folk practices, presented within this Russian-language story, unite to form an origin story for the Russian literary imagination – a Slavic alternative to the great works of classical antiquity appearing in translation at the turn of the nineteenth century in the Russian capital.[3]

Gogol''s Ukrainian stories may present a surrogate home to his Russian readers, but they also present a distant, exotic locale that is, like the imperial borders themselves, open to penetration by dangerous outside commercial forces. 'The Fair at Sorochintsy' begins as a love story: a dark-browed beauty, Paraska, falls in love with the young Hrytsko, and the two become engaged. To win the hand of his beloved, Hrytsko orchestrates the telling of a frightening folktale of a devil's red coat, a pig, and a Jew, who together wreak havoc at the Sorochintsy fair. This tale within a tale dramatizes anxieties about the peripheral marketplace, for it tells of the terrifying reproduction of marketplace matter. A demon pawns his red coat to a Jewish vodka merchant in Sorochintsy, who appraises the quality of the fabric: 'such cloth, even in Mirgorod you couldn't procure the likes of it!' (Gogol' 2001: I 82). The coat passes to a Pole, a merchant, and eventually a virtuous peasant, who chops the coat into pieces. Ever since, the devil returns to the fair each year in the form of a pig to gather the lost scraps of his jacket. The frightening red material that circulates throughout the fair is directly connected to the foreign merchants who handle the red cloak. (The Jew is the only one who makes a profit on the coat.) The porousness of the borderlands allows for this penetration. The fluid marketplace commerce between national groups that existed on the margins of the empire serves as a tangible symbol of imperial anxieties about its borders. The demonic reproduction of marketplace matter and materiality would return throughout Gogol''s oeuvre, from Sorochintsy to the Petersburg artist Chartkov, to the quintessential devilish buyer, Chichikov, whose quest for the dead souls of peasants patterned Gogol''s final artistic efforts. Art itself is prone to demonic reproduction and circulation – suffice it to recall that after his early novel in verse, *Gants Kiukhelgarten*, was panned by reviews, Gogol' attempted to buy up, and destroy, all extant copies.[4]

After the folktale is told (at night in a tavern), the listeners are frightened by a pig, whose face appears at the window. Paraska's frightened father, Solopy Cherevik, loses track of his horse and grain, and when Hrytsko, the trickster-suitor, returns them to him, Cherevik is grateful enough to give his

---

[3] Nikolai Gnedich would publish his translation of *The Iliad* into Russian in St Petersburg, a feat admired by many, particularly Pushkin, in 1829, the same year in which Gogol' began writing his *Dikanka* stories.

[4] As Stephen Hutchings (2004) has shown, Gogol' had similar anxieties about the reproducibility of the photographic image.

daughter's hand in marriage. The Ukrainian landscape, with its unsettling mixtures of ethnic outsiders and the tricks played between them, presents a comic, destabilizing force in the capital city. Gogol' highlights this with the introduction of his beekeeper-narrator, Rudyi Pan'ko, who mocks his Russian readers by apologizing for his audacious familiarity and vernacular themes: 'my dear readers, if you'll pardon the offense (you, perhaps, will get angry that a beekeeper would speak to you so directly, as if you were some kind of in-law or chum [kak budto kakomu-nibud' svatu svoemu ili kumu])' (2001: I 80) Using a colloquial narrative that the formalists would later term *skaz*, Gogol' creates an illiterate storyteller who entertains the educated Russian-language reader with his linguistic and cultural idiosyncrasies.

The Portrait

Gogol' was not writing in a vacuum. 'Little Russian' folk-style stories, mostly written in Russian, but some also in Ukrainian, were becoming popular among Russian readers. These ranged from Ivan Kotliarevs'kyi's Ukrainian-language Virgilic travesty, *Eneida* (1798), to Vasilii Narezhnyi's comic Russian-language novellas about the Ukrainian territories, which appeared between 1809 and 1824. A Ukrainian-language prose tradition was also emerging in the 1830s, and it echoed both the Ukrainian-language literature and Gogol''s Ukrainian-style stories. When Gogol' was writing, several Ukrainian romantic anti-imperialists were gaining prominence, the most famous being the poet and artist Taras Shevchenko (1814–61). Gogol''s contemporaries were acutely aware of his popularity. Shevchenko would dedicate a poem, 'To Gogol'' [Hoholiu, 1844], where he juxtaposed Gogol''s humour with his own seriousness: 'You laugh [...] while I must weep'. A Ukrainian-language prose tradition was also emerging in the 1830s, and it echoed both the Ukrainian-language literature and Gogol''s Ukrainian-style stories. Hryhorii Kvitka-Osnov'ianenko (Kvitka) was a generation older than Gogol', although the two wrote roughly at the same time.[5] Kvitka published his first popular work in Ukrainian, the short story 'A Soldier's Portrait' [Saldatskii patret, 1833] two years after Gogol''s 'Fair at Sorochintsy' appeared in *Evenings*. Kvitka portrays an artist who tests the veracity of a portrait he has painted by taking it to a fair (1968: III 23).[6] Like Gogol' before him, Kvitka flaunts the narrative potential of the Ukrainian

[5] Gogol' may have modelled his *Government Inspector* [Revizor] on Kvitka's *Guest from the Capital or Turmoil in a District Town* [Priezzhii iz stolitsy ili sumatokha v uezdnom gorode], which had circulated in draft form when Gogol' set pen to paper.

[6] Kvitka was, moreover, known to test his own Ukrainian stories by literally entering the rural marketplace and reading them aloud to vendors.

landscape by enumerating items at the fair, and includes a variety of ethnic types.

Just as Rudyi Pan'ko's pseudo-vernacular prepares the reader to enter the folk world of Gogol''s *Dikanka* tales, Kvitka accompanied his first Ukrainian stories with a mock apology: 'So what are we going to do? They don't understand our language, and they even snarl at our little book: This is some kind of crazy Finnish gobbledygook [neshto po-chuknons'ki] [...] why publish it when no one will understand it?' (1924: 9). Where Gogol''s *skaz* narrator apologizes for his Ukrainian accent, Kvitka's act involves a new level of audacity. His sarcastic introduction calls attention to his target audience (Ukrainians), his primary stumbling block (Russia's literary institutions), and his objective (to subvert these institutions with his Ukrainian stories).

Writing in Ukrainian challenged the supremacy of Russian language and culture in the tsarist empire, and the Russian literary critics of the day were quick to dismiss Ukrainian-language prose. Vissarion Belinskii, considered the leading critic in Russian literature of 1830s and 1840s, wrote:

> A peasant's life in itself is not particularly interesting for the educated person, so one needs a great deal of talent in order to idealize it to the point of poetry. This is a job for a Gogol', who knew how to blend the universal and the human in the Little Russian day-to-day [...] What deep significance we can draw from the fact that Gogol', who passionately loved Little Russia, would nonetheless become a writer in Russian, and not in Little Russian! (1859: 308–09; Luckyj 1971: 53)

Belinskii's attack on Ukrainian-language literature proves the audacity of Kvitka's project. Not only did Kvitka's stories, written in Ukrainian, challenge the Russian institutions of literature, 'A Soldier's Portrait' takes aim at the institutions of artistic authority. The story travesties an episode recounted by Pliny the Elder, in which the Alexandrian artist Apelles hides behind his painting to observe the responses of his critics.[7] When a shoemaker critiques the artist's portrayal of a shoe, the artist gratefully changes the portrait. But when the emboldened cobbler moves to critique the leg, the artist famously cries, 'Let the shoemaker stick to his last!' (Pliny 1991: 332). In Kvitka's rendition, the artist's masterpiece is a portrait of a Russian soldier (referred to as a *moskal* – the derogatory Ukrainian term for a Russian officer), designed to scare away crows at a wealthy estate, but so realistic that it frightens,

---

[7] Mykola Zerov (2003: 67) has called Kvitka-Osnov'ianenko's earliest works 'prose travesty', combining classical sources, caricatured descriptions of Ukrainian folk culture, and 'Kotliarevism' [kotliarevshchyna].

offends, or attracts the Ukrainian vendors who encounter it at the fair. Only when a young woman propositions the soldier and realizes her mistake is the artifice exposed and a critic insults the portrait. For Kvitka, the commercial landscape is at once a source of authentic Ukrainian behaviour and speech patterns and an allegory for the relationship between the peripheral market crowds and the institutions of authority.

Like Gogol''s ubiquitous, devilish pig, Kvitka's frightening portrait haunts the fair, at one point coming to life in the form of an actual Russian soldier who moves about the market, stealing products, and magically turning a profit:

> There and then a soldier appeared, and this time a real soldier, as lifelike as you and me [...] He swiped a bunch of onions from a cart, quickly selling them at half price, and did all of this so craftily and so cleverly, that not a single proprietor noticed. (1924: III 17–18)

The provincial fair, ever the site of uncanny transformations, trickery, and danger, is a site of mistaken identities where Russian officers and Ukrainian peasants frighten, criticize, and rob one another. It is possible that Gogol' had Kvitka's story in mind when he penned his tale of a money-lender's portrait – 'The Portrait' [Portret, 1835]. Where Kvitka's marketgoers eventually discover that the soldier is merely a painting, exposing it to criticism, Gogol''s portraitist only escapes the evil of his demonic creation by entering a monastery. Both writers, despite drastically different messages, convey the terrifying notion that even an artistic likeness, once exposed to the open market, can do harm.

Roman Koropeckyi and Robert Romanchuk (2017) have called attention to the 'Harkusha' figure in Little Russian literature in 1820s and 1840s. Harkusha is a noble bandit who not only robs the rich but also figuratively 'steals into the heart of the Great Russian literary system and unsettles it' (Koropeckyj & Romanchuk 2017: 310). The chaotic landscape of the Ukrainian fair – a surrogate for the Ukrainian borderlands itself – serves a similar function, but to drastically different ends, depending on who is writing and in what language. If Gogol''s works suggest the dangers which outside forces pose to the Slavic soul (as epitomized by the Ukrainian peasant in Sorochintsy, but including the Russian), Kvitka's fair presents a playful but nonetheless very real antagonism between a Ukrainian multi-ethnic fair, and Russian figures of authority.

The Goat

A Gogolian Ukrainian market town is also the setting for one of the best-known evocations of eastern European Jewish life – the Broadway musical *Fiddler on the Roof.* The musical was adapted from the Tevye stories of the Yiddish writer Sholem Aleichem (the pen name of Sholem Rabinovich). Sholem Aleichem spoke Russian with his family, wrote in Russian before he wrote in Yiddish, and adored Gogol'. He frequently cited Gogol' in correspondence, hung a portrait of Gogol' in his Kiev study, and kept a 'Gogol'-box' on his desk for works in progress (Frieden 1995: 103; Roskies 1996: 154; Wisse 2000: 48). Sholem Aleichem drew liberally from Gogol''s complex Ukrainian-Russian nexus in his modern Yiddish fiction. In addition to borrowing from Gogol''s setting and motifs, Sholem Aleichem carefully observed Gogol''s celebration of the Ukrainian folk in his stories, fitting folk themes into his own tales about a culture struggling to assert itself within a broader empire.

Sholem Aleichem, like Gogol' and Kvitka, was born in a small town in the Ukrainian territories. He too exported tales of the provinces to larger readerships. And he too portrayed the rural Ukrainian fair as a microcosm of the wider world: if Gogol''s and Kvitka's wider world was focused on Imperial Russia, which, under Nicholas I, was increasingly becoming a fortress empire, then Sholem Aleichem's wider world included not only his Jewish readers in Russia and Europe, but those who lived in the wider Yiddish-speaking diaspora – from the USA to Argentina and Palestine. Just as Gogol' creates a commercial landscape in his birth town of Sorochintsy, Sholem Aleichem renders his own hometown of Voron'kiv a memory space with a commercial flavour in his 1913 autobiographical novel *From the Fair* [Funem Yarid, 1913], which he wrote in the United States: 'A man, as he travels *to the fair*, is full of hope [...] But when he travels *from the fair*, he already knows the deals he's swung' (1926: 16). By setting his autobiography at a provincial fair – a space familiar to both the geography and literature of Russia's western borderlands, Sholem Aleichem provided a stage for the interactions taking place in the rapidly changing Jewish geography of the Pale of Settlement. The mass migration of close to 2 million Jews from the Pale of Settlement to the United States between 1881 and 1914 meant that he was not alone in leaving the metaphorical fair. For these emigrant Jewish readers, the Ukrainian fair was simultaneously the image of a dangerous place that one had to leave and, increasingly, a sanctified site of collective memory.

Although scholars have long identified the importance of Gogol' to Sholem Aleichem, the differences between the two writers' ideological and social agendas have remained an enigma, particularly given Gogol''s anti-Semitic reputation. But, significantly, whereas Gogol''s Jews are often in league with the devil, Sholem Aleichem's characters struggle to survive in Russia's marketplaces. A classic example is the protagonist in 'The Haunted Tailor' [Der farkishefter shnayder, 1901, 1909].[8] Shimmon-Elye-Sh'ma-Koleynu, a tailor, travels to Kozodoevka ('Goat-milking-town') to buy a milk goat for his wife. There he must navigate the town's unfamiliar marketplace. As he enters, confused market women shout to one another in Ukrainian:

> Listen, listen! How much for the hen?
> What hen? This is a rooster, not a hen!
> So let it be a rooster! Well how much for the hen?
>
> [Tshuiesh, tsuesh! A shto tobi za kurke?
> Iaka kurka? Tse piven, a ne kurka!
> Nehay bude piven! A sho tobi za kurke?]
>
> (Sholem Aleichem 1926: 22–23)

This scene recalls the sights and sounds in Gogol''s Sorochintsy that overwhelm Paraska and her father Cherevik. The peasant women, with their Ukrainian conversation about poultry, add an element of multilingual polyphony to the Yiddish-language story. The scene also rewards the multilingual reader with a hint of what is to come: the confusion among hens and roosters foreshadows the tailor's imminent confusion over the sex of his nanny goat.

The same circulatory marketplace magic that transforms Gogol''s devilish coat and Kvitka's soldier's portrait transform Sholem Aleichem's nanny goat, leading to Shimmon-Elye's demise. En route home to Zlodoevka ('Evildoer-town'), Shimmon-Elye stops for a drink at an inn managed by a distant, uneducated relative, Dodi, who bears some resemblance to Gogol''s Hrytsko – the handsome youth who craftily orchestrates the exchange of Cherevik's horse for a red sleeve following the potter's exit from a marketplace tavern – as well as to Kvitka's *moskal* rogue. Dodi exchanges Shimmon-Elye's nanny goat for a billy goat, exacting revenge on the boastful tailor. What was an 'angel of a goat' in Kozodoevka is unable to produce milk in Zlodoevka. When the tailor attempts to return the goat to Kozodoevka, he again stops for a drink and Dodi again exchanges the goat, rendering the tailor's plight increasingly hopeless.

In the final 1909 version of the story, the prank leads to unexpected tragedy: the tailor goes mad. Unlike Gogol''s Cherevik's temporary madness,

---

[8] This story was first titled 'A Tale without an End'. For a discussion of the publication history of this story, and an excellent analysis of the story itself, see Roskies (1996: 160, 377 n. 34).

however, the tailor's insanity leads to his untimely death and the Jews of Ukraine turn on one another: ignorant of Dodi's prank, Zlodoevka's residents prepare to wage war on Kozodoevka. The tale ends as a critique of a fragmented Jewish community whose members misdirect their frustrations at one another. The trickster Dodi – a rogue character straight from the Pale of Settlement – destabilizes the tailor's expected narrative, demonstrating, in the process the dangers and narrative potential of the multi-ethnic Ukrainian borderlands.

The Writer's Wares

Gogol''s 'Sorochintsy Fair' may be a joyous celebration of Ukrainian folk culture on the surface, but it ends with a premature wedding whose guests disappear into the soulless ubiquity of the market crowd. Gogol''s narrator leaves us on an abrupt note of dissatisfaction:

> Isn't it the same with happiness, a lovely and impermanent guest who flies from us, while for naught a single sound tries to express joy? [...] The one left behind is lonely [Skuchno ostavlennomu]! His heart remains heavy and sad, and nothing will help. (2001: I 97–98)

Gogol' would reiterate this expression of unexpected narratorial sadness throughout his oeuvre, most famously meditating on the sorrows of the author in his 'laughter through tears' soliloquy, which appears towards the end of *Dead Souls*, Part I:

> And for a long time yet a wondrous power has fated me to walk hand in hand with my strange heroes, to glimpse all of this enormously heaving life, to glimpse it through laughter visible to the world and unseen, invisible tears [skvoz' vidnyi miru smekh i nezrimye, nevedomye emu slezy]! (2001: VI 134)

Sholem Aleichem was said to have kept a copy of this passage from Gogol''s *Dead Souls* on his desk (Berkowitz 1958: 188–89). He would employ the idea of laughter through tears throughout his own oeuvre. In 'The Haunted Tailor', having left Shimmon-Elye to a tragic end, Sholem Aleichem's narrator employs his own model of Gogolian romantic irony to depart from his story:

> The story started out very happily, but it's left off, like so many happy stories, oy-vey, very sadly [...] And since you know the author of this story isn't gloomy and that he dislikes miserable and likes much

better happy stories, and since you know he dislikes a 'moral' and that sermonizing is not for him, let's laugh as the writer parts ways with you and leaves the thicket, laughing, and he wishes you, Jews, and all the people in the world, more laughter than tears. (1926: 68)

All three writers considered here pause on the irreconcilability of an idealized folk life and the world outside the Pale. Where Gogol' idealizes an innocent folk culture (and mourns its impossibility), Kvitka comically calls attention to the artifice that mediates Russians' and Ukrainians' perceptions of one another. Sholem Aleichem's unexpected, even disturbing, optimism leaves the Yiddish reader desiring change.

Literature itself is a product that can be bought and sold on the market. Its authenticity and corresponding value can be found in its language, its place of origin, and its desirability, based in part on imported fashion. Each of the stories discussed here contains a fragment of the devilish red cloak from Gogol''s dangerously porous fair at Sorochintsy. Gogol', a Ukrainian writing in the language of the tsarist empire, suggested the vulnerability of Slavic folk culture to dangerous outside forces. The devil's cloak in 'The Fair at Sorochintsy' reflects, in part, Gogol''s fear of those capitalist ventures (in which Jews are understood to be complicit) that threatened traditional Slavic culture. Ironically, Gogol''s fear of markets and foreigners proved to be a highly marketable, and translatable, element of his oeuvre. Kvitka-Osnov'ianenko wrote primarily for and about Ukrainians, demonstrating the risks inherent in the porous borderlands to the Ukrainian minority. The Russian soldier in Kvitka's story represents the frightening Imperial Russian presence. Sholem Aleichem, writing primarily for and about Jews, corrected a pervasive anti-Jewish stereotype, showing the vulnerable place of Jewish communities in the tsarist empire. For Sholem Aleichem, the Ukrainian marketplace, an increasingly frequent site of violence against Jews in the early twentieth century, represented a more immediate, physical danger.

The individual language literatures that emerged from Gogol''s fair moved in drastically different cultural directions. And yet what allowed them to do so was the presence of a borderlands prose. Ironically, Gogol', despite his Slavic-centred conservatism and xenophobic tendencies, provides a pretext for reading Russian literature transnationally. After all, if world literature, to quote David Damrosch (2003: 5), can be read as 'a mode of circulation and of reading', so too should we read Russian literary history as a history of circulation and exchange, whether through translation, travesty, plagiarism, or reception. Borders move, after all, and what had been part of the tsarist empire would eventually become independent Ukraine, and – for many Yiddish-speaking Jews – 'the old country'. Reading Russian literary history as internally transnational prompts us to scrutinize the porous, movable, and often multi-ethnic boundaries of empire – boundaries that have long been the sites where literary relationships are negotiated.

Works Cited

Anderson, Benedict. 1983. *Imagined Communities: Reflections on the Origin and Spread of Nationalism* (London: Verso).

Bakhtin, Mikhail. 1983. 'Rabelais and Gogol: The Art of Discourse and the Popular Culture of Laughter', trans. Patricia Sollner, *Mississippi Review*, 11(3): 34–50.

Belinskii, Vissarion. 1859. *Sochineniia V. Belinskogo* (Moscow: Izdanie K. Soldatenkova I. N. Shchepkina).

Berkowitz, Yitzhak (ed.). 1958. *Dos Sholem-Aleykhem bukh: Oytobiyografishe fartseykhenungen fun Sholem-Aleykhem*, 2nd edn (New York: YKUF).

Bojanowska, Edyta. 2007. *Nikolai Gogol: Between Ukrainian and Russian Nationalism* (Cambridge: Harvard University Press).

Casanova, Pascale. 2004. *The World Republic of Letters* (Cambridge, MA: Harvard University Press).

Damrosch, David. 2003. *What Is World Literature?* (Princeton, NJ and Oxford: Princeton University Press).

Frieden, Ken. 1995. *Classic Yiddish Fiction: Abramovich, Sholem Aleichem, and Peretz* (Albany, NY: State University of New York Press).

Glaser, Amelia. 2012. *Jews and Ukrainians in Russia's Literary Borderlands: From the Shtetl Fair to the St. Petersburg Bookshop* (Evanston, IL: Northwestern University Press).

Gogol', Nikolai. 2001. *Polnoe sobranie sochinenii i pisem* (Moscow: Nasledie).

Hohol'-Ianovskii, Vasilii Panasovich. 1918. *Prostak, abo khytroshchi zhinky perekhytreni moskalem: Komediia* (New York: Ukrainskoi knyharni imeni T. Shevchenka).

Hutchings, Stephen. 2004. *Russian Literary Culture in the Camera Age: The Word as Image* (New York and Abingdon: Routledge).

Koropeckyj, Roman, and Robert Romanchuk. 2017. 'Harkusha the Noble Bandit and the "Minority" of Little Russian Literature', *The Russian Review*, 76(2): 294–310.

Kotliarevs'kyi, Ivan Petrovych. 1989. *Eneida* (Kiev: Radians'ka shkola).

Kvitka-Osnov'ianenko, Hryhorii Fedorovych. 1924. *20-40 rokiv v Ukrainskoi Literatury*, ed. Oleksandr Doroshkevych, Shkil'na biblioteka (Kiev: Derzhavne vydavnytstvo).

——. 1968. *Tvory u vosmy tomakh* (Kiev: Dnipro).

Luckyj, George. 1971. *Between Gogol' and Sevcenko: Polarity in the Literary Ukraine, 1798–1847* (Toronto: University of Toronto Press).

Pliny (the Elder). 1991. *Natural History, a Selection,* ed. John F. Healy (London: Penguin).

Pratt, Mary Louise. 1992. *Imperial Eyes* (New York: Routledge).

Roskies, David. 1996. *A Bridge of Longing* (Cambridge: Harvard University Press).

Sholem Aleichem (S. Rabinovich). 1926. *Funem Yarid* (Vilne-Varshe: B. Kletskin).

Strich, Fritz. 1971. *Goethe and World Literature* (London: Routledge).

Wisse, Ruth R. 2000. *The Modern Jewish Canon: A Journey through Language and Culture* (Chicago: University of Chicago Press).

Zerov, Mykola. 2003. *Ukrainske pysmenstvo* (Kiev: Osnova).

3

The Empire Strikes East

Cross-cultural Dynamics
in Russian Central Asia

Olga Maiorova

In the nineteenth century, the rise of a national discourse in Russia went hand in hand with the spectacular advance of its imperial project. While Russian historians, writers, and painters focused on Russia's heartland and celebrated the ethnoculturally Russian people, the Romanov Empire was growing dramatically, expanding its borders and subjugating an increasing number of nationalities at a seemingly unstoppable rate. It was during this period that Russia annexed the Kingdom of Poland, the Caucasus, the vast Kazakh steppe, the Amur River, and finally – in its most spectacular imperial stroke – the Central Asian khanates and their adjacent lands bordering Iran, Afghanistan, and China. The diverse indigenous populations under Russian rule came to represent the Other against which Russians defined themselves as a progressive force of civilization projecting its power over 'barbarous' and 'inimical' peoples. Thus, Russia's imperial project inflected its national discourse, turning the empire into a stage on which the Russian people's historical drama unfolded.

Representations of the colonized as 'barbarous' – a typical way of justifying imperial conquest – seemed to erect insurmountable divides between 'us' and 'them'. Region-specific imperial policies further reinforced those divides. Driven by a desire to win the loyalty of its new subjects, the tsarist regime allowed many (though not all) ethnic groups under its control to continue their way of life and maintain some of their autochthonous institutions, putting local elites in charge. Although the Romanov Empire, like its European counterparts, sought to create a homogeneous state space by practising cultural imposition on and assimilation of the colonized, its 'Russification' policies gained momentum only in the late imperial era and varied widely across time and different areas of this huge empire. Towards the turn of the twentieth century, imperial authorities increasingly restricted the use of Ukrainian and Belorussian, imposed Russian education in Poland and Georgia, and discriminated against Jews, the indigenous peoples of Siberia, and many ethnic groups of the North Caucasus. Yet simultaneously a different dynamic developed: the regime made considerable concessions to some nationalities under its sway (e.g. Finnish, Lithuanian, and Chuvash, to name just a few) and even promoted their languages, limiting the influence of the non-Russian cultures bordering those nationalities (Swedish, Polish, and Tatar, respectively), and all this as a way of fostering their greater allegiance to the Romanovs. Thus, Russia grew into a particularistic empire that ruled through distinction by maintaining, and sometimes even reinforcing, differences among its subjugated populations (Sunderland 2010: 123–27; Kivelson & Suny 2017: 199–210).

Central Asia (or Turkestan, as it was then called; the territory roughly coinciding with modern Uzbekistan, Tajikistan, Kyrgyzstan, and Turkmenistan) was conquered piecemeal by the Russians between the 1860s and the 1880s (see the map in Fig. 3.1). In this region, the contrast between its native inhabitants and Russians was particularly stark. After defeating the Khiva and the Bukhara khanates, the tsarist regime granted them autonomy and ruled over them indirectly, through their native leaders, which fully preserved their traditional way of life. But even in those areas of Turkestan which were under imperial Russia's direct military rule (Kokand, Tashkent, Samarkand, Ashgabat, and adjacent territories), Muslims retained a larger degree of self-administration than their co-religionists in other parts of the empire (Crimea and the Volga–Ural area), which had been subjugated by the Romanovs much earlier. Central Asian Muslims were exempt from military conscription, native officials never adopted the imperial system of service ranks, and some of their indigenous judicial institutions remained in place up to the empire's collapse in 1917 (Khalid 2015: 8).

One of the unintentional results of these policies was the prolonged exposure of ethnically Russian subjects – especially those who made Central Asia their home – to the cultures of the colonized. All Russian observers familiar with the region spotlighted a cultural gap between 'Europeans' (as they called themselves) and 'Asians'. Most imperial accounts perceived the local cultures as backward, inferior, and doomed to decline or dissipation. They thus thought along the lines typical of European Orientalism, as defined by Edward Said – namely, as a cluster of academic and artistic discourses, cultural institutions, and political practices dichotomizing the world along the Orient-Occident binary and authorizing domination over the East as the degraded Other (Said 1978). The longer Russians stayed in the region, however, the more some of them grew engaged with and fascinated by the

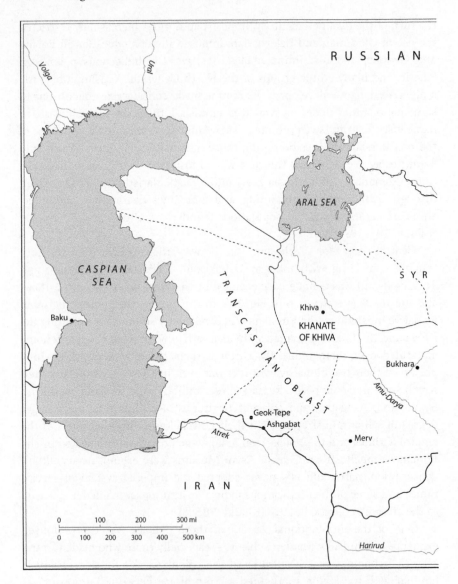

Fig. 3.1. Map depicting Central Asia at the height of Russian imperial
conquest, *c.* 1890.
Map by Bill Nelson.

colonized people and their culture. Several centuries of multifaceted interactions between Russia and its Asian neighbours contributed to the formation of this alternative attitude, but it was Russia's complicated position between East and West that was the decisive factor in its development.

While portraying itself as an agent of European civilization in the East, imperial Russia struggled with its profound ambivalence towards the West. A subject of centuries-long (at least since Peter the Great) government-led Westernization, the Romanov Empire sought to emulate Europe's social and cultural institutions, but at the same time suffered from an inferiority complex *vis-à-vis* the West and sought to valorize its standing as a nation distinguished by its own unparalleled qualities. Russia's position between East and West often figured as one of the unique qualities that Russians 'naturally' possessed. They boasted of their ability to comprehend, and interact with, both worlds. But the West, Russians bitterly complained, had long patronized, disparaged, and even mistreated them by placing Russia on the same side of the Orient-Occident divide as the Asians. Some Russian thinkers even grudgingly acknowledged Russia's latent Oriental nature. This inherent ambiguity in Russia's self-perception with regard to the East-West binary generated an environment where it was logical to destabilize boundaries, question cultural assumptions, and develop complex patterns of engagement with the Orient.[1]

Massive resettlement of Russians to Central Asia following the conquest of the region set these alternative attitudes in motion. Some segments of the Russian intelligentsia in Turkestan – especially those critical of Russian absolutism, explicitly oppositional to its repressive policies, and therefore exiled to Turkestan for their political views – not only developed expertise on Central Asia, but tended to refashion imperial discourse, dispel the negative stereotypes about the indigenous people, and even challenge cultural divides between colonizer and colonized. This chapter argues that such tendencies facilitated or at least set the stage for a set of cross-cultural encounters that have so far been under-studied, if not entirely overlooked.

Historians researching Russian rule in Central Asia have already recognized the collaboration of indigenous actors with the Bolsheviks in the Soviet era, but scholars tend to affirm the notion of a fundamental divide between Russians and native inhabitants of Turkestan during the imperial period. This chapter follows the most recent revisionist approach that explores reciprocal 'cross-cultural transfers' between the imperial centre and its newly acquired lands, and argues for the natives' agency in the process of

---

[1] For an informative discussion of Russian Orientalism from divergent viewpoints, see David-Fox et al. (2006).

knowledge-production and perception-formation regarding their motherland (Tolz 2015; Gorshenina & Tolz 2016). Substantial gaps must remain in our understanding of colonial history if we reduce it to a strict binary opposition of colonizers *versus* colonized and do not expand research beyond the confines of individual nation-building projects. This chapter focuses on the colonial encounters that led to dialogue and circulation of ideological constructs across national divides between native inhabitants of Central Asia and a group of Russian settlers in the area. As interactions between diverse actors in the colonies occurred and intensified, what at first seemed to Russians to be alien or dangerous in Turkestan came to represent practices with the potential to heal Russia's own ills, reorient it towards a more equitable society, and ultimately appeal to all of humankind. This profound intellectual shift stemmed from a radical rethinking of the imperial discourse established prior to the acquisition of Central Asia.

Imperial Rhetoric Revised

It was a belief in the Russian people's natural, mostly peaceful, expansion into new territories that underpinned the thematic repertoire of nineteenth-century imperial ideology, official and unofficial alike. As I have shown elsewhere (Maiorova 2010), that myth could take various forms. Some writers (like the historian Sergei Solov'ev and the journalist Mikhail Katkov) claimed that the Russian Empire came into existence as a result of sustained cooperation on the part of ethnically distinct groups under the leadership of the Russian people.[2] Others, like the famous Pan-Slavist Nikolai Danilevskii, depicted Russia's expansion as a benign process of predominantly non-violent colonization of adjacent lands, ultimately beneficial for the indigenous peoples. Danilevskii claimed that, over the centuries, 'weak, half-savage, and entirely wild native peoples were not only not destroyed or wiped off the face of the earth, but they were not even deprived of their freedom and property, nor turned into serfs by their conquerors' (1895: 201). Fedor Dostoevskii also elaborated on this point: from his perspective, Russia absorbed various ethnic groups not

---

[2] Sergei Solov'ev (1820–79), in his multi-volume *History of Russia from Ancient Times* (1851–79), emphasized Russia's multi-ethnic composition, which he described as continuing and expanding from its remotest past. He envisioned Russia as a European Christian state moving towards Western-type civil society. From the 1860s to the 1880s, Mikhail Katkov (1818–87), an influential political commentator of nationalist persuasion, used his widely acclaimed newspaper, *Moskovskie vedomosti* (Moscow News), to promote a state-centred vision of the Russian people as the main agent of empire-building that exercises power under the monarch's leadership.

to oppress or violate them, but to protect them, to give them the freedom to flourish without fear of greedy neighbours.[3] When these writers did recognize that Russia forcibly annexed some territories, they often presented it as a 'return' of 'our own' native lands, which had been taken from helpless Russia in the remote past when it was suffering from multiple invasions (a rhetoric that still persists in Russian official propaganda and resonates conspicuously with the justification of the 2014 annexation of Crimea under Putin). As Vera Tolz points out in her chapter in the present volume, all these nineteenth-century thinkers sharply contrasted benign Russian empire-building to that of western European powers that brutally 'usurped' someone else's – usually overseas – lands.

However, the tsarist army's merciless battles for Tashkent, Samarkand, Kokand, Geok-Tepe, and many other Central Asian strongholds flew in the face of this basic myth of Russian imperialism. Moreover, the conquest of Turkestan from the 1860s to the 1880s coincided with a series of ongoing crises, as the political, social, and economic problems of the Romanov Empire intensified, ultimately leading to its demise in 1917. With this traumatic experience rapidly unfolding, many Russian observers living in Central Asia felt increasingly at odds with the old image of Russia as a generous protector of its subjugated nationalities. The imperial rhetoric shifted away from the theme of non-violent expansion that was beneficial for the 'backward' natives to the theme of reciprocal cross-cultural collaboration that was advantageous for both the colonizers and the colonized.[4]

The majority of late-nineteenth-century representations of Turkestan prominently featured the motif of its wide open spaces and therefore its ability to accommodate settlers from European Russia without any negative consequences for the indigenous people. 'Nowhere in the world can the task of resettling people from the densely populated European areas of Russia be carried out as […] justly as it can in Turkestan', claimed Ivan Geier, one of the leading journalists in Turkestan, exiled to the colony for his participation in the 'going to the people' movement (1893: 83).[5] To support his argument Geier turned to irrigation:

---

[3] For a reconstruction of Dostoevskii's vision for the Russian Empire see Bojanowska (2012) and Maiorova (2015).

[4] On other efforts to refashion Turkestan from a 'backward colony', see Gorshenina and Tolz (2016).

[5] 'Going to the people' [khozhdenie v narod] was a large-scale movement of the 1870s and 1880s which saw educated youth of populist persuasion (often with a socialist and revolutionary agenda in mind), go to the countryside to immerse themselves in peasant life, educate the masses and improve their social conditions.

In Central Asia, due to the lack of water, the population density of the indigenous people in their lands remains low. But with the expansion of the irrigation system built by the Russians, huge new tracts will become available for cultivation, which will make it possible to place new settlers here without the slightest inconvenience to the natives. (1893: 83)

One certainly hears imperialist overtones in many of Geier's statements; however, his main theme is one of productive collaboration and exchange between the 'Europeans' and the 'Asians' – a process that, as he claimed, could transform both parties. Geier's belief in transformation is crucial. Of course, he utilizes the rhetoric of the civilizing mission transforming the colonized. However, he also highlights the potential of the colony to remedy the ills of the metropolis. Thus, referring to the disastrous 1892 famine in Russia's heartland, Geier states that Turkestan, once fully irrigated, would be able to rescue the entire empire from the fickle fate of uncertain harvests.

One can trace an even more radical inversion of the earlier imperial rhetoric in the works of the most influential Russian writer in Turkestan, Vladimir Nalivkin. An amateur linguist and self-trained ethnographer who lived for years among Central Asia's sedentary rural population (ethnic groups later designated as Tajiks and Uzbeks), he became fluent in several local languages and compiled the first Russian dictionaries in them. Nalivkin produced the most comprehensive accounts of the sedentary peoples of the region, winning praise from across the political spectrum both in Russia and abroad. He reversed the imperial discourse by ascribing to Uzbeks and Tajiks the same qualities that Russian literature celebrated as the unique features of the Russian people throughout the nineteenth century: 'moral strength', physical and mental endurance, adaptability, an innate ability to absorb the best accomplishments of neighbouring cultures – these were all traits he purportedly identified in local Muslims (Nalivkin 2015: 383).[6]

Nalivkin's attitude towards the peoples of the region was a mixture of admiration and guilt. Nalivkin acknowledged the incredible harshness of the conquest of Turkestan (in which he himself took part, to his later despair), but he believed that those atrocities had nonetheless paved the way for what had the potential to become harmonious relations between the colonizers and the colonized. '[We must] forget old scores', he wrote, addressing both the Russians and the indigenous peoples, 'we must turn our

---

[6] On the similarly sympathetic portrayal of Alei, the Muslim inmate in Dostoevskii's *Notes from The House of the Dead* [Zapiski iz mertvogo doma, 1860–62], see Geraci (2015: 213–14).

backs once and for all on old grudges and happily, as friends, embark hand in hand on the broad path of human progress and human unity'. Nalivkin reiterates this conciliatory plea twice, both opening and concluding his most famous ethnographic survey of the native population (2015: 381, 480). Moreover, at the beginning of this survey he presented Islam as a religion of peace, quoting from the Russian translation of the Quran: 'Peace is good'.[7] Lifting the phrase from its immediate scriptural context pertaining only to marriage and divorce, Nalivkin applied it as a more general statement. This semantic distortion – regardless of whether it was intentional or not – demonstrates his underlying inclination to switch gears in favour of the locals. More broadly, Nalivkin's work, though it at times employs negative stereotypes, represents a determination on the part of the Russian intelligentsia in Turkestan to reshape Russia's vision of its Asian periphery, challenge the power dynamic underlying Russian domination, incorporate eastern practices and intellectual constructs into the world view that they advocated, and thus elaborate a more inclusive ideological orientation, one that had the potential to appeal to all humankind.

Constructing the World of Universal Values

At the turn of the twentieth century, no Russian public figure expressed such an inclusive attitude towards ethnic and religious Others more explicitly and consistently than did Lev Tolstoi in his moral writings and teachings. Inspired by his transcultural humanism, criticism of modernity, and fascination with Eastern philosophy, non-Christian religions, and agricultural lifestyle, the Tolstoians who came to Central Asia sought to engage with and even adopt the perspectives of the indigenous sedentary peoples. However, it took Tolstoi's followers in Turkestan many years to organize themselves into a community and develop intellectual ties across ethnic divides.

In the summer of 1910, Tolstoi received a letter from one of his most devoted and long-term followers, Iurii Iakubovskii (1857–1929), who by that time had been living in Central Asia for 20 years. Forcibly relocated to Turkestan in 1890, Iakubovskii left St Petersburg for Samarkand with a suitcase stuffed with copies of Tolstoi's works which were banned for publication. 'When I came to Samarkand', Iakubovskii confessed to Tolstoi, 'manuscript copies of your works were my only solace in my hard and isolated life in the Asian borderland. But what are books to me now?!' With this

---

[7] 'Mir est' dobro' (chapter 4, verse 128). This Russian translation cannot be considered entirely accurate: the original text in modern English translations reads, 'Reconciliation is better'.

exclamation Iakubovskii interrupted his sad recollections to marvel at the public impact of Tolstoi's preaching on his contemporaries: 'Now, everywhere I see splendid people who grew up on your books and who live honest lives, according to the teachings laid out in those books'.[8] What could Iakubovskii, living in the remote borderlands of Central Asia, have seen that so impressed him as testimonies of the practical success of Tolstoi's teachings? How could Tolstoi's work prove relevant, even exciting, in that distant land?

In 1902 or 1903, Vasilii Repin, a Russian military officer who had been stationed in Central Asia a couple of years earlier, suddenly resigned his post to organize, with a group of Tolstoians, an agricultural community of people living and working together. Situated some 60 miles from Tashkent, the community lasted for nine years, even though it went through several crises and split up into smaller groups because of disagreements over religious issues and the philosophy of common property. Several times the community's leadership changed, and its philosophical agenda was altered when the poet Aleksandr Dobroliubov arrived in Turkestan to succeed Repin as leader. Dobroliubov's anarchistic views and his preaching of *oproshchenie* (the embrace of a simple life) and *strannichestvo* (wandering, in imitation of Christ's itinerant lifestyle) fit perfectly with the beliefs of the Tolstoians, but his esoteric mysticism radically diverged from Tolstoi's belief in the transparency and simplicity of Christian teaching. Yet Dobroliubov's charismatic personality fascinated the community's members and many of them followed his ideas.[9] The composition of the community was multi-ethnic and socially diverse: Ukrainian peasants of evangelical (Baptist) denomination; educated Jewish professionals; a group of peasants from Samara, who resettled in the region at Dobroliubov's initiative; Russian ex-military officers who had resigned like Repin (or with him); and pacifist Russian youth of noble background who refused to serve in the army.[10]

This relatively small, programmatically fluctuating, socially and ethnically heterogeneous community proved open to transnational contacts, increasingly engaging with the indigenous people. At first only bartering

[8] Letter from Iakubovskii to Tolstoi, 20 June 1910, Manuscript Division of the State Museum of L. N. Tolstoi, Moscow: Fond 1. No page numbers are available as the archive never paginated this document.

[9] My account of the community is based on the letters to Tolstoy by Iakubovskii and Mariia Repina, Vasilii's wife, in the Manuscript Division of the State Museum of L. N. Tolstoi, Moscow: Fond 1. We do not have information about each member of the community, but we know the names of those who visited Tolstoi and those who were under Tashkent police surveillance.

[10] Gosudarstvennyi Arkhiv Rossiiskoi Federatsii (GARF), f. 102 (Fond Departamenta Politsii), op. 244, d. 12 (Turkestanskoe general-gubernatorstvo. Agenturnye svedeniia).

and other economic interactions brought them together with the locals, but over nine years of living in close proximity to the *sarts* (a term for the sedentary population of Turkestan), the community's members came to admire the native practice of collective possession of land. Iakubovskii, who was close to the community but not a member, reported to Tolstoi, 'the interesting method of land use and ownership of dryland fields, which are considered common property, among the *sarts* of Samarkand. These practices', Iakubovskii observed, 'closely resemble those advocated by Henry George'.[11] Well aware of Tolstoi's fascination with the political philosophy of Henry George,[12] Iakubovskii was alluding here to the American economist's conviction that natural resources should belong equally to all members of society. The Tolstoians believed that indigenous practices of land ownership might provide a solution to the struggles they themselves were experiencing over the issue of collective property – and ultimately a solution to the predicaments that faced the entire world with the rise of capitalism, as Tolstoi understood it.

This surprising link between the autochthonous Central Asian institution of land ownership and Henry George's programme was filtered through Tolstoi's philosophy, and the way this connection appeared reveals an underlying mechanism of the transnational dynamic. The value of non-Russian culture rose in the eyes of Tolstoi and his followers, leading to their growing engagement with the colonized who now figured, for them, in the framework of worldwide developments and fuelled their inclusive vision of the world. But such a symbolic re-evaluation of the 'backward' local as the 'advanced' global could crystallize into an intellectual trend only when there emerged an agent of what Pascale Casanova (2004) calls 'transnational validation'. In order to reach some sort of agreement on the value of cultural expressions beyond the constraints of individual nations, a certain authority is needed to articulate and sanction the accord. Much as nineteenth-century Paris, according to Casanova, served as a centre for the transnational validation of artistic production, Tolstoi the philosopher figured as the authority refocusing the imperial gaze and validating the culture of the colonized as part of the global circulation of cultural expressions.

[11] Letter from Iakubovskii to Tolstoi, 20 June 1910, Manuscript Division of the State Museum of L. N. Tolstoi, Moscow: Fond 1.

[12] Tolstoi was interested in the work of the progressive American economist and journalist Henry George (1839–97) from at least the mid-1880s, when he was particularly excited about George's 1879 work *Progress and Poverty*, to the very end of his life, when he focused his attention on George's theory of single tax and his rejection of individual land ownership.

Indigenous cultures thus came to represent practices that were reminiscent of the teachings of Henry George and that were potentially appealing to all humankind. This construct challenged the colonial divide and the notion of progress being brought by the Russians to a 'barbarous' land. In the context of Tolstoi's philosophy, the theme of Islam, too, provided an occasion for cross-cultural contact. In 1910 Iakubovskii reported to Tolstoi: 'About a month ago I was visited by two Baha'is from Ashgabat. One was an old acquaintance of mine, the cousin of Izmailov, who visited you in 1908, and the other was a young man [...] – well-read, speaking excellent Russian, a typical Baha'i missionary'.[13] An avid reader of Tolstoi, Iakubovskii knew about Tolstoi's long-term interest in the Baha'i movement.[14] The movement had grown out of a relatively small Islamic community in Iran, initially including only Persian-speaking Shi'a Muslims, while Central Asian Muslims (as well as the majority of Muslims in the entire Russian Empire) were Sunni, with Turkic languages prevailing over Farsi. The Baha'is thus represented not merely Islam, but the remote world of Shi'ism, and even partial identification with them on the part of Tolstoi and his followers was a step towards the goal of creating a universal language of ecumenical religion. As Iakubovskii emphasized, the Baha'i missionaries brought him their books translated into Russian and claimed that the Baha'i faith 'was a teaching of Christian non-resistance'. These last words of course alluded to Tolstoi's preaching of non-resistance to violence. 'At present there is in Ashgabat a large Baha'i community', continued Iakubovskii, 'it would be very interesting to study the life of the community, with their "House of Justice", and their attitudes to the poor and non-resistance to the authorities'.[15]

Tolstoi had known about the Baha'i movement since 1890 and over the two subsequent decades he increasingly engaged with their beliefs in his writing, claiming that their teaching beautifully expressed his own philosophy (Standardo 1985). What he found particularly appealing in their teaching was their ecumenical zeal. As Tolstoi's secretary and devoted follower Dushan Makovitskii enthusiastically noted after a discussion of the Baha'i movement with Tolstoi, the Baha'is 'believe in universal brotherhood; no miracles, no dogma, just moral teachings [...] Altogether Baha'is number 18 million: in India, Persia, Turkey, Algeria, Egypt, and the United States.

---

[13] Letter from Iakubovskii to Tolstoi, 20 June 1910, Manuscript Division of the State Museum of L. N. Tolstoi, Moscow: Fond 1.

[14] The name of the Baha'i movement derives from the name of its founder, Baha'u'llah, which means 'Glory of God'.

[15] Letter from Iakubovskii to Tolstoi, 20 June 1910, Manuscript Division of the State Museum of L. N. Tolstoi, Moscow: Fond 1.

Among the faith's converts are both Christians and Jews' (1979: 203). The fact that Tolstoi grew interested in their teachings and read extensively about them prompted the Tolstoians in Turkestan to respond to the call of the local Baha'is. Baha'i books circulated in the Tolstoian community, which, in turn, disseminated *Posrednik* publications among the Baha'i.[16] But Tolstoi had very little first-hand exposure to the Baha'is and his understanding of their teachings was not always accurate. Contrary to his impressions, the movement did include a mystical message, absorbing elements of Sufism, and disapproved of all oppositional acts, even non-violent ones (Karlberg 2010). At the same time, like Tolstoi's teaching, the movement did indeed reject all forms of coercion, criticized social inequality, had no clergy, and proselytized the faith in terms of ecumenical persuasion. As scholars studying the Baha'i movement conclude, it sought to '[break] out of the cultural confines of its traditional [...] milieu' and to incorporate some elements of Christianity (Smith 2016: 230).

Regardless of how accurate the mutual perceptions of the locals and the Tolstoians were, this story reveals an important and largely overlooked aspect of the colonial dynamic in imperial Russia. Its brutal expansion led to bloody wars, centuries-long conflicts, mismanagement of the colonized, and traumatic experiences for a myriad victims. However, as a particularistic empire maintaining the differences between the subjugated populations, it also set the stage for transcultural exchanges outside of the institutions and jurisdiction of the state. Mutual engagement developed not only between the colonizers and the colonized but also across the multiple divides between various indigenous nationalities. The evidence suggests that we have seriously underestimated the scope and significance of multi-dimensional cross-cultural transfers in the Russian Empire. This kind of imperial history has not yet been written but deserves scholarly attention. The reciprocal dynamic on the imperial periphery provides a vantage point from which to re-evaluate the relevance of Russian culture for non-Russian subjects well beyond, outside, or despite state-promoted Russification. The study of these cross-cultural transfers may reveal a fuller picture of how the reorientation towards inclusivity that developed among Russians on the periphery led them to reject the ideology of insurmountable differences between 'us' and 'them'.

---

[16] Otdel rukopisei Rossiiskoi Gosudarstvennoi Biblioteki, f. 135, razdel II, karton 43, delo 36, ll. 1–2 (Iakubovskii's letter to V. G. Korolenko, 21 January 1911). *Posrednik* was the publishing house run by Tolstoi's followers.

Works Cited

Bojanowska, Edyta. 2012. 'Empire by Consent: Strakhov, Dostoevskii, and the Polish Uprising of 1863', *Slavic Review*, 71(1): 1–24.

Casanova, Pascale. 2004. *The World Republic of Letters* (Cambridge, MA: Harvard University Press).

Danilevskii, Nikolai. 1895. *Rossiia i Evropa* (New York: Johnson Reprint, 1966).

David-Fox, Michael, Peter Holquist, and Alexander Martin (eds). 2006. *Orientalism and Empire in Russia* (Bloomington, IN: Slavica).

Geier, Ivan Ivanovich. 1893. *Po russkim seleniiam Syr-Dar'inskoi oblasti*, vol. 1 (Tashkent).

Geraci, Robert. 2015. 'Islam' in *Dostoevsky in Context*, ed. Deborah Martinsen and Olga Maiorova (Cambridge: Cambridge University Press), 209–18.

Gorshenina, Svetlana, and Vera Tolz. 2016. 'Constructing Heritage in Early Soviet Central Asia', *Ab Imperio*, 4: 77–115.

Karlberg, Michael. 2010. 'Constructive Resilience: The Baha'i Response to Oppression', *Peace and Change*, 35(2): 222–57.

Khalid, Adeeb. 2015. *Making Uzbekistan, Nation, Empire and Revolution in the Early USSR* (Ithaca, NY: Cornell University Press).

Kivelson, Valerie, and Ronald G. Suny. 2017. *Russia's Empires* (New York and Oxford: Oxford University Press).

Maiorova, Olga. 2010. *From the Shadow of Empire: Defining the Russian Nation through Cultural Mythology, 1855–1870s* (Madison, WI: The University of Wisconsin Press).

——. 2015. 'Empire' in *Dostoevsky in Context*, ed. Deborah Martinsen and Olga Maiorova (Cambridge: Cambridge University Press), 86–97.

Makovitskii, Dushan Petrovich. 1979. *U Tolstogo (1904–1910). Iasnopolianskie zapiski. Literaturnoe nasledstvo*, vol. 90, book 3 (Moscow: Nauka).

Nalivkin, Vladimir Petrovich. 2015. *Polveka v Turkestane* (Moscow: Mardzhani).

Said, Edward W. 1978. *Orientalism* (New York: Pantheon Books).

Smith, Peter. 2016. 'Babi–Baha'i Expansion and "Geo-Cultural Breakthroughs"', *Journal of Religious History*, 40(2): 225–36.

Standardo, Luigi. 1985. *Leo Tolstoy and the Baha'i Faith* (Oxford: George Ronald Publisher, Ltd.).

Sunderland, Willard. 2010. 'The Ministry of Asiatic Russia: The Colonial Office that Never Was but Might Have Been', *Slavic Review*, 69(1): 120–50.

Tolz, Vera. 2015. 'Reconciling Ethnic Nationalism and Imperial Cosmopolitanism: The Lifeworlds of Tsyben. Zhamtsarano (1880–1942)', *Asia*, 69(3): 723–46.

4

Where the Nation Ends

Transnationalism and Affective Space in Post-Soviet Cinema

Dušan Radunović

On Territory, Nation, and the State:
The Post-Soviet Condition in Historical Context

It could be argued, with some simplification, that the rise of Western modernity, which is inseparable from the emergence of the sovereign nation state in seventeenth-century Europe, was predicated upon the drawing of territorial boundaries and the political demarcation of space. A certain 'sanctification' of national space and its becoming, through territorial delimitations, the constitutive element of national imagination and identity, emerged at the stage in European history when the old systems of allegiance and solidarity were abolished by the nationalist revolutions and new, horizontal ones came to be instituted as the political norm of the modern world (Suny 2001: 27 and *passim*). It was this territorial 'closure' that produced politically bounded national spaces with physical borders designed to separate, 'excluding those who are not felt to belong, drawing a dividing line between the familiar and the foreign' (Wimmer 2002: 33).

While the principle of national sovereignty was, since the end of the eighteenth century, becoming the pre-eminent, normative form of political governance in much of western and central Europe, the specificity of social and political conditions in Russia precipitated a fundamentally different historical experience in the territorially much larger and vaguer Eurasian geopolitical context.[1] If the processes of social and political modernization in

---

[1] On the specificities of ethnic and territorial traditions of nationhood in European political history and variations in the understanding of the concept of political sovereignty in the European tradition, see Brubaker (1992: 1–17).

Europe were not only accompanied by, but even premised upon, the principle of the political sovereignty of the nation state, the Eurasian political context, shaped by the Greater Russian Empire, resisted such political and social modernization in more than one way.[2] Although the Russian imperial state was, at least from the time of Ivan IV, consistently preoccupied with state-building, this ambition mostly took the form of ongoing territorial expansion, rather than the strengthening of the institutions of a nation state.[3] Indeed, it was spatial extension that was central to the Russian national and political imagination of the imperial era, and this process of sheer territorial expansion replaced more significant stratifications and demarcations, whether symbolic or physical.[4] The Russian imperial state failed, in fact, to politically appropriate its amassed space and map it according to the ethno-territorial principle on which the modern system of European nation states was built.[5]

By contrast, the state that then emerged from the ruins of the Russian Empire between 1917 and 1922 showed far greater consideration for the systematic political demarcation of this vast expanse to embark on what Bassin, Elly, and Stockdale have termed 'the absorption of space into the overall process of historical evolution and development' (2010: 7). Indeed, the new Soviet state was quick to add two important principles to its territorial organization, namely, 'the ethnic composition of the population and the economic affinity or cohesion [ekonomicheskoe tiagotenie] of the region' (Matsuzato 1997: 189). Through the scrupulous ethnographic mapping of the land with which the new Soviet nations were meant to identify, the early Soviet

[2] An attempt to reappraise the Russian imperial project as an enduring form of governance can be found in Jane Burbank and Mark von Hagen's article 'Coming into the Territory: Uncertainty and Empire' (2007: 1–27).

[3] On the confluence of national and imperial identity in Russian political imagination following Russia's vast territorial expansion in the sixteenth and seventeenth centuries, see Tolz (2001: 155–91), Plokhy (2006: 250–98), Miller (2015: 309–69), and, especially, Ther (2015: 573–91). On the ways in which the three land empires (Russian, Austro-Hungarian, and Ottoman) responded to the rise of the European nation state, see also Suny (2001: 29–30).

[4] Statistics show that the late-imperial Russian state divided its territory into a much smaller number of administrative units than its European counterparts. For example, while France in 1901 had '86 *départements* and 36,192 *communes*, each with an elected mayor [...] European Russia with nearly four times the population and five times the territory of France had only 51 *guberniias*, 511 *uezds* and 10,257 *volosts*' (LeDonne, cit. Matsuzato 1997: 183–84). See also Burbank and von Hagen (2007): 5–6.

[5] Pushkin's words from his 1836 letter to Petr Chaadaev, in which Russia's boundless spaces [*immense étendue*, neob"iatnye prostranstva] are ascribed a constitutive role in the shaping of the Russian national imaginary, cannot therefore be interpreted as a discourse on nationhood in the modern sense of the word.

state established a fundamentally new order of social organization, one that amalgamated the model of the ethno-territorial nation state (for each Union republic), with the principle of the multi-ethnic federation (for the Union as a whole).[6] This often precarious interplay between strategies of top-down supranational assimilation, on the one hand, and individual nation-building, on the other, continued practically until the collapse of the Soviet project itself. The dismantlement of the Soviet Union in 1991 ushered in a new set of nation-building processes in every part of the former Union. Unsurprisingly, at the heart of these lay what Brubaker and Cooper have termed 'languages of identity' – that is, discursive strategies whose aim was to enhance the 'sense of belonging to a distinctive, bounded group, involving both a felt solidarity or oneness with fellow group members and a felt difference from or even antipathy to specified outsiders' (2000: 19).

However, despite the prevalence, throughout the 1990s–2010s, of nation-building discourses in all post-Soviet states – discourses which continued to disintegrate the once unitary social and cultural sphere along the lines of national mobilization – there remained simultaneously a capillary network of counter-processes which continue to hold considerable influence over the lives of the people inhabiting the vast territory that was once the Soviet Union. Less visibly than official national narratives, these ostensibly marginal practices make their mark in the daily lives of post-Soviet societies and peoples: through trade routes (permitted or proscribed), migratory movements (deliberate or coerced), cultural flows (official and unofficial), communication networks (horizontal and vertical), and social imaginaries (old and new).[7] Indeed, through daily social, economic, and cultural flows that span state boundaries, an everyday transnational experience challenges the hegemony of the post-Soviet discourses of identity and exclusion. In particular, the high level of migration mobility in the post-Soviet sphere blurs the boundaries between legitimate and illegitimate political subjects, turning the hitherto excluded (refugees, diasporans, economic migrants, and other non-citizens) into active interlocutors in the social and political debate. According to Nancy Fraser, processes of this kind call into question the traditionally conceived normative public sphere, imagined as organized

[6] On the intricacies of early-Soviet policy towards nationalities, see Martin (2001) and Suny (2001). On the political conquest of nature as a strategy of Soviet nation-building, see Hirsch (2005).

[7] A 'social imaginary' is described by Charles Taylor (2002: 106 and *passim*) as the way in which ordinary people understand or 'imagine' their social surroundings in the widest possible sense, from political ideas and intellectual concepts to everyday human practices.

around the full citizens of nation states. For Fraser, the new (essentially transnational) form of society is a social assembly made of migratory subjects, 'legal aliens', and other fellow members joined together not necessarily by political legislation (that is, by being citizens of a given nation state) but 'by their co-imbrication in a common set of structures and/or institutions that affect their lives' (2014: 18, 30).

Fraser's vision of what might be called a transnational condition foreshadows some of the fundamental aspects of post-Soviet societies. Practically none of the new post-Soviet states, from Ukraine and Belarus to the Baltic, Transcaucasian, and Central Asian states, not to speak of the Russian Federation, have become homogeneous nation states – much as most of them would wish to be so. On the contrary, while actively pursuing the politics that would enable their greater internal cohesion on national grounds, the post-Soviet state remains a political entity in permanent tension between the unifying strategies of 'social closure' and the plethora of spontaneous transnational practices, which appear to run directly counter to them.

Space and/as Identity in Soviet and Post-Soviet Cinemas

The role that visual art, media, and cinema, in particular, have played in the shaping of Soviet and post-Soviet (trans)national imaginaries is nothing short of fundamental. As the French critic Jean-Michel Frodon has argued, there is a close correspondence between the nation and the moving image on several levels. According to Frodon, both cinema and the nation rest upon a certain 'projection'. Just like the moving image, which exists far beyond its sheer materiality, a nation transcends 'a territory and even a nation-state' to establish itself in the form of an image, a 'projection [that] is recognized both [...] by the population concerned, and at the same time, outside, by those who do not belong to it' (Frodon 1997: 136).

Indeed, 'the nation' exceeds the sum total of the biological substance of a group of people and the geographical space on which they live. And just like the moving image, in order for a nation to emerge, a projection or image of it – that is, of an integrated community and a shared, politically mapped, space – has to take shape.[8] No one understood the need for and the importance of the visual representation of space as a factor in this process better than the early Soviet policymakers and film practitioners. The film-makers

---

[8] Frodon here tacitly refers to Benedict Anderson's much-quoted pronouncement that nations are 'imagined communities' or unities of people who do not know of each other, but nonetheless 'in the minds of each lives the image of their communion' (Anderson 2006: 6).

of the Soviet era were on a mission to visually identify the endless localities of the new land, the unnamed natural space that was to be turned into the Soviet Union as a politically charted territory. Moreover, as Emma Widdis has put it in her account of the visual strategies of mediating physical space in early Soviet cinema, 'Understanding Sovietness, mean[t] understanding the space of Sovietness' (2003: 3). Widdis is right when she points out that at the heart of this visual mastering of space by early Soviet film-makers was Marxist ideology. The strategy of a visual appropriation of the new land was premised upon Karl Marx's idea of the 'appropriation' [Aneignung] of human reality – something deemed essential to alleviating human alienation and thus fundamentally transforming the way the world is experienced.[9] However, the putative philosophical overtones of a call for a symbolic appropriation of geographical space to be mapped as 'Soviet' should not obscure the state-building purpose *par excellence* of this cinematic procedure. As pointed out by Andrew Higson, the process of national identification in and through the moving image is always 'a hegemonizing, mythologizing process, involving the production and assignation of a set of meanings' (1989: 37). Higson's reminder here is an important one for our understanding of Soviet cinema's task in the building of the new state: to visually identify the vast and inarticulate space and then to hegemonically represent that space *qua* national space.

The visual strategies of the identification and assignation of space allow us to raise the key question that this chapter seeks to address: if the cinema of the early Soviet years was appropriating spaces, identifying them as politically and nationally mapped territories assigned to specific (Soviet) nations as their imaginary proprietors, how should we understand the opposite cinematic strategies in which the moving images 'dis-articulate' space and return the once-charted territories back to the state of nameless and unmapped landmass? Although neglected by the growing body of literature on cinematic nation-building in the post-Soviet era, this question is highly pertinent. In the post-Soviet political landscape, when new political elites are abundantly using the power of the moving image to 're-appropriate' their national spaces,[10]

---

[9] Marx advanced the concept of *Aneignung* in his early *Economic and Philosophical Manuscripts* (1844) and further developed it in the first volume of *Das Kapital* (1867).

[10] For example, by reintroducing the system of state commission [goszakaz] in 2008, the Russian Federation has legally formalized the utilization of the film industry for patriotic mobilization. In the words of Aleksandr Avdeev, the then Minister of Culture, the Russian state thus resumed its support for the films that 'espouse the ideas of humanism, spirituality, patriotism and other traditional moral values of Russia's peoples' (Fedina 2008).

we are at the same time witnesses to the rise of visual *counter-strategies* which, each in their own way, challenge the politics of national(ist) mobilization. These revisionist cinematic narratives strategically obscure territorial demarcations and disengage peoples from their designated 'national' spaces in order to make room for both individual agency and human affect to come to the fore.

The sections that follow will examine two post-Soviet film texts – Mikheil Kalatozishvili's *The Wild Field* [Dikoe pole] and Giorgi Ovashvili's *The Other Bank* [Gagma napiri] – which, each in their own way, challenge the hegemony of the post-Soviet discourses of identity through particular cinematic deconstructions of space as an enclosed and politically demarcated category.[11] As we shall see, by unsettling the territory-state-nation continuum, these films' undoing of territorial demarcations acts as a statement of distrust in the hegemonization of social space by nation state discourses and, in turn, as an affirmation of the powerful web of human relations, affects, and individual agency across and beyond any such demarcations.

The Disarticulation of Space in Mikheil Kalatozishvili's *The Wild Field*

Mikheil Kalatozishvili's film *The Wild Field* demonstrates an effort to eradicate the symbols of national identity on practically every level of production. Failing to attract any of the newly established national film-funding bodies (Russian, Kazakh, Azerbaijani, or Georgian), the film was produced by a small pool of private Russian investors. In a similar vein, the very title of the film suggests that extraterritoriality and an absence of boundaries will be one of its dominant themes. In use in sixteenth-century chronicles to describe the territories between the Dnepr River and the Black Sea, the term *dikoe pole* has carried the meaning of unbounded space, a landscape without social organization, or political jurisdiction.

By setting the film in a nameless, uncharted landmass (the locations of the shoot were the steppes of Kazakhstan, but the diegetic space remains conspicuously unnamed throughout the film; Fig. 4.1), Kalatozishvili

---

[11] Coterminous with the crisis of the state apparatus, the cinematic utilization of the uncharted geographical space emerged as a visual trope denoting an end to history and politics already in the late Soviet years. Since Andrei Tarkovskii's *Stalker* (1979) and Aleksandr Sokurov's *Dni zatmeniia* (1988), a number of film productions have articulated this dynamic, including *Lunnyi papa* (Khudoinazarov 1999), *Eiforiia* (Vyripaev 2006), *Tulpan* (Dvortsevoi 2008), *Kak ia provel etim letom* (Popogrebskii 2010), *Ovsianki* (Fedorchenko 2010), *V ozhidanii moria* (Khudoinazarov 2012), and *Ispytanie* (Kott 2014), to name but a few.

Fig. 4.1. *The Wild Field* [Dikoe pole], dir. Mikheil Kalatozishvili, 2008.
Reproduced with permission from Intercinema.

decentres the concept of mapped space or demarcated territory as a locus
of state power. This wide, uncharted land, which clearly signals a vacuum
of power, emerges, in fact, as the film's central protagonist, through which,
as one critic has observed, the 'trajectories of humans, animals and means
of transportation ephemerally traverse' (Razlogov 2008: 51). Indeed, the
diegetic space of the film is left without name or geographic coordinates
but, significantly, the episodic plot structure follows no particular narrative
logic and even the cardinal events in the film unfold as if of their own
accord. In this space without boundaries, with narrative action based around
human affects and drives, the centre of the film's moral universe is Dmitrii
Morozov, a young medical doctor who lives a solitary life in the middle of
the steppe with one goal: to help maintain the fragile equilibrium of the
boundless steppe.

The domineering vastness and wilderness of the steppe, precariously
organized not around any social structure, but the drives and affects of the
people who traverse it, situate *The Wild Field* tantalizingly close to the genre
of the Western. Yet this (in itself transnational) cinematic connection has its
limits insofar as the ideology of Kalatozishvili's film departs from the ethos of
this classical Hollywood genre. If the American Western symbolically legiti-
mizes the appropriation of landscape and turns conquest over nature into the
foundational myth of a rising nation (Simmon 2003: 51–54), *The Wild Field* is
doing precisely the reverse. By extolling the boundless space of the steppe and
by instituting human drives and instincts as its sole organizing forces, the film

Fig. 4.2. Incursion scene, *The Wild Field*.
Reproduced with permission from Intercinema.

puts forward a vision of primordial human associations in which elemental powers ultimately supersede organized forms of governance.[12]

This delegitimization of social order in the film is emphasized by the absence of any clear instances of the state, or any other authority. True, the lawman Riabov wears the insignia of a Soviet-era policeman [militsioner], but it is a minimal form of humanity that he enforces, rather than any kind of social institution of law and order. When, having survived an armed incursion of a group of outlaws, he stops one of the local men from violating the corpses of the intruders (Fig. 4.2), we learn that the local men 'did not swear an oath to Moscow' (Lutsik & Samoriadov 2010: 107). This archaic formulation signals a post-historical condition of civilizational regress, an undoing of modernity conditioned upon the system of social closures performed by the nation state. In contrast, the 'wild field' of the steppe, as it is represented in the film, enacts the world without closures. The only recognizable sign of authority in the film is a white flag with a red cross on it, which flies from Morozov's home surgery

---

[12] The steppe is, of course, a long-established trope of the Russian cultural imagination (e.g. see Chekhov's 1888 novella *The Steppe: History of a Journey* [Step'. Istoriia odnoi poezdki]). Kalatozishvili's own treatment of the steppe challenges the cinematic rendition of Central Asia known from early-Soviet cinematic practice, most notably Viktor Turin's monumental 1929 film *Turksib*, in which the previously inert and unutilized Kazakh steppe (along with its peoples) is triumphantly mapped, industrialized, and brought into civilization.

– a flag of no nation and an image generally associated with contested war zones. This too signals that the world of *The Wild Field* is a world of civilizational decline, in which every form of authority has been suspended.

The return to the primordial and the archaic in *The Wild Field* renders national identities superfluous, yet without, in fact, abolishing them as such. From Riabov's incident report we learn that the attackers were 'two unknown men of uncertain nationality, presumably Asian' (Lutsik & Samoriadov 2010: 106). The assault itself was staged irrespective of the identity of either the attacked or the attackers and the directorial decision to keep the bodies of the intruders outside of the camera's purview only confirms this. What this radical collapsing of territorial, state, and national identities seems to announce is that these categories not only have no agency, but they no longer appear to have a *raison d'être* in what is a post-national universe. Indeed, since the concept of a 'wild field' [dikoe pole] has neither centre nor periphery, it also has no insiders or outsiders, which renders the notion of social closure not only impossible, but also irrelevant.

Lastly, the film's dissociation of space, territory, and people not only suspends the political charting of space, but also puts an end to the subordination of that space to human agency, as well as, in turn, the subordination of individual agency to larger social structures. Nevertheless, Kalatozishvili's landscapes, which exist without social organization and political jurisdiction, are not simply natural or empty – they remain populated and traversed by affective human capacities (positive and negative) – drives, instincts, emotions. Indeed, the film's radical undoing of political space serves not only the purpose of rejecting the political (de)limitations of human geography; this is also a radical, precarious and in no way optimistic plea to look at this space as an affective space, in which basic human agency ultimately supersedes larger state-building ideologies.

The Reclamation of Space in Giorgi Ovashvili's *The Other Bank*

Resistance to the 'sacralization' of national territory assumes a central position in Giorgi Ovashvili's 2008 film *The Other Bank* [Gagma napiri]. This international co-production of private funding bodies from Georgia and Kazakhstan tells the story of 12-year-old Tedo (Fig. 4.3) – an 'internally displaced person' (the United Nations euphemism used to categorize victims of political or other discrimination who, having to leave their primary homes, find refuge in other parts of their own country).[13] In the aftermath of the 1992–93 military

---

[13] Just like *The Wild Field*, *The Other Bank* failed to attract any of the state film funders in the region, with the exemption of a contribution by the local Georgian

Fig. 4.3. *The Other Bank* [Gagma napiri], dir. Giorgi Ovashvili, 2008.
Reproduced with permission from Giorgi Ovashvili.

conflict in the breakaway Georgian region of Abkhazia, during which the
Georgian army was overpowered by the Russia-supported Abkhaz troops,
Tedo was forced out of his home together with other ethnic Georgians.[14] Now,
eight years on, the film's protagonist lives with his mother in a derelict cabin
on the outskirts of what the viewer assumes to be the Georgian capital Tbilisi.
The boy engages in petty crime and longs for a reunion with the father he has
left behind in Abkhazia.

Ovashvili narrates the story in a visually matter-of-fact manner, but it
takes even the informed viewer some effort to reconstruct the diegetic space
of the narrative – that is, to establish with any accuracy the historical and

National Film Centre. This lack of interest stands in contrast with the logic of Eurasian
and global film markets, in which films are increasingly joint transnational ventures.
It testifies to the fact that the greatest beneficiary of transnational production circuits
are commercial films and blockbusters. On the co-production and distribution
dynamic of Russian and other post-Soviet film markets, see the summary of the
European Audiovisual Observatory for 2016 (Talavera Milla & Fontaine 2016: 40–49).
[14] According to the last Soviet census (1989), ethnic Georgians made up 45.7%
of the overall population in Abkhazia, with ethnic Abkhaz making up 17.8%. The
1992–93 civil war, which inflicted over 10,000 casualties across both sides, resulted
in the expulsion and displacement of the entire Georgian population of Abkhazia,
approximately 240,000 individuals (Trier, Lohn & Szakonyi 2010: 17). For a succinct,
but well-documented look at the historical, political, and demographic aspects of the
Abkhaz-Georgian conflict, see Trier et al. (2010).

spatial coordinates within which the narrative unfolds. Indeed, although the geographical locations in *The Other Bank* are real and are either mentioned or indicated (the Enguri River; the Abkhaz town of Tkvarcheli; the capital of Georgia, Tbilisi), the spatial coordinates in the film are blurred by the conspicuous absence of standard cinematic signposts, such as road signs or recognizable landmarks. Rather than having a physical or geographical form, the narrative space of the film operates primarily as an affective and symbolic space. The space that Tedo traverses in the film is an emotive one and, as such, it is at all times in tension with this space's social organization and political demarcations (such as those exemplified by border posts). Ultimately, Tedo's paternal quest, the sole reason for his journey through no-go conflict zones, is an attempt to reappropriate this politically divided space of warring nations by transforming it into an intimate, personal one.

The film's optical minimalism, which restricts the representation of both cityscapes and landscapes to replace them with deliberately under-inscribed, insipid wastelands and suburban sceneries, successfully defamiliarizes the otherwise identifiable Georgian settings to achieve a more complex, emotive mapping of this space. However, this is not to say that, while unnamed, the liminal spaces in *The Other Bank* – bridges, railroads, border crossings, military buffer zones – are not heavily imbricated with social and political meanings (Fig. 4.4.). As one critic has put it, these non-neutral landscapes are etched with ongoing violence: they are Tedo's, and clearly everyone else's, 'pains of the past' (Pötzsch 2012: 186). The emotion Tedo feels for these landscapes of pain is precisely the driving force of his personal quest. Each step of his endeavour – his near-fatal train journey, the hitch-hiking and border crossing episodes during which he is a witness to rape and murder, or the equally precarious travels through Abkhazia – brings to bear this important, affective, reinscription of a defamiliarized, alien space.[15]

With the micro-political history of Transcaucasia in mind, one could say that Tedo's journey across interethnic divides *reclaims* the space of the Caucasus from social and political closures and thereby challenges the ongoing post-Soviet discourses of national mobilization. Returning to Marx's idea about the appropriation of human experience more generally, one might interpret Tedo's reach across contested nation state boundaries as an effort to reclaim the alienated world around him. If the post-Soviet nation-building strategies are about appropriating heterogeneous multi-ethnic spaces by various ethno-territorial closures (say, by declaring a particular territory an

---

[15] In his discussion of the relationship that pertains between human experience and space, Yi-Fu Tuan has argued that purposive movement and perception 'give human beings their familiar world of disparate objects in space' (1977: 12).

Fig. 4.4. Crossing of the Enguri River, *The Other Bank.*
Reproduced with permission from Giorgi Ovashvili.

area of high historical import and turning it into a national myth), Tedo's journey is then an attempt to undo these strategies and *re*appropriate the space as a space that has meaning for him, as *his* 'homeland', in a 'truer', non-exclusive, sense of the term.

However, practically all of Tedo's affective efforts seem to fail, with only one episode making an instructive exception. Having entered Abkhazia, Tedo stays overnight with an elderly Abkhaz couple who, we learn, lost their son in the 1992–93 conflict. When Tedo's feigned muteness (his survival strategy on Abkhaz soil) is foiled and his hosts realize that he is an ethnic Georgian, a certain antagonism arises, though he is eventually embraced by the couple in what could be understood as an act of symbolic adoption. Thus, the only instance when Tedo transforms the world around him is when he reaches out to the people whose world is, just like his own, shaped not by some state ideological inscriptions of nationhood, but by an affective, personal testimony of loss.

Having left his 'adoptive' Abkhaz 'home', Tedo's other sojourns yield little success. The much-desired paternal reunion comes to nothing when, upon returning to his former home, Tedo discovers that his father now has another family (Fig. 4.5) and when, on his way out of his birthtown, he is caught by an unknown armed group. When the ongoing violence and the omnipresent traces of terror finally overcome his attempts to reappropriate the disinte-grated spaces of his life and his former country, Tedo is left with no active strategy with which to perform his task. Instead, he mentally transports

Fig. 4.5. Tedo at his former home in Abkhazia, *The Other Bank.*
Reproduced with permission from Giorgi Ovashvili.

himself to a rather different kind of space by daydreaming of going on safari in Africa. The film ends with scenes from the African savannah, the product of Tedo's imagining a symbolically non-political space – unmarked by ethno-territorial boundaries, free from social closures and exclusions.[16]

Conclusion

The films of Mikheil Kalatozishvili and Giorgi Ovashvili deconstruct, in their different ways, the meanings of national space as a means by which the relationship between a modern polity and a human individual is established. Both films not only evade the limits and constraints of the dominant official nationalizing discourses, but explicitly counter these discourses through a strategy of de/re-territorializing nationally inscribed and politically mapped spaces. What the visual strategies deployed in these two films perform is: 1) the delegitimation of the authority of the nation state as a hegemonic social structure with the power to identify its subjects as members of a particular nation (with everything else that then follows as a consequence of this 'subjection'); and 2) the releasing of individual human agency, above all in its affective (rather than rational) figurations, as the true, universal subject of

---

[16] The film *Other Bank* is based on a novella titled 'A Journey to Africa' [Mogzauroba aprik'ashi] by the Georgian writer Nugzar Shataidze (2014).

historical processes. Through a deconstruction of key elements of national polities, these films ultimately question the applicability of certain political norms to the post-Soviet sphere and herald a vision of Eurasia as a fundamentally 'transnational' space.

Kalatozishvili's *The Wild Field* is set in a boundless unidentified corner of the Eurasian steppe, which renders the idea of territorial statehood pointless. Somewhat paradoxically, this boundless space is configured as one large borderline zone, in which the power of human affects is unleashed to ambiguous effect. In fact, Kalatozishvili takes his film to an uncertain, aporetic, if not pessimistic conclusion, insofar as the critique of state power and the affirmation of human individuality is shown to be by no means a necessarily creative force. Giorgi Ovashvili's *The Other Bank* challenges the legitimacy of the nation state to assign subjectivity in a different, but commensurable way. Unlike *The Wild Field*, *The Other Bank* is set in actual geographical locations, which are loaded with a history and politics that remain vital to the interpretation of the film. However, Ovashvili systematically defamiliarizes this 'real' space, while its road movie structure and the prevalence in it of what Hamid Naficy (2001: 222–61) has termed 'transitional spaces and sites' (homecomings, border crossings, bridges, train and bus travel) both highlights and contests the nation states' obsession with mapping territories, charting boundaries, and constructing nations, not least by means of violence.

Significantly, however, both films circumvent optimistic or redemptive endings. In *The Wild Field*, the absence of social norms and boundaries unleashes human affects often with destructive effects, while the protagonist of *The Other Bank* is forced to yield to the discourses of national exclusion despite the moral high ground that his position holds. Thus, in both films, the politics of transnationalism in post-Soviet Eurasia are rendered with scepticism: while being put forward as a corrective to ongoing state-building projects in the region, they come forth as either precarious or feeble political alternatives to these projects.

Works Cited

Anderson, Benedict. 2006. *Imagined Communities: Reflections on the Origin and Spread of Nationalism* (London: Verso).

Bassin, Mark, Christopher Ely, and Melissa K. Stockdale. 2010. *Space, Place and Power in Modern Russia: Essays in the New Spatial History* (DeKalb, IL: Northern Illinois University Press).

Brubaker, Rogers. 1992. *Citizenship and Nationhood in France and Germany* (Cambridge, MA: Harvard University Press).

Brubaker, Rogers, and Frederick Cooper. 2000. 'Beyond "Identity"', *Theory and Society*, 29(1): 1–47.

Burbank, Jane, and Mark von Hagen. 2007. 'Coming into the Territory: Uncertainty and Empire' in Jane Burbank, Mark von Hagen, and Anatolyi Remnev (eds), *Russian Empire: Space, People, Power, 1700–1930* (Bloomington, IN: Indiana University Press), 1–27.

Fedina, Anna. 2008. 'Kino podano', *Izvestiia*, 27 July <https://iz.ru/news/339059> [accessed 1 June 2018].

Fraser, Nancy. 2014. 'Transnationalizing the Public Sphere: On the Legitimacy and Efficacy of Public Opinion in a Post-Westphalian World' in Kate Nash (ed.), *Transnationalizing the Public Sphere* (Cambridge: Polity), 8–42.

Frodon, Jean-Michel. 1997. 'La projection nationale cinéma et nation', *Les cahiers de médiologie*, 1(3): 135–45.

Higson, Andrew. 1989. 'The Concept of National Cinema', *Screen*, 30(4): 36–46.

Hirsch, Francine. 2005. *Empire of Nations: Ethnographic Knowledge and the Making of the Soviet Union* (Ithaca, NY: Cornell University Press).

Lutsik, Petr, and Aleksei Samoriadov. 2010. 'Wild Field. Film Script', trans. Birgit Beumers, *Studies in Russian and Soviet Cinema*, 4(1): 95–122.

Martin, Terry. 2001. *Affirmative Action Empire* (Ithaca, NY: Cornell University Press).

Matsuzato, Kimitaka. 1997. 'The Concept of "Space" in Russian History – Regionalization from the Late Imperial Period to the Present' in Teruyuki Hara and Kimitaka Matsuzato (eds), *Empire and Society: New Approaches to Russian History* (Hokkaido: Slavic Research Center, Hokkaido University), 181–204.

Miller, Alexei. 2015. 'The Romanov Empire and the Russian Nation' in Alexei Miller and Stefan Berger (eds), *Nationalizing Empires* (Budapest and New York: Central European University Press), 309–69.

Naficy, Hamid. 2001. *An Accented Cinema: Exilic and Diasporic Filmmaking* (Princeton, NJ: Princeton University Press).

Plokhy, Serhii. 2006. *The Origins of the Slavic Nations: Premodern Identities in Russia, Ukraine, and Belarus* (Cambridge: Cambridge University Press).

Pötzsch, Holger. 2012. 'Imag(in)ing Painful Pasts: Mimetic and Poetic Style in War Films' in Asbjørn Grønstad and Henrik Gustafsson (eds), *Ethics and Images of Pain* (London: Routledge), 251–78.

Razlogov, Kirill. 2008. 'Evraziiskii khronotop. "Dikoe Pole", rezhisser Mikhail Kalatozishvili', *Iskusstvo kino*, 8: 50–52.

Shataidze, Nugzar. 2014. 'Puteshestvie v Afriku', *Novaia iunost'*, 6: 3–23.

Simmon, Scott. 2003. *The Invention of the Western Film: A Cultural History of the Genre's First Half-Century* (Cambridge: Cambridge University Press).

Suny, Ronald Grigor. 2001. 'The Empire Strikes Out: Imperial Russia, "National Identity", and Theories of Empire' in Ronald Suny and Terry Martin (eds), *A State of Nations: Empire and Nation-Making in the Age of Lenin and Stalin* (Oxford: Oxford University Press), 23–66.

Talavera Milla, Julio, and Gilles Fontaine (eds). 2016. 'European Film Production and Co-Production in Russia and the Export of Russian Films Abroad', Publication of the European Audiovisual Observatory <https://rm.coe.int/090000168078353d> [accessed 22 December 2017].

Taylor, Charles. 2002. 'Modern Social Imaginaries', *Public Culture*, 14(1): 91–124.

Ther, Philipp. 2015. '"Imperial Nationalism" as Challenge for the Study of Nationalism' in Alexei Miller and Stefan Berger (eds), *Nationalizing Empires* (Budapest and New York: Central European University Press), 573–91.

Tolz, Vera. 2001. *Russia* (London: Arnold).

Trier, Tom, Hedvig Lohm, and David Szakonyi. 2010. *Under Siege: Inter-Ethnic Relations in Abkhazia* (New York: Columbia University Press).

Tuan, Yi-Fu. 1977. *Space and Place: The Perspective of Experience* (Minneapolis, MN: University of Minnesota Press).

Vertovec, Steven. 2009. *Transnationalism* (London: Routledge).

Widdis, Emma. 2003. *Visions of a New Land: Soviet Film from the Revolution to the Second World War* (New Haven, CT: Yale University Press).

Wimmer, Mathias. 2002. *Nationalist Exclusion and Ethnic Conflict: Shadows of Modernity* (Cambridge: Cambridge University Press).

5

Vladimir Sorokin's *Telluria*

Post-imperial Eurasia, Fragmented Europe

Tatiana Filimonova

Sorokin and Eurasianism

Contemporary Russian speculative fiction often taps into the realm of geopolitics, redrawing maps, forming new states and destroying old ones, and creating transnational communities and protagonists who cross borders. Among such speculative fiction, alternate histories take a prominent place. Writers of the genre imagine how the present might look different if history had taken another course. Alternate histories usually introduce a plausible historical turning point that leads to a recognizable, if radically different, present. A striking example of the genre is Vladimir Sorokin's *Day of the Oprichnik* [Den' oprichnika, 2006], a sociopolitical dystopia that situates a fictional Russia within the context of larger Eurasia and imagines Russia's return to the sixteenth-century sociopolitical order. This chapter, however, will focus on a later work by Sorokin, his novel *Telluria* [Telluriia, 2013]. Here, Russia and Europe are divided into city states and self-declared republics, driven by disparate ideologies, governed by clashing elites, inspired by different religions. Set in a neo-medieval, fragmented Eurasia, the novel's imagined world challenges not only contemporary Russia's neo-imperial tendencies but also the sociopolitical and economic principles of the West, including international democratic alliances and globalization.

Why did Sorokin turn to alternate history in the 2000s? Born in 1955, the writer honed his craft in the Moscow underground in the 1980s, penning scandalous experimental works such as *The Norm* [Norma, written 1979–83] and *The Queue* [Ochered', written 1983] that satirized the Soviet Union, especially official Soviet discourse and aesthetics, though without engaging directly in political critique. Such works could not be published in the Soviet

Union, and circulated only in *samizdat* (i.e. underground self-publishing) or *tamizdat* (i.e. published abroad) forms. Sorokin's work became more widely known in the 1990s, with his provocative novel *Blue Lard* [Goluboe salo, 1999] causing outrage for its graphic depiction of homosexual encounters between Soviet leaders Stalin and Khrushchev. The panic around this novel coincided with the rise of Putin and Russia's move towards greater authoritarianism and social conservatism in the early 2000s, and this turn of events caused Sorokin to become more explicitly political. In a 2007 interview, he described his journey from being an 'apolitical' writer to a politically engaged one: 'the citizen in me has come to life' (Doerry & Schepp 2007). Although Sorokin's writing has always had an ideological resonance in a broad sense, it is true that he harnesses his subversive aesthetics to an immediate political critique of the present regime more obviously in his recent work. The alternate history is his weapon of choice, and one of his main targets is neo-Eurasianism: the ideology that celebrates the country's Asian roots and sees Russia as an imperial leader of the Eurasian continent, promoted explicitly by thinkers such as Aleksandr Dugin and used by the Putin government.[1] Sorokin is not the only writer of fiction to turn to Eurasian themes in contemporary Russia; rather, he provides an ironic, critical take on an ideology that is increasingly popular.[2]

At this point, it is necessary to recap the history of Eurasia as a concept and the movement associated with it. Eurasianism is an attempt to address what philosopher Nikolai Berdiaev famously called Russia's 'eternal' concern: that of 'East and West' (1990: 115). What Berdiaev saw as conflicting Eastern and Western elements in Russia provided fertile ground to Russian émigré intellectuals based in Europe in the aftermath of the 1917 revolution. Lamenting the Bolshevik usurpation of power, ideologues like linguist Nikolai Trubetskoi and geographer Petr Savitskii theorized about ways Russia could repair the damage inflicted on it by the Bolshevik regime, which – to their minds – would inevitably prove short-lived. Viewing capitalist western Europe as an aggressive predator whose domination of the world was detrimental to its colonial subjects, Eurasianists argued that, in order to prosper, Russia

---

[1] Mark Bassin and Gonzalo Pozo's recent edited volume examines the Russian government's co-option of Eurasianist ideas. See especially their introduction and chapters 8–10 (Bassin & Pozo 2017).

[2] Many notable examples of Eurasianism in literature occur in novels by lesser-known authors like Pavel Krusanov and genre writers like Khol'm van Zaichik (see Filimonova 2015; Suslov 2017). Neo-imperialist discourse also interests major writers such as Viktor Pelevin, Aleksandr Prokhanov, Dmitrii Bykov, and Vladimir Sharov, thereby encompassing both mass-market fiction and high-brow literature (Lipovetskii 2002; Noordenbos 2011; Suslov 2016).

needed to follow a unique path, a 'third way' that would combine elements of capitalism with socialist and Orthodox principles in its government, economy, and society (Trubetzkoy 1991). They believed that Russia had to unite Eurasian peoples under an imperial banner because of their shared historical destiny and ethnic and cultural proximity (Savitskii 2003). At a time when theories of western Europe's decline abounded, they hailed Russia's Eastern Orthodox spirituality and its multi-ethnic cultural heritage as a source of salvation for all of Eurasia. Moreover, they directed anticolonial rhetoric at leading European empires long before the rise of postcolonial thought more broadly (Tolz 2015).

Despite the Eurasianists' predictions, the Bolshevik regime endured while Eurasianism petered out as an ideology. However, in the 1990s, neo-imperialist ideas of a strong Eurasia regained popularity in Russia, coinciding with state-level economic agreements and cultural bonds to rival those of the West.[3] As Russia has become more assertive on the world stage, Eurasianism has been used by ideologues not only to challenge the West but also to contain the xenophobic sentiments of Russian nationalists at home and promote Russia's dominance in post-Soviet space as a nexus for transnational connections among peoples of the former Soviet republics.

Post-Soviet neo-Eurasianism promoted the idea of a strong multi-ethnic empire under the leadership of Orthodox Russia. Ultra-conservative political thinker and provocateur Aleksandr Dugin was instrumental in reviving Eurasianism and reinforcing the geopolitical emphasis at the movement's ideological core. Dugin added the idea of multipolarity to Eurasianist discourse, asserting Russia's messianic role in challenging the dominance of North America in global culture and economics.[4] Lev Gumilev's Eurasianist-inspired theories of ethnogenesis, which appeared in print in the 1980s and 1990s, aided Dugin in expanding the theoretical basis of neo-Eurasianism and reaching wider audiences.[5] Widely circulating reprints of Eurasianist texts,

---

[3] This trend started with Evgenii Primakov's promotion of Russia's alliance with China and India, and continued with Putin's Eurasian Economic Union and associated projects.

[4] Dugin wrote that 'at the core of the geopolitical construction of this Empire should be [...] the principle of a "common enemy". The repudiation of Atlanticism, the rejection of the US's strategic control, and of the primacy of economic, liberal market values – these provide the common basis of civilization, that shared impulse that will pave the way for a durable political and strategic union and will create the backbone of the coming Empire' (1999: 216).

[5] Lev Gumilev (1912–92), a Russian historian and geographer, developed theories which – though largely debunked as unscientific – gained popularity in Russia in the 1990s. His 'passionarity theory of ethnogenesis', set out in his monograph

and Dugin's successful promotion of his views in universities and the political arena, meant that Russians – consciously or not – started to perceive their country not just as a state but as the major part of a continent; society as a whole began to think about Russia in geopolitical terms. Continental Eurasia was more often contrasted with the 'Atlantic West', while neo-Eurasianist terminology seeped into political life and was embraced by Putin himself in the mid-2000s (Hill & Gaddy 2012: 26). Corresponding with this political and intellectual trend, and facilitated by Dugin's links with leading cultural figures, Eurasianism penetrated the literary milieu of Putin's Russia, boosting the production of alternate histories, prompting many authors, including Sorokin – who eagerly parodied Eurasianist scenarios in his novels – to embrace this genre.

Eurasianist Alternate Histories

Scholars have sought the explanation for the Russians' hunger for alternate histories, including Eurasianist ones, in the country's history of rapid regime change, which prompted constant rewriting of history (Marsh 2007), as well as in its population's disillusionment with the newly discovered past, or indeed with their present condition (Vitenberg 2002). Alexander Etkind coined the concept 'magical historicism' to describe such works, with their 'bizarre but instructive imagery that has evolved out of a postcatastrophic, post-Soviet culture'. Noting how 'memory [is] turning into imagination' within this culture, Etkind reflects that 'many authors and readers seem to share a desire for a poetic re-enactment of the catastrophic past' or to imagine alternative outcomes to it (2009: 631). For Sorokin, it was not so much the rewriting as the repeating of history that prompted a dabbling in the alternate history genre. In a 2007 interview focused on *Day of the Oprichnik*, Sorokin expressed his concern about the darkest pages of Russian history entering contemporary reality: 'There is much talk about Russia being a fortress. Orthodox churches, autocracy and national traditions are supposed to form a new national ideology. This would mean that Russia would be overtaken by its past, and our past would become our future' (Doerry & Schepp 2007). This world of the past, portrayed in *Day of the Oprichnik*, was ideologically modelled as a Eurasianist dystopia, including elements such as Russia's turn to Orthodoxy, the implicit nationalism within a state that flaunts multi-ethnic harmony, and an autocratic government.

Ethnogenesis and the Earth's Biosphere [Etnogenez i biosfera zemli, 1993], asserts that history is governed by the interactions of various ethnoses with each other and with their geographical environments.

This rise of neo-Eurasianism in twenty-first-century Russia and the intensifying authoritarianism in its politics and society simultaneously fascinated and repelled Sorokin. Sorokin created a genre that blended alternate history with 'magical' elements of science fiction and satirical dystopia and used the conservative neo-Eurasianist movement as a source for his irony. Written within the span of five years, *Day of the Oprichnik*, *Sugar Kremlin* [Sakharnyi Kreml', 2008], and *The Blizzard* [Metel', 2011] – forming an interconnected 'Oprichnik cycle' – were immediately interpreted as critiques of Putin's neo-imperialist policies (Aptekman 2009). In this novelistic cycle, Sorokin imagines a retrograde self-contained Russian-Eurasian empire and exaggerates China's economic power to gigantic proportions, reimagining Russian space, the flow of peoples within it, and the roles of its ethnically or socio-economically segregated communities. The author's gaze in these novels transcends national borders, broadening their scope to include eastern Eurasia despite their primary focus on Russia. Much of *Telluria* has a strong political impetus but, unlike the Oprichnik cycle, its fictional world is less dependent on a critique of neo-imperialism. Here, Sorokin's irony focuses on globalization across Eurasia, including responses to the transnational movements of people and ideas in western Europe and a commentary on Russia's 'third way'.

Geopolitics and Globalization in *Telluria*

Even though Sorokin's early works inevitably had political resonance, until the Oprichnik cycle the author had styled himself as 'apolitical' (Doerry & Schepp 2007) and he engaged, rather, in the playful deconstruction of established literary discourses and aesthetic planes. As Sorokin's interest in politics grew, his deconstructive lens focused increasingly on sociopolitical trends like the growing rift between the Putin-era elite and the masses, and the government's return to Soviet-style propaganda, among others. In *Telluria*, by using the alternate history genre to create a fictional world of great ethnic diversity – a place in which real-world colonial history no longer manifests itself, and where empires have broken down into city states and republics – Sorokin deconstructs the discourse of post-imperial globalization. In *Telluria* the critique of Russia's neo-imperialism evident throughout the Oprichnik cycle transforms into a questioning of geopolitical formations and social doctrines of the present day, including the liberal democratic principles that uphold globalization and promote diversity as state-building strategies, thus suggesting the ultimate failure even of democratic semi-imperial formations. The novel turns a defamiliarizing gaze not just onto Russia but equally onto the West, revealing the author's scepticism also about liberal global alliances such as the European Union.

The Oprichnik cycle imagines how Eurasianism, infused with nationalist, segregationist, and fundamentalist religious ideas of fictional imperial Russia, prompts a complete geopolitical remake of Eurasia. With *Telluria*, Sorokin foresees not an imperialist revival but rather a disintegration of nations and societies that follows this neo-imperial period. Stretching across most of Eurasia, the Russia of *Day of the Oprichnik* possesses clearly delineated borders ('the Great wall'). In *Telluria*, the once-great empire is balkanized into pockets of nationally and temporally bound locales, creating a fictional world in which neither Russia nor Europe are recognizably present. Instead, a neo-medieval Eurasia is fragmented into a set of principalities driven by various ideologies and characterized by socio-economic and cultural trends of the past: carnivalesque Rhineland Westphalia exists alongside Islamist Stockholm while, east of the Urals, the Stalinist Soviet Socialist Republic rivals the Communist Baikal Republic. Each of *Telluria's* 50 chapters boasts a unique literary style matching or, often, challenging the diverse ideological, historical, or philosophical content (for example, Chapter 6, set in the neo-Stalinist 'Ural Republic' imitates the propagandistic style of Soviet war reports). The fictional principalities, republics, and city states mimic a wide assemblage of state discourses, and the novel's reader navigates through various cultural codes and versions of national character, shaped by contemporary developments fuelled by globalization, migration, and cosmopolitanism. Tellurium, a precious hallucinogenic metal, drives interaction and travel among fictional states. It also serves to thematically unite the disjointed chapters.

Some critics have likened *Telluria* to *Day of the Oprichnik* by classifying it as 'politically engaged prose' and a 'dystopia' (Schwartz 2016: 290), while portraying Sorokin as 'a relentless prophet' (Narinskaia 2013). While *Telluria* certainly includes dystopian elements, the novel successfully combines an ideological critique akin to that in the Oprichnik cycle with an expanded array of stylistic experiments characteristic of Sorokin's earlier conceptualist work, many of which are humorous for the sake of being humorous, and include elements of political or, at times, moral critique rather as a sideline. Chapters 9 and 42 illustrate the two different Sorokins in this novel. The former chapter is set during the city council meeting of Orthodox-Communist Muscovy, conducted almost entirely in bureaucratic Soviet jargon. By combining the stylistic register of Soviet bureaucracy with the trappings of a medieval Russian state, Sorokin makes a critical comment about the persistence of authoritarianism throughout seemingly disparate periods in Russian history. A satirical message is here achieved through the absurd incongruity of historical settings and discursive styles. Counterbalancing this overtly ideological content, Chapter 42 is motivated almost entirely by a playful linguistic experiment.

It features an inter-species love story narrated in a peculiar version of Old Church Slavonic by a heartbroken domesticated centaur. However, even here one can find a moral imperative: the chapter rests on the problematic practice of keeping a semi-rational being as branded livestock-turned-pet.

While in earlier novels, such as *Blue Lard*, stylistic experimentation was fed largely by Russian or Soviet historical and cultural references, *Telluria* ventures beyond Russia. By extending the geographical scope of the novel, Sorokin creates more room both for playful stylization and for ideological satire, with western Europe providing new sources for the pseudo-historical settings of some chapters, allowing for underlying ideological commentary on European affairs more broadly. Here, Sorokin's literary and linguistic devices are enriched by the theoretical underpinnings of post-Soviet neo-imperial ideas, as well as by broader public responses to globalization. In this fictional world, the economic and political processes driving cross-cultural contact differ drastically from reality, although many of the political actors form easily recognizable, albeit paradoxical and therefore highly entertaining, blends. Sorokin, for example, mocks European conservatives' fears of Islamic fundamentalism and of mass immigration from the Middle East by describing a Stockholm that is under tight Wahhabi control and a Cologne that has just been liberated from Taliban occupation. Wahhabis are, moreover, depicted as leading the 'liberating' Islamist war against 'crusaders' in western Europe. Chapters 8 and 25 are narrated from the Wahhabis' point of view, and do not shy away from stereotypical representations of them as misogynists and extremists. Literary experimentation feeds into ideological concerns and elements of the plot influence the diversity of narrative styles: Chapter 8, stylized as a *mujahid* prayer, features an assemblage of vivid but clichéd metaphors: it calls for 'Jihad's thunder' to 'shake up the walls' of 'old Europe'. Here, typically for Sorokin, the violence reaches absurd, hyperbolic, even grotesque levels, as the narrator describes with gusto the rape of European women by 'valiant Mujahideen' warriors (2013: 72).

Western liberals, however, are also a target of Sorokin's critique. Chapter 5, which starts with an enthusiastic television report from the revived Carnival in Cologne, a report that highlights the ethnic and religious diversity of Rhineland Westphalia's liberation heroes – ends up lambasting western European telejournalism for its sanctimoniously patriotic enthusiasm by exposing the poverty and hypocrisy of the reporter and revealing his drug addiction.

Another powerful political actor – Orthodox communism – controls Muscovy, the former backbone of a powerful empire. Coining this paradoxical religious ideology, Sorokin points to the recent co-option of both the Orthodox Church and Soviet history by the Russian government. This peculiar blend of ideologies allows him to create the absurd sermon in Chapter 3, the language of which combines the Old Church Slavonic vocabulary of Orthodox prayer with Soviet acronyms and the capitalist jargon of post-Soviet Russia:

> If his Majesty's top-manager summons to the glory of the CPSU [Communist Party of the Soviet Union] in the name of all saints and for the happiness of all people and merely by God's will, by the dictate of world imperialism, by the command of enlightened Satanism, by the fervour of the Orthodox patriotism.[6] (Sorokin 2013: 20)

Cultural critic Boris Paramonov has praised Sorokin for providing a 'succinct treatise on Russian history' in Chapter 11 and, simultaneously, 'an instant photograph of contemporary Russia' insofar as its three pages, which read like a sermon, list 'all of Russia's events and hopes' (Genis & Paramonov 2013). Similarly, in Chapter 3, Sorokin mockingly lists nearly all of the 'isms' that dominated Russian cultural discourse during the last century: communism, Orthodox fundamentalism, national bolshevism, anti-Americanism, globalism, and many more.

When Sorokin creates imaginary city states, he questions not only Russia's but also western Europe's tendencies towards globalization, drawing on the rich fictional potential that the imaginary cities offer in regard to transnationalism. Social anthropologist Nina Glick Schiller writes that 'transnationality' places cities within the synergies and tensions of the mutual construction of the local, national, and global' (2012: 31). By populating many of his imaginary states with diverse individuals whose background suggests a transnational past, and by creating a cumulative image of a diverse metropolis even in the unlikely 'Ural Republic', Sorokin explores the cities' potential to represent the narrow local identity, the multicultural melting pot, and the setting for transnational connections that stretch across Eurasia. In their introduction to *Minor Transnationalism*, Francoise Lionnet and Shu-Mei Shih emphasize the importance of decentralization for transnational processes to occur: 'The transnational [...] can be conceived as a space of exchange and participation wherever processes of hybridization occur and where it is still possible for cultures to be produced and performed without necessary mediation by the center' (2005: 5). *Telluria*, without making 'the transnational' central to its plot, imagines a version of a decentralized world where transnational experiences abound. Although some chapters focus on Moscow, the Russian capital has ceased to exist as such, appearing merely as a fragment of the former

---

[6] All translations of excerpts from *Telluria* and other Russian-language sources are my own.

empire. Chapter 1, describing a planned assault on the Kremlin, warns of a potential conflict over fictional Moscow's governing body. Yet the author hardly returns to that storyline. The Kremlin's fate ceases to matter, and Moscow is relegated to the periphery of the novel, revealing a sense of its fictional world's political multipolarity.

Ironically, the calls for a multipolar world that entered Putin's political discourse via Dugin's neo-Eurasianism and aimed at turning Moscow into a key 'pole' result here in a different kind of multipolarity, one which undermines Russian hegemony. Sorokin follows a key neo-Eurasianist idea through to a logical conclusion that is not necessarily palatable to Moscow: the emerging chief economic and political actors, the 'poles' of the fictional Eurasia, are located outside of Moscow's control. Much of the transnational exchange in the novel occurs as a result of the demand for tellurium, and wars are fought over ideological disagreements about its use as a drug. Nestled in the Altai Mountains, Telluria is a utopian state that controls the mining, distribution, and even administering of the drug. Led by a beneficent French-born president and populated by ethnic Kazakhs and Russians, Telluria becomes a powerful political actor on the continent, but has yet to establish diplomatic relations with some of the existing states. In Chapter 23, Telluria witnesses a historic day: it is officially recognized by the Baikal Republic, clearing the path for more exports, and paving the way for Telluria to become a chief actor in the newly forged multipolar world (Sorokin 2013: 223–24).

Moscow's downfall is aptly described through the words of an English visitor. In the second chapter, cosmopolitan traveller Leo writes a convincing account of Russian history to his lover in 'neo-imperial' England (little is known about this seemingly outdated political formation in this fragmented fictional world). Concisely characterizing the Russian Empire as an 'Asian-Byzantine despotic government combined with the indecently oversized colonial geography, harsh climate and timid population', Leo narrates twentieth-century history, which he accomplishes by extending Lenin's memorable metaphor of the Russian Empire as a rotting corpse (Lenin 1967–70: 409). Following the revolution, this corpse is first propped up by the 'groaning caryatids' Lenin and Trotskii, then prettied up and frozen for freshness, this time held up by millions of dead bodies during Stalin's reign (Sorokin 2013: 16–17). Defrosting and freezing in turn, after the fall of the Soviet Union the 'post-Soviet imperialists were ready to turn into caryatids' to prop up the empire's corpse. At this point Sorokin's authoritative control of the text interprets the historical reality of contemporary Russia creating a projected alternative history for its future, starting with Putin's Russia. Although Putin is not named, he is recognizable in the narrator's portrait of 'a nondescript man [...], a great liberal and psychotherapist' who, having spent a decade and a half 'speaking about reviving the empire', 'did everything for the corpse to successfully fall apart [...] After the collapse of the empire Moscow went through [...] hunger, new monarchy + bloody *oprichnina*, social estates, constitution, MKP, the parliament'. Leo finally classifies the current political regime of Muscovy as 'enlightened theocratocommunifeudalism' (Sorokin 2013: 17).

The epistolary style here blends with that of a political treatise. In a break with Sorokin's earlier characteristic style, the narrator demonstrates a keen interest in interpreting Russia's past, defining its national and historical identity, and, as a result, operating within the same neo-imperialist discourse as neo-Eurasianist ideologues, albeit critical of the discourse's political connotations. Communicated through the words of a westerner, this historical treatise suggests that had the revolution of 1917 led to the empire's break-up into 'several states of a reasonable size; everything would be quite in the spirit of contemporary history, and the peoples that have been held back by the crown would at last develop their post-imperial national identity and start to live freely' (Sorokin 2013: 15). The forceful revival of the empire in *Telluria*, however, leads to tumultuous changes, political instability, and its eventual disintegration.

Neo-Medievalism in *Telluria*

Telluria's post-neo-imperial world approaches the 'new Middle Ages' – echoing the concept that adherents of a cyclical approach to history had used in the early twentieth century. Berdiaev, pondering 'the fate of Russia and Europe' in the 1924 essay 'The New Middle Ages', evoked this historical period in regard to post-revolutionary Europe, referring 'to the rhythmic succession of eras, the transition from the rationalism of Modern history to the irrationalism or the supernationalism[7] of the medieval kind', and suggesting that 'religious struggle [and] polarization' characterized this new era (Dugin 2014). Dugin embraces Berdiaev's 'new Middle Ages' as a viable model for post-Soviet society, suggesting that this 'medieval paradigm presupposes a religious, heroic, and hierarchical society as opposed to the materialistic, commonplace, pragmatic, mercantile order that dominates our time' (2014). Through Dugin, neo-medievalism has entered Putin's political discourse and thus become another ideological point of departure for stylization or critique in contemporary speculative fiction

---

[7] Berdiaev's concept of *sverkhnatsionalizm* implies a humanitarian concern for all people and is opposed to nationalism, which promotes chauvinistic interests of a specific people or nation.

and film.[8] A character in *Telluria*'s Chapter 28, which recounts conversations of the world's best 'carpenters' travelling from Telluria to Europe (the 'carpenters' administer tellurium to users by nailing it into their skulls), also uses Dugin's geopolitical jargon: 'after the collapse of ideological, geopolitical, and technological utopias, the Eurasian continent was submerged into the blessed enlightened Middle Ages' (Sorokin 2013: 286).

Sorokin's 'new Middle Ages' partially draw on Berdiaev's and Dugin's characterization of that period: the carpenter describes this epoch as 'enlightened'. In Dugin's view, a return to the Middle Ages is the preferred path for Russia because it presupposes a 'religious' and 'heroic' society (Dugin 2014). While Sorokin's former Russian Eurasian states appear much more nationalistic than Berdiaev would like to see, they are driven by religious struggle. However, Sorokin's neo-medieval world appears enlightened even by the standards of Western liberalism and does not show the ethnic and religious hatred sometimes associated with the medieval era in the historical imagination. Race and ethnicity seem to have disappeared as markers of belonging. The fictional states feature ethnically diverse populations, but often in contexts that preclude religious diversity and political freedom. Characters, endowed by the writer with carefully selected, ethnically marked names, appearances, and linguistic habits, display little to no awareness thereof. Their backgrounds are irrelevant within *Telluria*'s fictional world; however, they point to a past characterized by transnational processes associated with globalization, such as colonial and postcolonial migration.

An example of an ethnically progressive but politically rigid space appears in Chapter 6, set in the warring Communist 'Ural Republic'. Meticulously imitating the clichéd and optimistic *agitprop* style of Soviet war correspondents, the chapter reports on the progress of a guerrilla squadron in the war effort. The squadron bears the name of Miguel Eliazar, the Republic's military hero, which suggests both a connection with the Spanish Civil War and the Hebrew Bible, but also alludes to the contemporary Russian writer Mikhail Elizarov, whose vivid texts exhibit a certain nostalgia for the Soviet past, and who has been criticized for nationalist and even fascist leanings (Latynina 2009). The soldiers' names imply the squadron's ethnic diversity, including Slavic, French, Anglo-Saxon, and Arabic roots. While the organized struggle of this diverse group for the dominance of communism cleverly reflects the internationalist ideas of the early Bolsheviks, one should not interpret this conglomeration of ethnicities merely as a mockery of

---

[8] Aleksei German's screen adaptation of the Strugatskii brothers' *Hard to be a God* [Trudno byt' bogom, 2013] serves as another example of a contemporary fictional adaptation that emphasizes the medieval aspects of the original.

Communist internationalism. In the alternative history of Sorokin's fictional world, Bolshevism had played its role in globalizing the world in the distant past, followed by a number of wars, state formations, and political regimes, creating a world where Russian territory is fragmented anew after successive periods of Soviet imperialism, democracy, and neo-nationalism. On the one hand, therefore, the Ural Republic features an almost ideally globalized model society in which the successful integration of migrants into a dominant ethnos is not questioned but has become part of history. On the other hand, by setting this cosmopolitan society into the frame of the rigid, doctrine-driven socialist realist discourse inspired by the armed guerrilla struggle for communism, Sorokin in fact questions the ability of ideologies that downplay ethnic differences and national or local identity to pursue liberal causes. The Ural Republic's neo-socialist society reminds readers that multiracial ideologies are often repressive, despite their progressive outlook on ethnicity.

Furthermore, the absurd alternative historical reality of the novel's fictional world, in which national, ethnic, religious, and even local affiliations drive political life – such as, for example, the threat from the airborne forces of the Mongol empire or the bellicose 'Wahhabi separatists' – reminds the readers that racial, religious, or ethnic diversity does not guarantee political liberalism at state level. A globalized world where ethnic differences cease to matter appears possible only in an artificially constructed society or within a text whose relation to reality is purely tangential, and which is based on a utopian ideology from the start.

The most authoritative judgements of the fictional world's geopolitical status and the prognosis for Europe's future come from the carpenters mentioned earlier. Travelling in a tent attached to a giant horse, the motley group includes, among others, Russian, French, Chinese, and Jewish men. This 'carpenters' guild' is headed to 'Europe, the cradle of civilization. Dear old lady. She had it hard. The Wahhabi hammer had struck it. The strike was merciless, cruel. But Europe survived this blow [...] It is fragmented, squished. But alive' (Sorokin 2013: 268). As they travel, bringing with their drug the salubrious sleep that will 'cure' the continent, the carpenters disclose their views on the world, echoing Lev Tolstoi's philosophical digressions in *War and Peace*. Inevitably, some characters express critical judgement of fictional Russia's history. In a casual conversation, one reveals the fate of the Great Russian Wall that was being erected by characters in *Sugar Kremlin*: the wall – Russia's 'last imperial illusion' – was never finished because the construction adminis-trators pilfered too many bricks in the process (Sorokin 2013: 260). Ivan Il'ich, a character whose name refers to Tolstoi's protagonist famous for discovering life's purpose on the verge of dying, bluntly concludes that 'the great idea of reviving the Russian Empire crashed against bricks' (Sorokin 2013: 261).

But perhaps the most ironic and, at the same time, powerful statement comes from the guild's foreman, Vitte (a tongue-in-cheek allusion to one of Russia's greatest promoters of industrialization and international investment, late-imperial prime minister Sergei Witte). After rejoicing at the newly established 'enlightened Middle Ages', Vitte ponders:

> The world has taken on a human scale. The nations have discovered themselves. Man stopped being a mere sum of technologies [...] People have discovered the sense of things anew [...] Genetic engineering is helping men feel their true size. Man has reclaimed his faith in the transcendental. He has reclaimed the sense of time. We are no longer in a hurry. And, most importantly, we now understand that there can be no technological paradise on earth. No kind of paradise, for that matter. (Sorokin 2013: 286–87)

Vitte suggests that embracing this neoprimitive ideology made humans appreciate time and realize that a paradise was not possible on Earth. Yet the novel's conclusion asserts the possibility of a paradise away from 'civilization', one that feeds off these neoprimitive sentiments but rejects tellurium. Poet and critic Dmitrii Kuz'min voted *Telluria* down in favour of another novel for the Nos literary award, remarking that its last chapter featured the only authentic character, the 'voluntary Robinson' of the novel's 'Boschian panorama': 'In the end, it turns out that the only character who is "alive", who is not just a puppet, is the man who takes off to the woods and plans to survive there in complete solitude, foraging for food' (Morev 2015). Paradise it may be, but Gavrila Romanych's solitary existence in the middle of the woods, presented in a diary written in a folksy style, also reads as a travesty of the recent 'authentic' lifestyle trend associated with escaping cities and their attendant elements of globalization to move to the depths of nature. Avoiding the 'enlightened Middle Ages', Sorokin's Gavrila avoids the challenges of the contemporary world, albeit relying on its technological achievements to build his temporary abode. A namesake of Gavrila Romanovich Derzhavin – the most prominent poet of the Russian late-eighteenth-century Enlightenment – Sorokin's Gavrila Romanych stands for what Derzhavin's times opposed. Piously venerating the Slavic pagan deity Iarilo, he envisions a self-sufficient foraging existence in nature, and ascetically refutes the blessings of civilization, dismisses drugs and their attendant wars, money and authority, and even procreational human needs. Such an ending resembles a post-apocalyptic beginning, a modernist search for a new life, and for the author – yet, at the same time, just another literary form and intertextual reference to complete the diverse array of *Telluria*'s chapters.

Conclusion

Like his novels, Sorokin himself exemplifies a certain form of transnational experience: he frequently spends time in western Europe, attracting diverse audiences to his readings. A widely travelled cosmopolitan, he too is a *Bildungsnomade* travelling in pursuit of learning and entertainment, utilizing his knowledge of the world in his writing.[9] Sorokin's latest novels reveal the author's awareness of the growing international appeal of his work, which increasingly focuses not just on Russian affairs, as it did in the early 2000s, but now also scrutinizes the West. His cosmopolitan outlook permeates his narratives and *Telluria* marks the beginning of Sorokin's conscious efforts to reach broader Western audiences.

Sorokin is not the only contemporary writer whose prose examines transnational encounters. In recent decades, Russian-language narratives reflecting Soviet resettlement policies, post-Soviet migration and immigration, born out of Russia's imperial and Soviet history, have been gaining visibility in the West, thanks to translations into English, German, French, and other languages. Narratives like those by Liudmila Ulitskaia (e.g. *Medea and Her Children*, 1996) and Petr Aleshkovskii (e.g. *Fish: A History of One Migration*, 2006), grounded in realism, have resonated with readers who lived through the immediate post-Soviet period that created a generation of misplaced persons and global nomads, eliciting moral and political commentary. Conservative opinions on migration and globalization, bearing a nationalist tint – such as those by Zakhar Prilepin and Aleksandr Prokhanov – have also been gaining visibility abroad and popularity among Russian readers.

In the context of this realist tradition, authors writing at the confluence of genres and relying on elements of speculative fiction have had the advantage of expressing political opinions while at the same time keeping a greater distance from reality. In such works, irony becomes an intrinsic element of political critique – whether of nationalism, neo-imperialism, or globalization. Beyond Sorokin, a vivid example of such writing is that of his intellectual counterpart Viktor Pelevin, whose recent novels interrogate ethical aspects of new sociopolitical trends in Russia, Europe, and beyond.[10] Such narratives appear more valuable to readers who strive to find in the experience of reading the thrill of genre fiction coupled with aesthetic pleasure, alongside political

---

[9] The term *Bildungsnomade* suggests parallels between the 'nomadic' lifestyle of a regularly travelling author and the formative impact of such travels on their character and psychology, as in a *Bildungsroman* (Herrmann 2015: 31).

[10] See, for example, Pelevin's simultaneous critique of misogyny and political correctness in his 2011 novel *S.N.U.F.F.* (Lalo 2014).

relevance. Although some of Sorokin's and Pelevin's imaginary scenarios have come dangerously close to reality, the absurdity of their fictional worlds makes their critique more palatable to a sophisticated reader by preventing these writers from transforming into political pamphleteers. Preserving the postmodernist scepticism of teleological narratives, its nuanced self-irony, narrated by a multitude of voices and situated within a collage of styles, historical, and geographical frames, the political critique in Sorokin's *Telluria* might be more effective than the targeted message of the Oprichnik cycle. Stylistically and ideologically, this novel destroys imperial and geopolitical formations from both ends of the political spectrum: it continues to condemn neo-imperialist Russia, but it also probes the integrity of the European Union, its values and actions. Sorokin's deconstructive lens is equally successful when tackling conservative neo-Eurasianist and liberal European imperialisms. Director and critic Konstantin Bogomolov praised Sorokin, saying that he 'still remains number one in his attempt to explode the linguistic environment, literary reality, in his attempt to find approaches to forms and meanings that have outlived themselves' (Morev 2015). More broadly, *Telluria* shows that Sorokin is capable not only of exploding literary reality but also of challenging intercultural assumptions and problematizing the sometimes myopic views on globalization by dissecting cultural discourses and literary conventions alike.

Works Cited

Aptekman, Marina. 2009. 'Forward to the Past, or Two Radical Views on the Russian Nationalist Future: Pyotr Krasnov's *Behind the Thistle* and Vladimir Sorokin's *Day of an Oprichnik*', *Slavic and East European Journal*, 53(2): 241–60.

Bassin, Mark, and Gonzalo Pozo. 2017. *The Politics of Eurasianism: Identity, Popular Culture and Russia's Foreign Policy* (London: Rowman and Littlefield International).

Berdiaev, Nikolai. 1990. *Sud'ba Rossii* (Moscow: Mysl').

——. 1994. *Filosofiia tvorchestva, kul'tury i iskusstva* (Moscow: Iskusstvo).

Doerry, Martin, and Matthias Schepp. 2007. 'Spiegel Interview with Author Vladimir Sorokin. "Russia Is Slipping Back into an Authoritarian Empire"', *Der Spiegel Online*, 2 February <http://www.spiegel.de/international/ spiegel/0,1518,463860,00.html> [accessed 26 January 2018].

Dugin, Aleksandr. 1999. *Osnovy geopolitiki. Geopoliticheskoe budushchee Rossii. Myslit' prostranstvom* (Moscow: Arktogeia-tsentr).

——. 2014. 'Nikolai Berdiaev: Nonsystem as Method', *Evraziia. Informatsionno- analiticheskii portal* <http://evrazia.org/article/2572> [accessed 26 January 2018].

Etkind, Alexander. 2009. 'Stories of the Undead in the Land of the Unburied: Magical Historicism in Contemporary Russian Fiction', *Slavic Review*, 68(3): 631–58.

Filimonova, Tatiana. 2015. 'Eurasia as Discursive Literary Space at the Millennium', in David Lane and Vsevolod Samokhvalov (eds), *The Eurasian Project and Europe: Regional Discontinuities and Geopolitics* (Basingstoke: Palgrave Macmillan), 117–27.

Genis, Aleksandr, and Boris Paramonov. 2013. '"Telluriia" Sorokina', *Radio Svoboda* <https://www.svoboda.org/a/25187148.html> [accessed 30 May 2018].

Gumilev, Lev. 1993. *Etnogenez i biosfera zemli* (Moscow: TOO Mishel' i ko).

Herrmann, Elisabeth. 2015. 'How Does Transnationalism Redefine Contemporary Literature' in Elisabeth Herrmann, Carrie Smith-Prei, and Stuart Taberner (eds), *Transnationalism in Contemporary German-Language Literature* (New York: Camden House), 19–42.

Hill, Fiona, and Clifford Gaddy. 2012. 'Putin and the Uses of History', *The National Interest*, 117: 21–31.

Lalo, Alexei. 2014. 'New Trends in Russian Intellectual Anti-Americanism: The Strange Case of Viktor Pelevin's Novel *S.N.U.F.F.*', *Slavonica*, 20(1): 34–44.

Latynina, Alla. 2009. 'Sluchai Elizarova', *Zhurnal'nyi zal* <http://magazines.russ.ru/novyi_mi/2009/4/la13.html> [accessed 26 January 2018].

Lenin, V. I. 1967–70. *Polnoe sobranie sochinenii v 55 tomakh*, Vol. 36 (Moscow: Izdatel'stvo politicheskoi literatury).

Lionnet, Françoise, and Shu-Mei Shih. 2005. 'Introduction: Thinking through the Minor, Transnationally' in *Minor Transnationalism* (Durham, NC and London: Duke University Press), 1–23.

Lipovetskii, Mark. 2002. 'PMS (postmodernizm segodnia)', *Zhurnal'nyi zal* <http://magazines.russ.ru/znamia/2002/5/lipov.html> [accessed 26 January 2018].

Marsh, Rosalind J. 2007. *Literature, History and Identity in Post-Soviet Russia, 1991–2006* (Bern: Peter Lang).

Morev, Gleb. 2015. 'Ot Sorokina ozhidat' deiatel'nosti po perechisleniiu deneg v fond nel'zia. Konstantin Bogomolov i Dmitrii Kuz'min ob"iasnili Glebu Morevu, kak i pochemu oni golosovali na premii "Nos"', *Colta.ru* <http://www.colta.ru/articles/literature/6240> [accessed 24 July 2017].

Narinskaia, Anna. 2013. 'Neumolimyi prorok', *Kommersant* <https://www.kommersant.ru/doc/2320979> [accessed 26 January 2018].

Noordenbos, Boris. 2011. 'Ironic Imperialism: How Russian Patriots Are Reclaiming Postmodernism', *Studies in East European Thought*, 63(2): 147–58.

Savitskii, Petr. 2003. 'Geograficheskiie i geopolitisheskiie osnovy evraziistva' in K. Korolev (ed.), *Klassika geopolitiki. XX vek* (Moscow: Izdatel'stvo AST), 677–87.

Schiller, Nina G. 2012. 'Transnationality and the City' in Stefan Kraetke, Kathrin Wildner, and Stephan Lanz (eds), *Transnationalism and Urbanism* (New York: Routledge), 31–45.

Schwartz, Matthias. 2016. 'Utopia Going Underground: On Lukyanenko's and Glukhovsky's Literary Refigurations of Postsocialist Belongings between Loyalty and Dissidence to the State', *Russian Review*, 75(4): 589–603.

Sorokin, Vladimir. 2013. *Telluriia* (Moscow: Corpus).

Suslov, Mikhail. 2016. 'Of Planets and Trenches: Imperial Science Fiction in Contemporary Russia', *The Russian Review*, 75(4): 562–78.

——. 2017. 'Eurasian Symphony: Geopolitics and Utopia in Post-Soviet Alternative History' in Mark Bassin and Gonzalo Bozo (eds), *The Politics of Eurasianism: Identity, Popular Culture and Russia's Foreign Policy* (London: Rowman and Littlefield International), 81–100.

Tolz, Vera. 2015. 'The Eurasians and Liberal Scholarship of the Late Imperial Period', in Mark Bassin, Sergey Glebov, and Marlene Laruelle (eds), *Between Europe and Asia* (Pittsburgh, PA: University of Pittsburgh Press), 27–47.

Trubetzkoy, N. S. 1991. *The Legacy of Genghis Khan and Other Essays on Russia's Identity* (Ann Arbor, MI: Michigan Slavic Publications).

Vitenberg, Boris. 2002. 'Ob istoricheskom optimizme, istoricheskom pessimizme, i gosudarstvennom podkhode k istorii (Po povodu novykh knig A.L. Ianova i Iu. N. Afanas'eva)', *Novoe literaturnoe obozrenie*, 54 <http://magazines.russ.ru/nlo/2002/54/viten-pr.html> [accessed 17 July 2017].

Part II

Beyond and Between Languages

6

World Literature, War, Revolution

The Significance of Viktor Shklovskii's
A Sentimental Journey

Galin Tihanov

Viktor Shklovskii (1893–1984) was one of the foremost exponents of Russian Formalism.[1] At the same time, his work was embedded in the discourses and practices of what was later to emerge as 'world literature': a specific focus in the study of literature that emphasizes the travel and circulation of texts across cultural environments in a multitude of languages. This chapter seeks to uncover Shklovskii's previously overlooked engagement with this discursive domain; as such, it is an original contribution not just to understanding his *A Sentimental Journey* [Sentimental'noe puteshestvie, 1919–23], arguably the richest part of Shklovskii's 1920s memoir trilogy, but also to honing a transnational approach to his writing. Shklovskii's work has already been discussed through the prism of mobility and nomadism (Dwyer 2009, 2016);[2] the present study shifts the discussion towards Shklovskii's so far unexplored involvement in, and reaction to, early Soviet discourses and practices of 'world literature'.[3] I begin by placing his work in the larger context of Russian literary

This article is the outcome of research conducted and funded under the auspices of the AHRC OWRI Research Programme 'Cross-Language Dynamics: Reshaping Community'. I am grateful to Stephen Hutchings, Catherine Davies, and Andy Byford for the productive collaboration within this programme.

[1] The Russian formalists were an influential group of literary scholars and critics, mostly born in the 1890s and writing in the 1910s and 1920s. Other major exponents of the school included Boris Eikhenbaum, Iurii Tynianov, and Roman Jakobson. As their name suggests, the formalists paid particular attention to the form of literary works, preferring to analyse literature as an autonomous discourse grounded in the specific use of language. For background on Russian formalism, see Tihanov (2012a).

[2] On nomadism in Russian culture, see, most recently, Hansen-Löve (2017).

[3] On Shklovskii and world literature, from a very different perspective that does not

theory (notably the writings of Mikhail Bakhtin) and its engagement with world literature; I then proceed to take a fresh look at *A Sentimental Journey* as a document of war and revolution, but also as an intervention in debates on literary theory and world literature.

Today the legacy of modern literary theory is not available in a pure and concentrated fashion; instead, it is dispersed, dissipated, often fittingly elusive. The reason for this is that this inheritance is now performing its work in a climate already dominated by a different regime of relevance, which it faces directly and must negotiate. The patrimony of literary theory is currently active within a regime of relevance that evaluates literature based on its market and entertainment value, with only residual recall of its previously highly treasured autonomy. This regime of relevance has engendered a distinctive interpretative framework that has recently grown and gained enormous popularity, not least in the classroom, as 'world literature'. I place these words in quotation marks for they now tend to refer to a particular liberal Anglo-Saxon discourse grounded in assumptions of mobility, transparency, and recontextualizing (but also decontextualizing) circulation that supports free consumption and unrestricted comparison of literary artefacts.

A look at Russian literary theory during the interwar decades reveals that some of its major trends are highly relevant, obliquely or more directly, to this new framework of understanding and valorizing literature in the regime of its global production and consumption. Mikhail Bakhtin begins his book on Rabelais with a reference precisely to world literature: 'Of all great writers of world literature, Rabelais is the least popular, the least understood and appreciated' (1984: 1). Bakhtin, however, pays lip service to the then powerful notion of world literature as a body of canonical writing: he ostensibly compares Rabelais to Cervantes, Shakespeare, and Voltaire. But this understanding of world literature does not really interest him. Instead, he takes a different route, reconceptualizing the study of world literature as a study of the processes that shape the novel to become a world genre, a global discursive power. Of course, Bakhtin is here indebted to the Russian formalists: for him, too, the novel is the underdog of world literature, whose discursive energies are at first feeble and scattered, unnamed for a long time, until they begin to coalesce and rise to prominence.[4]

Bakhtin's engagement with world literature holds a distinctly non-Eurocentric and, I would emphasize, non-philological charge. He works

engage with the historical context or with Shklovskii's *A Sentimental Journey* and his hands-on involvement in Gor'kii's 'World Literature' project, see Hamilton (2018).

[4] For another inscription of Bakhtin in the context of Russian engagements with world literature during the 1930s, see Clark (2011).

with the novels he lists mostly in translation, as did Shklovskii before him. While Bakhtin appears to be relying on a Western canon to validate his theses, his primary interest lies in the literature and culture of pre-modernity, when Europe was not yet a dominant force and did not see itself as the centre of the world. Bakhtin is fascinated by the subterranean cultural deposits of folklore, of minor discourses, of ancient genres, of anonymous verbal masses – all of which long predate European culture of the age of modernity (beginning roughly with the Renaissance, but especially since the eighteenth century, when the doctrine of cultural Eurocentrism was worked out by the French *philosophes*, only to witness its first major crisis in the years immediately after the First World War), which is the only *dominant* (Eurocentric) European culture we know. Even Rabelais's novel interests Bakhtin above all for its traditional, premodern, folklore-based layers. He performs a flight away from Eurocentrism not by writing on non-European cultures, but by writing on pre-European cultures, on cultures that thrive on the shared property of folklore, rites, rituals, and epic narratives, centuries before Europe even began to emerge as an entity on the cultural and political map of the world; his is an anti-Eurocentric journey not in space but in time.[5] Bakhtin's contemporaries, the semantic palaeontologists Nikolai Marr and Ol'ga Freidenberg, whose writings he knew, achieved something similar in their work on myth and pre-literary discourses (Tihanov 2012b). Seeing Bakhtin in this new light allows us to enlist him as an early predecessor of the non-Eurocentric and translation-friendly thrust of today's Anglo-Saxon academic programmes in world literature. One can thus appreciate that Shklovskii was far from alone in his engagement with the agenda of world literature; but he embraced this agenda earlier, and – as we shall see later on in this chapter – his work had seminal implications for the future methodology of this particular paradigm.

War, Revolution, World Literature

The publication history of Viktor Shklovskii's *A Sentimental Journey* in Russia is indicative of the turmoil Shklovskii captures in his memoir. Written and published in parts between June 1919 and January 1923, it is a book begun in Russia and completed in emigration. It is a book about war, revolution, literary

---

[5] This is not to say that Bakhtin did not appreciate the need to undertake serious research on literatures beyond Europe and the West; see his praise for Nikolai Konrad's important book *West and East* (Bakhtin 1986: 2). Konrad was the foremost Soviet Japanologist and Sinologist during the 1950s and 1960s; he was the engine behind the multivolume Soviet *History of World Literature* at the early stages of working out its methodology.

theory, yet it also deals with world literature in ways that have not previously been appreciated and discussed. The memoir first appeared in its entirety in January 1923 in Berlin; the many Russian editions since 1923 would omit various portions of the book (deemed to be incompatible with official dogma), all through to 2002 when the Berlin edition was eventually republished in Moscow.[6] Thus *A Sentimental Journey* is also about exile and the long journey home, which sometimes comes to an end only posthumously (Shklovskii had passed away in Moscow in December 1984).

On first reading, *A Sentimental Journey* is a book about two revolutions (the February and October revolutions of 1917) and the ensuing civil war that engulfed Russia and its empire. It starts with memorable passages about Shklovskii's life before the revolutions: dullness, dreariness, and constant oppression through the tedious passage of time make up the dominant mood in the opening paragraphs. The beginning is thus mutely suggestive of cataclysm and estrangement waiting to happen, mitigating this unbearable sense of flatness. Estrangement is very much Shklovskii's master technique in *A Sentimental Journey*: he often chronologically reshuffles the episodes he narrates, leaves entire semantic entities dangling without resolution, and resurrects the tradition of wit and paradox in order to present the reader with a non-linear exposition of the war and the two revolutions. Ultimately, he eschews taking sides, working instead across political divides. In an extraordinary passage on the death of his brother, Evgenii, Shklovskii states: 'He was killed by the Reds or the Whites. I don't remember which – I really don't remember. But his death was unjust' (1970: 156). Rarely can one find a better example of political withdrawal in favour of a strong ethical judgement; only Kolia, Gaito Gazdanov's protagonist from his émigré novel *An Evening with Claire* [Vecher u Kler, completed in 1929 and published as a book the following year], rivals this reluctance to commit politically when he says that joining the Whites was mere accident – he might just as easily have joined the Reds.

While the concept of estrangement in Shklovskii may have had a number of sources in various scholarly and philosophical traditions with which he may have been (often indirectly) familiar, the crucial formative factor that contributed to the rise of this concept was undoubtedly the First World War (Tihanov 2005). The war was the propitious ground on which a materialist, substance-orientated view of the world grew strong and flourished amidst and out of – ultimately as a protest against – the cacophony and chaos of

---

[6] All quotations are from the English translation (Shklovsky 1970), occasionally modified for the sake of accuracy. For the first full republication of the 1923 Berlin edition in Russia, see Shklovskii (2002).

annihilation. Facilitating a return to the pristine nature of things seemed to be for so many other writers of the war generation the greatest gift that the progress of technology, industry, and warfare, so evident on the eve of the war and during it, could give back to a frustrated Europe. Estrangement was a technique designed to assist this process by equipping the reading public with the required acuteness of perception. The time is ripe to place the early Shklovskii – even more forcefully than has been done on occasion in the past – in his proper context, that of the First World War, and to see him as an author participating in the larger constellation of brilliant European essayists whose work and ideas were rooted in their war experience. At the same time, we need to be aware of the role the October Revolution played in Shklovskii's evolution after 1917. The revolution no doubt added to his war experience, amplifying and throwing into relief his main dilemma, that of aesthetic innovation (ambiguous and at times shaky) *vis-à-vis* social and political conservatism. It was this dilemma that led him to reject the October Revolution as a member of the Socialist Revolutionary Party – but also to highlight its attractiveness, its sheer incommensurability, scale, and purifying force. The revolution superimposed a new political dynamic which, while not cancelling the dispositions of the war experience, demanded different responses; in other words, in Shklovskii's memoir the war and the revolution are to be thought together without being conflated. Remarkably, Shklovskii's memoir weaves into these powerful narratives a third one: an examination of Jewish identity and anti-Semitism during the war (in the East, in Persia, Shklovskii notes the absence of anti-Semitism as a factor that helps his reconciliation with, and acceptance of, the locals). *A Sentimental Journey* is thus a book that straddles intense self-reflection and unmitigated self-abandonment to fate: Shklovskii refers to Spinoza's famous example of the 'falling stone' (Shklovsky 1970: 133) in order to quip, self-ironically, that 'a falling stone does not need to think'.[7]

Shklovskii's memoir is not just about war and revolution, however, but also about world literature. His involvement in the emergent Russian debate on world literature was direct and, as often with Shklovskii, marked by commitment and distance in the same breath. He joined Gor'kii's 'World Literature' project in 1919.[8] This was a large-scale publishing project,

---

[7] Spinoza used the example of the falling stone to suggest that free will was an illusion: if the stone were endowed with self-consciousness, it would still be convinced that it was moving of its own accord, even if it had been thrown by someone or otherwise obeying the force of gravity.

[8] Gor'kii's project was called 'Vsemirnaia literatura' in Russian, a term that can be translated as both *world literature* and *universal literature*.

educational and socially ameliorative at its core. The idea was for a new, expanded canon of world literature to be established in post-revolutionary Russia, including – for the first time – not just works from Western literatures but also from the literatures of Asia, the Middle East, and Latin America. These works had to be translated (in some cases retranslated to replace poor existing translations), equipped with proper introductions and apparatus, and made available in reliable but cheap scholarly editions to those previously disenfranchised: the workers, peasants, and soldiers, in short, the classes of the oppressed. The project was centred in Petrograd, and its infrastructure included a publishing house which, at its peak, would employ around 350 editors and translators, as well as a translators' studio which was meant to familiarize younger translators with translation theory, literary theory, and other cognate fields.[9]

It is to this studio that Shklovskii was recruited by Gor'kii in 1919 to give lectures in literary theory. One has to recall that at that time Petrograd was a city ravished by famine and civil war, in the grip of dire poverty and utter insecurity. In *A Sentimental Journey*, Shklovskii laconically notes his aunt's death from starvation; it is in this atmosphere that he threw himself into Gor'kii's project. The ambition to promote a non-Eurocentric approach to world literature was particularly important: early on, Gor'kii established an editorial committee on oriental literatures chaired by his friend of long standing and dean of Russian Indology, academician Sergei Ol'denburg; the committee also included the brilliant sinologist Vasilii Alekseev, the renowned Arabist Ignatii Krachkovskii, the already famous archaeologist and linguist Nikolai Marr, journalist and writer Aleksandr Tikhonov, and Gor'kii himself.[10] The paradox at the heart of this project was not, of course, the fact that Gor'kii set out to redress decades of social injustice; he regarded his project precisely as an instrument of radical social transformation, in which previously disadvantaged layers of society would be offered access to the greatest works of literature. But this radical social transformation, meant to facilitate upward mobility for millions of people, was to be achieved through the most conservative of methods: by invoking a secure (if augmented) canon

[9] On Gor'kii's project, see, most recently, Khotimsky (2013) and Tyulenev (2016); for a more essayistic account, see the chapter 'Petrograd, 1918' in David (2011). On Soviet engagements with world literature between the two world wars, see, more generally, Epelboin (2005).

[10] When Gor'kii later published his journal *Beseda* (1923–25) in Berlin, he once again sought to recruit Ol'denburg and Alekseev as contributors (Yedlin 1999: 158); according to Khodasevich, the idea of founding *Beseda* (initially under the title *Putnik*) was actually Shklovskii's (Yedlin 1999: 157–58).

of, to recall Matthew Arnold's definition of culture from *Culture and Anarchy*, 'the best that has been thought and said'. Gor'kii's radical project was thus tempered by his humanist notion of world literature as a canon of texts and a tool for inculcating the virtues of civility and erudition (or 'learnedness', in the language of that epoch). This understanding of 'world literature' goes back to the late eighteenth and early nineteenth century, when Wieland (not by accident the author of the first important German novel of education), some 25 years before Goethe, in a somewhat elliptical manner talked about world literature as an instrument of self-improvement that teaches us to better communicate with others and supplies knowledge of the world to which we would otherwise not have access.[11]

The translators' studio established in 1919 had contributions from some of the best contemporary Russian writers and translators: Evgenii Zamiatin, Nikolai Gumilev, Kornei Chukovskii (one of the best translators of literature from the English language who had already produced translations of Walt Whitman's poetry); of the Russian formalists, Boris Eikhenbaum was also invited to contribute. Shklovskii notes in his memoir that the translators' studio quickly evolved into a 'literary studio', where drafts of literary works were discussed and literary theory and criticism were on the agenda. 'I never in my life worked the way I did that year', he writes (Shklovsky 1970: 186). Before a young audience, Shklovskii was teaching *Don Quixote* and Sterne, and wrote, in conversation with his students, the chapters on Cervantes and Sterne that were to be included in his book *Theory of Prose* [O teorii prozy, 1925; second, expanded edition, 1929).

The Portability of Literariness: Shklovskii's Enduring Relevance

At this juncture, it is important to place Shklovskii's commitment to the idea of world literature in the broader context of our present debates on the subject. To understand 'world literature' as a specific construct, we must ask the unavoidable question about the location of 'world literature' *vis-à-vis* language, which has important consequences for how we interpret the dispersed legacy of modern literary theory (founded, undoubtedly, by Shklovskii and the Russian formalists). This question appears to be banal at first sight; yet there could not be a more fundamental question when it comes to how we think about literature than the question of language. Here we need to confront the issue of translation and recognize its legitimacy, not just with reference to current debates (between those who champion the beneficial role of translation and those who treasure the idea of untranslatability as a way of

---

[11] See Tihanov (2011: esp. 143).

opposing politically dubious equivalences),[12] but by going to the very origins of modern literary theory and the work that Shklovskii himself was doing in 1919/1920, some of which he succinctly captures in *A Sentimental Journey*.

My contention here is that we need to begin to understand the current Anglo-Saxon discourse of world literature, in which the legitimization of reading and analysing literature in and through translation plays a pivotal role, as an echo of, and a late intervention in, a debate that begins in the early days of classic literary theory.[13] By 'classic literary theory', I mean here the paradigm of thinking about literature that rests on the assumption that literature is a specific and unique discourse whose distinctiveness crystallizes around the abstract quality of 'literariness'. This way of thinking about literature begins around the First World War – with Shklovskii and his fellow formalists – and is largely dead by the 1990s. In *A Sentimental Journey*, Shklovskii rages against those who think of literature primarily as a conveyor of political ideas and civic values rather than as a specific, self-sufficient use of language: 'How strange to substitute the history of Russian liberalism for the history of Russian literature' (Shklovsky 1970: 192). But classic literary theory does not disappear without leaving behind a dissipated legacy consisting in rehearsing, in various ways, the question of the centrality – or otherwise – of language in how we understand literature. The current debate on 'world literature' is part and parcel of this dissipated legacy of classic literary theory, re-enacting the cardinal debate on whether one should think literature within the horizon of language or beyond that horizon. It is incumbent upon us to recognize that the current polemics on 'world literature' in the Anglo-American academy are an extension of these earlier debates on language and literariness originating in classic literary theory, not least because, like so many other discourses of liberal persuasion, the Anglo-Saxon discourse of world literature, too, often passes over in silence its own premises, leaving them insufficiently reflected upon, at times even naturalizing them.

As is well known, the Russian formalists agreed that what lends literature its specificity is literariness. But we tend to forget that they disagreed on what constitutes literariness.[14] Roman Jakobson (mentioned once in *A Sentimental Journey*, but more frequently in Shklovskii's only slightly later memoirs, *Zoo, or Letters not about Love* and *Third Factory*) believed that literariness is lodged

---

[12] For these two positions, see, respectively, Damrosch (2003) and Apter (2013).

[13] This argument is more fully developed in Tihanov (2017a).

[14] For an early and insightful interpretation, from a different perspective, of the split within Russian formalism over how literariness should be understood and captured, see Hopensztand (1938), of which there is a passable English translation: cf. Hopensztand (1989).

in the intricate, fine-grained workings of language. To him, only the language of the original matters, as this intricacy cannot be captured in translation. Not by chance does Jakobson spend his entire career (when it comes to his work as a literary scholar) analysing texts written in verse, basing these analyses on the language of the original. Shklovskii, Eikhenbaum, and (to some extent) Tynianov, on the other hand, believed that the effects of literariness are also (and, in a sense, primarily) produced on levels above and beyond language. In a striking difference from Jakobson, Shklovskii in particular chose to analyse prose rather than poetry, and to do this in translation. This is precisely the work he was doing in the translators' studio in Petrograd, about which he reminisces in *A Sentimental Journey*. It is the level of composition, rather than the micro-level of language, that claimed Shklovskii's attention when trying to explain the effects of literariness. His famous distinction between *fabula* and *siuzhet*, for example, works with undiminished validity also when we read in translation.[15] We do not need the language of the original to appreciate the transposition of the material and its reorganization through retrospection, retardation, etc. (techniques which Shklovskii, sometimes following Sterne, himself abundantly employs in *A Sentimental Journey*).[16] Moreover, Shklovskii and Tynianov proved that even on the level of style the language of the original is not the only vehicle of literariness. The parodic aspects of *Don Quixote*, for instance, can be gleaned and grasped also in translation, provided we have some background knowledge of chivalric culture and its conventions. Thus the Russian formalists' internal debate on what constitutes literariness – and Shklovskii's belief in its portability beyond the language of the original – had the unintended consequence of lending today ammunition and justification to those who believe in the legitimacy of reading and analysing literature in translation.

Let me repeat: the current discourse of 'world literature' is an iteration of this principal question of classic literary theory: should one think literature within or beyond the horizon of language? This specific iteration recasts the question, while retaining its theoretical momentum. Shklovskii (who was blissfully monolingual and taught Cervantes and Sterne in translation in the translators' studio), together with Eikhenbaum (who, despite being a reader of English who could – and did – work with texts of fiction in the original, would also often highlight the fact that literariness materializes on the level of

---

[15] For the Russian formalists, *fabula* was the chronological sequence of events as they progress from the start to the end of a narrative text, while *siuzhet* was the way in which these events are reorganized to appear (through devices such as retrospection, prolepsis, retardation, and so on) in the literary work of art (a novel, a story, etc.).

[16] On Shklovskii's uses of, and debt to, Sterne's prose, see Finer (2010).

composition rather than solely on the micro-level of language), was facing the foundational conundrum of literary theory: how to account for literariness with reference to both individual languages and language per se. If Shklovskii's response was to be seminal in terms of *theory*, it had to be a response that addressed both the *singularity* of language (the language of the original) and its *multiplicity* (the multiple languages in which a literary text reaches its potential audiences in translation). No claim to theory would lawfully exist unless literariness could be demonstrated to operate across languages, in an act of continuous estrangement from the language of the original.

The Anglo-Saxon discourse on world literature, foremost in the work of David Damrosch, has proceeded – so it seems to me – in the steps of Shklovskii by foregrounding the legitimacy of working in translation. Damrosch has implicitly confronted the tension between the singularity and multiplicity of language by concluding that studying a work of literature in the languages of its socialization is more important than studying it in the language of its production, not least because this new priority restricts and undermines the monopoly of methodological nationalism in literary studies. (The languages of creation and socialization can, of course, coincide, and the implications flowing from this, especially where this coincidence involves a global language such as English, are something worth thinking about; equally, there are cases in which more than one language can be deployed in producing a work of literature – but never as many as the plethora of languages that provide the infrastructure for its circulation.)[17]

Shklovskii's *A Sentimental Journey* is thus not just a monument to the February and October revolutions and the ensuing civil war; it is also a monument to one of the most seminal moments in classic literary theory which still reverberates in our current debates on world literature. The wide-ranging implications of Shklovskii's highlighting the legitimacy of reading and analysing literature in translation mitigates, at least to some extent, the concerns of some of his contemporaries that the formalists' concept of literariness was based on the discussion of an overwhelmingly Eurocentric (and thus relatively narrow and insufficiently representative) corpus of texts.[18]

Yet one should not assume that Shklovskii embraced Gor'kii's project unreservedly. In a splendid passage from *A Sentimental Journey*, he ironically distances himself from what he clearly perceived as a project on too grand a scale, and one that sought to revolutionize culture through the conservative

[17] On the political and cultural baggage of English (and hence the dangers of asserting it as a seemingly transparent medium of translation), see, e.g. Mufti (2016).

[18] For a more detailed discussion of these concerns, see Tihanov (2017b: esp. 426–27).

educational tools of the canon. In the passage in question, Shklovskii refers to both Gor'kii's world literature project and the publishing house:

> 'World Literature'. A Russian writer mustn't write what he wants to: he must translate the classics, all the classics; everyone must translate and everyone must read. Everyone will read everything and will know everything, absolutely everything. No need for hundreds of publishing houses; one will do – Grzhebin's. And a catalogue projected to one hundred years, a catalogue one hundred printers' signatures long; in English, French, Indo-Chinese, and Sanskrit. And all the literati and all the writers will fill in the schemes according to rubrics, supervised by none other than S. Ol'denburg and Alexandre Benois, and then shelves of books will be born, and everyone will read all the shelves and know everything. No heroism or faith in people is needed here. (Shklovsky 1970: 189; translation modified)

This is Shklovskii at his best: both passionate and restrained, ironically distanced yet committed. He clearly objects to Gor'kii's project of world literature, as he sees in it a coercive instrument with which to impose a non-negotiable canon ('the classics'); he even seems to suggest that Gor'kii's project is a form of censorship, of contempt for the freedom of expression. There is also a dormant nationalism in Shklovskii's indictment of Gor'kii's implied criticism of Russian literature as provincial compared to the canon of world literature. The enumeration of languages into which the overambitious catalogue of the 'World Literature' publishing house was to be printed is – without a shadow of a doubt – only half-serious in tone ('Indo-Chinese' is Shklovskii's way of mockingly referring to a non-existent (single) language of the East; 'Sanskrit' was by that time a language endowed with huge cultural capital accumulated over centuries, but nonetheless strongly reduced in its vernacular use). As a matter of fact, Gor'kii's World Literature publishing house published two separate catalogues (both in 1919): one containing a list (marked 'provisional', as the catalogue put it) of translations of literary works from Europe and North America, and one of (intended) translations from non-Western literatures (titled 'The Literature of the Orient'); the first catalogue featured an essay by Gor'kii and editorial apparatus, both also translated into French, English, and German, while the second catalogue had a brief unsigned introduction and editorial apparatus, both available in the catalogue solely in Russian and French (Katalog 1919a and Katalog 1919b). Even before the criticism voiced in his memoir, Shklovskii had openly written to Gor'kii about his discontent with the project's extensive understanding of world literature, which was in danger of reproducing a mechanical view of it as the sum total of its parts, and accounting for its variety in merely spatial terms: 'Grzhebin's publishing house, and the House of Scholars, and "World Literature" (real name: "the whole of the world" [literature]) – this is also a [case of] spatial perception' [Grzhebinskoe izdatel'stvo, i Dom uchenykh, i "Vsemirnaia literatura" (nastoi-ashchee nazvanie: vsia vsemirnaia) – tozhe prostranstvennoe vospriiatie].[19] Shklovskii's irony was shared by Eikhenbaum who in his 1925 article 'O. Henry and the Theory of the Novella' referred to 1919–24 as the time when, in Russia, Russian literature 'lost its seat to "world literature"' under the pressure of a flourishing translation industry; Eikhenbaum deliberately put the words 'world literature' in quotation marks to signal his sarcasm (1927: 166).

The fascination of *A Sentimental Journey* for today's reader lies in its idiosyncratic, sometimes even whimsical, portrayal of war and revolution – a memoir which zigzags through five years of history, from Russia to Galicia to northern Iran to Russia, then to Ukraine, back to Russia, back to Ukraine, and then on again to Russia, to Finland and Germany, capturing acts of profound historical transformation through the ephemera of daily life; a memoir displaying Shklovskii's blissful disregard for dates – he cannot recall whether he married in 1919 or 1920 (Shklovsky 1970: 177) – and his playful employment of compositional techniques of estrangement *à la* Sterne. But Shklovskii's *A Sentimental Journey* is also a valuable piece of engagement with literary theory through fiction: an early – and at the time pioneering – attempt to practise theory without a theoretical meta-language. This daring attempt, which begins with *A Sentimental Journey*, intensifies in the next two memoirs written by Shklovskii (*Zoo, or Letters not about Love* and *Third Factory*); it foreshadows post-structuralism's own endeavour (especially visible in Roland Barthes's later work) to amalgamate productively fiction and theory in an uncharted journey through the text. Paradoxical, ironic, difficult, at times soberly pessimistic, Shklovskii's greatest achievement in his *A Sentimental Journey* is the realization that one has to confront and test the language of (formalist) literary theory against the language of fiction by staging their symbiotic existence within a single work. Through Shklovskii's early memoirs – including his *A Sentimental Journey* – Russian formalism comes into its own, realizing that the most significant Other of literary theory is literature itself.[20]

It is this twofold relevance of Shklovskii's text – as a quirky document of its time and as an intervention in consequential debates on literary theory and on world literature – that extends its life across time and space. Shklovskii

---

[19] Shklovskii's letter to Gor'kii (April 1922), quoted in Shklovskii (2018: 191); my translation.

[20] For more on this, see Tihanov (2016).

was to continue his engagement with the Soviet discourse of world literature during the 1930s, especially in the several different versions of his *Marco Polo*,[21] a narrative about travel to and from East Asia that, in fact, staged a journey across land masses which were to become a part of the Asian territories of the Soviet Union. Orientalism, empire, and world literature[22] were to meet in this deceptively modest book in a way that was both fascinating and ideologically profoundly ambivalent.

Shklovskii was thus directly engaged with the Soviet discourse and practices of world literature; but his single most important contribution, in my view, was to have posed the question about what constitutes literariness – and to have answered it in a way that continues to impact our current polemics around world literature. His insistence that the literary core of literature travels well – his belief, in other words, that literariness is in the end portable – remains an unavoidable argument in these disputes, even when the academic practitioners of 'world literature' are not always prepared to acknowledge this. Shklovskii, then, furnishes an ideal example of the diffuse, subterranean afterlife of Russian literary theory in our own century.

Works Cited

Apter, Emily. 2013. *Against World Literature: On the Politics of Untranslatability* (London: Verso).

Bakhtin, Mikhail. 1984. *Rabelais and his World*, trans. Hélène Iswolsky (Bloomington, IN: Indiana University Press).

——. 1986. *Speech Genres and Other Late Essays*, trans. Vern McGee, ed. Caryl Emerson and Michael Holquist (Austin, TX: University of Texas Press).

Clark, Katerina. 2011. *Moscow, the Fourth Rome: Stalinism, Cosmopolitanism, and the Evolution of Soviet Culture, 1931–1941* (Cambridge, MA: Harvard University Press).

Damrosch, David. 2003. *What Is World Literature?* (Princeton, NJ: Princeton University Press).

David, Jérôme. 2011. *Spectres de Goethe: les métamorphoses de la 'littérature mondiale'* (Paris: Les Prairies Ordinaires).

Dwyer, Anne. 2009. 'Revivifying Russia: Literature, Theory, and Empire in Viktor Shklovsky's Civil War Writing', *Slavonica*, 15(1): 11–31.

---

[21] Different incarnations of this text were published over more than 35 years, from 1931 into the late 1960s; particularly influential was the 1936 version in the book series 'The Life of Remarkable People' [Zhizn' zamechatel'nykh liudei] founded by Gor'kii (Shklovskii 1936).

[22] Suffice it to mention the importance of Marco Polo's travelogue for Coleridge, Kafka, Borges, and Calvino, amongst others.

——. 2016. 'Standstill as Extinction: Viktor Shklovsky's Poetics and Politics of Movement in the 1920s and 1930s', *PMLA*, 131(2): 269–88.

Eikhenbaum, Boris. 1927. 'O Genri i teoriia novelly' in Eikhenbaum, *Literatura: Teoriia. Kritika. Polemika* (Leningrad: Priboi), 166–209.

Epelboin, Annie. 2005. 'Littérature mondiale et Révolution' in Christophe Pradeau and Tiphaine Samoyault (eds), *Où est la littérature mondiale?* (Saint-Denis: Presses Universitaires de Vincennes), 39–49.

Finer, Emily. 2010. *Turning into Sterne: Viktor Shklovsky and Literary Reception* (Leeds: Legenda).

Hamilton, Grant. 2018. 'Defamiliarization and the Act of Reading World Literature' in Roisi Braidotti et al. (eds), *Deleuze and the Humanities: East and West* (London: Rowman & Littlefield), 11–26.

Hansen-Löve, Aage. 2017. 'Russkie kak kochevniki: Kontsepty nomadizma v russkoi kul'ture' in Nikolai Poseliagin and Mikhail Trunin (eds), *Verba Volant, Scripta Manent: Festschrift k 50-letiiu Igoria Pil'shchikova* (Zbornik matitse srpske za slavistiku, Vol. 92), 317–30.

Hopensztand, Dawid. 1938. 'Filozofia literatury formalistów wobec poetyki futuryzmu', Życie literackie, 5: 182–92.

——. 1989. 'Formalist Literary Philosophy versus Poetics of Futurism', trans. Bogdan Lawendowski, *Literary Studies in Poland/Études Littéraires en Pologne*, 21: 107–19.

Katalog 1919a. *Katalog izdatel'stva 'Vsemirnaia literatura' pri narodnom komissariate po prosveshcheniiu. Vstupitel'naia stat'ia M. Gor'kogo/Catalogue des éditions de la 'Littérature mondiale' paraissant sous le patronage du Commissariat de L'Instruction Publique. Préface de M. Gorky. Pétersbourg* (St Petersburg: Vsemirnaia literatura).

Katalog 1919b. *Katalog izdatel'stva 'Vsemirnaia literatura' pri narodnom komissariate po prosveshcheniiu. Literatura Vostoka/Catalogue des éditions de la 'Littérature mondiale'. La littérature de l'Orient. Pétersbourg* (St Petersburg: Vsemirnaia literature).

Khotimsky, Maria. 2013. 'World Literature, Soviet Style: A Forgotten Episode in the History of an Idea', *Ab Imperio*, 3: 119–54.

Mufti, Aamir. 2016. *Forget English: Orientalisms and World Literatures* (Cambridge, MA: Harvard University Press).

Shklovskii, Viktor. 1936. *Marko Polo* (Moscow: Zhurnal'no-gazetnoe ob"edinenie).

——. 2002. 'Sentimental'noe puteshestvie' in Shklovskii, *Eshche nichego ne konchilos'...*, ed. A. Galushkin (Moscow: Propaganda), 15–266.

——. 2018. *Sobranie sochinenii*, Vol. 1: *Revoliutsiia*, ed. Il'ia Kalinin (Moscow: Novoe literaturnoe obozrenie).

Shklovsky, Viktor. 1970. *A Sentimental Journey: Memoirs, 1917–1922*, trans. Richard Sheldon (Ithaca, NY: Cornell University Press).

Tihanov, Galin. 2005. 'The Politics of Estrangement: The Case of the Early Shklovsky', *Poetics Today*, 26(4): 665–96.

——. 2011. 'Cosmopolitanism in the Discursive Landscape of Modernity: Two Enlightenment Articulations' in D. Adams and G. Tihanov (eds), *Enlightenment Cosmopolitanism* (London: Legenda), 133–52.

——. 2012a. 'Russian Formalism' in *The Princeton Encyclopedia of Poetry and Poetics*, 4th ed. (Princeton, NJ: Princeton University Press), 1239–42.

——. 2012b. 'Framing Semantic Paleontology: The 1930s and Beyond', *Russian Literature*, 72(3–4): 361–84.

——. 2016. 'Pamiat' teorii: o nasledii russkogo formalizma' in S. Zenkin and E. Shumilova (eds), *Russkaia intellektual'naia revoliutsiia 1910–1930-kh godov* (Moscow: Novoe literaturnoe obozrenie, 2016), 58–63.

——. 2017a 'The Location of World Literature', *Canadian Review of Comparative Literature*, 44(3): 468–81.

——. 2017b. 'On the Significance of Historical Poetics: In Lieu of a Foreword', *Poetics Today*, 38(3): 417–28.

Tyulenev, Sergey. 2016. '*Vsemirnaia Literatura*: Intersections between Translating and Original Literary Writing', *Slavic and East European Journal*, 60(1): 8–21.

Yedlin, Tovah. 1999. *Maxim Gorky: A Political Biography* (London: Praeger).

7

The Transnational Vladimir Nabokov, or the Perils of Teaching Literature

Marijeta Bozovic

Nabokov and Transnational Russian Literature

Despite – or perhaps, because of – the controversy that he inspired in the last decades of his life, Nabokov has been acknowledged as the 'first among Russian-born literati to attain the "interliterary stature of a world writer"' (Shapiro 2009: 101).[1] An unconventional but influential cultural ambassador, he reimagined the international relevance of the Russian literary tradition as well as the stylistic and thematic possibilities of the late-twentieth-century transnational novel. Russia's liminal position both inside and outside of European culture arguably proved an advantage, and Nabokov, a model for how other writers might break into and decentre the networks of cultural capital that shape and define literary canons.[2]

Nabokov presents an exceptional yet paradigmatic case study of transnational literature, fraught with mid-century canon wars and cultural capital

---

[1] While writers and critics use many terms to describe 'more than national' literary phenomena (interliterary, international, supranational, world literature, etc.), I follow John Burt Foster Jr. and the editors of this volume in my preference for 'transnational': 'If "inter" assumed orderly, almost diplomatic processes of give-and-take among well-defined units, "trans" posits a more active, less regulated, even unpredictably creative surge of forces across borders that no longer seem as firmly established' (Foster 2013: 2).

[2] I develop the canon formation argument in *Nabokov's Canon: From Onegin to Ada* (Bozovic 2016). The monograph examines the cultural translation that Nabokov attempts to perform in his two most controversial works, the *Eugene Onegin* translation project and the novel *Ada*, annexing what he feared was a vanishing Russian tradition to that of the English-language modernist novel.

rivalries. Primarily due to the *succès de scandale* of *Lolita* (1955), but then delivering hit after hit with *Pnin* (1957), *Pale Fire* (1962), *Speak, Memory* (1967), and the translated Russian oeuvre, Nabokov carved out a place for himself in a number of canons.[3] He began to establish himself, *pace* Roman Jakobson, as both the elephant and professor of zoology.[4]

Nabokov managed to escape the marginal status of a Russian émigré writer to become, in the 1960s and 1970s, the most famous world writer alive; moreover, he managed to convince readers that the Russian tradition was central to a world canon of literary masterpieces. In this regard, he resembles less other Russian émigré writers than their artistic and musical compatriots, who had an easier time translating their life's work to European and American soil: the painters Wassily Kandinsky and Marc Chagall, the composer Igor Stravinsky, or the choreographer George Balanchine, all of whom have been defining voices of international modernism in their respective media.

Working within the literary medium, Nabokov managed not only to escape marginalization, but through his literary output and lifelong aesthetic propaganda campaign, to shape the playing field. Towards the end of his life and in the decades since, Nabokov has come to hold symbolic value for artists and writers across the globe – of a densely allusive and parodic prose style, of a rare virtuoso multilingualism, of an uncompromising stance on artistic autonomy, and of a Cold War-era (some would say, reactionary) modernism. Nabokov has even been accused of infecting a generation of writers with his prose style and performative posturing. Yet the many artists and thinkers who have paid him homage reflect a wide range of aesthetic – and political – projects.

Two writers on whom Nabokov's oeuvre and transnational status have had a notable impact are the Iranian Azar Nafisi and South African J. M. Coetzee. Both Nafisi and Coetzee hold PhDs in English literature from major American universities; both write in English; and, like Nabokov, both join the world republic of letters from the outside.[5] In the space of four years, both Nafisi

---

[3] Nabokov has also been partly assimilated into an American modernist canon: *Lolita*, *Pnin*, and *Pale Fire* especially are often included in university syllabi on American modernism.

[4] Roman Jakobson famously objected to the proposal that Nabokov join the ranks of the Harvard Slavists in 1957 with the quip, 'Gentlemen, even if one allows that he is an important writer, are we next to invite an elephant to be Professor of Zoology?' (Boyd 1991: 303).

[5] See Casanova (2004). Works written in imperial languages fare dramatically differently on the global market than do works in so-called 'minor languages': it is, of course, when he begins to write in English that Nabokov attains the status of world

and Coetzee produced books that in some sense rewrite Nabokov's most infamous novel, *Lolita*. In the stylized 'memoir in books' *Reading Lolita in Tehran* (2003) and the novel *Disgrace* (1999), Nafisi and Coetzee respectively pick up on the pedagogical perils of transnational literary canon formation, but to dramatically different ends. The former is enthusiastic of the tribe of 'Nabokov's children', the latter more ambivalent. Both are now émigrés – and both, like Nabokov, retain the cultural capital that comes with privileged outsider status.

Lolita and the Bad Professor

John Guillory builds on the work of Pierre Bourdieu to define literary canon formation as the 'constitution and acquisition of cultural capital', linked specifically to the school and university syllabus as 'the institutional form by means of which this knowledge is disseminated' (1993: ix). As an example, Guillory examines the New Critical revision of American universities' English curriculum. T. S. Eliot used his authority as a literary figure to insist on an alternative tradition that, tautologically, had 'a good deal to do with the legitimation of his poetic practice' (Guillory 1993: 147). A fundamental battleground for canon formation, the syllabus – as a culturally and politically fraught list of valued texts to be read, taught, and imbibed – invites the co-creation of precursors.

Syllabi, lists of books, and scenes of teaching haunt Nabokov's fiction and non-fiction works alike. Nabokov's preferred canon runs 'counter' to quite a few alternative visions of literary history: the Soviet canon of Russian literature, the American Slavic studies canon of Russian literature, but also the modernist canon of the reigning Anglo-American literary elites Nabokov encountered on the college campuses where he spent so many years.[6] In each case, Nabokov pushed against a nationally or linguistically bounded canon in favour of a more fluid (if hardly egalitarian) model of cultural flow: for James Joyce to be read in the company of Lev Tolstoi rather than Eliot. Of course,

writer. I have written about Nabokov's use of English and the (geo)politics of translation elsewhere, see Bozovic (2017). See also Lawrence Venuti's groundbreaking work on the politics of translation for a larger discussion of this global phenomenon (Venuti 2008).

[6] For example, we might remember the 'pressures exerted on Nabokov by the Russian faculty at Wellesley College, where he was teaching, to include Socialist Realist novels in his courses. In several letters, Nabokov expressed his reluctance to compromise on his assertion that "Communism and its totalitarian rule have prevented the development of authentic literature during these last twenty-five years"' (Norman 2012: 89). See also Boyd (1991: 90–91).

the implicit natural heir to such a list of precursors was always the multilingual and cosmopolitan Nabokov himself.

Nabokov's most transnational fictions collide and merge strands of
English, French, Russian, and other literatures. Yet such literature is fraught
with paradoxes and perils. If Nabokov liked to rewrite syllabi so as to include
himself more centrally, he also liked to include visions of that project going
terribly wrong in his fiction. Nabokov's oeuvre contains countless failed
doubles, evil twins, and nightmare versions of transnational literary teaching.
The *mise en abyme* created by Nabokov's many doubles is indeed a signature
quirk that irritates some readers of his fiction. J. M. Coetzee wrote in 1974:
'*Pale Fire* is after all another version of the same Romantic myth [...] that an
ironic consciousness permits transcendence of a bad infinity of exegesis' (6).

Nabokov's most extreme case study of abysmal pedagogy is the failed poet/
pervert Humbert Humbert. *Lolita*'s narration is drenched with anguished
wonder at Humbert's inability to seduce Lolita in any sense, including with
the 'wonderland' of literature he has to offer her. Humbert becomes Hunter,
Hummer, and Humbug in the novel, but he is certainly no Scheherazade who
can win the affections of others through storytelling. Or, as Humbert inimi-
tably puts it, 'I could persuade [Lolita] to do so many things – their list might
stupefy a traditional educator; but no matter how I pleaded and stormed, I
could never make her read any other book than the so-called comic books or
stories in American magazines for females' (1989: 173). Judging by his references ('Reader! Bruder!', 1989: 264) Humbert offers the very American Lolita a
canon dictated by continental tastes, even in its New World inclusions.

When Stanley Kubrick condensed Humbert's pedagogical struggles into a
single scene for the 1962 film adaptation of *Lolita*, he picked a passage from
Nabokov's comically overlong script, where Humbert reads Edgar Allan Poe's
elegiac elocution piece 'Ulalume' (1847) to a sceptical Lolita. The passage
reads as follows:

> Humbert: Would you like me to read you some poetry?
> Lolita (bored, rolling her eyes): Sure, why not.
> Humbert: This is my favorite poet. It was ...
> Lolita (interrupting): Who's the poet?
> Humbert: The divine Edgar.
> Lolita: Who's the divine Edgar, Edgar who?
> Humbert: Edgar Allan Poe, of course.
> Lolita: Uhm.
> Humbert: It was night in the lonesome October of my most immemorial
> year. Notice how he emphasizes this word. It was hard by the dim lake
> of Auber, in the misty mid region of Weir. You see, he takes a word

like 'dim' in one line, and twists it, you see? It comes back as 'mid region of Weir'.

Lolita: Mid region. And he twists it to dim. Ah, that's pretty good. Pretty clever.

Humbert: Thus I pacified Psyche and kissed her, and conquered her scruples and gloom, and we passed to the end of the vista, but were stopped by the door of a tomb, and I said: what is written, sweet sister? She replied: Ulalume, Ulalume.

Lolita: Well, I think it's a little corny, to tell you the truth.

(Nabokov 1997: 121)

The ridiculous scene parodies and intercuts the fear of failing to reach students with that of romantic failure: classroom erotics exposed, as it were. I will not dwell here on the erotics of reading in Nabokov, as Eric Naiman has done so brilliantly in *Nabokov, Perversely*, the cover of which alone suffices to illustrate that once we have seen the world through Nabokovian lenses we cannot unsee any of it.[7] I turn instead to similar scenes of failed teaching and colliding cultures in Nafisi's and Coetzee's rewritings of *Lolita*, to trace the directions taken by Nabokov's unexpected heirs in exploring the ethics and aesthetics of transnationalism into the twenty-first century. Each 'adaptation', as it were, brings to the surface colonial tensions latent but lurking in the original(s).

Exposing *Lolita in Tehran*

Asar Nafisi's *Reading Lolita in Tehran* intercuts episodes from a home seminar on Western literature that Nafisi hosted for seven young Iranian women with the story of her academic career, expulsion from the University of Tehran, and eventual decision to emigrate. The book is structured in four parts, named after seminal characters and authors: 'Lolita', 'Gatsby', 'James', and 'Austen'. The opening section, dedicated to *Lolita*, interprets Nabokov's novel as an allegory about the oppression of women that is surprisingly relevant to 1990s Iran:

Reading Lolita in Tehran was initially received with popular and critical fanfare, but has since been panned on aesthetic and ethical

---

[7] The cover photograph depicts a group of children at a drinking fountain, but despite the literal focus on the foreground, all eyes dart to the blurry figure of a solitary man watching from a bench, rendered sinister by the monograph's title (Naiman 2010).

grounds alike. In 'Reading Nafisi in the West: Feminist Reading Practices and Ethical Concerns', Catherine Burwell, Hilary E. Davis, and Lisa K. Taylor summarize the initial splash: A contemplation on Nafisi's experience living and teaching classics of Western literature in revolutionary Iran, this rich literary work topped the *New York Times* bestseller list for more than ninety weeks, sold more than one million copies and received enthusiastic reviews from critics across the West [...] The book is appearing on course syllabi across North America in the disciplines of women's studies, international relations, English studies and anthropology, with course titles such as 'Understanding Totalitarianism', 'Understanding Culture and Cultural Difference' and, of course, 'Women and Islam'. (Burwell, Davis, & Taylor 2008: 63–84)

Burwell, Davis, and Taylor question the timing of this surge in popularity of Iranian women's memoirs and fiction, citing scholar Gayatri Spivak's imperative 'to render transparent the interests of the hegemonic readership' (Burwell et al. 2008: 64). Why are we reading Iranian women's memoirs right now, they ask?

While Burwell interrogates the discourses that produce the imagined 'Third World woman' as 'without agency and in need of rescue', Davis draws attention to two problematic modes of reading: empathic identification and reading for truth: 'Empathetic identification is problematic because it is inherently egocentric, while reading for understanding problematically assumes that the text offers a truth about the world which is complete and objective rather than partial and constructed' (Burwell et al. 2008: 68). Strikingly, both modes echo Nabokov's own descriptions of bad reading from the *Lectures on Literature, Strong Opinions*, and throughout his fictional works: Nabokov emphasizes the intellectual failures of bad reading where Davis foregrounds the ethical and political problems, but the two critiques harmonize.

While Davis focuses on the way *Reading Lolita in Tehran* has been read, reviewed, and taught by contemporary publics, the most vehement critics point to the author's politics. In the tellingly titled 'Native Informants and the Making of the American Empire', Hamid Dabashi reads Nafisi as a colonial agent, inviting American military intervention in the Middle East. He argues that the body of literature best represented by Nafisi's *Reading Lolita in Tehran* is 'partially responsible for cultivating the US (and by extension global) public opinion against Iran', complete with the Orientalist fantasy of saving Muslim women from their men: '"White men saving brown women from brown men," as the distinguished postcolonial feminist Gayatri Spivak puts it in her seminal essay, "Can the Subaltern Speak?"' (Dabashi 2006).

Dabashi goes a step further to connect the geopolitical stakes of fostering anti-Islamic sentiment among American and global readers with the canon struggles still alive and well across American universities:

> With one strike, Azar Nafisi has achieved three simultaneous objectives: (1) systematically and unfailingly denigrating an entire culture of revolutionary resistance to a history of savage colonialism; (2) doing so by blatantly advancing the presumed cultural foregrounding of a predatory empire; and (3) while at the very same time catering to the most retrograde and reactionary forces within the United States, waging an all-out war against a pride of place by various immigrant communities and racialised minorities seeking curricular recognition on university campuses and in the American society at large. (Dabashi 2006)

Let us confine ourselves to looking at what Nafisi does with *Lolita* and with pedagogy, as indicative of her larger project. Her scenes of subversive gatherings of women reading forbidden literature are seductive on the surface, but they are as condescending to the reader as they are to the stylized students, whose lives are moved by Nafisi's seminar leadership to an extent that shades into evident professorial fantasy. We might expect Nafisi to downplay the erotic charge in her writing, yet her prose does anything but:

> I spent longer than usual choosing my clothes that first morning, trying on different outfits, until I finally settled on a red-striped shirt and black corduroy jeans. I applied my makeup with care and put on bright red lipstick. As I fastened my small gold earrings, I suddenly panicked. What if it doesn't work? What if they won't come? (2003: 12)

Since the novel is a professorial fantasy of the first order (diverging equally from reality and the anxiety dreams many faculty face at the start of each semester), the students do all come, tremulous but eager. She greets students like Mahshid, who has 'grace and a certain dignity. Her skin is the color of moonlight, and she has almond-shaped eyes and jet-black hair' (2003: 13). Of the same student elsewhere, Nafisi writes:

> Mahshid's hair [...] was meticulously styled and curled under. Her short bangs gave her a strangely old-fashioned look that struck me as more European than Iranian. She wore a deep blue jacket over her white shirt, with a huge yellow butterfly embroidered on its right side. I pointed to the butterfly: did you wear this in honor of Nabokov?' (2003: 12)

Here is one final description:

> I had never seen Sanaz without her uniform, and stood there almost
> transfixed as she took off her robe and scarf. She was wearing an
> orange T-shirt tucked into tight jeans and brown boots, yet the most
> radical transformation was the mass of shimmering dark brown hair
> that now framed her face. She shook her magnificent hair from side
> to side ... (2003: 16)

'I wonder if you can imagine us' (2003: 39), Nafisi teases her reader, after
passages of dwelling on the hair, skin, and (inevitably almond-shaped) eyes
of her charges. They wait to be imagined, just as they eagerly await emancipation via the Western canon – and a Western canon that includes Nabokov
as its first and most important emissary. Nafisi, for one, unquestioningly takes
Nabokov at his elephant and zoologist word.

Dabashi has a few things to say about the erotic imaginaries of *Reading
Lolita in Tehran*. Focusing on the book's title and cover, he exposes what he
terms Nafisi's 'tantalising addition of an Oriental twist to the most notorious
case of pedophilia in modern literary imagination' (Dabashi 2006). Dabashi
is less interested in questioning Nafisi's reading of Nabokov than in locating
both (Nabokov in passing) on the wrong side of the culture wars. The cover
image in question depicts two Iranian teenagers with covered heads reading
something unseen:

> The twist rests on the fact that the picture of these two teenagers
> on the cover of *Reading Lolita in Tehran* is in fact lifted from an
> entirely different context. The original picture from which this cover is
> excised is lifted off a news report during the parliamentary election of
> February 2000 in Iran. In the original picture, the two young women
> are in fact reading the leading reformist newspaper *Mosharekat* [...] In
> its distorted form and framing, the picture is cropped so we no longer
> see the newspaper that the two young female students are holding in
> their hands, thus creating the illusion that they are 'Reading Lolita'
> – with the scarves of the two teenagers doing the task of in Tehran.
> (Dabashi 2006)

In Dabashi's analysis, Nafisi and her publisher have doctored the photograph
so as to 'usher' these young women into an imagined colonial harem.

This is certainly one reading of Nabokov: Nafisi tries to repeat the master's
move, writing herself into her chosen transnational canon with a sexy
bestseller. In doing so, however, she cleans up Nabokov's morally complex and

deeply ambiguous fabula and skips past *Lolita*'s distancing frames. *Reading Lolita in Tehran* seems to miss the essence of the parable of failure and force in the pedagogical fantasy she adopts. Instead, Nafisi unwittingly steps right into the role of Humbert for her Lolitas.

Open *Disgrace*

For a similar scene of failed cross-cultural communication centred on the teaching of literature, but one that provides a counter-example of the directions contemporary writers might take in Nabokov's wake, we can turn to Coetzee's *Disgrace*. Here is a plot summary of the novel as read by Spivak – whose insights underwrite so many of the critiques referenced in this essay:

> David Lurie, a middle-aged male professor, sentimental consumer of metropolitan sex-work, seduces a student, and is charged with sexual harassment by the appropriate committee. He refuses to utter the formulas that will get him off. He leaves the university and goes to his possibly lesbian daughter Lucy's flower farm. The daughter is raped and beaten, and he is himself beaten and badly burnt. The daughter is pregnant and decides to carry the child to term. One of the rapists turns up at the neighboring farm and is apparently a relative of the owner. This farmer Petrus, already married, proposes a concubinage-style marriage to Lucy. She accepts. The English professor starts working for an outfit that puts unwanted dogs to sleep ... (2012: 320)

In a novel whose first part reads obliquely but persistently as yet another dialogue with *Lolita*, Coetzee delivers several memorable scenes of failed transnational literary teaching. David Lurie attempts to seduce Melanie with, as he puts it, old words. He tells her that a woman's beauty does not belong to her alone:

> Smooth words, as old as seduction itself. Yet at this moment he believes in them. She does not own herself. Beauty does not own itself.
> 'From fairest creatures we desire increase', he says, 'that thereby beauty's rose might never die.'
> Not a good move. Her smile loses its playful, mobile quality. The pentameter, whose cadence once served so well to oil the serpent's words, now only estranges. He has become a teacher again, man of the book, guardian of the culture-hoard. She puts down her cup. 'I must leave, I'm expected.' (Coetzee 2000: 16)

Mere pages later, Lurie tries again with Wordsworth instead of Shakespeare, this time in the classroom setting. He lectures at the indifferent (and, we recognize, racially different from him) students:

> Wordsworth seems to be feeling his way toward a balance: not the pure idea, wreathed in clouds, nor the visual image burned on the retina, overwhelming and disappointing us with its matter-of-fact clarity, but the sense-image, kept as fleeting as possible, as a means toward stirring or activating the idea that lies buried more deeply in the soil or memory.
>
> He pauses. Blank incomprehension. He has gone too far, too fast. How to bring them to him? How to bring her? (Coetzee 2000: 22)

Lurie fails, again and again, to cast the familiar spell with words that both are and are not in the language of the land. It is as if the crumbling empire attempts to hold on through sheer prestige and the lingering memories of its once unquestionable cultural superiority. Coetzee brings to the surface the colonial foundations of the erotic and pedagogical failure already present in Nabokov's own work: the delusion and hypocrisy that lurks behind the generously proffered syllabus and its implicit power narratives.

Where does Coetzee's fiction differ from Nafisi's memoir? In what compelling direction does he take Nabokov's literary legacy? What makes this novel more than a story about the nostalgic sufferings of an old white man in post-apartheid South Africa, realizing he has lost his colonial power and privileges? The profound technical accomplishment of Coetzee's novel, as Spivak points out, is that it confines the narrative to David Lurie while exposing all the limitations and unattractiveness of the character:

> *Disgrace* is relentless in keeping the focalization confined to David Lurie [...] When Lucy is resolutely denied focalization, the reader is provoked, for he or she does not want to share in Lurie-the-chief-focalizer's inability to 'read' Lucy as patient and agent. No reader is content with acting out the failure of reading. This is the rhetorical signal to the active reader, to counterfocalize [...] This provocation into counterfocalization is the 'political' in political fiction – the transformation of a tendency into a crisis. (2012: 323–24)

To focalize, in narrative theory, means to focus a text on a particular perspective, such as the consciousness of the protagonist. To counter-focalize, then, is to read against the dominant perspective: by reading actively, to break free. What Spivak does not mention is that Coetzee borrows this technique too, as well as trace aspects of the fabula, from Nabokov. Counter-focalization is the key to reading *Lolita* past Humbert's narrative: the invitation to 'read better' than the morally blind villain-protagonist is one of the signatures of Nabokov's late fiction. Lurie's relationships with Melanie and Lucy, respectively, reflect in fragmented form Humbert's sexual and parental relationship with Lolita, allowing Coetzee to interrogate his own protagonist's failure to read the other from multiple angles and in obsessive iterations.

Nafisi tried to make the teaching of literature à la Nabokov seem unproblematic in her own attempt to break into a canon of world literature and fizzled fast. Coetzee brought the anxiety to the surface and succeeded – in the process even winning the Nobel Prize in literature that had eluded Nabokov.

The Divergent Legacies of a Transnational Nabokov

What might such painful parodies of literary pedagogy teach us about transnational Russian literature? From a linguistically and nationally minded perspective, *Lolita*, *Reading Lolita in Tehran*, and *Disgrace* are all English-language books and therefore fall outside the traditional bounds of Slavists' enquiry. Moreover, teaching scenes such as the ones above reveal anxiety over precisely the emancipatory promises of literature 'beyond' nation – anticipating ongoing debates about world literature as an institutional enterprise.[8] Rephrased more bluntly, do these scenes express the fear that, one way or another, literature beyond nation becomes a euphemism for the literature of empire, of one kind or another – that the seductive multicultural syllabus is neither seductive nor multicultural, and that it thinly veils an invitation to subjugation?

The debate is worth returning to in our context and for our project, which looks to celebrate the roots and legacies of a Russian literature beyond Russia. On the one hand, we feel the genuine excitement and potential of the hybrid (à la Homi Bhabha); something of the science fiction fantasy of conjuring new cultures into being. (Nabokov's *Ada* is a brilliant example, but Russian

---

[8] David Damrosch suggests that 'world literature is not an infinite, ungraspable canon of works but rather a mode of circulation and of reading' (2003: 5). Mads Rosendahl Thomsen argues, 'It is only within the last decades that the concept of culture has gradually been more and more widely defined as non-essentialist, hybrid and contingent, something that has not been reflected in the practice of literary history, but which in all likelihood is one of the main reasons behind the renewed interest in world literature' (2008: 3). See also Pizer (2006) and Prendergast (2004).

Brooklyn is often no less fantastical.) On the other, we sense the violence of the colonial flipside, hidden in plain sight in a European haircut and butterfly blazer in Iran.

Nabokov proves paradigmatic in more ways than one, including the embarrassing politics that likely cost him the Nobel. As Nataša Kovačević has noted, Nabokov and Orientalism share plenty of rhetoric: we need only remember 'Nabokov's legitimization of Western liberal democracy as *the* ideal political system' and 'the lack of any systemic critique when it comes to US politics, which leads Nabokov to his embarrassing endorsement of the Vietnam War and collaboration with the CIA and FBI' (Kovačević 2008: 21). In Kovačević's reading, Nabokov understood all too well that he must play the exotic other and perform cultural difference – 'what Gayatri Spivak calls the "staging" of "culture" – to his American audiences on both the left and the right (and the shades in between), if he is to interest them in the story of his exile' (2008: 22).[9]

The twenty-first-century legacy of Vladimir Nabokov, transnational Russian provocateur, may well be that he demands the study and discussion of both of his divergent legacies: enthusiastic native informant and suspicious counter-focalizer extraordinaire. Reading *Lolita* 'transnationally', alongside texts such as *Reading Lolita in Tehran* and *Disgrace*, forces us to see what cannot then be unseen: the power dynamics present in every syllabus, in every classroom lecture, in every invitation to 'imagine us'. Teaching such books together might even encourage pedagogical practices that are genuinely emancipatory.[10]

[9] Kovačević stresses the 'conservative oddity' Nabokov must have seemed among the left-liberal intelligentsia where he published and worked: yet 'the left-liberal intellectual and social milieu was itself somewhat of an oddity in relation to the American mainstream, anti-communist sentiment, particularly in the postwar period. The mainstream, in fact, is the wave on which Nabokov's career rides' (2008: 24).

[10] See Hong and Ferguson: 'Defining humanities teaching as the "noncoercive rearrangement of desire," Spivak theorizes a role for literary training that would interrupt the reflexes and habits of knowing that the global dominant instills through university education – habits of self-centering, sanctioned ignorance, and strategic exclusion that enable the reproduction of global class apartheid' (2011: 8).

Works Cited

Boyd, Brian. 1991. *Vladimir Nabokov: The American Years* (Princeton, NJ: Princeton University Press).

Bozovic, Marijeta. 2016. *Nabokov's Canon: From Onegin to Ada* (Evanston, IL: Northwestern University Press).

——. 2017. 'Nabokov's Translations and Canon-Formation', *Translation Studies*, 10: 1–13.

Burwell, Catherine, Hilary E. Davis, and Lisa K. Taylor. 2008. 'Reading Lolita in the West: Feminist Reading Practices and Ethical Concerns', *Topia*, 19: 63–84.

Casanova, Pascale. 2004. *The World Republic of Letters* (Cambridge, MA: Harvard University Press).

Coetzee, J. M. 1974. 'Nabokov's Pale Fire and the Primacy of Art', *UCT Studies in English*, 5: 6.

——. 2000. *Disgrace* (New York: Penguin).

Dabashi, Hamid. 2006. 'Native Informers and the Making of the American Empire', *Al-Ahram Weekly On-line*, 797, 1–7 June <http://weekly.ahram.org.eg/2006/797/special.htm> [accessed 20 June 2018].

Damrosch, David. 2003. *What is World Literature?* (Princeton, NJ: Princeton University Press).

Foster, John Burt Jr. 2013. *Transnational Tolstoy: Between the West and Russia* (New York: Bloomsbury).

Guillory, John. 1993. *Cultural Capital: The Problem of Literary Canon Formation* (Chicago, IL: University of Chicago Press).

Hong, Grace Kyungwon, and Roderick Ferguson (eds). 2011. *Strange Affinities: The Gender and Sexual Politics of Comparative Racialization* (Durham, NC: Duke University Press).

Kovačević, Nataša. 2008. *Narrating Post/Communism: Colonial Discourse and Europe's Borderline Civilization* (Milton, UK: Routledge).

Nabokov, Vladimir. 1989. *Lolita* (New York: Vintage Books).

——. 1997. *Lolita: A Screenplay* (New York: Vintage Books).

Nafisi, Azar. 2003. *Reading Lolita in Tehran: A Memoir in Books* (New York: Random House).

Naiman, Eric. 2010. *Reading Nabokov Perversely* (Ithaca, NY: Cornell University Press).

Norman, Will. 2012. *Nabokov, History and the Texture of Time* (New York: Routledge).

Pizer, John. 2006. *The Idea of World Literature: History and Pedagogical Practice* (Baton Rouge, LA: Louisiana State University Press).

Prendergast, Christopher (ed.). 2004. *Debating World Literature* (London: Verso).

Shapiro, Gavriel. 2009. *The Sublime Artist's Studio: Nabokov and Painting* (Evanston, IL: Northwestern University Press).

Spivak, Gayatri Chakravorty. 2012. *An Aesthetic Education in the Era of Globalization* (Cambridge, MA: Harvard University Press).

Thomsen, Mads Rosendahl. 2008. *Mapping World Literature: International Canonization and Transnational Literatures* (London: Continuum).

Venuti, Lawrence. 2008. *The Translator's Invisibility: A History of Translation*, 2nd ed. (New York: Routledge).

8

Bringing Books across Borders

Behind the Scenes in Penguin Books

Cathy McAteer

Introduction

Russia's literary canon – what we think of today as the Russian 'classics' – started coming across national borders *en route* to the UK in the latter part of the nineteenth century. In the absence of Russian–English translators at that time, the first English translations of Russian texts were often made from German or French versions, as is the case with the initial English versions of Turgenev's *Sportsman's Sketches* [Zapiski okhotnika] and Tolstoi's *War and Peace* [Voina i mir]. After centuries of Russophobic sentiment in the UK (Phelps 1958), Britain's acknowledgement at the end of the nineteenth century that Russia had a worthy literary canon of its own proved a significant realization in Anglo-Russian cultural relations, one which Donald Davie famously describes in elevated terms in his essay '"Mr Tolstoy, I presume?" The Russian Novel through Victorian Spectacles': 'the awakening of the Anglo-Saxon people to Russian literature [...] should rank as a turning-point no less momentous than the discovery of Italian literature by the generations of the English Renaissance' (1990: 276). The reality, though, of the UK's assimilation of nineteenth-century Russian culture, including literature, is observed more objectively and judiciously by Philip Bullock:

> Because Russia was geographically remote, its language known to only a handful of the most dedicated linguists, its culture and history unfamiliar, and its character disputed even by its own inhabitants, familiarity with Russia in England was always going to be the province of a particularly select group of specialists and enthusiasts. (2009: 20)

Britain's acquaintance with Russian culture and literature was dependent therefore on these specialist agents: skilled, dedicated, and usually more knowledgeable on Russian matters than the rest of the field. The following agents played significant roles in the early reception of Russian literature in English translation: the philosopher, jurist, and legal reformer Jeremy Bentham (1748–1832) and his protégé John Bowring (1792–1872), an early advocate and translator of Russian poetry; the Russian novelist Ivan Turgenev (1818–83), who was singled out and publicized by Henry James (1843–1916) for being the ideal foreign (and the first Russian) novelist to suit English tastes with his continental writing style; the publishers Henry Vizetelly (1820–94) and William Heinemann (1863–1920), who acted upon the implementation of the Forster Education Act to produce foreign literature in translation for a new, mass audience; and, finally, the translator Constance Garnett (1861–1946), who 'with Herculean productivity, gave the English reader virtually all the Russian prose classics' (Rayfield 2001: 28), producing over 70 volumes' worth in English translation. Once under way, the translation of Russian literature into English 'was achieved in a remarkably short period of time: almost the entire body of nineteenth-century prose was translated in the space of forty years, between roughly 1885–1925' (Beasley & Bullock 2011: 283–84).

Collectively, therefore, these agent-enthusiasts introduced the British to a positive notion of Russian culture – challenging the 'ready tradition of native Russophobia' (Bullock 2009: 24), first voiced in accounts by sixteenth-century sea merchants (Phelps 1958: 418) and compounded by hostility during the Great Game and the Crimean War in the eighteenth and nineteenth centuries – which, in turn, prepared the way for Penguin's relaunch of the Russian classics in the mid-twentieth century. At the start of the twentieth century, Russian literature had been used for specialist language teaching in universities and had been 'promoted as reflecting "more directly currents of thought and problems of human life"' (Beasley 2013: 186). Penguin's Russian classics represent a literary development which not only continued to serve university undergraduates (and even national servicemen on the Cambridge Russian programme[1] (Briggs 2014)) but, crucially, they also inspired a mass audience of Anglophone lay readers. Thanks to Penguin, their cutting-edge publishing developments – modern distribution channels, striking book design, and a translation strategy which made Russian literature accessible and appealing – lay readers of Russian literature in translation were able for the first time to enjoy a 'bourgeois feeling of familiarity in the presence of an interesting, but domesticated, foreigner in the drawing room' (Burnett 2000: 370).

---

[1] Private email to C. McAteer, 18 August 2014.

This chapter analyses Britain's appreciation of Russian literature by adopting an archive-based case study of a publishing house – Penguin Books – and its approach to literary translation via its Penguin Classics series. Conscious of needing to appeal to an 'uninitiated' post-war readership, Penguin's approach to translation was one of domesticating – or 'Englishing' – Russian literature. In practice, this meant translating and packaging what had previously been a distinctly foreign experience into something more akin to nineteenth-century British literature. To achieve this effect consistently, across all Russian titles, Penguin pooled expertise from a constellation of agents and translators. My chapter argues that Penguin's translation and publishing methods, designed to emphasize the familiarity and minimize the strangeness of Russian literature, reshaped the way that Russian literature was received by a readership now keen to learn about Russia via the classics. This chapter examines the institutional, editorial, and commercial factors behind commissioning and publishing such translations, and translators' practices too. Until recently, translation theorists consistently discussed translation in largely text- or audience-centric terms, while the agents of translation and their practices have frequently been overlooked (Simeoni 1998). However, the so-called 'sociological turn' – applied more recently to translation studies by scholars at the end of the 1990s – forces a finer-grain analysis of the fully diverse nature of collaboration between key agents (Simeoni 1998). Robert Crowe argues that 'A full(er) understanding of what is going on in books, and more precisely why, cannot be achieved without dogged enquiry into the shadowy world of a publication's genesis, and a serious attempt to come to terms with the world into which the book is delivered' (2012: 209). This chapter introduces just such an analysis to examine how and why the Penguin Russian collaboration – overlooked until now – resulted in a reinvigorated interest in Russian literature which spanned nearly 50 years and reached socially diverse Anglophone markets in the UK and beyond. Having made the Russian greats accessible to a mass readership with little previous exposure to foreign texts, Penguin achieved something that no publisher had previously realized to the same extent: it assimilated Russian texts into a recognizable canon.

The Sociological Turn and the Penguin Archive

The sociological turn analyses the personal, commercial, and political motivations behind the transnational movement of texts, asking, 'Who are the discoverers, and what interest do they have in discovering these things?' (Bourdieu 1999: 222). The cross-border movement of a text requires combined agency by specialists, and the rise of a foreign literary canon relies on target audience receptiveness. The commissioned literary translator is inextricably linked to the commissioner (usually the publisher and editors), and both are responsible for book sales. The deployment of archived information – a practical methodology recently advocated by Jeremy Munday (2014) – enables us to understand the commissioners, the translators, their life experiences, and resulting translation practice. Careful and judicious scrutiny of archival content may be used to build a picture, a 'microhistory' (Munday 2014: 65) which reveals how agents interact, produce their texts, and, ultimately, come to shape the reception of a new literary canon. This is an area of interrogation which, according to Munday, cannot be deduced from the study of the primary text alone. The contents of an archive can be utilized effectively to demonstrate how 'interactions govern not only the choice of translator and titles for translation but the way the text is translated' (Mason 2014: 123). In the case of Penguin, it is particularly rewarding (and rare) to have an archive that encompasses correspondence for the early Russian classics' translators. Cross-examination reveals patterns in translators' backgrounds and practices but, coupled with text-based analysis, also identifies common domesticating criteria which became recognized as Penguin's trademark style.

An analysis of correspondence stored in the Penguin archive (housed at the University of Bristol, UK) between Allen Lane, the founder of Penguin Books, the Penguin Classics editors Emile Victor Rieu and A. S. B. Glover, and their first freelance translators, Gilbert Gardiner, Elisaveta Fen, Rosemary Edmonds, and David Magarshack, provides valuable insight into the commissioning, translating, and publishing of Russian texts. It contributes to the hitherto under-studied field of twentieth-century Russian–English literary translation and publishing – a lacuna in our knowledge (Beasley & Bullock 2011: 285) – and represents a period when publishing/translation practices became more streamlined. Penguin's Russian classics form a bridge between the early, isolated discoverers of Russian literature and the now plentiful, contemporaneous modern retranslations of the Russian classics.

The Penguin Classics Vision

The Medallion Titles were the earliest incarnation of the Penguin Classics series, which began in 1946 with E. V. Rieu's translation of Homer's *The Odyssey* and lasted until its transition in 1962 to Black Cover Titles (Edwards, Hare, & Robinson 2008: 127). The Medallion Titles, so called because of the roundels on their front covers (Schmoller 1994: 58–59), represent a period of intense activity when ideas and translation commissions flourished. Correspondence levels are high as questions over titles, translators, pay, royalties, and translation style are raised for the first time. The earliest details of how Rieu met and commissioned a new translator are, unfortunately, often absent (lost, it seems, in a sociable haze of dinner discussions which were never officially recorded). What is clear, though, is that in October 1944, Rieu wrote to Lane notifying him that he would be able to devote one day a week as General Editor 'of your new Translation Series from the Greek, Latin and other classics' (Hare 1995: 186). There is a sense of great anticipation in his letter. Rieu reveals that he has already compiled a list of 40 Greek and Roman authors to be included in the series, that he has plans for a similar list of French authors, and is ready to set 'one or two Scandinavian translations afoot' (Hare 1995: 186). He explains that he might consult friends over which books should feature on the French list. His letter just two days later to H. D. F. Kitto (Professor of Greek at the University of Bristol) testifies as much:

> Any comments you may care to make on my lists will be most welcome, and I shall be particularly grateful for any help you can give me in finding first-class men (possibly among the younger scholars not yet clear of the war) who are likely to be fired with the idea. What a chance![2]

The unprecedented success of Rieu's own translation of *The Odyssey* (it sold over 3 million copies and was Penguin's best seller until the publication of *Lady Chatterley's Lover* in 1960) not only secured the drive for an expanded Penguin Classics series but also positioned Rieu as an ideal in-house reviewer of the Penguin Classics translations. He set his personal benchmark for general Penguin translation practice: Penguin Classics translations must be linguistically accessible and appealing to the mass lay reader, 'high art' must reach the wider audience (Bourdieu 1993: 129). Rieu initially gave academics an opportunity to submit sample translations, but famously rejected their efforts on the grounds that 'very few of them could write decent English, and most were enslaved by the idiom of the original language' (Edwards et al. 2008: 26). He elucidates some of his key considerations in his early correspondence with Kitto, whom he urges to use 'the bare minimum of footnotes, if any', adding: 'It is the translator's job to make the text explain itself, remembering always that it is not erudition we want to teach but appreciation'.[3]

---

[2] Letter from Rieu to Kitto, 21 October 1944, Ref. DM1938, Penguin Archive, Bristol University Arts Library, Special Collections.

[3] Letter from Rieu to Kitto, 21 October 1944, Penguin Archive, Bristol University Arts Library, Special Collections.

Rieu's initial expectations of a Penguin Classics translation are outlined more publicly in a copy of the in-house publicity booklet, playfully (and ambiguously) titled *Penguins Progress*:

> The series is to be composed of original translations from the Greek, Latin and later European classics, and it is the editor's intention to commission translators who could emulate his own example and present the general reader with readable and attractive versions of the great writers' books in good modern English, shorn of the unnecessary difficulties and erudition, the archaic flavour and the foreign idiom that renders so many existing translations repellent to modern taste. (1946a: 48)

Committed to the aspiration of producing translations in 'good modern English' to appeal to a new, post-war generation of lay readers, Rieu reiterates in his next *Penguins Progress* contribution, 'Translating the Classics', the one principle to which 'I pin my faith and from which I deduce all minor rules and decisions' (1946b: 37): the principle of equivalent effect. Rieu defined this principle as the 'lodestar of the translator's art', explaining that 'the translation is the best which comes nearest to giving its modern audience the same effect as the original had on its first audiences' (Rieu & Phillips 1955: 153). Rieu's perception of the 'good' 'Penguin' translation strikes a balance between accuracy, authenticity, and accessibility, and commends the advice of the seventeenth-century poet John Dryden, to paraphrase.

Rieu's *Penguins Progress* announcement concludes by listing authors who will be included in the series (Homer, Xenophon, Ibsen, Chekhov, Ovid, Voltaire, Turgenev, Gor'kii, Maupassant) and stating those who already exist (Sayers's translation of Dante's *Inferno* and Watling's translation of Sophocles's *Theban Plays*). The Medallion Titles were dominated by translations from Greek and French literature (29 and 28 translations, respectively), followed by Latin and Russian literature, each with 16 translations (Edwards et al. 2008: 127). It is something of a surprise that Russian literature should have commanded such a high position in the early hierarchy of the Penguin Classics publications. The Penguin archive offers no explanation as to why, but one can hypothesize a number of commercial, professional, and socio-cultural factors which could have contributed to such a robust Russian representation. These include: Rieu's awareness of the average translation's shelf life, with an acknowledgement that fresh, modern translations were long overdue (some of Garnett's translations were 50 years old); recognition of Russia's own high regard for and pride in its nineteenth-century classics; a corporate, competitive awareness of which classic titles were being tackled by other publishers (as Rieu and his fellow copy editor A. S. B. Glover note, they were keen 'to get ahead' of their publishing competitor Hamish Hamilton,[4] which had published some Turgenev classics and Gogol''s *Dead Souls* in the late 1940s and early 1950s).

Rieu's Penguin Classics pledge to 'select works that have a perennial value (for all and not for scholars only)' intimates his desire for a nation's cultural heritage to transcend modern, political obstacles, which may explain why there is no mention in the Penguin archive of a Cold War motivation behind Penguin's publishing of Russian titles. Lane (who courted speculation throughout his career about having left-leaning political tendencies[5] (Hare 1995: 71)) could not initially see any literary merit, for example, in publishing Solzhenitsyn's *One Day in the Life of Ivan Denisovich*; he suspected it 'may well become a dead duck quite soon'.[6]

Whilst the list was supplemented with further translations from Italian (eight titles), early English (six), and a smattering of other languages, these were significantly fewer in number. Each language category was given its own easily identifiable colour code (Edwards et al. 2008: 58) with translations of Russian literature signified by red borders on the cover and spine. The front cover of each novel in the series had a specially designed black-and-white roundel (medallion). The medallion was a non-lingual, paratextual clue intended to pique the reader's curiosity by revealing a significant moment, theme, or character from the novel. What precisely was featured on the medallion was often discussed in advance with the translator.

Where some of the first Penguin Books (Agatha Christie, for example) would be regarded more as popular than 'quality' literature, the same cannot be said for the Penguin Classics series. Rieu attempted to combine popularity and quality, packaged at an affordable price (less than the cost of a packet of cigarettes), and playing to a post-war mood of 'relaxation, pleasure, expansion and reconstruction' (Radice & Reynolds 1987: 14). This popular quality literature presented itself in 'rather cosy introductions and a "house style" of translation' (Radice & Reynolds 1987: 14). In terms of a corporate translation style, no specific document setting out clear guidelines has ever been discovered in the Penguin archive, but Rieu, nevertheless, set a concise,

---

[4] Letter from Glover to Rieu, 30 July 1946, Ref. DM1107/L4, Penguin Archive, Bristol University Arts Library, Special Collections.

[5] Lane's political views synchronized with a national shift to the left after the Second World War, seeing the election of a Labour government and the birth of the National Health Service (Lewis 2006: 130).

[6] Memo from AL [Allen Lane] to AG [Antony Godwin], 4 February 1963, Ref. DM1107/2053, Penguin Archive, Bristol University Arts Library, Special Collections.

unambiguous standard: 'Dr Rieu's object was to break away from that academic idiom in which so many of the world's classics have been put before the general reader, and to present them in contemporary English without any transgressions of scholarship or textual accuracy' (Williams 1956: 19).

Translingual Gatekeepers

Rieu, acting as the editorial bridge between translator and publisher, undertook the role of negotiator to match the classic novel to be translated with the 'right' sort of translator, someone with proven skill and expertise, preferably with a flair for literary translation, and a professional bent towards Penguin's (and his own) benchmarks of readability and equivalent effect. Adrienne Mason argues that Rieu 'took a fairly cavalier attitude to the depth of a translator's first-hand knowledge of the source language or culture' (2014: 127) and as he was unable to understand a Russian source text himself, there is some truth in this. However, in terms of experienced Russian-English literary translators, Rieu did not have an infinite choice at his disposal and he put his trust in the available translators, his 'gatekeepers' (Marling 2016: 6). Aside from a brief biographical sketch on the opening pages of a Penguin Classic translation (and even then, biographies only appear to have been included once the series was well established, from 1963 to 1970 as Black Cover classics), the extent to which Penguin's Russian translators remain relatively hidden, and some almost forgotten, is surprising considering their importance. The Penguin translators are described as having been 'vital, but often underappreciated' (Yates 2006: 149), validating Theo Hermans's statement that translators are generally 'hidden, out of view, transparent, incorporeal, disembodied and disenfranchised' (2000: 7).

Since the era predated the birth of translation studies as a discipline by two decades, any knowledge of translation theory and a formalized translation strategy would have been self-taught, and of those whom Rieu commissioned, with the possible exception of Rosemary Edmonds, it is most probable that they possessed intuitive (in some cases, bilingual) or vocational translation skills. Whilst Penguin's early Russian translators might have acquired and used their language skills in different settings, both professional and personal, their backgrounds unanimously reflect a Europe in transition. Elisaveta Fen (neé Lydia Vitalievna Zhiburtovich) (Penguin's translator of Chekhov's plays), and David Magarshack (Penguin's translator of Dostoevskii, Goncharov, Gogol', and Chekhov) immigrated to the UK in 1925 and 1920, respectively, from a turbulent post-revolutionary Russia. Rosemary Edmonds (Penguin's translator of Tolstoi, Pushkin, and Turgenev) worked as a senior wartime translator, funded later by de Gaulle to study Russian at the

Sorbonne. With background details such as these, it becomes less surprising that these individuals eventually found work transposing their language and cross-cultural skills to the field of translation in peace-time Britain, and where better to do this than Penguin Classics, the publisher of the moment?

According to Rita Wilson, the term 'translingual' suggests 'an understanding of translation as not only something that happens after the story ends, but is a crucial part of the narrative itself' (2011: 235). She identifies that translingual writers, 'in attempting to navigate between languages and the associated social contexts, bring both linguistic and cultural translation into play as processes fostering encounter and transformation' (Wilson 2011: 235). As 'on-the-job' translators rather than the scholarly dons whom Rieu first dismissed, the first Penguin Russian translators were well placed to navigate between languages and cultures and, therefore, to satisfy Rieu's expectation to render Russian classics idiomatically, in 'good modern English'. They used vernacular language to domesticate the otherworldliness of Russian culture. In turn, the prospect of a career riding a potential wave of Penguin commissions would have held great appeal to every freelancer seeking regular and potentially lucrative work. The parameters of mutual dependency were set; the safe, timely, and satisfactory delivery of a text on the one hand, in return for contractual, financial, and potentially reputational benefit on the other. As Rieu pronounced to Kitto, 'What a chance!'[7]

Clear in their views on what a Penguin Classics translation should deliver to its target readers, there remained the question of what Penguin's 'rather cosy introductions' should deliver, the crucial, paratextual framing of the translation. Paul Foote, translator of *A Hero of Our Time* (1966), asked exactly this question of editor James Cochrane in June 1964. Cochrane's comprehensive reply not only outlines all the ingredients for a model Penguin introduction but also identifies Penguin's typical target reader as an 'intelligent and sophisticated adult'.[8] Foote must assume that his target reader knows nothing about the source author, the book itself, and very little about Russian literature in general. He is advised to enlighten the target reader as to 'why he ought to get to know this book' and provide information 'which will make the acquaintance pleasant and profitable', including positioning Lermontov and his work in the context of European literature.[9] There are

---

[7] Letter from Rieu to Kitto, 21 October 1944, Ref. DM1938, Penguin Archive, Bristol University Arts Library, Special Collections.

[8] Letter from Cochrane to Foote, 17 June 1964, Ref. DM1107/L176, Penguin Archive, Bristol University Arts Library, Special Collections.

[9] Letter from Cochrane to Foote, 17 June 1964, Ref. DM1107/L176, Penguin Archive, Bristol University Arts Library, Special Collections.

clear instructions for Foote to 'sell' the book to his target reader, to make 'the highest possible claims for it'.[10] The introduction should be a cultural and literary crash course, preparing an inquisitive but uninitiated reader for something new, an experience which may propel them out of Anglophone comfort zones and into a foreign land.

In the field of production, the translator is generally regarded as ideally positioned to provide such essential cross-cultural insight: who else could know each word and culture-specific detail, the sociocultural background and historical context to a source text and source author in the same way as the translator? Translators were privileged to act as literary commentators on the source authors' works, though Garnett declined this opportunity (Garnett 2009: 306–07). However, the remit for composing a Russian Medallion introduction did not encompass a linguistic dissection of the text. During the early Penguin Classics years, the Russian translators used their introductions to provide some biographical background to the source author, then to position the text in its socio-historical/political source culture context. The translation process (i.e. the translator's practice-based rationale) is never discussed, therefore, and the translator as linguistic expert remains invisible (perhaps because such matters were deemed of little interest or significance to the general reader).

David Magarshack (1899–1977): A Case Study on 'Englishing' Russia

Archival research has shown that the reasons for translators to embark on a contractual agreement with Penguin varied, as did the nature of their professional interactions with the publisher, often depending on their personal and professional backgrounds. Although little is known about Gilbert Gardiner (translator of Penguin's very first Russian classic, Turgenev's *On the Eve* (1950)), for example, the archive reveals that he waited 26 years for royalties on his translation, suggesting that translation was not his sole income. For Magarshack, whose many archived papers reflect his 15-year tenure at Penguin and seven publications of major works, financial need to support his family drove him to fulfil Penguin commissions in haste. An émigré with little English on arriving in the UK, Magarshack graduated in English language and literature and, having tried unsuccessfully to forge a career as a British crime writer, he turned to translation in order to earn a living. As Rieu noted to fellow editor A. S. B. Glover after initial interactions with Magarshack, 'he lives by

---

[10] Letter from Cochrane to Foote, 17 June 1964, Ref. DM1107/L176, Penguin Archive, Bristol University Arts Library, Special Collections.

his translations'.[11] Magarshack was notably more assertive with editors over matters of pay than his fellow freelancers; having agreed to an annual royalty payment (7.5% on books sold),[12] Magarshack was assiduous in ensuring that bookshops kept a plentiful stock of his translations.

It is uncertain whether Magarshack's translation style conformed to Rieu's by coincidence or by careful design on his part to secure re-employment and book sales, but Magarshack earned his living by delivering accessible translations. When interviewed for the *Chicago Tribune* about his method, he stated that 'if I can translate my translation back to Russian quickly – then it is a bad translation. It has not been Englished as a work of imagination' (Igoe 1963). Magarshack's translations generally bring the source text and culture to the reader (Schleiermacher 1813) rather than force the uninitiated reader to stretch beyond their comfort zone (and capabilities) in order to meet the source text. He achieved this aim through idiomatic, lexical, and social equivalence. Rather than rely on a 'plain and easy'[13] or literal rendering of a nation's phraseology, and risk distorting the way in which the nation is received by the target audience, Magarshack believed that the translator should capture equivalent sense through accurate paraphrase. He domesticated culture-specific references as necessary, a prime example of this being his use of the English 'Mr' and 'Mrs' and omission of Russian patronymics. In the absence of a ready idiomatic equivalent, he recommended that translators devise their own comparable idioms which may, in time, become incorporated into the English language.[14] He applied Dickensian-style dialect to his Dostoevskii characters, a departure from Garnett's prose, which Brodsky criticized for assuming only one voice: her own (Burnett 2000: 369). Magarshack's dialects, though, have since been evaluated as being 'possibly too much like a London barfly' (May 1994: 44). Nevertheless, in his review of the Penguin translation of *The Idiot* (1955), George Gibian writes that 'again and again [...] Magarshack is idiomatic and fluent, whereas Constance Garnett puts an undesirable, even if only thin, curtain of awkwardness and unnaturalness between the reader and the novel' (1958: 153). For Magarshack, a translator's careless lexical choices risk perpetuating false impressions and national stereotypes, all of

---

[11] Letter from Rieu to Glover, 20 January 1949, Ref. DM1107/L23, Penguin Archive, Bristol University Arts Library, Special Collections.

[12] Letter from Rieu to Glover, 20 January 1949, Ref. DM1107/L23, Penguin Archive, Bristol University Arts Library, Special Collections.

[13] Magarshack, General Principles of Translation from the Russian, n.d.: 14, Magarshack Archive, MS1397. Leeds: Leeds University Special Collections.

[14] Magarshack, General Principles of Translation from the Russian, n.d.: 15, Magarshack Archive, MS1397. Leeds: Leeds University Special Collections.

which are accepted by the target culture and ultimately become difficult to reverse. It is clear from his notes how keenly he felt that the translator has a responsibility to convey a 'faithful' likeness of the original text, but not a literal copy, and he argues that Garnett's distorted image of the Russian 'has today become so generally accepted that it even colours the views of serious authors on Russian affairs'.[15]

Conclusion

By today's standards, the post-war Penguin translations of the Russian classics are often regarded as *over*-domesticating – an assessment which has since led to a swathe of 'corrective' retranslations (May 2000: 1208). It could be argued, however, that Penguin had in fact set something of a benchmark in Anglophone Russian literary translation by experimenting with different methods of bringing the text closer to the everyday reader. This chapter, which uses a broadly sociological perspective to evaluate Penguin's relaunch of Russian literature in English translation, demonstrates the intertwining of commercial, editorial, and translation strategies that together made up the distinctive 'Penguin approach' of making the 'foreign' accessible to the 'masses'. Penguin and translators like Magarshack made it their priority to bring Russian classics into 'the (English) drawing room', both literally and metaphorically. While their own very specific way of going about eliminating cultural foreignness is hardly appropriate for our own times, there is no doubt that they enabled Russian literature to take root in the Anglophone world as never before, and that in many ways they prepared its readership for the Soviet literature which came next. In the midst of the Cold War, they cultivated a perception of Russia and its cultural heritage that was designed not simply to transcend politics but also, crucially, to be assimilated, appropriated, and appreciated by *all*. This deeper democratic legacy of the Penguin approach, where the ultimate goal is indeed a given culture's 'domestication' by a mass readership, can in fact be seen in much of the translation and publishing practice of the literary marketplace of today.

---

[15] Magarshack, General Principles of Translation from the Russian, n.d.: 18, Magarshack Archive, MS1397. Leeds: Leeds University Special Collections.

Works Cited

Beasley, Rebecca. 2013. *Russia in Britain, 1880–1940: From Modernism to Melodrama* (Croydon: Oxford University Press).

Beasley, Rebecca, and Philip Bullock (eds). 2011. 'Introduction: The Illusion of Transparency', *Translation and Literature*, 20(3): 283–300.

——. 2013. *Russia in Britain, 1880–1940: From Modernism to Melodrama* (Croydon: Oxford University Press).

Bourdieu, Pierre. 1993. *The Field of Cultural Production* (Cambridge: Polity Press).

——. 1999. 'A Conservative Revolution in Publishing', trans. Ryan Fraser (2008), *Translation Studies*, 1(2): 123–53.

Bullock, Philip. 2009. *Rosa Newmarch and Russian Music in Late Nineteenth and Early-Twentieth Century England* (Farnham: Ashgate).

Burnett, Leon. 2000. 'Fedor Dostoevskii 1821–1881, Russian Novelist, Short-Story Writer and Journalist' in Olive Classe (ed.), *Encyclopedia of Literary Translation into English A–L*, Vol. 1 (Chicago and London: Fitzroy Dearborn Publishers), 365–71.

Crowe, Robert. 2012. 'How to Fillet a Penguin' in Stephen Harrison and Christopher Stray (eds), *Expurgating the Classics, Editing Out in Greek and Latin* (London: Bloomsbury Press), 197–212.

Davie, Donald. 1990. '"Mr Tolstoy I Presume?" The Russian Novel through Victorian Spectacles' in Donald Davie, *Slavic Excursions: Essays on Russian and Polish Literature* (Manchester: Carcanet), 271–80.

Edwards, Russell, Steve Hare, and Jim Robinson (eds). 2008. *Penguin Classics*, rev. ed. (Exeter: Short Run Press).

Garnett, Richard. 2009. *Constance Garnett – A Heroic Life* (London: Faber and Faber).

Gibian, George. 1958. 'Review: *The Idiot* by Fyodor Dostoyevsky, David Magarshack', *The Slavic and East European Journal*, 2(2) <http://www.jstor.org/stable/304328?seq=2#page_scan_tab_contents> [accessed 12 June 2017].

Hare, Steve. 1995. *Penguin Portrait: Allen Lane and the Penguin Editors, 1935–1970* (London and New York: Penguin).

Hermans, Theo. 2000. 'Shall I Apologize Translation?' <http://discovery.ucl.ac.uk/516/1/Ep_Apologizetrans.pdf> [accessed 26 May 2017].

Igoe, W. J. 1963. 'The Gift of Tongues', *Chicago Tribune*, 20 October.

Lewis, Jeremy. 2006. *Penguin Special, The Life and Times of Allen Lane* (London: Penguin).

Magarshack Archive, MS1397. Leeds: Leeds University Special Collections.

Marling, William. 2016. *Gatekeepers: The Emergence of World Literature and the 1960s* (New York: Oxford University Press).

Mason, Adrienne. 2014. 'Molière among the Penguins, John Wood's Translations for the Early Penguin Classics' in Katja Krebs (ed.), *Translation and Adaptation in Theatre and Film* (Abingdon: Routledge), 122–39.

May, Rachel. 1994. *The Translator in the Text: On Reading Russian Literature in English* (Evanston, IL: Northwestern University Press).

——. 2000. 'Russian Literary Translation into English' in Olive Classe (ed.), *Encyclopedia of Literary Translation into English, M–Z*, Vol. 2 (London: Fitzroy Dearborn), 1204–09.

Munday, Jeremy. 2014. 'Using Primary Sources to Produce a Microhistory of Translation and Translators: Theoretical and Methodological Concerns', *The Translator*, 20(1): 64–80.

Penguin Archive, Bristol University Arts Library, Special Collections.

Phelps, Gilbert. 1958. 'The Early Phases of British Interest in Russian Literature', *The Slavonic and East European Review*, 36(87) (June): 418–33.

Radice, William, and Barbara Reynolds (eds). 1987. *The Translator's Art* (Harmondsworth: Penguin).

Rayfield, Donald. 2001. 'Prince among Professors', *Times Literary Supplement*, 13 April <https://www.the-tls.co.uk/articles/private/prince-among-professors/> [accessed 24 November 2017].

Rieu, Emile Victor. 1946a. 'The Penguin Classics', *Penguins Progress*, 1 (July).

——. 1946b. 'Translating the Classics', *Penguins Progress*, 2 (October).

Rieu, Emile Victor, and John B. Phillips. 1955. 'Translating the Gospels', *The Bible Translator*, 6(4) (October): 150–59.

Schleiermacher, Friedrich. 1813. 'On the Different Methods of Translating' in Lawrence Venuti (ed.), *The Translation Studies Reader*, 2nd ed. (New York: Routledge), 43–63.

Schmoller, Tanya. 1994. 'Roundel Trouble' in Russell Edwards, Steve Hare, and Jim Robinson (eds). 2008. *Penguin Classics*, rev. ed. (Exeter: Short Run Press), 58–59.

Simeoni, Daniel. 1998. 'The Pivotal Status of the Translators' Habitus', *Target*, 10(1): 1–39.

Williams, William E. 1956. *The Penguin Story* (Aylesbury: Hunt, Barnard & Co.).

Wilson, Rita. 2011. 'Cultural Mediation through Translingual Narrative', *Target*, 23(2): 235–50.

Yates, Martin (ed.). 2006. *The Penguin Companion* (Chippenham: Octoprint).

9

'Sewing up' the
Soviet Politico-cultural System

Translation in the Multilingual USSR

Sergey Tyulenev and Vitaly Nuriev

Introduction

In his 1953 *Introduction to Translation Theory*, one of the Soviet Union's first and leading translation scholars, Andrei Fedorov, wrote:

> The Soviet Union is a multi-national state, where people speak, write, and create in a multitude of languages [...] Translation is the most direct path by which peoples of the USSR can become acquainted with the literary treasures of other peoples, and in this way serves as an effective means for the continued development of Soviet culture. (cit. Baer 2016: 56)

On the one hand, the Union of Soviet Socialist Republics (USSR) was intent on building a unified – Soviet – politico-cultural system; on the other, as a state, it was a union of diverse (ethno-)nations, each of which was understood to have, as a key attribute of nationhood, its own national language. Translation, therefore, came to be understood as one of this system's vital binding elements. Yet it would be misleading to think that translation functioned equally in the USSR between all its languages. There was one language – Russian – which assumed a special, pivotal, position in the Soviet system of translation.

The Russian language was, of course, the first language of the multinational USSR; building on the legacies of the Russian Empire, it became the USSR's lingua franca. However, the role that Russian performed in the USSR as a means of communication between its nations cannot be reduced simply and straightforwardly to its status of lingua franca. As this chapter will argue, Russian also performed a distinctive role as a 'translation medium', in the sense that translation from and into Russian became the primary facilitator, but at the same time the key controller, of the circulation of literary and sociopolitical works, and thus of the meanings and messages contained in them. This was the case, firstly and principally, within the multinational politico-cultural system of the USSR itself; and secondly and rather more loosely, across the politico-cultural system of the broader socialist international in which the USSR took on a central and dominant role. To address the broader question of the transnational role of the Russian language both within the USSR and beyond it, it is important, first, to describe the place and identity of Russian in this historically and politically distinctive federative state; and second, to identify and analyse the specific politico-cultural functions that translation from and into Russian assumed within the USSR's system of cultural and ideological production.

The Transnationalism of the Russian Language in and beyond the USSR

The USSR was constructed as a conglomeration of nationalities – ethnonational groups, each endowed with a set of canonized cultural attributes (not least language), as well as material (territorial, administrative, and infrastructural) supports associated with nationhood. At the same time, Soviet nationalities were ultimately understood to belong to one nation – the Soviet people – united by a common ideology and sociopolitical organization, that of Marxism-Leninism.

The early Soviet nationalities policy brought together two strange bedfellows – internationalism and nationalism (Martin 2001). As Baer puts it, 'a commitment to the progressive Communist ideal of internationalism did not prevent the regime from promoting the opposing ideology of Romantic nationalism' (2016: 49). Indeed, the Soviets built on what Andrew Wachtel has described as the 'synthetic nature of the Russian national project' (1999: 56), the idea that 'Russia's manifest destiny was to absorb other civilizations rather than destroy them', from which 'followed logically that they all had to be translated into Russian, to be made available for the grand synthetic project whose realization was to occur in the future' (1999: 53). This was one of the most striking paradoxes of Soviet culture, emanating from the Bolsheviks' efforts to renegotiate Russia's imperialist legacy while at the same time resorting to forms of universalism typical of certain prominent strands of Russian nationalism (Wachtel 1999: 67–72). In consequence, one of the main dilemmas of the Soviet language policy, as part of its wider nationalities policy, was how to reconcile a single Communist linguo-cultural identity with a commitment to assisting all Communist nations in preserving and developing their respective ethno-national identities, not least their languages and literatures (see the 1931 decree of the Presidium of the Central Executive Committee of the USSR 'On Publishing Literature in the Languages of National Minorities').

More specifically, what emerged as a problem to be solved was how to develop a system of politico-cultural communication across a multilingual union while simultaneously fostering, rather than repressing, the linguistic and cultural identities of the respective Soviet nations.[1] The most obvious solution to this problem of transnational communication was that of instituting a Union-wide lingua franca. And yet, what seemed vital here was for this lingua franca to serve as a neutral bond, rather than itself be a form of national expression. This was why early in the history of looking for solutions to this problem, some went as far as to propose Esperanto as the language that would be best positioned to connect the different nations of the USSR (Schlapentokh 2011: 63).

In reality, it was Russian, of course, that acquired this role, owing to its established status as the most widely spoken language of what had once been the Russian Empire. Indeed, according to the 1920 population census (PS 1920), out of the former empire's total population of 131,546,045, the majority (82,594,643) lived in the Russian Soviet Federative Socialist Republic (RSFSR), and 66,485,972 of the latter lived in its European part. Most of those people spoke Russian, whether as their only language or as one of the languages in their command.

However, the manner in which the Russian language was then promoted as lingua franca of the Union is significant, for it was consistently contrasted with all the other languages of the Union, as the only one that was effectively non- or supranational. As Witt points out, 'Russian as the dominant ethnicity was unmarked' (2013: 146, n. 19); the adjective 'national' [natsional'nyi] was used, in turn, principally with reference to non-Russian ethnicity.

Contrary to the other Soviet languages, Russian was the first language of the RSFSR, which was itself a complex multinational and multilingual federative unit. The RSFSR was, moreover, considered the 'nucleus' of the USSR (Gorbachev 1987: 18) and the springboard of the entire international revolutionary movement (Lenin 1969: 303). Russian was thus, from the Bolshevik perspective, imagined as the language not of a nation state but a proletarian state – the first state of this kind, in fact.

It was in this context that Russian was then actively promoted as the USSR's lingua franca, mostly through the education system, but also by other

---

[1] Among the initiatives that leaned towards the standardization of the communicative form among the Union's many languages was, for example, the idea to convert the writing systems of all Soviet peoples into a single alphabet, Cyrillic.

means, such as the national military service. Russian became viewed as a powerful means of connecting proletarians belonging to different nationalities, furthering their economic and cultural development down the path of Soviet modernization. In effect, Russian was the language of Soviet modernity, the language of historical progress and civilizational advancement, both of which were always framed in ideological terms. It was in this sense that Russian was understood as an essential element in 'improving' 'national' (non-Russian) cadres in scientific and technical domains. Moreover, knowledge of Russian became an essential cultural capital for non-Russian Soviet citizens, enhancing their geographical, social, and professional mobility, providing access to higher levels of education and white-collar jobs.

Russian was also promoted beyond the borders of the USSR as the leading language of a transnational Communist culture – the language through which the 'proletarians of all nations' could be united. After the Second World War, Russian was imposed as a standard feature of the school curriculum in all the countries of the Soviet-led socialist bloc and was also promoted actively in the countries of the 'Third World' – for example, by inviting foreign students to study at Soviet universities where pre-sessional courses in the Russian language were indispensable.

Thus, the Soviets promoted Russian as a 'world language' with universal claims. It was, thanks to the USSR's superpower status, the lingua franca of the Communist world (a world which was expected to grow, extending, in theory, to the entirety of the globe). But Russian was also expected to embody *trans*nationalism in another sense – that of *transcending* (going beyond or over) sheer 'nationality' as such.

However, developing Russian as a non-, supra-, and transnational lingua franca was not in and of itself sufficient to 'sew up' the politico-cultural system that was the USSR, let alone the Communist International, both of which, despite the drive for unity and integration, were still being built explicitly and emphatically as multinational and multilingual. And while all of the above was effective in promoting Russian to a common linguistic 'thread' that helped interlink the system together, it was not the 'thread' itself that did the 'sewing'. What was still needed was the 'needle', and that was *translation*. Indeed, the development of translation became vital as the means through which common (Soviet) political, social, and cultural values crossed the linguistic and cultural boundaries between the different Soviet and socialist nations, 'sewing' them together even while ensuring the legitimate preservation of their individual existence as linguistically, culturally, and historically distinct entities.

At the same time, however, translation interconnected the different Soviet and socialist nations in another way as well. Since, in the context of the

Soviet nationalities policy, a given language was conceptualized as a defining attribute of a matching nationality (even if, in practice, one's official nationality and one's linguistic identity often did not coincide), translation also became understood as a form of *transnational exchange* (i.e. as the means by which the different nations shared their respective cultural riches), building thereby one common cultural treasure trove. Initially, this common fount was itself envisaged as multilingual. In 1934, Maksim Gor'kii stated that he wanted to see 'every work of every ethnic group in the Soviet Union [...] translated into the languages of all the other ethnic groups' (Baer 2016: 56).

However, this vision of multilingual translation was never realized. Instead, it was *translation from and into Russian* that became the hub of the Soviet translation system, which meant that the linguistic form of the common repository was Russian. For sure, the choice of the Union's lingua franca as the pivotal language in a potentially highly complex multilingual translation system seems entirely logical as a practical solution to what was certainly a practical problem. However, this problem was never just practical: it was also a supremely political and ideological issue, intimately tied to the broader Soviet languages and nationalities policies that went, in fact, to the core of the Soviet political and cultural organization more generally.

The aforementioned construction of the Russian language as non-, supra-, and transnational was politically and ideologically essential if translation from and into Russian was to become the hub of the Soviet translation system both within and beyond the USSR's borders. Translating into Russian became tantamount to translating from a 'national' (i.e. secluded, separated, isolated) realm into a shared, common, universal realm. For a 'national' work to be translated into Russian did not only allow more people to read it; it also meant that the work in question assumed a higher, universal value, as a work that was worth sharing both across the Soviet realm and beyond it. Crucially, however, by this very fact, translation from and into Russian acquired another important function as well – it was quickly turned into a mechanism of politico-cultural control. The next section describes what this meant in practice.

Russian as Translation Medium in the USSR

Translation was vital to the way in which the USSR as a multilingual state operated in the first two decades of Bolshevik rule. In their desire to eschew 'Great Russian' imperialism and avoid appearing to impose Russian on other nations at the expense of these nations' own languages, the Bolsheviks gave a major boost to translation across the different languages of the Union, and this, at first, principally in the domain of state administration. In the

1920s and early 1930s, administrative documents were actively circulated in translation and, as a result, existed both in Russian and in the languages of other Soviet nations (Rudnev 2007). However, by the late 1930s, this practice came to be perceived as much too onerous, multiplying the paperwork and sometimes leading to misunderstandings, especially when the translator happened to be underqualified. The system was consequently discontinued, and all state documents had to be produced in Russian. This went hand in hand with the reinforcement of the policy of the obligatory teaching of Russian in all Soviet schools.

However, in the domains of both ideology and literature, translation to and from the languages of the Union continued to thrive. What occurred, though, was a split between the centre and the periphery in terms of how translation was organized. According to the 1931 decree 'On Publishing Literature in the Languages of National Minorities', Soviet nations were encouraged to publish literature in their own languages locally, while central publishing in the languages of the various peoples of the USSR was to be discontinued. A portion of publishing in the local languages included translations into those languages – especially, though not only, from Russian. This was true both of the 'major' Soviet languages (i.e. the languages of the Soviet republics – Estonian, Kazakh, Moldavian, etc.) and of the 'minor' ones (i.e. the languages of the Soviet peoples who did not have their own republics, including Abkhaz, Bashkir, Chechen). It was assumed that the USSR's national languages would be enriched in significantly by translations of Russian classics, including pre-revolutionary greats, such as Pushkin, Gogol', Lermontov, Ostrovskii, Tolstoi, Turgenev, and Chekhov; recognized poets of the revolution, like Maiakovskii; but also the works of contemporary establishment writers, notably Dmitrii Furmanov, Mikhail Sholokhov, Aleksandr Korneichuk, Aleksandr Fadeev, and Nikolai Tikhonov (Witt 2013).

An even greater portion of translation work focused on the classics of Marxism-Leninism (with the works of Lenin and Stalin taking precedence over those of Marx and Engels in terms of completeness of coverage). Here, too, even some of the founding works of Communist ideology, such as the *Manifesto of the Communist Party*, reached non-Russian nationalities through translations from Russian rather than directly from the original (Tyulenev 2010).[2]

The centre, by contrast, became responsible for publishing collected volumes and anthologies of the gems of all-Union literature in Russian

---

[2] This was the case, for instance, with the Tatar edition of the Communist Manifesto, which was in fact a bilingual Tatar and Russian edition (Marx and Engels 1979).

translation, such as *Sovetskii rasskaz* (1975) or *Sovetskaia poeziia* (1977), establishing also an important literary journal – *People's Friendship* [Druzhba narodov] – as an outlet for translations (Witt 2013: 144–45). Translations from the languages of Soviet nationalities into (supranational) Russian were used to establish a new kind of Soviet literary canon based on 'the mutual enrichment of [the] fraternal literatures of the nationalities of the USSR' (as stated in the 'Draft Resolution of the First All-Union Conference of Translators', cit. Witt 2013: 183).[3]

Once a work entered this canon, it did not seem to matter which language the Soviet writer had created it in originally. The translation of the work into Russian ensured the author's place in the pantheon of great Soviet writers and, through that, potentially, the pantheon of world literature as well. Even folk poets from hitherto illiterate nations stood a chance. A typical example is the Kazakh bard Dzhambul Dzhabaev, whose 'songs were included in Soviet school anthologies and became compulsory reading also in the post-war socialist-realist canon exported to the Eastern bloc' (Witt 2013: 147; see also Witt 2011). Indeed, Russian mediated both between individual Soviet 'nationalities' and between the Soviet Union and the rest of the world, starting with the socialist bloc.

Terms such as 'Soviet literature' [sovetskaia literatura], 'literature of the peoples of the USSR' [literatura narodov SSSR], and 'literature of the socialist countries' [literatura sotsialisticheskikh stran] became the accepted way in which literary canons were framed in the Soviet Union. The noun 'literature' [literatura] was here invariably used in the singular, denoting, despite the multiplicity of national cultural traditions that were being assembled, a single body of literature, a single 'cultural repository', in the words of Aleksandr Fadeev, chairman of the Union of Soviet Writers between 1946 and 1954 (cit. Baer 2016: 57).

The inclusion of a particular work in this repository automatically raised the prestige and visibility of that work. This was especially the case when the translation was carried out by a Russian writer of note. For example, in 1935, the influential Soviet literary critic Dmitrii Mirskii described the translations of Georgian poetry by Boris Pasternak and Nikolai Tikhonov as 'a most valuable contribution to our common poetical heritage' (cit. Zemskova 2013: 191). This was not, however, just the perspective of the Russian centre.

---

[3] To be sure, collections of socialist writers' works were also translated into national languages and published in the national republics. For Latvia, see Plēsuma (1970) and Krauliņš (1975); for Armenia, see Zaryan (1938); see also Witt (2013: 146). However, these collections were fewer in number, different in status, and their readership was inevitably restricted.

A similar point was made by one of the delegates from Azerbaijan at the First All-Union Congress of Soviet Writers in 1934:

> We have a lot of poets and Russian writers who have been translated into Turkic [*sic*]. Our poetry, however, the verse of Soviet Azerbaijan, has been translated into Russian and other languages poorly. For the Georgians, comrades Pasternak and Tikhonov have done a lot. They have considerably raised the prestige of Georgian poetry, and rightly so, for Georgia has wonderful poets [...] Translation should be strengthened. It should be arranged that Tikhonov and Pasternak translate not only Tabidze [a famous Georgian poet], but also [...] other poets of the Soviet Caucasus. (cit. Zemskova 2013: 190)

This quotation reveals three things: firstly, that simply being translated into Russian might have enabled a work to be admitted to the central, overarching canon of Soviet literature, but the quality and prestige of a translation was a significant factor in determining the position of value that a work occupied in the canon; secondly, that a prestigious translation into Russian was valued not just for helping enrich the overall cultural repository of 'Soviet literature', but also for serving the cause of the *national* literature to which the work belonged; and thirdly, that the way in which translation was organized and supported by the relevant institutions of the Soviet state (in terms of both how much and how well a given national literature was being translated into Russian) influenced the 'rank' that a given national literature occupied within the wider Soviet canon relative to other national literatures. Indeed, translation into Russian was never a simple aggregator of works into a unified 'Soviet canon' – the process of canonization through the Soviet system of translation was far more complex and greatly affected the canons of the individual national literatures as well.

Furthermore, translation into Russian did something else as well – it also 'sewed' into a 'Soviet canon' works of 'world literature', that is the vetted, approved, appropriated, and mediated literary and political 'classics' in foreign languages.[4] The construction of a Soviet canon of world classics started early on (1919–24) through such ambitious translation enterprises as Maksim Gor'kii's 'World Literature' [Vsemirnaia Literatura] project (Tyulenev 2016). The world literature built into the Soviet canon was inevitably selective. It included, for example, works by Homer, Dante, Shakespeare, Molière, Swift,

---

[4] An example of the construction of a 'translation canon' of this kind can be found in the materials of the First All-Union Conference of Translators, which took place in Moscow in 1936 (see Witt 2013: 164).

Goethe, Schiller, Heine, Balzac, Stendhal, and Flaubert, but also writers such as Henri Barbusse, member of the French Communist Party and author of a 1936 hagiography of Stalin.

Significantly, many of these 'world classics' were then introduced into the national languages via Russian. For example, an Azerbaijani translation of Dante's *La Divina Commedia* was made from a Russian translation (Dante 1988). Russian translations also played the role of intermediary in the rendering of Shakespeare's plays and sonnets, as well as Goethe's works, into a number of languages of the USSR, including Armenian, Azerbaijani, Bashkir, Kara-Kalpak, Karachay-Balkar, Kyrgyz, Moldavian, Ossetian, and Turkmen.

In some cases, a Soviet translation was produced from a Soviet-era Russian translation specifically in order to replace pre-existing translations that were deemed politically unsuitable. For instance, the Soviet Latvian translation of Defoe's *Robinson Crusoe* by Ed. Mārēns (1946) was produced not from the English original but from Kornei Chukovskii's 1935 Russian translation (Defo 1946). The two earlier, pre-war, Latvian translations that had been made directly from the original and followed it closely, retained, among other things, the novel's strong religious component. In contrast, Chukovskii's Russian translation, first published in 1935, had taken considerable liberties with the original text, given that the translator's target audience was children raised in an atheistic society. For example, in Defoe's English original the word 'God' is used as many as 161 times; in Chukovskii's version it occurs only four times and is always written in the lower case – 'god(s)' as *bog(i)*. Thus, by purging unwanted, ideologically problematic elements, translation from and into Russian served as a distinct form of censorship that determined what was included in the Soviet canon and what then filtered into the various national languages.

It would be fair to say that in the Soviet Union 'world literature' existed principally in Russian. Indeed, even publishing houses in the non-Russian republics usually published foreign texts in a Russian translation first, on the pragmatic assumption that this would make the text accessible to the widest possible readership both within and beyond the republic. For instance, in 1987, in Tbilisi, Georgia, Cicero's *Catiline Orations* was published in Russian not Georgian (Tsitseron 1987), even though no Georgian translation of this work then existed. Relatedly, in the non-Russian Soviet republics, university programmes in literary studies relied predominantly on Russian translations of world literary masterpieces, as these were far more numerous; translations of foreign literature into the languages of other Soviet nations were on the whole sporadic and selective. The situation, of course, varied from republic to republic: in Latvia, for instance, literary studies programmes were able to use a combination of different translations, Latvian and Russian, depending on what was available in which language (Zalite & Abeltinya 1980: 19–22). This was only possible, however, because Latvia had enjoyed an established domestic tradition of literary translation before becoming part of the USSR.

For sure, this pivotal role that Russian played in the Soviet translation system as the medium through which everything passed, was hardly the free choice of the Soviet republics. And it is clear that the Russian language acquired this role not simply for practical reasons, but because the translation system of which it was a part was ultimately serving the interests of the Soviet state which needed to shape its politico-cultural system in a very particular, complex way. The statistical data found in the UNESCO catalogue of published translations of books, called the Index Translationum (IT), confirms this.[5] In the period from 1979, when the IT's electronic database began to be collected, to 1991, the year of the collapse of the USSR, Russian features as the principal source language for translations made into the languages of all the former republics of the USSR. However, when one compares the number of translations from these other languages spoken in the USSR into Russian *before* and *after* 1991–92, one sees a drastic decrease (Table 1; the Ukrainian, Kazakh, and Georgian cases are used as illustrations of a broader trend). A comparable decrease post-1991 can be observed in translations from Russian into the languages of the peoples of the USSR (Tyulenev 2010).

Table 9.1. Translations into Russian within the USSR
(Σ represents the total number of translations
in a given direction registered on IT)

	1979–91	*1992–2010*
Ukrainian ⇒	Σ2321	Σ371
	Russian 972	Russian 99
Kazakh ⇒	Σ900	Σ26
	Russian 659	Russian 4
Georgian ⇒	Σ1121	Σ69
	Russian 647	Russian 13

The comparison of the two periods (1979–91 and 1992–2010) confirms that the Soviet translation system was both dependent on and reflective of the USSR's political structure. This is further corroborated by the fact that the

---

[5] Index Translationum <http://www.unesco.org/xtrans/bsform.aspx?lg=0> [accessed 13 May 2017].

most actively translated publications belonged to the most ideologically charged domains of discourse – law, social sciences, education, political writing. The most translated individual works were, in fact, those of the leaders of the Soviet state and the classics of Marxism-Leninism.

The second most actively translated domain was literature, but among the translated titles one does not find any works which might be considered ideologically 'dangerous'. For instance, in the period 1979 to 1991 there are no translations of any of the works by Pasternak into Ukrainian, Kazakh, or Georgian. There were also no translations of works by, say, Bulgakov into Ukrainian and Kazakh. One can, however, find five translations of Bulgakov into Georgian, but only during the 1980s, in the years marked by the weakening of Moscow's political grip on the national peripheries.

When compared with the number of translations of the writings of Lenin (136 publications into Ukrainian, 62 into Kazakh), even translations of nineteenth-century classics, such as Chekhov or Tolstoi, occupied only a modest place in the total production. Indeed, according to the IT statistics, there were only two translations of Chekhov into Ukrainian and two into Kazakh, and only six translations of Tolstoi into Ukrainian and four into Kazakh. As far as translations into Georgian are concerned, there were five translations of Chekhov and as many as 11 of Tolstoi, although this was still considerably fewer than the 17 translations of works by Lenin. Ideological control was obviously at work here and translation was clearly one of its key mechanisms.[6]

Conclusion

Translation played a major role in the multinational and multilingual USSR. It became one of the key means through which a unified cultural-political system was to be 'sewed up' while still maintaining the policy of fostering a union of diverse nations, each with its own language and literature as critical attributes of national worth. The translation system that emerged in the USSR was predicated on the Russian language serving not only as the Union-wide lingua franca but also as a 'translation medium' – a pivotal hub, from and into which the bulk of Soviet translation was being carried out, thus enabling both cultural and political control.

For this to happen the Russian language had to be more than just a lingua franca – it had to do more than simply interlink the different nationalities of the Union. Russian was certainly not to be seen as the language of the former

---

[6] For a more detailed discussion of translation flows from and into Russian based on the IT data, see Tyulenev (2010).

imperial hegemons; it was instead cast as the language of the first proletarian state, and as such the bearer of the most progressive universal values.
More importantly still, Russian needed to be construed differenty from all
the other, 'national' languages of the USSR: it was thus consistently framed
as non-national, supranational, and transnational – the latter in the sense
of being able to transport (through translation into it) a national form and
meaning from a state of (national) isolation into a state of universal acknowledgement and appreciation.

Works of sociopolitical writing and literature formed the bulk of what
was being translated across the languages of the USSR. However, translation
did not just play a role in disseminating an ideological world view or leader
cult across the Union (and then also beyond it to the world at large); it also
created a canon of literary culture identified as 'Soviet'. What this 'Soviet'
canon meant was rather more complex than it looks, however, for it contained
several juxtaposed layers. It certainly implied the creation of a kind of 'melting
pot' of canonical 'Soviet literature' in which the national origins of a particular
work did not seem to matter much and where a work's inclusion into the
'sanctified' corpus was far more important than its origins. And yet, insofar
as the translation of the 'best' literature from and into Russian simultaneously
entailed a form of 'elevation' of individual national literatures – confirming,
but also distributing, potentially unequally, their individual worth relative
to one another (introducing even a degree of competition between them) –
translation also helped stimulate the individual nationalities' consideration of
their respective cultural self-worth.

Finally, the Soviet translation system effectively appropriated into the
Soviet politico-cultural canon a body of works of 'world literature', which
both made world classics 'Soviet' and at the same time allowed the Soviet
politico-cultural system to extend itself beyond works produced in the
USSR itself. Crucially, though, this appropriation, which included both the
translation of foreign classics into Russian and the subsequent translation of
these translations into the Soviet 'national' languages, also entailed forms of
politico-ideological control and censorship, through the ideological reshaping
of the source text.

The fact that this translation system collapsed at exactly the same time
as the Soviet political system itself demonstrates how integral it was to the
larger Soviet project. What is perhaps more important, though, is that it
reveals the complex nature of the USSR's *trans*nationalism, which can be
understood here as an attempt to overcome the challenges of the USSR's
*multi*nationalism. What this chapter has argued more specifically is that
the Soviet system of translation played a critical role in this. Finally, even
though the Soviet translation system seemed to have tried to simplify itself

as it reached the 1930s – precisely by turning translation from and into Russian into the system's pivotal hub – what the above analysis has revealed is that this very solution was not that simple in the end. It was premised on particular negotiations of the identity of the Russian language away from nationhood as such, while it did not seem to do away with complexity at another, deeper level, as the Soviet politico-cultural system continued, in fact, to remain precariously stretched between the national, the multinational, and the universal.

Works Cited

Baer, Brian James. 2016. 'From International to Foreign: Packaging Translated Literature in Soviet Russia', *Slavic & East European Journal*, 60(1): 49–67.

Dante Alighieri. 1988. *Ilahi komedija*, trans. Äliağa Kürčajly from the Russian (Baku: Jazyčy).

Defo, Daniels [Defoe, Daniel]. 1946. *Robinsons Kruzo*, trans. Ed. Mārēns from the Russian translation by Koreni Chukovskii (Riga: LVI).

Gorbachev, Mikhail. 1987. *Perestroika: New Thinking for Our Country and the World* (New York: Harper & Row).

Krauliņš, Kārlis (ed.). 1975. *PSRS tautu literatūra* [The Literature of the Peoples of the USSR] (Riga: Zvaigzne).

Lenin, Vladimir. 1969. *Polnoe sobranie sochinenii*, Vol. 38 (Moscow: Izdatel'stvo politicheskoi literatury).

Martin, Terry. 2001. *The Affirmative Action Empire: Nations and Nationalism in the Soviet Union, 1923–1939* (Ithaca, NY: Cornell University Press).

Marx, Karl, and Friedrich Engels. 1979. *Kommunistlar partijase manifesty* (Kazan': Tatarskoe knizhnoe izdatel'stvo).

Plēsuma, V. (ed.). 1970. *PSRS tautu rakstnieki: literatūras rādītājs* [Writers of the USSR] (Riga: Viļa Lāča Latvijas PSR Valsts bibliotēka).

PS. 1920: 'Territoriia i naselenie (Po perepisi 28 avgusta 1920 goda)' <https://yadi.sk/i/f9A5tSsM3Gtx2RT> [accessed 13 April 2017].

Rudnev, Dmitrii. 2007. 'Iazykovaia politika v SSSR i Rossii: 1940–2000 gg.' in *Gosudarstvennaia iazykovaia politika: problemy informatsionnogo i lingvisticheskogo obespecheniia* (St Petersburg: Filologicheskii fakul'tet SPbGU), 120–38.

Schlapentokh, Dmitry. 2011. 'The Fate of Nikolai Marr's Linguistic Theories: The Case of Linguistics in the Political Context', *Journal of Eurasian Studies*, 2(1): 60–73.

Sovetskaia poeziia, 2 vols (Moscow: Khudozhestvennaia literatura, 1977).

Sovetskii rasskaz, 2 vols (Moscow: Khudozhestvennaia literatura, 1975).

Tsitseron, Mark Tullii [Cicero, Marcus Tullius]. 1987. *Rechi protiv Katiliny* (Tbilisi: Tbilisskii universitet).

Tyulenev, Sergey. 2010. 'Through the Eye of the Needle of the Most Proletarian Language', *mTm (Minor Translating Major, Major Translating Minor, Minor Translating Minor)*, 2: 70–89.

——. 2016. '*Vsemirnaia Literatura*: Intersections between Translating and Original Literary Writing', *Slavic & East European Journal*, 60(1): 8–21.

Wachtel, Andrew. 1999. 'Translation, Imperialism, and National Self-Definition in Russia', *Public Culture*, 11(1): 49–73.

Witt, Susanna. 2011. 'Between the Lines: Totalitarianism and Translation in the USSR' in Brian James Baer (ed.), *Contexts, Subtexts and Pretexts: Literary Translation in Eastern Europe and Russia* (Amsterdam: John Benjamins), 149–70.

——. 2013. 'Arts of Accommodation: The First All-Union Conference of Translators, Moscow, 1936, and the Ideologization of Norms' in Leon Burnett and Emily Lygo (eds), *The Art of Accommodation: Literary Translation in Russia* (Bern: Peter Lang), 141–84.

Zalite, Tamara, and Renata Abeltinya. 1980. *Programme for 'Twentieth Century Foreign Literature' Course* (Riga: Peter Stuchka Latvian State University).

Zaryan, Nairi (ed.). 1938. *Khoryrtayin eritasard groghner: Almanakh: Nver leninyan komeritmiucyan p'arapants XX-amyakin* [Young Soviet Writers' Anthology. Gift on the Occasion of the 20th Anniversary of the Glorious Leninist Komsomol] (Yerevan: Gosizdat Armenii).

Zemskova, Elena. 2013. 'Translators in the Soviet Writers' Union: Pasternak's Translations from Georgian Poets and the Literary Process of the Mid-1930s' in Leon Burnett and Emily Lygo (eds), *The Art of Accommodation: Literary Translation in Russia* (Bern: Peter Lang), 185–211.

10

The Politics of Theatre

'New Drama' in Russian, across Post-Soviet Borders and Beyond

Julie Curtis

New Drama in Russia – and Beyond ...

The first decade of the twenty-first century saw the emergence in Russian theatre of a phenomenon known as 'New Drama'. After the collapse of the USSR in 1991, and as the Soviet state doctrine of socialist realism faded into irrelevance, the most visible transformation in mainstream theatre had initially been in the direction of commercially driven mass entertainment; Western-style musicals and translated blockbusters flourished. A hitherto somewhat closed society thus became more open to the transnational influences of Western capitalism. But if the early years of post-Soviet culture saw an influx of Western models and values, the present century has seen a resurgence of Russian-language writing for the theatre, both in Russia and in the former republics of the Soviet Union such as Ukraine and Belarus. Authors from these three countries already knew each other well and often collaborated; they met frequently at festivals, entered or judged the same playwriting competitions, travelled freely to one another's countries, and shared New Drama workshops as something that was by no means narrowly specific to their own nations. The creation of New Drama was thus a transnational phenomenon from its inception, with leadership and influences shaping Russian theatre culture from other Russian-speaking nations as well as being themselves shaped by Russian models. In more recent years Russian-language theatre has survived as a trans-national phenomenon across some former member states of the USSR, even as certain individual states begin to pull further away from one another, and away from their hitherto shared use of the Russian language.

Most accounts of the beginnings of New Drama mention a range of festivals of contemporary drama in the capitals, and in provincial cities such as Ekaterinburg and Togliatti, which emerged in the late 1990s. Amongst these was the Moscow New Drama Festival founded in 2002 (Beumers & Lipovetsky 2009: 31; Freedman 2014: 5). Meanwhile, Sasha Dugdale, the leading British translator of contemporary Russian drama, who was then working for the British Council in Moscow, facilitated visits of seminal importance by British theatre professionals which brought some of the ideas of 'British New Writing'/'In-yer-face' drama to Russia. In particular, a couple of projects starting in 1999 and involving work with younger Russian-language playwrights, led by practitioners such as Elyse Dodgson (International Director at the Royal Court Theatre), inspired two major developments which shaped New Drama (Dugdale 2009: 14). The first of these was a renewed prioritization of the playwright's work – and specifically his or her text – over the role of the theatre director. The second development was the promotion of documentary or verbatim theatre, drawing on the authentic language of official documents, or of natural speech derived from interviews, as the basis for creating new dramatic texts. The contemporary world suddenly became a vital subject for drama. John Freedman, theatre critic of *The Moscow Times* throughout this period (from 1992 until 2015), admits that trying to define New Drama narrowly leads to 'a knot of contradictions'; but he nevertheless affirms that 'Russian theatre before and after New Drama are two vastly different cultural spaces' (2014: 7).

These innovations were taken up enthusiastically by a number of playwrights and theatres, and were reflected in most festivals showcasing new writing. Dugdale points here to the crucial importance of Elena Gremina, who with her husband Mikhail Ugarov would go on to found the best-known theatre of New Drama, Moscow's Teatr.doc, in 2002 (2009: 17).[1] The motto of Teatr.doc proclaims that this is 'A theatre for everyone, a theatre in which people don't play roles' (Teatr.doc n.d.): in Russian as in English this is a play on words, reflecting the seriousness of their undertakings as well as a move away from the artifice of more conventional theatre.

Since 2002, documentary drama in particular has emerged as a vehicle through which to address all sorts of controversial topics and issues that mainstream Russian theatre ignored: political scandals, police brutality, censorship and the persecution of artists, and the pressures of a resurgent social conservatism. This conservatism has manifested itself in state legislation banning the use of obscenity on stage (as well as in literature and film, and even

---

[1] The world of New Drama was profoundly shaken by the premature deaths in rapid succession in the spring of 2018 of both Mikhail Ugarov and Elena Gremina. The future of the New Drama movement in Moscow, and the fate of Teatr.doc and its associated activities, remains to be clarified.

social media); laws restricting the use of blasphemy; laws banning the 'propaganda of non-traditional [sexual] relations' to minors; and laws controlling how historical issues such as the Stalinist Terror can be represented in art. In *The Pagans* [Iazychniki, 2010], a play full of obscenities and blasphemy, questions are asked about the extent to which the use of pious speech truly reflects the moral integrity of the speaker (Blasing, 2017 conference).[2] The play's Ukrainian author, Anna Iablonskaia, who wrote in Russian, was tragically killed at the age of 29 in the 2011 suicide bombing at Domodedovo Airport in Moscow. The play was staged at Teatr.doc and defiantly remains in their repertory, despite legislation since the Pussy Riot scandal of 2012 which has repeatedly threatened to fine theatres and other public venues that do not 'protect the feelings of audiences' in deference to 'the traditional values of Russian society', citing as examples 'patriotism, the feelings of believers, national and aesthetic values' (Ministerstvo kontrkul'tury 2017). New Drama has been innovative with technology (including an increasingly inventive use of multimedia), but also draws upon unvarnished spoken language as well as documentary sources such as text messages, legal documents, blogs, and so on. Some critics have argued, however, that authenticity and sincerity have been achieved in New Drama at the expense of certain traditional playwriting elements, such as dramatic structure and character development: other traditional features of theatre productions such as a curtain and proscenium arch, costumes, sets, and props are also largely dispensed with. In 2005 Marina Davydova, a distinguished theatre critic, deplored the ways in which, inspired by European and above all British models, Russian theatre had come to focus on the small-scale and the marginal, in contrast to the weighty productions of the past created by great directors: 'We are living through the end of the theatrical epoch' (2005: 36, 38–40, 56–58).

The widespread use of *mat*, the language of Russian obscenity, in New Drama has attracted a great deal of comment – and official opprobrium. This phenomenon reflected the irruption into literary texts of the language actually used by great swathes of the population in their everyday discourse, even though the use of obscenity in print had been taboo throughout

---

[2] References to '2017 conference' are to communications by participants at 'Playwriting Without Borders. Conference on 21st-century theatre (Russia, Ukraine, Belarus)', which was held at Wolfson College, University of Oxford, 6–7 April 2017. Some comments cited in this paper were made by participants during round-table discussions (Elyse Dodgson; Molly Flynn; Nadiia Miroshnychenko; Tania Arcimović; Natalia Koliada), others were in the form of formal papers, namely: Molly Blasing, '"Ne skvernoslov", otets moi": *Mat* and the Language of Faith and Family in Anna Yablonskaya's *The Pagans*'.

the Soviet era. As Beumers and Lipovetsky put it: '*Mat* in documentary theatre as the language of aggression and of reaction to violence unites such disconnected subcultures as the worlds of prisoners, the homeless, illegal immigrants and corporate managers, television producers and gays. *Mat* is the common denominator, effectively the only meta-language of modern Russia' (2009: 221).

Another, associated feature of New Drama was the representation of physical violence, often linked with sexual acts, and sometimes extreme in nature. In the play *Oxygen* [Kislorod, 2003] written by Ivan Vyrypaev, the most distinguished Russian playwright of New Drama, obscenities are brilliantly combined with blasphemy to produce a subtly poetic and musical text describing a man's brutal murder of his wife. In the same author's *July* [Iiul', 2007], blasphemy and obscenities are again woven into a monologue by a man who has murdered several people, dismembering one body and eating part of another. What makes the play in performance even more startling is that according to the stage directions the role of the male murderer is to be voiced by a woman, not a man. Beumers and Lipovetsky's seminal study focuses specifically on the centrality of violence to New Drama:

> Violence, its languages and manifestations are intrinsically linked with the performativity of language in New Drama, where it acquires at least three aesthetic functions. First, violence demonstrates the disintegration of the Soviet social order, indicating cultural chaos. Second, violence arises as a reflection of new, post-Soviet social practices connected with the redistribution of authority, property, symbolic and economic capital. Third, violence functions as a denotation of the sacred, of the ritual of transgression. (2009: 43)

It is striking that in 2009, for these scholars as for the practitioners of New Drama, the issue of the nationality of the authors and the choice of language for writing drama was not a significant issue. Elyse Dodgson (2017 conference) has noted that Elena Gremina of Teatr.doc was determined from the very start to ensure that Russian-speaking voices from Ukraine and Belarus should continue to be heard in Moscow. In the seminars which Dodgson conducted over many years on behalf of the Royal Court Theatre and the Royal Shakespeare Company (RSC), she worked with a whole range of playwrights, such as the Durnenkov brothers Mikhail and Viacheslav from Russia, but equally with Natalia Vorozhbit and Maksim Kurochkin from Ukraine, and Pavel Priazhko from Belarus. A notable feature of playwriting in a number of the newly independent states that emerged from the collapse of the USSR (especially Ukraine and Belarus, but also to some extent in the

Caucasus, and the former Baltic and Central Asian republics) is that drama-tists continued to use the Russian language for their writing and shared artistic projects. This was especially the case with New Drama during the first decade of the twenty-first century: in the early 2000s, drama written in Russian continued to provide a network linking far-flung practitioners across an enormous region, overstepping national frontiers.

The degree to which this was echoed in their native theatrical spheres varied, however. The Italian scholar Erica Faccioli has suggested that Ukrainian and Belarusian playwrights tend in fact to look in somewhat different directions: Belarusian dramatists still have a desire for recognition in modern-day Russia, the country's close ally, whereas Ukrainians have started to be more inclined to seek new audiences in western Europe (2016: 24). By contrast, the Franco-Belarusian researcher Virginie Symaniec has argued that Belarus has really always been pulled in two directions, between Poland and Russia (cit. Faccioli 2016: 81). Nevertheless, the specific transnational cultural bond between these three post-Soviet states, established through the use of Russian, remains very powerful. One major theme of New Drama which is in itself 'transnational' is of course the legacy of the 1986 disaster at Chernobyl, the Soviet nuclear power station based in Ukraine which spread contamination around the world, but caused most damage to its immediate neighbour, Belarus. This catastrophe, which ignored geopolitical frontiers, has been reflected by several authors across the entire region, such as the Ukrainian Pavlo Ar'e in his play *In the Beginning and the End of Times* [V nachale i v kontse vremen, 2013].

In Russia itself, New Drama was pronounced to be on the wane or even dead by the end of its first decade. Beumers and Lipovetsky declared that the 'New Drama' festivals were essentially repeating themselves as early as 2007 and 2008: their view was that by this point the most significant figures in the movement were turning towards cinema instead (2009: 303–04). In the Foreword to their volume, the leading director Kirill Serebrennikov argued in similar terms:

> New Drama is a transitional phenomenon; the term should be forgotten, or applied to the late 1990s and early 2000s when there was a surge of a new truth, a social truth, in the theatre. Those people who previously had no voice in the theatre, such as marginal groups, victims of violence, people from the lowest social classes, were the 'heroes of the time' and New Drama gave them a voice. But once this had been done – what should happen next? This next step was a cul-de-sac and the movement led nowhere. (2009: 9–10)

What is certainly true is that New Drama has never become mainstream, and in this respect its reach has only extended to a relatively narrow circle of intellectuals interested in experimental theatre forms and subversive subject matter. Nevertheless, it is this drama which has had the greatest success in the twenty-first century in reaching beyond national frontiers and getting noticed and staged abroad (rather like dissident literature of the late Soviet period). It has also enthusiastically embraced social media and the internet. It might seem remarkable to a Western, commercially motivated cultural scene that the full texts of about 30 plays selected for readings during the Liubimovka festival are simply posted on the internet every year by the organizers, together with videos of their rehearsed readings and transcripts of the audience discussions of the works. The Belarus Free Theatre (BFT) regularly live-streams its performances to a global audience as well, providing English-language surtitles to overcome any difficulties in understanding the Russian or Belarusian languages beyond the former Soviet republics. While this apparent lack of concern for intellectual property rights has potentially problematic implications for the income stream of authors and performers alike, the free availability of texts and performances online means that the wider transnational impact and significance of New Drama, within Russia and internationally, should not be underestimated.

What has happened since 2009, when Beumers and Lipovetsky argued, together with Kirill Serebrennikov, that the wave of New Drama was already ebbing into insignificance? In particular, what has happened to that shared endeavour across Russia, Belarus, and Ukraine, which the use of a common language had facilitated during a fascinating period of experimental creativity? Political developments of the second decade of the twenty-first century have significantly influenced the further development of transnational playwriting in Russian. Far from declining since 2009, contemporary drama written by those youthful playwrights who drove the New Drama movement has proved to be a medium which continues to flourish. One of the ways in which this activity has manifested itself is in the form of ongoing as well as new festivals and annual playwriting competitions run in Belarus and Ukraine as well as Russia. These regularly attract hundreds of entries, driving up quality and giving a voice not just to established writers but also to individuals from outside the major cities, to women, and to the young. In Russia prizes for new writing are now awarded at the influential Golden Mask theatre festival in Moscow, at the Eurasia drama competition run by the playwright Nikolai Koliada in the Urals city of Ekaterinburg, and many others. At Teatr.doc, Gremina and Ugarov continued to take an interest in issues from across the entire region, as with their play *Two People in Your House* [Dvoe v tvoem dome, 2012], about the house arrest of the Belarusian opposition politician Vladimir

Nekliaev. The role of the Belarusian protagonist was originally performed in Russian in Moscow by the Ukrainian dramatist Maksim Kurochkin. However, there have been considerable changes and important developments in New Drama since 2012, the year of the scandalous Pussy Riot performance and its aftermath, which have been exacerbated since the traumatic events of 2014 which set Russia and Ukraine at odds with each other.

New Drama in Ukraine

In Ukraine the Russian language has always been used very extensively, irrespective of whether people identify themselves as ethnically Ukrainian, Russian, or as a mixture of the two. Commentators have observed that until recently one's choice of language in Ukraine was not on the whole regarded as a controversial issue, and Russian and Ukrainian were used fairly interchangeably, with many people effectively bilingual (Flynn, 2017 conference; Miroshnychenko, 2017 conference). But events since late 2013 – the Maidan protests which led to the Ukrainian revolution, the 2014 Russian annexation of Crimea, and the ongoing sporadic fighting in the east of Ukraine – have served to change that situation. To use Russian rather than Ukrainian is now sometimes interpreted as reflecting a linguistic – and therefore political and cultural – conflict, even though it would be quite wrong to assume that Russian speakers were automatically pro-Russian and that Ukrainian speakers were all pro-European.

Few cultural figures in Russia were prepared to speak out as Russian-Ukrainian relations descended into crisis. But in December 2014 police interrupted the showing at Teatr.doc of an 'unlicensed' film by the Babylon 13 collective presenting the events of Maidan in a positive light, *Stronger than Arms* [Syl'nishe nizh zbroia / Sil'nee chem oruzhie, 2015], and Gremina received an official warning. Shortly afterwards, and perhaps not coincidentally, Teatr.doc was notified that its premises no longer satisfied fire regulations, and since then it has been forced to move more than once (in 2018 the company is once again facing eviction). Undaunted, it has continued to stage controversial plays on this subject. Since 2014, dramatists from Ukraine have still brought their plays to the Teatr.doc venue in Moscow, and to the annual Liubimovka festival held there, thereby keeping open a rare and slender channel of cultural communication. Nevertheless, there were the first signs of a beginning of a parting of the ways in a comment by the dramatist Anastasiia Kosodii, from Ukraine, during the 2015 Liubimovka festival:

> It seems to me that a line has to be drawn between Russian and Ukrainian culture. When cultural traditions are so tightly intertwined,

one way or another one of them starts to suffocate the other. I like Russian culture and Russian theatre, but we will work better when we begin to understand how we differ from one another, and what we can take from one another. (Liubimovka 2015b)

All the same, one of the organizers, the playwright Evgenii Kazachkov, warmly welcomed her 2015 contribution to the Moscow Liubimovka festival, expressing the hope that it might be precisely dramatists who would find a constructive way of approaching the subject of what had happened in the political sphere, and a language that would contribute to healing the wounds (Liubimovka 2015a).

The events of Maidan, the occupation of Crimea, and the fighting in the east of the country have formed the backdrop for a difficult period in the life of one of Ukraine's best-known New Drama playwrights, Natalia Vorozhbit. After a number of early successes in Russia, Ukraine, and abroad, she was commissioned by Sir Michael Boyd at the RSC in Stratford to write a play of Shakespearean scope. The result, *Grainstore* (2009), about the Ukrainian famine of the 1930s, which she provocatively presents as contrived deliberately by Stalin to subdue the Ukrainian people, was first developed and staged in English, at Stratford. Only later did it appear in Ukraine, in Russian. The events at Maidan led to her writing (with Andrei Mai) a verbatim-style documentary piece called *Maidan: Voices of the Uprising* [Dnevniki Maidana, 2014]. It reflected the reality of people's experience of those events, and therefore naturally alternated between material in Ukrainian and in Russian, a translingual linguistic feature which was of course lost when it was staged in English at the Royal Court in the same year. These shifts within texts between two languages (Russian and Ukrainian, or Russian and Belarusian) are one of the features which have characterized many successful transnational projects. But Vorozhbit has in recent years moved more to writing in Ukrainian, citing the 'impossibility' of continuing to function only in Russian in the present political circumstances. On the other hand, she spoke about the problems of her choice of language – and also subject – at a London performance of her work in progress *Can I or Can't I* (developed as *Bad Roads* for the Royal Court in 2017). She observed that with this very intimate piece, in which she describes the exhilaration of a sexual encounter during a visit to the battleground of Donetsk airport to research a drama project, she was not even sure that she would want to show the piece either in Ukraine or in Russia, where audiences might be shocked by the erotic theme superseding political trauma. Furthermore, she had to acknowledge that as a dramatist with a significant profile in Britain, she was in some ways dependent on writing in the Russian language: a theatre expert like Dugdale translates from

Russian, not Ukrainian, and it might be hard to find as good a translator for a Ukrainian text (Vorozhbit 2015). In her recent project, called 'The Theatre of Displaced People', she has sought to create for Ukraine a theatre which would adopt some of the New Drama techniques developed at Moscow's Teatr.doc, in order to provide a voice for local inhabitants during this period of political upheaval, and to offer an outlet which could be both transformative and therapeutic. Thus, recent circumstances have tended to oblige someone like Vorozhbit to come down on the side of Ukrainian identity, where before her mixed identity had seemed relatively unproblematic.

New Drama in Belarus

In Belarus only 15% of the population are ethnic Russians, but Russian is effectively the national language, with Belarusian used only rarely: 85% of books are published in Russian, and only 10% of the population claims to use Belarusian in their everyday lives (Barushka 2015). This situation is of course a legacy of the USSR, when Russian was the dominant language of the entire Soviet empire. After the collapse of the Soviet Union in 1991, Belarus not only retained Russian as its official language but also did the least of all the former republics of the USSR to shed its Soviet authoritarian past. President Aleksandr Lukashenko, described in 2005 by the Bush administration as 'Europe's last dictator', has been continuously in power since 1994, and he has done much to promote Russian still further over the Belarusian language.

New Drama was much slower to establish itself in Belarus than in Russia. One of the first theatre groups to adopt the methods of New Drama was the Belarus Free Theatre (BFT), which was founded in 2005 as a theatre 'where you could say what you think and make art out of that' (Jones 2016). In that same year the BFT's organizers also inaugurated an International Contest of Contemporary Drama (ICCD), which focused on the complex issue of identity by inviting Russian-language dramatists from any country to respond to the simple question, 'Who are we?' (Symaniec, cit. Faccioli 2016: 92). But in the aftermath of police brutality and a clampdown in December 2010 following widespread protests against the authorities, claiming that the presidential elections had been rigged, the three founders of the BFT were forced to seek asylum in Britain in 2011. They describe themselves as the only European theatre in political exile, and now have a worldwide reputation and reach: 'The BFT has to date created more than 25 productions and performed in over 40 countries. In 2015 alone it performed to live audiences of over 10,000 people internationally and more than 500,000 viewed online performances of its work' (BFT 2016: viii). International patrons of the theatre have included the late Václav Havel and Sir Tom Stoppard.

The leading Belarusian theatre critic Tania Arcimović has described how, in the years that followed, experimentation was frowned upon, and Belarusian theatres largely reverted to a safe, traditional repertory (Arcimović, 2017 conference). The BFT has continued to stage clandestine productions in Belarus itself, conducting rehearsals by Skype from London. Both actors and audiences who attend performances, at very short notice and in discreetly arranged venues, are at risk of arrest. But many Belarusian playwrights have had to look outside Belarus to be staged. Pavel Priazhko's play *Panties* [Trusy, 2006] was selected for the New Drama Festival and staged in St Petersburg and Moscow, where it was directed by Ivan Vyrypaev. As Dugdale notes, 'Critics greeted this work as having the potential to change the course of new writing in Russia' (2015). Leading Russian theatre critic Pavel Rudnev has observed that the Belarusian writer Priazhko has indeed had an enormous influence on the development of New Drama in Russia itself: 'It was he who shifted New Drama away from the drama-turgy of themes towards a dramaturgy of language' (2010). This is another example of the fact that New Drama is by no means a phenomenon which was created by Russians and then taken up elsewhere: Belarusian and Ukrainian contributions to the aesthetics of New Drama were equally important to its evolution in Russia. And indeed, Priazhko turns out to have been the single most frequently performed playwright between 2006 and 2016 at Moscow's annual Liubimovka Festival of Contemporary Drama, which has been a showcase for New Drama. Only in the last three or four years has the situation within Belarus altered somewhat, with a number of Belarus playwrights (Priazhko, Dmitrii Bogoslavskii, Pavel Rassol'ko), whose work had already been widely performed and celebrated at 'New Drama' festivals in Russia and Ukraine, finally having their works staged in Belarus itself. By 2013, productions were organized in Belarus of *Patris* (by Sergei Antselevich, Viktor Krasovskii, and Bogoslavskii), a new documentary play which in some respects revisits the BFT's original question – 'Who are we?' – by exploring what contemporary Belarusian citizens understand by the concept of patriotism. There have indeed been some indications more recently that the Belarusian language is being heard rather more frequently on stages in Belarus, especially since the 2014 events in Ukraine provoked a resurgence of nationalist feeling, manifested in the championing of local languages, right across the Slavic nations of the former USSR (Barushka 2015; Arcimović, 2017 conference).

We may trace the way things have developed in the last few years in Belarus by looking at the ICCD, which has been run in association with the BFT since 2005. The internet provides a space to run the contest despite state persecution, although it is suspected that the apparent destruction of some of the webpages of the ICCD competition dating to its early years may have been due to the malicious actions of state-backed hackers (Koliada, 2017 conference). The ICCD awards prizes for Russian-language plays, some of which are then published. Winners have included playwrights such as Anna Iablonskaia (Ukraine), Aleksei Shcherbak (Latvia), Pavel Priazhko (Belarus), and the Durnenkov brothers (Russia). In his 'Introduction' to the 2014 volume of winning texts, one of the BFT founders, Nikolai Khalezin comments: 'The publication which you are holding in your hands has by the will of fate become a symbol of the current complex time which is being experienced in three East European nations struggling with authoritarianism: Belarus, Ukraine and Russia' (BFT 2014: 10). Pavel Rudnev, the Russian co-chair of the jury, added: 'A huge problem in Russia, Belarus and Ukraine today is a trend to self-closure, to tightness, to artificial isolation. One of the major themes of the new post-Soviet drama is the catastrophic destruction of communication between people, generations, genders and countries' (BFT 2014: 14).

It remains striking that these two cultural commentators, from Belarus (via London) and Moscow, respectively, both take it for granted that the political problems facing Russia, Ukraine, and Belarus are in some ways naturally and inevitably a cause for shared concern. This was reflected in the fact that the 2016 award ceremony for the ICCD plays, which could be submitted in Russian, Belarusian, or Ukrainian, was held simultaneously in London, Minsk, Kiev, and Moscow.

Conclusion

Another example of the transnational in action – in the sense of the Russian language being used in order to speak to three national cultures at once – can be seen in the BFT's remarkable production *Burning Doors* (2016). This project came about after Nikolai Khalezin and Natalia Koliada from the BFT got to know Maria Alekhina, who had been imprisoned after her participation in the 2012 Pussy Riot events in Moscow. As Koliada has said: 'What's happening now is the next Iron Curtain. We cannot make changes without you. First we need to understand each other, have a dialogue between the people of Europe and the people of Russia and Belarus' (Jones 2016). *Burning Doors* weaves together the story of Alekhina (who re-enacted her own experiences of prison violence in the production) with the stories of the Ukrainian film director Oleg Sentsov, sentenced by the Russian authorities to 20 years in prison in 2015 for his protest actions at the time of the 2014 occupation of Crimea, together with the story of the Russian performance artist Petr Pavlenskii, notorious for staging a number of protest acts including nailing his scrotum to the cobbles of Red Square in 2013.³ The production was dedicated to the memory of the Belarus-born investigative journalist Pavel Sheremet, a Russian citizen who was killed by a car bomb in Ukraine in July 2016, during the first week of rehearsals. As Natalia Koliada put it: 'When it [the murder] happened, we knew exactly why we were doing this show' (Koliada, 2017 conference). *Burning Doors* is thus a production staged in Britain by a company from Belarus, about political persecution and violence suffered by human rights activists and journalists in Russia and Ukraine; and it is performed in Russian with English surtitles. As a cultural event, it thereby achieves truly transnational scope, bridging political issues involving Russia, Ukraine, and Belarus for a British audience through the medium of the Russian language – and addressing British issues as well. The urgency of the BFT's campaigns to defend free speech and human rights throughout the world is undiminished, as shown by the events it organized (including one at the House of Commons) to get people to discuss the threat of censorship in Britain, after the highly controversial cancelling of Nadia Latif's *Homegrown*, a play about Islamic radicalization commissioned by the National Youth Theatre (*Burning Doors*, post-show discussion September 2016; Farrington 2015).

The Russian language, and shared political and theatrical values, have allowed playwrights and theatre directors in Russia, Ukraine, and Belarus to maintain a dialogue – where this still seems feasible – in which they address issues of common interest, and to continue to explore the possibilities of drama within a shared framework of creative endeavour. Their festivals and competitions continue to be judged collectively by juries made up of individuals from all three countries. In a situation where aggressive feelings can be whipped up by a single Croatian World Cup player posting a nine-second clip in which he shouts, 'Long Live Ukraine!', provoking loud Russian boos heard by a global audience every time he touched the ball thereafter (Rumsby 2018), the merits of such transnational cultural and theatrical contacts and collaborations become even more apparent. On a personal level, it has been a matter of considerable regret for some Russians and Ukrainians who have worked together in the past that they find it increasingly difficult to establish a geographical space where they can meet and continue to share ideas and projects, against the backdrop of mounting international tensions. On the positive side, however, the transnational dimension of the professional activities of Russian, Ukrainian, and Belarus theatre practitioners in turn opens them out through a variety of channels to wider interactions with European partners, and to emergence on to a world stage.

³ At the time of writing, Oleg Sentsov was nearly two months into a hunger strike in the remote Siberian prison camp in which he was detained.

Works Cited

Barushka, Katerina. 2015. 'After Decades of Russian Dominance, Belarus Begins to Reclaim its Language', *Guardian*, 28 January <https://www.theguardian.com/world/2015/jan/28/-sp-russian-belarus-reclaims-language-belarusian> [accessed 12 July 2018].

Belarus Free Theatre. 2014. *Belarus Free Theatre: New Plays from Central Europe. The VII International Contest of Contemporary Drama* (London: Oberon Books).

——. 2016. *Belarus Free Theatre: Staging a Revolution. New Plays from Eastern Europe. The VIII International Contest of Contemporary Drama* (London: Oberon Books).

Beumers, Birgit, and Mark Lipovetsky. 2009. *Performing Violence: Literary and Theatrical Experiments of New Russian Drama* (Bristol: Intellect).

Davydova, Marina. 2005. *Konets teatral'noi epokhi* (Moscow: OGI).

Dugdale, Sasha. 2009. 'Preface' in Birgit Beumers and Mark Lipovetsky, *Performing Violence: Literary and Theatrical Experiments of New Russian Drama* (Bristol: Intellect), 13–25.

——. 2015. Programme notes for P. Priazhko's *Harvest*, staged at the Ustinov Studio in Bath, March and April.

Faccioli, Erica (ed.). 2016. *I teatri post-sovietici. Ucraina, Bielorussia, Estonia, Lettonia, Lituania* (Rome: Universitalia).

Farrington, Julia. 2015. 'The Arts, the Law and Freedom of Speech', *Guardian*, 7 August <https://www.theguardian.com/stage/2015/aug/07/arts-law-freedom-speech-legal-knowledge-packs-arts-organisations> [accessed 24 July 2018].

Freedman, John. 2014. *Real and Phantom Pains: An Anthology of New Russian Drama* (Washington, DC: New Academia Publishing).

Jones, Alice. 2016. '"I don't feel fear": Pussy Riot's Maria Alyokhina on making her stage debut', 31 August https://inews.co.uk/essentials/i-dont-feel-fear-pussy-riots-maria-alyokhina-making-stage-debut-535154 [accessed 24 July 2018]

Liubimovka. 2015a. 'Nevozmozhno molchat'', 15 September <https://lubimovka.ru/blog/151-nevozmozhno-molchat> [accessed 24 July 2018].

——. 2015b. 'Znat' drug druga, no ne slivat'sia', 17 September <https://lubimovka.ru/blog/160-znat-drug-druga-no-ne-slivatsya> [accessed 24 July 2018].

Ministerstvo kontrkul'tury. 2017. 'Rossiiskie deputaty zashchitiat obshchestvo ot "amoral'nogo iskusstva"' <https://moc.media/ru/1554> [accessed 24 July 2018].

Rudnev, Pavel. 2010. 'Pavel Priazhko. Zakrytaia dver'', *Topos*, 22 June.

Rumsby, Ben. 2018. 'Croatia's Domagoj Vida Could Face FIFA Sanction after Shouting "Glory to Ukraine" after Defeating Russia', *The Telegraph*, 8 July <https://www.telegraph.co.uk/world-cup/2018/07/08/croatias-domagoj-vida-could-face-fifa-sanction-shouting-glory/> [accessed 12 July 2018].

Serebrennikov, Kirill. 2009. 'Foreword' in Birgit Beumers and Mark Lipovetsky, *Performing Violence: Literary and Theatrical Experiments of New Russian Drama* (Bristol: Intellect), 9–11.

Teatr.doc. n.d. <http://www.teatrdoc.ru/> [accessed 24 July 2018].

Vorozhbit, Natalia. 2015. Q&A at the Grad Gallery (London), 14 May (author's notes).

Part III

Cultures Crossing Borders

11

A la russe, mais à l'étranger

Russian Opera Abroad

Philip Ross Bullock

Writing in 1914, Rosa Newmarch, then the leading British authority on Russian music, claimed that Russian opera 'is beyond all question a genuine growth of the Russian soil; it includes the aroma and flavour of its native land "as the wine must taste of its own grapes"' (395). This vision profoundly shaped Western perceptions of Russian music throughout much of the twentieth century (Bullock 2009), yet the nationalist interpretation of the history of Russian music has been extensively challenged by scholars such as Richard Taruskin (1997) and Marina Frolova-Walker (2007). Other scholars have exposed the striking receptivity of Russian music to foreign influences. Studies of Mikhail Glinka by Elena Petrushanskaia (2009) and Daniil Zavlunov (2010, 2014) have replaced an emphasis on his supposed Russianness with a new focus on his debts to Italian models. More generally, Rutger Helmers (2014) has traced a cosmopolitan genealogy within nineteenth-century Russian opera, focusing on works by Glinka, Aleksandr Serov, Petr Chaikovskii, and Nikolai Rimskii-Korsakov. Drawing on such revisionist scholarship, this chapter shifts the focus of attention away from matters of composition and reception, examining instead how the institutional structures of opera performance facilitate the circulation of key works across national borders. This emphasis on the transnational circulation of cultural artefacts opens up new ways of reading Russian opera against a widespread nationalist approach, even when individual works seem organically linked to the Russian cultural consciousness.

Pushkin and Chaikovskii: *Evgenii Onegin* as Cosmopolitan Palimpsest

Chaikovskii's *Evgenii Onegin* (1877–78) epitomizes the perceived 'Russianness' of Russian opera, partly because of the canonicity of its source text (Aleksandr Pushkin's eponymous 'novel in verse', 1823–31, published 1833), and partly because of that text's affectionate portrayal of Russian identity. The novel abounds in evocations of *starina* ('bygone days', 'old-fashioned ways'), which are juxtaposed with the superficiality of the Europeanized culture of the Russian capital, St Petersburg. In particular, Tat'iana enjoys a close relationship with her peasant nanny, who represents a source of folk wisdom and wholesome common sense. The early-nineteenth-century critic Vissarion Belinskii described *Evgenii Onegin* as 'an encyclopaedia of Russian life' (Hoisington 1988: 17–42), and in a famous speech given at the opening of a statue to Pushkin in Moscow in 1880, Fedor Dostoevskii referred to Tat'iana as the personification of Russian womanhood; steadfast and self-sacrificing, Tat'iana becomes the progenitor of a long line of exemplary Russian literary heroines, whose virtues are set against the shortcomings of their male counterparts (Hoisington 1988: 59–63).

Dostoevskii also argued that although Pushkin never left the boundaries of the Russian Empire, his Russianness was forged through a creative dialogue with foreign literatures: 'Undoubtedly, European poets did greatly influence the development of Pushkin's genius and continued to do so throughout his life. Nevertheless, even Pushkin's first poems were more than mere imitations; already the extraordinary originality of his genius shone brightly in them' (cit. Hoisington 1988: 56). Dostoevskii's argument was a nationalist one, rooted in the messianic pan-Slavism of the second half of the nineteenth century, yet it opens up a way of thinking about *Evgenii Onegin* that can simultaneously accommodate its obvious Russianness and its equally obvious receptivity to other literary traditions. Tat'iana reads little but English and French senti-mental novels ('she fell in love with all the fancies / of Richardson and of Rousseau'), and for all her association with the Russian countryside, she writes her confession of love to Onegin in French. Onegin is a parody of Byron and Byronism ('a Muscovite in Harold's dress'), whereas Lenskii ('a poet, and a Kantian sage') evokes German romanticism (Pushkin 1979: 77, 188, 66).

A similar set of arguments can be made about Chaikovskii's opera, whose Russianness is rooted in a series of cosmopolitan encounters. The perceived national identity of the opera is in part the product of the fact that Tat'iana is far more central to its action than Onegin; Tat'iana's famous 'letter scene', for instance, lacks the narrator's ironic commentary about it having been originally written in French. At the same time, *Evgenii Onegin* is the product of a dialogue with a number of other operatic models. Italian opera, for instance, provoked a strong antipathy in Chaikovskii, not least because in the mid-century, Italian works dominated Russian stages and enjoyed great popularity with audiences. In particular, *Evgenii Onegin* was conceived as an antidote to Giuseppe Verdi, whose *Force of Destiny* [La forza del destino, 1861–62] had been premiered in St Petersburg in 1862, and whose *Aida* was explicitly in Chaikovskii's mind in the mid-1870s. As he wrote to his friend, the composer Sergei Taneev, in January 1878:

> I assure you that not for all the riches in the world could I now write an opera with such a plot, since I need people, not puppets; I would willingly tackle any opera in which, even if it lacked any powerful and unexpected effects, I found beings like me, who experience emotions which I too have experienced and can understand. The emotions of an Egyptian princess, of a Pharaoh, of some hysterical Nubian, I cannot know or understand. (Chaikovskii 1959–83: VII 21)

Wagner too provoked a great deal of ambiguity in Chaikovskii. He had heard a number of his works in concert in the 1860s, including during Wagner's visit to Russia in 1863, but his most significant encounter was in the summer of 1876, when he was dispatched to cover the inaugural Bayreuth Festival for a Moscow newspaper. Chaikovskii's reactions are complex, but in broad outline, he recognized Wagner's skill as a composer of orchestral music, yet thoroughly disliked his handling of dramatic form:

> Maybe the *Nibelungen* is a very great work, but it is probable that there has never before been anything more boring and tedious than this rigmarole. The accumulation of the most complicated and refined harmonies, the colourlessness of everything that is sung on the stage, the endlessly long dialogues, the total darkness in the theatre, the absence of anything interesting and poetic in the plot – all of this exhausts one's nerves to the utmost degree. (1959–83: VI 65)

If Verdi and Wagner proved to be negative influences on Chaikovskii, then Mozart and Bizet proved more productive. Chaikovskii adored *Don Giovanni*, and in 1875 translated *The Marriage of Figaro* [Le nozze di Figaro, 1785–86] into Russian for a student performance at the Moscow Conservatory. He wrote to Taneev about a performance of *Figaro* he heard in Paris in 1883: 'My God, how divinely beautiful this music is in its unpretentious simplicity!' (Chaikovskii 1959–83: XII 102).

As for Bizet, Chaikovskii first encountered the score of *Carmen* (1873–74) soon after its premiere in Paris in 1875, and heard the opera for himself whilst in the French capital in early 1876. In early 1878, he wrote to his patron, Nadezhda von Meck: 'It is music without pretension to depth, but so charming in its simplicity, so lively, so sincere rather than invented, that I have almost learnt the whole opera by heart from beginning to end!' (Chaikovskii 1959–83: VI 330). A letter from 1880 sheds yet more light on what Bizet meant to him: 'in truth, I know nothing in music that could more rightly be said to represent that feature which I refer to as *prettiness, le joli* [...] Bizet is an artist who pays tribute to his age and to modernity, yet who is imbued with sincere inspiration' (Chaikovskii 1959–83: IX 197). Chaikovskii's debt to Bizet may even have an unexpectedly Russian dimension, given that Prosper Mérimée, the author of the novella on which *Carmen* was based, was one of the earliest translators of Russian literature into French, and his *Carmen* has a number of affinities with Pushkin's narrative poem *The Gypsies* [Tsygany, written 1824–25, published 1827] (Lowe 1996). Chaikovskii may have been unaware of the connection, yet it suggests that for all their emphasis on national colour, opera plots can be readily transposed across borders, and often encode a transnational sensibility even when composed within a seemingly national framework.

This insight can also be carried over into the study of the reception of Russian opera abroad, where it might at first appear that European and North American interest conforms to a traditional binary opposition between West and East, civilized and barbarian, self and other. Yet, as Tamsin Alexander (2012, 2014, 2015a, 2015b) has argued, the relationship between Russia and the West around the turn of the twentieth century was closer to a continuum and was often negotiated through an overlapping set of national, regional, and local concerns. Institutional factors shaped performance practices too, and Russian operas were often mediated through other national traditions. The first Russian operas to be heard in Britain were Anton Rubinstein's *Demon* (premiered 1875) and Mikhail Glinka's *A Life for the Tsar* [Zhizn' za Tsaria, 1836], yet they were given in Italian rather than Russian (as *Il Demonio* and *La vita per lo Czar*, respectively), partly because performers would have been unfamiliar with Russian, but also because of the status of Italian as a musical lingua franca. When it comes to Chaikovskii, the first of his operas to be performed outside of Russia was not *Evgenii Onegin*, but *The Maid of Orleans* [Orleanskaia deva, written 1878–79, premiered 1881], which was staged in Prague in 1882. Here, generic and national concerns came together since *The Maid of Orleans* conforms more closely to the conventions of French *grand opéra* than any of Chaikovskii's other stage works, and hence was potentially more legible within an international context. Yet regional factors also determined the choice of an opera that dealt with the story of Joan of Arc. In the 1880s, Bohemia was a centre for Slavic patriotism, and a Russian opera dealing with a nation's attempt to overthrow a foreign oppressor accorded with widespread anti-German sentiment.

Evgenii Onegin was soon taken up in the internationalized context of opera performance. Having established itself in theatres throughout the Russian Empire in the 1880s, it was subsequently seen in Prague (1888), Hamburg (1892, conducted by Gustav Mahler), London (1892 and 1906), and New York (1920). Yet as the opera became an accepted part of the international canon, it also found itself carrying the burden of its Russianness. As with other Russian operas, most notably Aleksandr Borodin's *Prince Igor* [Kniaz' Igor', 1869–87], Modest Musorgskii's *Boris Godunov* (1868–69, revised 1871–72) and *Khovanshchina* (1872–81), or the 15 stage works of Rimskii-Korsakov, *Evgenii Onegin*'s production history reveals an overwhelming tendency to treat its evocation of Pushkinian *starina* with loving fidelity. Whilst this practice can certainly be justified by the subject matter of many of these operas, it also reveals a widespread assumption that an opera by a Russian composer must be treated in a manner that accords with its supposed origins.

There has, however, been a tradition of resistance that seeks to situate *Evgenii Onegin* in unexpected contexts and thereby reaccent its significance for contemporary audiences. Although *Evgenii Onegin* has never been subjected to a treatment as radical as Vsevolod Meierkhol'd's 1935 production of Chaikovskii's *Queen of Spades* [Pikovaia dama, 1890], which attempted to bring the opera closer to Pushkin's original short story, Dmitrii Cherniakov's 2006 production for Moscow's Bol'shoi Theatre (also seen in Paris in 2008) trespassed against years of tradition by dispensing with much of the opera's *starina* and imposing an absurdist rather than a psychological reading of the main characters' moral predicaments. It is, however, the German school of *Regietheater* (a tradition that argues for a director's right to propose radically inventive interpretations of stage works that go against the author's intentions) that has come up with new interpretations of *Evgenii Onegin* that challenge both its Russianness and its historical setting. In 2007, the Polish director Krzysztof Warlikowski mounted a production at the Bavarian State Opera in Munich that reinterpreted the opera as an allegory of repressed homosexual desire. Nicknamed 'Brokeback *Onegin*' (in homage to Ang Lee's 2005 film version of Annie Proulx's short story 'Brokeback Mountain'), it proposed an erotic reading of the relationship between Onegin and Lenskii, updated the action to the post-war era, and made use of a chorus of semi-clad cowboys. Criticized by some for imposing a 'narrow' interpretation on the supposedly 'universal' emotions evoked by the score, Warlikowski's approach (evoking, of course, Chaikovskii's own homosexuality) reveals how readily the national contexts of opera can be undone through productions that look elsewhere for inspiration.

Leskov and Shostakovich: Soviet Opera in the World

While Chaikovskii's *Evgenii Onegin* has in the international context been made to embody the Russianness of Russian opera, Dmitrii Shostakovich's *Lady Macbeth of the Mtsensk District* [Ledi Makbet Mtsenskogo uezda] has been turned into an exemplar of an apparently native Soviet tradition. Written between 1930 and 1932, and first performed in 1934, it is based on a short story of the same name by Nikolai Leskov (dating from 1865), whose subject matter is firmly rooted in the reality of Russia's nineteenth-century merchant community. As its Shakespearean name suggests, *Lady Macbeth* is a universal tale of desire and destruction, yet one that takes place in a specific milieu (the 'Mtsensk District'). The eventual fate of *Lady Macbeth* reinforces the sense of its embeddedness in Soviet culture. Stalin attended a performance at Moscow's Bol'shoi Theatre on 26 January 1936 and was supposedly shocked by its amoral depiction of human sexuality and a score which he found cacophonic; two days later, a denunciation of the opera appeared in *Pravda*. Written on the eve of the great purges, *Lady Macbeth* has frequently been interpreted as a turning point in the relationship between Soviet artists and state power.

Yet despite the fact that Leskov's 'Lady Macbeth' is rooted in Russian nineteenth-century provincial life, it is a tale that has significant transnational dimensions too (a 2016 film version by British director William Oldroyd, for instance, adroitly relocates it to a nineteenth-century setting in the north of England). Similarly, although based on a work of nineteenth-century Russian literature, Shostakovich's opera borrows much of its musical language and dramatic argument from a number of contemporary European operas – such as Alban Berg's *Wozzeck* (1914–22) – that were performed in Leningrad in the 1920s (Clark 1995). Moreover, alongside the establishment of a Soviet operatic canon, one of the major tasks of Soviet cultural politics was the creation of a body of works suitable for export. In the 1920s, the state music publishing house entered into a collaborative agreement with Universal Edition in Vienna (Bobrik 2011), and contacts between East and West were further facilitated by bodies such as PresLit (Patterson 2009). Most notably, VOKS (Vsesoiuznoe obshchestvo kul'turnoi sviazi s zagranitsei – the All-Union Society for Cultural Relations with Foreign Countries) coordinated the publication and performance of Soviet works abroad and facilitated exchanges between Soviet and foreign creative artists (David-Fox 2002: Mikkonen & Suutari 2016). As Katerina Clark (2011) has argued, despite the inward turn and emphasis on nationalism that was characteristic of Soviet culture in the 1930s, the Soviet Union still perceived itself as a global power at the vanguard of progressive politics. The promotion of Soviet culture worldwide was one important way of combining politics, ideology, and propaganda, and would become central to cultural policy in the post-Stalin era, when music competitions and the training of virtuoso Soviet performers became a prominent strategy within the geopolitics of the Cold War (Tomoff 2015).

Before it was removed from the repertoire, Shostakovich's *Lady Macbeth* was performed 83 times at Leningrad's Malyi ('Small') Opera Theatre and 94 times at Moscow's Nemirovich-Danchenko Theatre. This success – unprecedented for a contemporary opera by a Soviet composer – was widely reported in the foreign press; the publication of piano scores in English translation in 1935 further served to promote the work's reputation abroad. Yet the international reputation of *Lady Macbeth* was above all the result of performances outside the Soviet Union (Haußmann 2011). Its first foreign performance took place in Cleveland on 31 January 1935 in a Russian-language production that transferred to New York's Metropolitan Opera on 5 February and to Philadelphia on 5 April. The first European performances – at the Royal Opera in Stockholm and the National Theatre in Bratislava – also took place that year. Even after the attack on the opera in *Pravda*, it continued to be performed widely. It was presented at Prague's New German Theatre on 29 January 1936, followed by performances in Zurich and Ljubljana in February. A single concert performance was given (in English) at the Queen's Hall in London on 18 March 1936 (a young Benjamin Britten was in the audience and there are evident affinities between *Lady Macbeth* and his own *Peter Grimes* [1944–45]). A Danish-language version opened in Copenhagen on 10 October 1936, running for 15 performances, and the opera was also heard in Zagreb in May 1937.

Lady Macbeth then fell out of the international repertoire, other than two performances at Venice's La Fenice theatre in September 1947, and a production that opened in Düsseldorf in November 1959. Yet Soviet cultural politics suddenly intervened to rehabilitate the opera. Now titled *Katerina Izmailova* and subjected to a number of revisions to the libretto which downplayed the eroticism of the original, a new version of the opera opened in Moscow on 8 January 1963 (Fay 1995). This edition enjoyed even great worldwide success than the original, with productions in the Soviet Union (Riga, Gor'kii, Kazan', Kiev, Leningrad), the Eastern bloc (Zagreb, Brno, Pécs, Berlin, Dresden, Ruse, Budapest, Poznań, Leipzig, Prague, Ljubljana, Warsaw, Tallinn), and the West (London, Milan, Nice, San Francisco, Vienna, Wiesbaden, New York, Florence, Buenos Aires, Basel, Augsburg, Copenhagen, Aachen, Oslo, Innsbruck). The reputation of this revised version was further cemented by the release of a film version directed by Mikhail Shapiro (1966), which was subtitled into a number of foreign languages and heavily promoted abroad. Yet when it came to Soviet opera, *Katerina Izmailova*'s success abroad was the exception rather than the rule. Kirill Molchanov's *The Dawns Are Quiet Here* [Zori zdes' tikhie, 1972] was a critical disaster when it was performed at New York's Metropolitan Opera in 1975, when socialist realist aesthetics and Cold War politics served as a barrier to Western comprehension (Taruskin 1976). The success of *Katerina Izmailova*, by contrast, can be traced to the fact that not only was it a Soviet opera (and one, moreover, with a dramatic backstory of censorship and artistic persecution) but it also reflected continuities with the nineteenth-century tradition and was hence more legible within an international context of performance and reception.

The interaction between the Soviet and international contexts of Shostakovich's *Ledi Makbet/Katerina Izmailova* changed once again in 1979, when the 'original' version of the opera was published in Hamburg and recorded in London for EMI. Starring Galina Vishnevskaia and conducted by Mstislav Rostropovich, this version derived its cachet and 'authenticity' from the fact that it featured performers who had been forced into exile as a result of their support for Aleksandr Solzhenitsyn (Vishnevskaia had also taken the lead role in Shapiro's film version of the opera). The opera – in its two versions – thus came to embody a distinction between West and East, émigré and Soviet, and even modernism and socialist realism, with the original score representing what many people took to be Shostakovich's uncompromised vision of a radical score that could be championed only outside of the composer's homeland, especially at a time when the Russian avant-garde was much in vogue in the West, but still largely taboo within the Soviet Union itself, at least officially.

Shchedrin and Nabokov: *Lolita* and the Post-Soviet Russian Imaginary

The collapse of the Soviet Union posed almost insuperable problems for the effective functioning of the arts after 1991, not least in the field of opera, which is both financially draining and administratively complex (Quillen 2014). St Petersburg's Mariinskii Theatre, led by its energetic musical director, Valerii Gergiev, coped with such challenges by entering into a number of strategic international collaborations, most notably a high-profile recording contract with the Philips label. Covering the canonical nineteenth-century repertoire from Glinka to Rimskii-Korsakov (and making room for Prokof'ev too), this arrangement effaced the Soviet tradition and positioned the Mariinskii Theatre as the guardian of an imperial legacy that could be readily marketed to foreign audiences, whether through high-profile foreign tours or the promotion of the opera house as an exclusive tourist destination.

But what of contemporary composers and their relationship to Russian opera? Here, two related phenomena stand out: the number of premieres given abroad and the foreign origins of many libretti. In fact, these features reach back into the late Soviet era, when state control of the arts meant that more experimental composers had to look elsewhere for opportunities to have their operas performed. Based on a novel by Boris Vian, Edison Denisov's *The Foam of the Days* [*L'écume des jours*, also translated into English as *Froth on the Daydream*, *Foam of the Daze*, and even *Mood Indigo*, 1977–81], was first performed in Paris in 1986 (its Soviet premiere took place in Perm' in 1989). Dmitrii Smirnov's two operas based on works by William Blake – *Tiriel* [Tiriel', 1983] and *The Lamentations of Thel* [Zhaloby Teli, 1985–86] – were likewise premiered in western Europe in 1989, the first in Freiburg, the second at London's Almeida Festival. The three completed operas of Al'fred Shnitke were all premiered outside of Russia: *Life with an Idiot* [Zhizn' s idiotom, to a libretto by Viktor Erofeev, 1991] in Amsterdam in 1992, *Gesualdo* (1994) in Vienna in 1995, and *Historia von D. Johann Fausten* (1983–94) in Hamburg in 1995. In Amsterdam, Dutch National Opera commissioned two notable modern Russian operas: Aleksandr Knaifel"s *Alice in Wonderland* [Alisa v strane chudes, 1995–99], first staged in 2001, and Aleksandr Raskatov's *Heart of a Dog* [Sobach'e serdste, 2008–9], based on a story by Mikhail Bulgakov, in 2010.

Yet the most singular instance of Russian opera's recent engagement with global culture is Rodion Shchedrin's *Lolita* (1992), premiered in Stockholm in 1994 (Shchedrin 2012: 179–88; Karetnyk 2016). Shchedrin's long and productive career is a fascinating example of how a creative artist can astutely navigate the shifting contexts of cultural politics. His first opera – *Not only Love* [Ne tol'ko liubov', 1961] – is a lyric comedy set on a collective farm that encapsulates the turn towards emotional verisimilitude that was typical of Khrushchev's 'Thaw' after the grandiloquent historicism of the Stalin era. His *Dead Souls* [Mertvye dushi, based on Nikolai Gogol"s novel] of 1976 illustrates the Soviet practice of adapting literary texts for the stage, not least in the more conservative years of the Brezhnev era.

Lolita, however, reinforces the impression that by 1994 the main focus of Russian opera had shifted beyond the geographical boundaries of the Russian Federation. Moreover, the choice of Vladimir Nabokov's infamous English-language novel (1955) attests not just to a more cosmopolitan range of literary influences but also to a particular engagement with Russian culture's own transnational contexts. As an émigré, Nabokov was excluded from the Russian literary canon as it had been interpreted in the Soviet Union; Shchedrin's *Lolita* represents, therefore, a musical response to the novel that reunites both the Soviet and the émigré branches of twentieth-century Russian culture in the post-Soviet era.

Yet it does so through the prism of a text originally written in English and which takes as its subject matter many of the most prominent clichés of post-war American culture. Indeed, it was precisely Western readers' familiarity with *Lolita* that made it such a promising source for the opera's libretto, and there is therefore something paradoxical about the novel being made to stand in for the Russian literary tradition. The work was, moreover, originally commissioned by Rostropovich on behalf of the Paris Opera, which was searching for 'a new opera [...] on a Russian subject, and for its composer to be from Russia' (Shchedrin 2012: 180). However, the opera fell victim to intrigue and innuendo, and was salvaged only by the intervention of the Swedish Royal Opera. At this point, rights issues meant that the opera had to be translated into Swedish for performance, so Nabokov's English-language novel, which Shchedrin had set in the author's own Russian translation, was eventually performed at two removes from its original linguistic context. The opera was not performed in its 'original' Russian until 2003, when it was staged in Perm' (followed by another production in Moscow the following year). A further linguistic transposition was effected in Wiesbaden in 2011, when the opera was performed in German.

What is most striking about Shchedrin's subsequent operatic work is that he has renounced the linguistic polyvalency of *Lolita* and returned to a more stable vision of the Russian literary canon. Premiered in New York in 2002, his concert opera based on Leskov's folkloric odyssey *The Enchanted Wanderer* [Ocharovannyi strannik, 1992] offers something more conventionally 'Russian' than *Lolita*. Thereafter, Shchedrin's operas have returned to Russia itself and propose models for post-Soviet cultural identity that have their roots in pre-revolutionary and even premodern Russia. *Morozova, the Boyar's Wife* [Boiarina Morozova, 2006], first heard at the Moscow Conservatory in 2006, looks back to a key episode in Russian history – the seventeenth-century religious schism in the Russian Orthodox Church that led to the repression of the Old Believers. *The Lefthander* [Levsha, 2012–13] and *A Christmas Tale* [Rozhdestvenskaia skazka, 2015] further develop Shchedrin's interest in the writings of Leskov (in the second case, a translation from the Czech of a fairy tale by Božena Němcová). First heard at St Petersburg's Mariinskii Theatre in 2013 and 2015 respectively, these works suggest – in keeping with political developments more generally – that after a period when a hybrid, transnational configuration of Russian opera was the norm, a more ethnocentric, national vision now looks likely to prevail.

Envoi

Music offers a particularly productive way of analysing the transnational contexts of Russian culture, since it seems to be simultaneously situated at two opposing extremes of the continuum between the global and the local. For some critics (such as Rosa Newmarch or many nineteenth-century nationalists), music represents a powerful vehicle for expressing national sentiment. For other commentators, music – unlike verbal language – constitutes an idealized form of supposedly 'universal' language, able to communicate truths across national and linguistic boundaries without any obvious form of translation. Opera offers a useful modulation of such views, inasmuch as it fuses 'abstract' musical expression with a literary text that requires explicit mediation and even, when performed abroad, some form of translation (indeed, it is tempting to see the composer's score as the first process in interpreting that particular literary text for the audience). Like much Russian music, Russian opera has often been viewed from an exclusively nationalist perspective, both by native critics keen to emphasize its contribution to the formation of national consciousness and by foreign commentators keen to subscribe to a myth of Russian 'otherness'. Yet, as this chapter has argued, by attending to the institutional framework of performance around the globe, it becomes possible to expose a countervailing tradition of reading Russian opera against the grain, thereby revealing the transnational influences that at are work in even the most seemingly straightforward expressions of the national spirit.

Works Cited

Alexander, Tamsin. 2012. 'An "Extraordinary Engagement": A Russian Opera Company in Victorian England' in Anthony Cross (ed.), *A People Passing Rude: British Responses to Russian Culture* (Cambridge: Open Book Publishers), 97–112.

——. 2014. 'Too Russian for British Ears: *La Vita per lo Czar* at Covent Garden, 1887', *Tekst. Kniga. Knigoizdanie*, 2: 30–48.

——. 2015a. 'Tchaikovsky's *Yevgeny Onegin* in Britain, 1892–1906: Slipping between High and Low, Future and Past, East and West', *Musiktheorie*, 3: 223–34.

——. 2015b. 'Decentralising via Russia: Glinka's *A Life for the Tsar* in Nice, 1890', *Cambridge Opera Journal*, 27(1): 35–62.

Bobrik, Olesia. 2011. *Venskoe izdatel'stvo 'Universal Edition' i muzykanty sovetskoi Rossii* (St Petersburg: N. A. Novikov).

Bullock, Philip Ross. 2009. *Rosa Newmarch and Russian Music in Late Nineteenth and Early Twentieth-Century England* (Farnham: Ashgate).

Chaikovskii, P. I. 1959–83. *Polnoe sobranie sochinenii: literaturnye proizvedeniia i perepiska* (Moscow: Gosudarstvennoe muzykal'noe izdatel'stvo).

Clark, Katerina. 1995. *Petersburg: Crucible of Cultural Revolution* (Cambridge, MA and London: Harvard University Press).

——. 2011. *Moscow, the Fourth Rome: Stalinism, Cosmopolitanism, and the Evolution of Soviet Culture, 1931–41* (Cambridge, MA: Harvard University Press).

David-Fox, Michael. 2002. 'From Illusory "Society" to Intellectual "Public": VOKS, International Travel and Party-Intelligentsia Relations in the Interwar Period', *Contemporary European History*, 11(1): 7–32.

Fay, Laurel E. 1995. 'From *Lady Macbeth* to *Katerina*: Shostakovich's Versions and Revisions' in David Fanning (ed.), *Shostakovich Studies* (Cambridge: Cambridge University Press), 160–88.

Frolova-Walker, Marina. 2007. *Russian Music and Nationalism: From Glinka to Stalin* (New Haven, CT: Yale University Press).

Haußmann, Rüdiger. 2011. *Dmitri Schostakowtischs Oper 'Lady Macbeth von Mzensk (Katerina Ismailowa) und ihre Inszenierungen* (Berlin: Ernst Kuhn).

Helmers, Rutger. 2014. *Not Russian Enough? Nationalism and Cosmopolitanism in Nineteenth-Century Russian Opera* (Rochester, NY: University of Rochester Press).

Hoisington, Sonia Stephan (ed. and trans.), 1988. *Russian Views of Pushkin's 'Eugene Onegin'* (Bloomington and Indianapolis, IN: Indiana University Press).

Karetnyk, Bryan. 2016. 'Staging *Lolita* (and "Saving" Humbert): Nabokov, Shchedrin and the Art of Adaption', *Slavonic and East European Review*, 94(4): 601–33.

Lowe, David A. 1996. 'Pushkin and "Carmen"', *19th-Century Music*, 20(1): 72–76.

Mikkonen, Simon, and Pekka Suutari (eds). 2016. *Music, Art and Diplomacy: East-West Cultural Exchanges and the Cold War* (Farnham: Ashgate).

Newmarch, Rosa. 1914. *The Russian Opera* (London: Herbert Jenkins).

Patterson, Ian. 2009. 'The Translation of Soviet Literature: John Rodker and PresLit' in Rebecca Beasley and Philip Ross Bullock (eds), *Russia in Britain, 1880–1940: From Melodrama to Modernism* (Oxford: Oxford University Press), 188–208.

Petrushanskaia, Elena. 2009. *Mikhail Glinka i Italiia: zagadki zhizni i tvorchestva* (Moscow: Klassika-XXI).

Pushkin, Alexander. 1979. *Eugene Onegin*, trans. Charles Johnston (London: Penguin).

Quillen, William. 2014. 'Winning and Losing in Russian New Music Today', *Journal of the American Musicological Society*, 67(2): 487–542.

Shchedrin, Rodion. 2012. *Autobiographical Memories*, trans. Anthony Phillips (Mainz: Schott).

Taruskin, Richard. 1976. 'Molchanov's *The Dawns are Quiet Here*', *Musical Quarterly*, 62(1): 105–15.

——. 1997. *Defining Russia Musically: Historical and Hermeneutical Essays* (Princeton, NJ: Princeton University Press).

Tomoff, Kirill. 2015. *Virtuosi Abroad: Soviet Music and Imperial Competition during the Early Cold War, 1945–1958* (Ithaca, NY: Cornell University Press).

Zavlunov, Daniil. 2010. 'M. I. Glinka's 'A Life for the Tsar' (1836): An Historical and Analytic-Theoretical Study' (unpublished PhD Thesis, Princeton University).

——. 2014. 'Constructing Glinka', *Journal of Musicology*, 31(3): 326–53.

12

On Russian Cinema Going West (and East)

Fedor Bondarchuk's *Stalingrad* and Blockbuster History

Stephen M. Norris

Released in October 2013, Fedor Bondarchuk's blockbuster film *Stalingrad* set box office records in Russia by making $51.8m domestically and $68m in total, making it the highest-grossing film in Russian history (KinoPoisk n.d.). That a Russian film about the Second World War should become the biggest box office success in domestic cinema history is hardly a surprise. The victory over Nazi Germany in what Russians call the Great Patriotic War continues to serve as an anchor for contemporary Russian national identity. Although the cult of the war that once flourished in Brezhnev's USSR dwindled in the late 1980s, since he became president in 2000 Vladimir Putin has overseen its reconstruction (see Wood 2011: 172–200; Norris 2011: 201–29; Tumarkin 1995). Bondarchuk's blockbuster represents an important component to this memory turn: heavily promoted, the film enjoyed immense press coverage and a wide release both at home and abroad.

Yet the story of *Stalingrad* is a deeper, more interesting one than is suggested by just this brief sketch. If we apply transnational perspectives to contextualize the film, we get a richer tale. Film is an inherently transnational phenomenon. Tracking film technology and film reception across national borders gets at the heart of Akira Iriye's basic definition of transnational history as one of 'the study of movements and forces that cut across national borders' (2004: 213). A transnational history of a single film can help us comprehend how Russian cinema has tried to go global with varying degrees of success. Applying this approach – one that centres on the concept of cross-border flows, or how ideas and objects can cut across national boundaries – to Bondarchuk's *Stalingrad* does not downgrade its domestic significance in terms of how it contributed to Putin-era patriotic culture (van der Vleuten 2008: 978). Instead, it enhances our own understanding of how these trends developed by showcasing the entanglements between countries; the relations, circulations, and connections across and through several countries; and the ways that these connections have changed across time (Saunier 2013: 2–4). In a sense, contemporary Russian patriotic culture itself is a product of these transnational forces.

As we shall see, the story of *Stalingrad* told from a transnational perspective allows us to appreciate that concepts such as patriotism and national identity develop from the flow of ideas and technologies across borders (in this case, between Russia, the United States, and China). A transnational study of *Stalingrad* helps us grasp how Russian cinema experienced a revival influenced by ideas derived from Hollywood accompanied with expectations that a new national cinema would finally have an impact in the USA. It reveals, in other words, that the concept of the nation and definitions of patriotism matter in transnational studies, even if it shows that these concepts are often in flux and have unintended consequences. *Stalingrad* was marked for box office success not just in Russia, but in the United States. Instead, because Bondarchuk signed a partnership with Sony Pictures International, it was released and did extremely well in China, paving the way for other Russian films to enter that market.

Act I: Russian Cinema Goes Hollywood, 1998–2008

At the time of its collapse, the Soviet Union was one of the most film-going nations on earth. During the 1960s and 1970s, for example, the average Soviet citizen went to the cinema 20 times per year (Beumers 1999: 871–96). Major studios such as Mosfilm, Lenfilm, and Gorky Film Studio, as well as Republic studios from Odessa to Almaty, combined to put out over 150 films per year. Soviet history was bound up in cinema. Lenin famously declared it the 'most important of the arts'. Pioneering directors such as Sergei Eisenstein and Dziga Vertov helped to make Soviet cinema famous worldwide, whilst Stalinist musical comedies and historical films such as *Chapaev* made film an essential part of Soviet everyday life. Thaw-era films provided audiences with nuanced depictions of the past and present of Soviet life, and Brezhnev-era comedies and dramas brought millions into cinema halls.

When the Soviet system collapsed, so too did its film industry and, to a certain extent, these traditions (see Norris 2012). The state no longer provided subsidies for films, film studios, or cinema halls. Many of these sites transitioned into furniture stores, car washes, and automobile repair shops. By the mid-1990s, Russian cinema had become a shadow of its former self: according to one 1996 study, only one in four Russian citizens went to a film more than once that year. By that time, American films had deluged what remained of the film market. As the post-Soviet economy tanked, the once-vaunted film industry followed it. The few films produced tended to capture the dark mood of the time. Known as *chernukha*, these films, which first appeared in the late 1980s, might best be understood as a 'blackening of Soviet and post-Soviet reality' (Graham 2013). Films in this genre focused on dirty locales, dysfunctional families, casual (and sometimes explicit) violence, cruelty, and rape. *Chernukha* culture played no small part in the cultural malaise that led to the USSR's collapse; it also helped to define the view of the 1990s as a dark, depressing, violent, and chaotic period.

A series of events in 1998 began to turn things around for Russian cinema. The Russian government defaulted on its IMF loans in August, sending the economy into another depression. Just before those events, at an extraordinary meeting in May of the Russian Film-makers' Union, newly elected president Nikita Mikhalkov called on members to put an end to the *chernukha* culture and to make new Russian heroes for new Russians. He was not alone: Daniil Dondurei, editor of the influential journal *The Art of Cinema*, argued that films from the late Soviet and early post-Soviet era had failed their audience, creating a culture of national inferiority. Calling Hollywood a myth-maker par excellence, Dondurei suggested that Russian spectators had become proud of American heroes, for no Russian heroes existed onscreen. Mikhalkov made similar comments, stating that Hollywood had forced the world to recognize American values and heroes through its movies. It was time, he intoned, for Russian movies to create Russian heroes for Russian audiences; it was time for Russian cinema to become the most important of the arts again.

Mikhalkov was not alone. Although far less bombastic, Karen Shakhnazarov sounded similar notes. In 1998, the well-respected director took over as general director at Mosfilm studio. The venerable Soviet institution had fallen on hard times, and Shakhnazarov joked that his immediate goal was to produce a single movie. At the same time, like his colleague Mikhalkov, Shakhnazarov believed *chernukha* had run its course and had contributed to the despondency of the late Soviet and early post-Soviet eras. For Russian cinema to survive, it had to become more 'audience friendly'. Both Mikhalkov and Shakhnazarov agreed on how to meet this goal: Russian cinema had to become more like Hollywood. It needed higher-quality films, more action, more special effects, more stars, uplifting storylines, better PR. The key was to marry these most Hollywood of approaches to 'Russian' content. It worked. By the mid-2000s, Russian films were besting Hollywood blockbusters at the box office. Mikhalkov and Shakhnazarov, who made their own contributions to the renewed Hollywood-style Russian national film culture in *The Barber of Siberia* [Sibirskii tsiriul'nik, 1999] and *A Rider Called Death* [Vsadnik po imeni smert', 2002], were joined by a host of directors, producers, actors, and others who took part in this revitalization project. The successful formula proved to be copying Hollywood-style techniques with explorations of Russian history, Russian culture, and Russian locales. The attitude that summed up this success was best expressed by Konstantin Ernst, the head of Russia's main television broadcaster, Channel One and the major film producer of the post-Soviet revitalization. In an interview, Ernst stated that Russians should be 'eternally grateful to Hollywood' because 'Hollywood forced our lazy, fat Russian moviemakers to make films, to edit them, to make special effects, to talk in a language teenagers understand'. 'We are grateful', he noted, 'but now we will make our cinema ourselves', criticizing what he believed was Hollywood's attempt to 'conquer' Russia and 'convert us' (*Seance* 2006).

Timur Bekmambetov, whose films were produced by Ernst's Channel One, proved to be the most successful first practitioner of the new Russian blockbuster formula. Bekmambetov's *Night Watch* [Nochnoi dozor, 2004] was the first post-Communist Russian film to win the box office; its 'defeat' of *Lord of the Rings: The Fellowship of the Ring* made victory even sweeter. The sequel, *Day Watch* [Dnevnoi dozor], also directed by Bekmambetov, shattered records in 2006, earning $32m domestically and $38m overall. Both films were released in the United States amidst hopes that, because of their special effects and storylines, they would make a dent in the American market. Neither did so. Bekmambetov beat his own box office record with his sequel to the Soviet classic, *Irony of Fate: Continuation* [Ironiia sud'by. Prodolzhenie, 2007], which earned $50m in Russia and $55.6m overall. Bekmambetov's Russian blockbusters may not have impacted American cinemas, but he initially ended up making a mark there: he moved to Hollywood and made *Wanted* (2008), which placed second in the world box office after *WALL-E*, setting records in Russia and South Korea (his next two Hollywood films – 2012's *Abraham Lincoln, Vampire Hunter* and 2016's *Ben-Hur*, did not do as well at the box office).

Between the two *Watch* films, Fedor Bondarchuk scored a massive hit with his Afghan War blockbuster, *Ninth Company* [9-aia rota]. In 2005, it surpassed *Night Watch*, earning $25m domestically (*Day Watch* would beat it – one memorable scene in that sequel featured a car blasting through a *Ninth Company* billboard). The son of Sergei Bondarchuk, the Academy Award-winning Soviet director, and Irina Skobtseva, the Soviet actress who played Hélène in Bondarchuk's *War and Peace* [Voina i mir, 1966–67], Fedor studied at VGIK (the All-Russian State University of Cinematography) under Iurii Ozerov. While Fedor was still Ozerov's student, he acted in Ozerov's 1990 film, *Stalingrad*, playing a sniper named Ivan. After the collapse, Fedor initially made a name for himself directing music videos (he teamed up with Nikita Mikhalkov's son, Stepan). Fedor also continued acting, gaining critical acclaim for his portrayal of Prince Myshkin in 2002's *Down House* [Daun Khaus], an adaptation of Dostoevskii's *The Idiot* [Idiot, 1868–69]. *Ninth Company* was Fedor's debut as director: in addition to its box office success, the film was critically acclaimed, receiving both the Nika and Golden Eagle for Best Picture (the Russian equivalents of the Oscar and Golden Globe).

Ninth Company is a perfect example of the Russian turn to Hollywood (see Norris 2012: 143–66). Based on the exploits of the Ninth Company of the 345th Guards Airborne Unit in Afghanistan but adapted for dramatic effect, Bondarchuk's film attempted to remember and to memorialize the last generation of Soviet soldiers who fought in that war. In meeting these professed aims, Bondarchuk also employed a big budget, a huge PR campaign, and Hollywood-style special effects. The film itself, as many critics in Russia and the West noted, drew openly on American Vietnam films, most notably Stanley Kubrick's 1987 *Full Metal Jacket*. Bondarchuk understood the domestic, patriotic elements to his film, and held a special screening for veterans of the Afghan War and for Vladimir Putin: afterwards, the Russian president praised the film for scoring a 'direct hit on the soul'. While many debated the film's borrowing from Hollywood and pondered the meanings of the patriotic culture conveyed onscreen, few questioned the overall impact of the film and how it captured the mid-2000s desire to revitalize Russian cinema. Putin, for his part, declared Russian film 'reborn' after he saw *Ninth Company*. Afterwards, Bondarchuk would go on to direct the two-part sci-fi epic, *The Inhabited Island* [Obitaemyi ostrov, 2008], which also triumphed at the box office.

The period between 1998 and 2008 was not the first time Russian cinema had turned to or away from Hollywood. Throughout its 100-year history, Russian and Soviet directors had engaged in an intense dialogue with Hollywood movies. The early film pioneers such as Eisenstein wanted to create a 'Soviet' cinema based on montage theory and practice that would challenge Hollywood; Soviet audiences, however, mostly preferred Douglas Fairbanks and Mary Pickford. Eisenstein's co-director Grigorii Aleksandrov went to Hollywood in 1930 and, inspired by what he saw, developed his smash musical comedies of the 1930s. After the Second World War, film served as a weapon in the cultural Cold War: movie exchanges between the two superpowers served as opportunities to promote values, histories, and cultures. This cultural competition, however, was largely one-sided: Soviet cinema, as a recent history illustrates, 'spent a lot of time reacting to what the American government and American cinema were saying about the USSR' while Hollywood 'spent little time denouncing Soviet propaganda' (Shaw and Youngblood 2010: 217). The values promoted by Hollywood thus

Fig. 12.1. Official Russian poster for *Stalingrad*,
dir. Fedor Bondarchuk, 2013.
Reproduced with permission from Art Pictures Studio.

appeared to be 'natural', while Soviet values had to be defended, making them seem artificial.

The rise of the new Russian blockbuster, however, took place in a changed economic landscape, one where Russian producers had the money to fund big-budget films. It was also widely reported, generating a host of newspaper pieces, journal articles, and television commentaries. Shakhnazarov thought the new Russian *blokbaster* – yes, it even generated a Russian word – was necessary, but warned that it would be successful only if its content was 'Russian', not 'American': the Russian *blokbaster* had to 'not only borrow forms, to master technologies, and to develop new habits, they also have to introduce something of our national culture'. Critics despaired that the adoption of this idea would destroy true 'Russian' cinema; the director Vadim Abdrashitov lamented that Russian blockbusters would become 'our contribution to the worldwide process of cinema-hamburgerization' (cit. Norris 2012: 12–14).

The decision to go Hollywood, to turn West in order to 'save' Russian cinema, becomes clearer when viewing it through this transnational framework. Fedor Bondarchuk made this turn and his *Stalingrad* represents an important moment in it. It was the first Russian film shot in IMAX 3D and many, including Bondarchuk himself, hoped that Russian films would from now on out-Hollywood Hollywood.

Act II: *Stalingrad* as Transnational Cinema Project

One key component in the decision to turn to Hollywood techniques was the influence, or at least perceived influence, of American films about the Second World War. More specifically, when Steven Spielberg's *Saving Private Ryan* debuted in Russia in October 1998, several prominent voices in the Russian film world grumbled about it. Shakhnazarov cited Spielberg's film as the motivating factor for his formula of borrowing Hollywood techniques and adding 'Russian' content, complaining that 'it was obvious we needed such a film [a Second World War epic]' in order to combat 'the American films with their own evaluation of the war constantly thrust upon us'. When Mosfilm bankrolled Nikolai Lebedev's 2002 hit *Star* [Zvezda], initiating a wave of feature films and television serials about the 'Great Patriotic' that has not abated, Shakhnazarov expanded:

> In recent decades there has formed some kind of atmosphere – actually it's not clear any more who won the war. I know that in Europe people believe from an early age that the Americans won the war. But the most amazing thing is that even in our country, our young people, deluged by American film productions, which the Americans do very

well, seem to have the notion that the victory was not our achievement
at all. ('Interv'iu' 2002)

Just as the turn to the *blokbaster* resulted from a perceived influence of
American films, alongside the deleterious effects of *chernukha* on young
Russians, so too did the turn to war films result from similar beliefs. In both
cases, Hollywood was cited as shorthand for the need to rebuild national
culture, particularly among young people.

Saving Private Ryan touched a nerve not just because it seemingly gave
all the credit for victory to the Americans. Its seriousness, its reverence, and
its treatment of the war as sacred, seemed to infringe upon the sacredness of
the Great Patriotic War in Russia. In a 1999 review for *Art of Cinema*, Igor'
Mantsev noted that Spielberg's film flew in the face of recent American war
films, which tended to treat both the Second World War and the Korean
War as absurd or disgusting; instead, he wrote, *Ryan* is a 'serious film', one
where 'Spielberg, like the masters of the Soviet school, perceive the war as
the will of the gods, as super-personal action, a mystery, as an instrument of
justice' (Mantsev 1999). The framing at the beginning and end of Spielberg's
film means that 'Power and the State' are the 'all-powerful gods' to which the
characters make their sacrifices, an all-too-Soviet view. In a sense, Mantsev
concluded, Spielberg constructed a 'contemporary myth', and he compared its
abstract idealism of sacrifice for the American nation to Soviet classics such
as Sergei Bondarchuk's 1974 *They Fought for their Motherland* [Oni srazhalis'
za Rodinu, 1999].

When *Star* debuted in 2002, Russian audiences and critics interpreted it
as a direct response to Spielberg. Critic Ekaterina Barabash was one of many
who called it 'necessary' and 'our accurate response to *Private Ryan, The Thin
Red Line, Pearl Harbor*, etc.' (Barabash 2002). In *Art of Cinema*, Elena Stishova
reviewed *Star* as a film best understood as a 'reaction of our collective soul
to the Hollywood expansion into the forbidden territory of national memory
about the sacredness of our war' (Stishova 2002). After years of Hollywood
cinematic salvos within Russian movie houses, she concluded, *Star* offered a
chance for 'revenge', which also came after years of Russian self-abasement on
screen. *Star's* restoration of national values provided audiences with a sense
of pride. Over the course of the decade, as more and more films and serials
saturated Russian screens, regardless of what critics and audiences thought
about the artistic merits of these films, the general consensus was that 'our'
victory had been restored to 'us' through cinema. The impact of American
films – or at least the debates about their impact – helped to generate films
that bolstered domestic patriotism, an indication of how transnational flows
often serve to revitalize the nation.

Fedor Bondarchuk's *Stalingrad* should be understood within this transnational framework. From 2002 through 2013 (and, for that matter, through 2018, as I write these words), innumerable films about the Great Patriotic War have sought to restore a sense of pride and of patriotism to Russian culture. *Stalingrad* represents the apex of this trend; not only did it shatter box office records, easily besting Hollywood offerings in October 2013, it also 'defeated' Hollywood at its own game, becoming the first Russian IMAX 3D movie. At the same time, as a result of the competition that the 'Russian blockbuster' debate had initiated, many in the Russian film industry hoped that *Stalingrad* would make an impact in Hollywood itself, not just defeat Hollywood films at the domestic box office.

Given the way *Saving Private Ryan* was hotly debated in Russia, the framing of Bondarchuk's epic makes a little more sense. Spielberg's film begins and ends in the present, at the American cemetery in Normandy, where an elderly James Ryan visits the graves of his fallen comrades. Over the course of the film, we learn that Ryan has survived in part by government order (the president commands his rescue because of the deaths of his brothers, a plot derived from the real-life Sullivan brothers), in part by luck, in part through the sacrifice of his fellow soldiers. As he dies, Captain John Miller (played by Tom Hanks) tells Ryan that he should earn his survival; earlier, Miller and his squad suggested Ryan better invent something useful in order to justify the gift of being rescued. At Miller's grave, Ryan asks his wife whether he has earned his survival. These scenes, which bracket the film, provide its interpretative framework: most reviewers saw them, along with the American flag that waves during them, as Spielberg's attempt to honour the patriotic sacrifices Americans made in the Second World War and the heavy burden of guilt placed on those that survived.

Stalingrad is also framed from the present day. It opens in March 2011, after the earthquake and tsunami that devastated Japan. A plane carrying foreign aid workers lands in Japan; it contains a Russian doctor who has come to help out. He is directed towards five people trapped in the rubble; they are Germans and he speaks to them in their language as they are rescued. One of the Germans, Nina, laments that her father has died, to which the doctor replies that he had five fathers and they all died. When Nina expresses disbelief, the Russian begins to tell her the tale of how he had five dads. It is a story, as the narrator recounts at the end, of those 'who gave their lives for the freedom of millions of people on earth'. The narrator, conceived during the Battle of Stalingrad and given the name Sergei, has carried this Russian gene of willingness to sacrifice oneself for the greater good into the 2011 Japanese crisis. He has earned the gift of survival. Take that, Private Ryan!

Built upon this frame, *Stalingrad* follows two basic stories. The first explores the last remaining resident of one of Stalingrad's apartment complexes, 19-year-old Katia, who has refused to leave. She interacts with five soldiers defending the building: they will become the 'five fathers' of her baby. Much like the platoon in *Saving Private Ryan* (and, for that matter, a common trope in both American and Soviet films about the war), the men embody different types who came to the city to defend it. Gromov, the captain (and therefore the Captain Miller/Tom Hanks character), is a salt-of-the-earth hero who has witnessed too much death already but who is steadfast in preserving his honour as a professional soldier. Poliakov, nicknamed 'Angel', is older than the captain and is defined by his devout Orthodox belief. Sasha Nikiforov, the third, was a cultured opera singer before the war but has become a cold-blooded killer. Chvanov is a villager who is also a sharpshooter-turned-sniper with an axe to grind against the Germans. Sergei Astakhov (played by Bondarchuk's son, Sergei) is nicknamed 'sissy' because he failed in an earlier mission. This part of the plot follows their heroic actions to defend the house and, with it, Katia; they are clear that she represents the 'motherland', which does not automatically include Stalin (thus challenging the notion that soldiers fought for both). All five die, but not before impregnating Katia and her son with their heroism: the biological father, as the film reveals, is Sergei.

The second story focuses on the German enemies of the five Russian soldiers, in particular on Captain Kahn (played by Thomas Kretschmann). Here, too, *Stalingrad* engages with a Hollywood film that received significant press coverage in Russia: Jean-Jacques Annaud's 2001 French-American co-production about snipers in the battle for Stalingrad, *Enemy at the Gates*. Featuring a fictionalized version of the Soviet marksman Vasilii Zaitsev (played by Jude Law) engaged in combat with a purely fictional German sniper Erwin König (Ed Harris), Annaud's film presents both sides as victimized by their totalitarian systems. The film also featured so-called 'blocking units' [zagradotriad], Soviet troops charged with firing at anyone who retreated from battle. These units appeared after Stalin issued his infamous order no. 227 in July 1942, which became famous for its line 'not one step back!' The prominent film critic Viktor Matizen, writing in *The Art of Cinema* (2001), pointed out that *Enemy at the Gates* contained visually striking scenes reminiscent of *Saving Private Ryan* while also being the first film screened in Russia to reference Stalin's infamous order. Matizen praised it, while other critics disagreed about whether or not the plot was 'too Hollywood' for a film about Russia's war.

Bondarchuk's second story in *Stalingrad* responds to these issues. Kahn has raped a Russian woman, Masha, but also sees himself in part as her

Fig. 12.2. The city in ruins, *Stalingrad.*
Reproduced with permission from Art Pictures Studio.

protector from other traumas. He tells her that the war, and the Soviet enemy, has turned him from a soldier into a beast. Eventually the two come to love each other and Kahn promises he will save Masha once the battle is won. With the exception of a stereotypical colonel who is characterized as a unrepentant beast, most of the German soldiers are depicted as human counterparts to the Soviets, much like *Enemy at the Gates*. In this sense, Bondarchuk's film also follows changes first introduced in post-Soviet movies that followed *Star*, such as Aleksei German Jr.'s *Last Train* [Poslednii poezd, 2003] and Mikhail Segal's *Franz + Polina* [2008], which both cast Germans more sympathetically than in Soviet-era films.

What made Bondarchuk's *Stalingrad* stand out, as most critics and viewers noted, were the special effects used to render the city and the battle for it. In an otherwise negative review, one prominent film critic wrote that 'the battle scenes are not only cruel, but beautiful: the director relishes them' (Gladil'shchikov 2013). Another critic, who praised the film, noted that Bondarchuk's use of the 3D IMAX format created a world onscreen that helped spectators enter it (Tsyrkin 2013; Kostetskaya 2016: 1–15). We can see the city smoulder and in ruins; we run through the claustrophobic spaces in which the battle occurs as ashes fall around us; we see missiles fall on the city from the point of view of the missile itself; we can gaze from above and through holes in buildings at the destruction war brings: through state-of-the-art computer technology, Bondarchuk turns Stalingrad into a mythic space.

Vladimir Medinskii, the minister of culture, declared *Stalingrad* to be a 'socially meaningful blockbuster', one that combined high-quality effects with high levels of patriotism (cit. Roth 2013). Bondarchuk also stated in an interview that he 'went to Vladimir Putin [Ia prishel k Vladimiru Putinu]'

Fig. 12.3. The battle seen through a destroyed building, *Stalingrad.*
Reproduced with permission from Art Pictures Studio.

and told him his plans about the film and its proposed budget. Bondarchuk explained that the visit was needed because 'we planned to make a film on a theme sacred for our country, using the latest Hollywood technology' and knew therefore 'how it might be received by conservative parts of our society' (cit. Iusipova 2013). He received the funds and Putin's blessing. In one review, again in *The Art of Cinema*, Elena Stishova, while criticizing the over-the-top patriotism of the movie, encouraged potential spectators to 'forget all the movies about the Great Patriotic' they know and to 'start with a clean slate, free of stereotypes and mythologies' before seeing *Stalingrad* (Stishova 2013). In these and other pronouncements, Bondarchuk had helped to slay the beasts of Private Ryan, Jude Law, and Soviet war myths all at once.

As an addendum to this engagement with Hollywood war films, the Russian Wikipedia entry for *Spasti riadovogo Raiana* (as of this writing anyway) erroneously claims that Spielberg borrowed the story from a Soviet cinematic source: Iurii Ozerov's ponderous Brezhnev-era epic *Liberation* recounted the story of the four Stepanov brothers, three of whom died in the war. Their history was used in the 1989 film *Stalingrad*, which 'was attended by American and British actors and film-makers'. Regardless of this rather tendentious connection, Russian Wikipedia is clear: 'In general, there were many similar cases [of brothers dying], but on the Soviet front, where losses were at least double, the probability of such incidents was higher than on the Western front' (Wikipedia n.d.).[1]

---

[1] Here Wikipedia is wrong: Ozerov's film was from 1990, not 1989, and the Stepanov brothers, of whom there were eight, all died in the war.

Act III: Production Companies, IMAX, and Transnational Reception

Of course, the Holy Grail in these transnational skirmishes would be for a Hollywood-style Russian blockbuster to win the American box office. Konstantin Ernst put high hopes on Timur Bekmambetov's *Watch* films, but both achieved only modest success in their limited American releases. Bekmambetov did become the first Russian director to do well at the worldwide box office in 2008, but that came with his English-language film *Wanted*, which starred Angelina Jolie and James McAvoy.

Similar hopes were placed on *Stalingrad*. Bondarchuk founded his own production company, Art Pictures Studio, in 1992, and reorganized it after the success of *Ninth Company*. With *Stalingrad*, he also entered into a partnership with Sony Pictures and Columbia Pictures in order to get a wide release for the film. Once again, the high hopes placed on a Russian film to deliver box office gold in Hollywood did not meet reality; foreign films, it seems, will always be foreign in the USA.

That being said, *Stalingrad* received unusual coverage for a Russian film in the North American press. *Rotten Tomatoes* did not certify it fresh (they rated it 49% based on the critical response), but did link to 70 reviews. Liam Lacey of Canada's *Globe and Mail* called it 'a bizarre concoction, part Putin-era patriotic chest thumping and part creaky war melodrama, all set in a superbly recreated ruined city', while also highlighting 'the awkward Japanese bookends to the film' (Lacey 2014). Chris Nashawaty of *Entertainment Weekly* liked it a little more, even though he characterized it as 'pretty much your standard band-of-brothers narrative, with each soldier defined by one specific character trait (the sniper with ice in his veins, the quiet killer who was an opera tenor before hell came to town, the German with an unexpected human streak)' (Nashawaty 2014). Most reviewers concurred with these assessments: in North America, *Stalingrad* seemed like a fairly ordinary Hollywood war film.

Interestingly, and perhaps appropriately, Russian film critics came to similar conclusions. Kinopoisk, a central website devoted to cinema that acts as a Russian Rotten Tomatoes of sorts, linked to 59 critical reviews, 61% of them positive. The site also saw more than 64,000 people give it an average rating of 5.7/10, while 549 spectators posted reviews, 51% of them positive (KinoPoisk n.d.).[2] Viktor Matizen (2013), president of the Russian Film Critics Guild, who liked *Enemy at the Gates*, did not like Bondarchuk's film, citing its poor screenplay, its attempt to make a present-day statement, and its unpersuasive, unrealistic plot points inside of Stalingrad. Matizen noted that *Stalingrad* also included the 'not one step back' order, the same one he referenced in his praise

---

[2] The statistics are accurate as of 17 May 2017.

of Annaud's 2001 film, but this time considered its inclusion blasé. In the end, he praised the look of Stalingrad rendered onscreen as its most impressive achievement. Iurii Gladil'shchikov was a little more critical, calling his overall impressions of the film 'strange' [strannye]. Among the strange parts he listed were the 'Immaculate Conception' element to the plot, the 'fairy tale' aspect to the military battle itself, its 'ultra-contemporary' vision combined with its 'old-fashioned' patriotic appeals with their forced reliance on Orthodoxy, and its overall messiness (Gladil'shchikov 2013).

The film did do well, however, in China, where nearly 2 million spectators saw it. It made $8.65m in its opening weekend, becoming the first non-Chinese, non-Hollywood film ever to do so (Kinopoisk n.d.). The Chinese critical reception, however, sounded similar notes. One reviewer noted that it abandoned traditional narrative structures – citing the beginning and end – to tell a human story; the experience was like watching a 'dynamic oil painting'. The only hesitation, many Chinese critics noted, sounding like American audiences, was that the subtitles and Russian names might confuse spectators. The *Beijing Youth Daily*, by contrast, reviewed it negatively, describing it as a Russian-American co-production and noting that Chinese audiences wanted to drink a little Russian vodka, but got Coca-Cola instead (Xiao 2013). The review concluded that the film had its moving scenes, but represented a Hollywood mode of storytelling packed with Russian historical themes and values.

Stalingrad did leave some footprints, however. The film apparently attracted middle-aged Chinese spectators, and one was quoted in the English-language daily paper *Global Times* stating, 'I was greatly impressed by the authentic, horrifying, touching scenes in the film' (*Global Times* 2013). The same paper covered the opening of the film, as well as linking its Chinese success to the better relations between China and Russia, culminating in two trips to Russia by Chinese President Xi Jinping. The use of 3D IMAX technology in order to draw spectators into the city depicted onscreen, it seems, could work across national boundaries.

Stalingrad illustrates how the transnational flow between Hollywood and Russia still mostly travels one way.[3] Hollywood-like Russian films, however, can now travel successfully to China: *Stalingrad*'s success helped to smooth the path towards more cinematic cooperation between the two nations, eventually producing a 2015 agreement between Central Partnership in Russia and the China Film Group to distribute more films. Subsequent partnerships were signed between China's Shanghai Media and Russia's

---

[3] The exception would be the relative success of art-house Russian films (Andrei Zviagintsev's, for example) among American cinephiles.

Gazprom Media and through the creation of a China-Russia Media Exchange Year in 2016. The transnational story of *Stalingrad* – one focusing on cross-border flows between film – also illustrates how the nation still matters in transnational approaches. Bondarchuk's film, created as part of a wave of Russian blockbusters that borrowed from Hollywood techniques appeared with an ambition to conquer American box offices. Instead, it mostly served as a vehicle to strengthen national imaginings in Russia by forming a key component of the increasing focus on patriotism as a national idea during Putin's second tenure as president. Bondarchuk's business arrangement with Sony, meanwhile, created an unexpected opening across another border, resulting in two-way cinematic exchanges.

Works Cited

Barabash, Ekaterina. 2002. 'Otdykhajte spokoino, Riadovoi Raian', *film.ru*, 12 April <https://www.film.ru/articles/otdyhayte-spokoyno-ryadovoy-rayan> [accessed 16 October 2019].

Beumers, Birgit. 1999. 'Cinemarket, or the Russian Film Industry in "Mission Possible"', *Europe–Asia Studies*, 51(5): 871–96.

Gladil'shchikov, Iurii. 2013. 'Fedor Bondarchuk i voina mirov', *Moskovskie novosti*, 15 October <http://www.mn.ru/blogs/blog_cinemagladil/88340> [accessed 21 August 2018].

Global Times. 2013. '*Stalingrad* Tops Box Office', 6 November <http://www.globaltimes.cn/content/822970.shtml> [accessed 21 August 2018].

Graham, Seth. 2013. 'Tales of Grim', *The Calvert Journal*, 18 January <http://www.calvertjournal.com/opinion/show/57/chernukha-little-vera-cargo-200> [accessed 21 August 2018].

'Interv'iu s K. Shakhnazarovym', 2002. Included as an extra on Ruscico DVD edition of *Zvezda* [Star], directed by Nikolai Lebedev.

Iriye, Akira. 2004. 'Transnational History', *Contemporary European History*, 13(2): 211–22.

Iusipova, Larisa. 2013. 'Spasibo Putinu za "Stalingrad"', *Izvestiia*, 28 October <http://izvestia.ru/news/559639> [accessed 21 August 2018].

KinoPoisk: *Stalingrad*. n.d. <https://www.kinopoisk.ru/film/stalingrad-2013-468196/> [accessed 4 October 2018].

Kostetskaya, Anastasia. 2016. 'Stalingrad Re-Imagined as Mythical Chronotope: Fedor Bondarchuk's *Stalingrad* in IMAX 3D', *Studies in Russian and Soviet Cinema*, 10(1): 1–15.

Lacey, Liam. 2014. '*Stalingrad*: A Bloody Battle Becomes a Bizarre Concoction', *The Globe and Mail*, 28 February <http://www.theglobeandmail.com/arts/film/film-reviews/stalingrad-a-bloody-battle-becomes-a-bizarre-concoction/article17138067/> [accessed 21 August 2018].

Mantsev, Igor'. 1999. 'Tridtsat' tri neschast'ia', *Iskusstvo kino*, 1 <http://kinoart.ru/archive/1999/01/n1-article4> [accessed 21 August 2018].

Matizen, Viktor. 2001. 'Korolevskaia okhota na Zaitseva', *Iskusstvo kino*, 7 <http://kinoart.ru/archive/2001/07/n7-article9> [accessed 21 August 2018].

——. 2013. 'Dom bez fundamenta', *Novye izvestiia*, 16 October <http://www.newizv.ru/culture/2013-10-16/190766-dom-bez-fundamenta.html> [accessed 21 August 2018].

Nashawaty, Chris. 2014. 'Stalingrad', *Entertainment Weekly*, 8 March <http://ew.com/article/2014/03/08/stalingrad-movie/> [accessed 21 August 2018].

Norris, Stephen M. 2011. 'Memory for Sale: Victory Day 2010 and Russian Remembrance', *Soviet and Post-Soviet Review*, 38(2): 201–29.

——. 2012. *Blockbuster History in the New Russia: Movies, Memory, Patriotism* (Bloomington, IN: Indiana University Press).

Roth, Andrew. 2013. 'Russia's "Stalingrad" Is a Hit on Screen', *New York Times*, 11 November <http://www.nytimes.com/2013/11/12/arts/international/russias-stalingrad-is-a-hit-on-screen.html?_r=0> [accessed 21 August 2018].

Saunier, Pierre-Yves. 2013. *Transnational History* (New York: Palgrave Macmillan).

Seance. 2006. 'Sobesednik: Konstantin Ernst', 29/30 <http://seance.ru/n/29-30/portret-konstantin-ernst/sobesednik-konstantin-ernst/> [accessed 21 August 2018].

Shaw, Tony, and Denise Youngblood. 2010. *Cinematic Cold War: The American and Soviet Struggle for Hearts and Minds* (Lawrence, KS: University Press of Kansas).

Stishova, Elena. 2002. 'Odinochestvo zvezdy', *Iskusstvo kino*, 8 <http://kinoart.ru/archive/2002/08/n8-article3> [accessed 21 August 2018].

——. 2013. 'Mne ne bol'no', *Iskusstvo kino*, 4 October <http://kinoart.ru/blogs/mne-ne-bolno> [accessed 21 August 2018].

Tsyrkin, Nina. 2013. 'Kak nevestu rodinu liubim', *Iskusstvo kino*, 9 October <http://kinoart.ru/blogs/kak-nevestu-rodinu-my-lyubim> [accessed 21 August 2018].

Tumarkin, Nina. 1995. *The Living and the Dead: The Rise and Fall of the Cult of World War II in Russia* (New York: Basic Books).

Van der Vleuten, Erik. 2008. 'Toward a Transnational History of Technology: Meanings, Promises, Pitfalls', *Technology and Culture*, 49(4): 974–94.

Wikipedia. n.d. 'Spasti riadovogo Raiana' <https://ru.wikipedia.org/wiki/Спасти_рядового_Райана> [accessed 4 October 2018].

Wood, Elizabeth. 2011. 'Performing Memory: Vladimir Putin and the Celebration of World War II in Russia', *Soviet and Post-Soviet Review*, 38(2): 172–200.

Xiao, Yang. 2013. '*Stalingrad*: Vodka with Cola', *Beijing Youth Daily*, 4 November <http://ent.sina.com.cn/r/m/2013-11-04/13434036275.shtml> [accessed 4 November 2018].

13

Queer Transnational Encounters in Russian Literature

Gender, Sexuality, and National Identity

Connor Doak

In 2006, Iurii Luzhkov, then Mayor of Moscow, banned a proposed Gay Pride parade in Russia's capital city. Justifying his decision, he called homosexuality 'unnatural' and declared that 'such activities were more suited to European countries, more "advanced" [prodvinutykh] on this issue than Russia' (cit. Kovaleva 2006), thereby pinning Russian national identity to a supposedly 'natural' heterosexuality, in opposition to a decadent and gay-friendly Europe. Luzhkov's decision not only caused disappointment among local lesbian, gay, bisexual, and transgender (LGBT) communities in Russia, but also attracted international condemnation from Western human rights groups and activists. In the decade that followed, tensions have grown as gay rights have become a new fault line in relations between Russia and the West. While Western countries increasingly embrace pro-gay policies such as anti-discrimination laws and same-sex marriage, Russia has become more restrictive. A key turning point was Russia's adoption of a law in 2013 that criminalized 'the propaganda of non-traditional sexual relations among minors' (Rossiiskaia Federatsiia 2013). Dubbed the 'anti-gay law' in the West, the law was condemned internationally, and the fallout overshadowed international sporting and cultural events, such as the Sochi Winter Olympics of 2014, when gay rights activists both inside and outside Russia held protests against the law.[1] The conflict has also played out in the international legal

I would like to thank Brian Baer, Katherine Bowers, Andy Byford, Vitaly Chernetsky, Tatiana Filimonova, Stephen Hutchings, and Oliver Taslic for their thoughtful feedback on a draft version of this chapter.

[1] For background on how the conflict over LGBT rights played out in the case of the Sochi Olympics, see Edinborg (2017: 132–34) and Sykes (2017). See also Baker (2017)

arena, with the European Court of Human Rights (ECHR) finding the law discriminatory in 2017 and ordering Russia to pay damages to the plaintiffs who brought the case against the state. The Russian government rejected the ruling.[2]

The growing rift between Russia and the West over LGBT rights is an issue that cuts across politics, society, and culture. As such, it has been addressed by scholars in multiple fields. Historians have located the issue within a broader tradition of Russian homophobia: Dan Healey suggests the roots of modern Russian homophobia lie in Stalinism and its surveillance state (2018: 158), though he also points out that, ironically enough, in the early modern period, western European travellers often critiqued the Russians for their leniency towards homosexuality (1999: 39–43). International relations (IR) scholars have developed a subfield of Queer IR, drawing attention to how gender and sexuality – both overtly and covertly – have become a battle-ground for sovereign states (Richter-Montpetit 2018). Queer IR, moreover, also recognizes how states cast themselves in gendered and sexualized roles when interacting with one another, as Cynthia Weber (1999) has shown.[3] While western European states see themselves as liberal champions of sexual minorities around the globe, Russia has cast itself as 'the saviour of European civilization' (Moss 2017: 195), styling itself as the last bastion of 'traditional' gender norms and sexuality. Although few Western scholars are sympathetic to Russia's anti-gay law, some are troubled by the self-congratulatory attitude of certain Western activists and leaders who imagine the rift as a conflict between a liberal, enlightened West and a benighted Russia, a simplified picture that erases the significant divisions *within* the West and Russia, as well as the West's own – still recent – history of homophobia. Jasbir Puar coined the term homonationalism to critique what she sees the use of liberal

---

on the sexual politics of the Eurovision Song Contest. Gessen and Huff-Hannon (2014) provide a collection of testimonies from gay, lesbian, and bisexual Russians about how their lives were affected by the anti-gay laws, leading to persecution and violence, and forcing many to flee the country. The book, which is bilingual in English and Russian, was published to coincide with the Winter Olympics at a time when Russia was on the international stage.

[2] The 2017 ruling is the latest in a series of disputes between Russia and the ECHR. See Bartenev (2017) on how the conflict between Russia and ECHR on gay rights has developed and deepened since the introduction of the anti-gay propaganda law.

[3] A landmark publication in this topic is Cynthia Weber's *Faking It: U.S. Hegemony in a 'Post-Phallic' Era* (1999). Weber investigates how the United States styles itself in gendered and sexualized terms in relation to Latin America, especially Castro's Cuba: 'the United States [...] continued to pursue Cuba as an idealized feminine object, even once its mistress had grown a beard' (2).

gay rights discourse as a means to 'continue or extend the project of U.S. nationalism and imperial expansion endemic to the war on terror' (2007: 2). While Puar speaks primarily about homonationalism in terms of justifying Islamophobia, the concept has also been applied to Western critiques of Russian homophobia (Edinborg 2017: 78–80; Sykes 2017: 157–62).

This chapter explores how imaginative literature is implicated in, and responds to, the political and cultural rift between Russia and the West on issues of gender and sexuality. Rather than looking at mega-events such as the Winter Olympics or international institutions such as the ECHR, where battle lines are often drawn in predictable ways, I suggest that literary texts can provide a subtler understanding of the intersection of sexuality and national identity when contemporary Russian writers depict queer communities or individuals in the West. Looking at how writers represent queer people switches our attention away from big players on the global stage – states, global institutions, international broadcasters – towards actors who work on a smaller scale, but nevertheless exist within the transnational arena, as Ulf Hannerz (1996: 6) reminds us. Moreover, while the literary texts I discuss deal with individuals who express queer desires or behaviours, I argue that these texts are engaged nevertheless in a broader project of a queer reimagining of relations between Russia and the West.

At this point, it is helpful to clarify my terminology. In line with contemporary queer theorists, I use the term 'queer' not simply as a catch-all term for lesbian, gay, bisexual, and transgender. Rather, 'queer' covers a wide range of non-normative gender performances and sexual expression that 'aggressively challeng[e] hegemonies, exclusions, norms and assumptions' (Giffney & O'Rourke 2009: 3). 'Queer', therefore, is an anti-identarian term that first and foremost signifies resistance to categorization in terms of gender and sexuality, but it also points to a broader project of subverting both political systems and aesthetic norms.[4] The term 'transnational' similarly operates on multiple levels. Just as 'queer' challenges the organizing categories of gender and sexuality, so 'transnational' questions essentialist definitions of nation and national identity. When I speak of 'queer transnational encounters', at the most literal level I refer to same-sex relationships between Russians and foreign characters, which has been a recurring trope in Russian queer writing since the early twentieth century. However, at a deeper level, I suggest that these texts are queer and transnational in a political and aesthetic sense: they are experimental narratives that challenge contemporary assumptions

---

[4] This view of queer theory as an oppositional, anti-identitarian movement is elaborated by Halperin, who explains: 'Queer is by definition *whatever* is at odds with the normal, the legitimate, the dominant' (1995: 62).

about gender and sexuality as well as the construction of 'Western' and 'Russian'. I should also add here that this chapter is a transnational critique in another sense, namely insofar as I am a non-Russian, Western-identified, gay reader commenting on Russian texts. While I am aware that my positionality makes me open to charges of the kind of homonationalism that Puar criticizes, I would add that my outsider status allows me to engage in readings that fall outside the authors' intentions precisely because I am *not* the intended reader.

In what follows, I begin by tracing briefly the appearance of queer transnational encounters in Russian literature as the start of the twentieth century, before turning to two contemporary case studies. Both are short stories which feature Russian protagonists who encounter LGBT people and communities in the West. First, 'The Violet Suit' [Lilovyi kostium, 1999] by Viktoriia Tokareva depicts a Russian violinist's brief lesbian dalliance with a German translator in France. Ostensibly, this story provides an outsider's, almost ethnographic view on Western metropolitan gay culture at the turn of the millennium. However, behind the story's façade of sexual experimentation, I argue that Tokareva constructs a peculiarly reactionary Russian version of female heterosexuality based on the idea of the Russian woman – and the Russian nation – as martyr. Tokareva's treatment of gender and sexuality reveals how Russia on the cusp of the twenty-first century began to move towards more conservative notions of gender and sexuality, which are inextricably bound up with Russia's new nationalism and its turn away from the West. Yet I suggest that, oddly enough, Tokareva's story ends up celebrating a strangely queer, non-normative version of Russian heterosexuality even as she seeks to distance herself from Western gay rights discourse.

The second story, 'Mr Esposito' [Mister Esposito, 2008] by Margarita Meklina, depicts an aspiring Russian novelist who has emigrated to the USA. He tries unsuccessfully to gather information about the life story of the trans woman Tamara Raval, hoping to write her story to launch his career. Here, Meklina creates a homology between the transgender experience and the transnational, a connection that proves productive as Meklina reveals how the constructed nature of both national and gender identities depend on one another. I read 'Mr Esposito' as a critique of the kind of ethnographic narrative that Tokareva produces. Meklina lays bare the devices of this type of narrative: that is, she exposes how it is constructed, and in so doing, she critiques the aspiration that lies behind it and the effects on its audience. Ultimately, Meklina's story becomes an enquiry into the ethics of reading and writing about queer people, particularly in a transnational context.

My approach here builds on recent scholarly work on representations of homosexuality in Russian literature.[5] The link between representations of homosexuality and national identity has received particular attention from Baer (2009, 2014), who rightly points out that Russian depictions of homosexuality are always overdetermined, serving to comment not only on sexuality or gender, but also issues such as 'individuality, aesthetics, spirituality, victimhood, and, yes, even Russianness' (2009: 3). Baer's final chapter in *Other Russias* dwells on how postmodernist writers such as Viktor Pelevin and Vladimir Sorokin deploy homosexuality to 'figure a self-reflexive aestheticism' (2009: 250), although one worries that the lived experience of queer people can disappear in texts that emphasize the metaphorical value of sexuality. This chapter builds on Baer's work, but attempts to keep one eye on the depiction of queer people as individuals while also thinking specifically about how their transnational encounters throw into relief larger, state-sponsored narratives about national identity.

Coming Out as Transnational Journey

A long tradition, present in both Western and Russian gay literature, links sexual discovery and coming out with the crossing of national borders, either literally or metaphorically. One sees this connection in symbolist writings, such as Zinaida Gippius's proto-lesbian poetry, although it is strongest in Mikhail Kuzmin's *Wings* [Kryl'ia 1906], often called Russia's first gay novel. *Wings* depicts the love between a Russian adolescent, Vania Smurov, and his tutor, Larion Shtrup, who is English (or half-English; the text is intentionally unclear about his background).[6] Vania takes lessons in Ancient Greek language and literature from Shtrup, and learning a new language and culture becomes a cipher for his discovery of his own homosexuality and his feelings for his tutor. When Shtrup stresses the importance of Vania reading the

[5] Simon Karlinsky's pioneering work in the 1970s and '80s revealed an underground current of Russian gay literature repressed by the Soviet Union (e.g. Karlinsky 1976 and 1989). He penned the introduction to Kevin Moss's *Out of the Blue* (1996), an anthology of Russian gay texts in English translation. The Silver Age period has received attention from scholars (e.g. Burgin 1998; Malmstad and Bogomolov 1999) and recently both Russian and Western scholars have begun to investigate the contemporary representations of LGBT people in the post-Soviet period (e.g. Baer 2009; Chantsev 2007; Chernetsky 2007: 146–82).

[6] Bershtein discusses Shtrup's Englishness, suggesting a connection to the Oxford aesthetes Walter Pater and John Addington Symonds, whose Hellenism and celebration of Ancient Greece had a 'strong and not terribly subtle homosexual subtext' (2011: 80).

Greek texts in the original language, as opposed to in Russian translation, he is also expressing the joys of same-sex love:

> A whole world, entire worlds are closed for you, Vania [...] Reading in translation is like having a soulless doll, something manufactured by a craftsman, instead of a flesh-and-blood person, smiling or glum, whom you can love, kiss, or hate, whose blood you can see coursing through his veins, and in whose naked body you can see natural grace. (Kuzmin 1984: 195)

In other words, Shtrup equates accepting one's homosexuality with the ability to cross linguistic and cultural borders so seamlessly that translation or mediation is no longer required. True to his symbolist heritage, Kuzmin sees homosexual love as an aesthetic, even spiritual experience.[7] Homosexuality allows Vania to escape his immediate environment of Russian upper-class society with its petty prejudices into an idealized Hellenic world of beauty, although that Hellenism is of course itself a British invention of the late nineteenth century (Dowling 1994). It is not so much that Vania escapes to 'Greece', another nation; rather, he escapes to a Hellenic chronotope that exists outside space and time. Homosexuality is thus imagined as a way of transcending such temporal categories as national identity altogether.

The idea that discovering one's homosexuality also involves transnational crossings is found in Western literature, too, throughout the twentieth century. James Baldwin's *Giovanni's Room* (1956), for example, is a story of same-sex love between an American and an Italian barman in Paris; the novel itself illicitly crossed national borders as Russian translations were smuggled into the Soviet Union of the 1970s (Baer 2014: 432). Transgender writing, too, often evinces an interest in the transnational: as the shared prefix *trans-* suggests, crossing between countries can readily – if problematically – be metaphorized as a crossing between genders. For example, in Jan Morris's *Conundrum* (1974), an autobiographical account of male-to-female transition, the Welsh author dwells on her long career as a foreign correspondent and travel writer, suggesting that her 'incessant wandering [is] an outer expression of [her] inner journey' (1974: 101). The transnational paradigm remains a productive one in LGBT world literature even today, although few contemporary writers share the unmitigated utopianism of a Kuzmin when

---

[7] A much more negative take on the idea of homosexuality as a spiritual experience is found in Vasilii Rozanov's tract *People of the Moonlight* [Liudi lunnogo sveta, 1911]; Rozanov criticizes what he sees as a loss of virility among men in the Russia of his time leading to the spread of a spiritual homosexuality (Baer 2014: 430).

it comes to depicting relationships across borders, often highlighting the difficulty of reconciling national and sexual identities in a globalized world. For example, Shyam Selvadurai's novel *The Hungry Ghosts* (2013) features a Sri Lankan immigrant who brings a critical outsider's gaze to the Canadian gay community, and who ultimately breaks up with his Canadian boyfriend because his own experiences and memories tie him to a Sri Lankan past and identity that his partner cannot understand.

Contemporary Russian literature features a similar ambivalence about the West. As writers began to depict same-sex encounters more openly after the fall of the Soviet Union, homosexuality became associated in the minds of many Russian writers with Westernization. Often, the West figures as providing an escape from the repressive homophobia of Russian society, as in Yelo Vermin's story 'The Green Hills of Wales' [Zelenye kholmy Uel'sa, 2006], a story in which a young gay Muscovite dreams of exchanging homophobic Russia for a sexually liberated Wales. He insists to his sceptical boyfriend: 'You can casually drop into conversation that you're gay. It's not like Russia' (Vermin 2006). His dreams appear close to fruition when he meets Chris, a ginger-haired Welshman at a Moscow club. He promptly discards his Russian boyfriend and prepares to leave for the United Kingdom. However, the story ends with news of his death when his Moscow–London flight crash-lands into the English Channel, interrupting his transnational romance and dreams of gay liberation. In this text, Wales functions not as a lived environment, but a fantasy space 'where people still believe in elves' (Vermin 2006), a queer Utopia that can only exists in dreams, not reality.

Such ambivalence towards the West reappears in more recent texts, such as Dar'ia Vil'ke's young adult novel *The Jester's Cap* [Shutovskoi kolpak, 2013], in which one of the main characters, Sam, a gay teenager, leaves Russia for the Netherlands after suffering a homophobic beating.[8] Yet Vil'ke concentrates not on the potential joys that await Sam in Amsterdam, but on the pain of emigration, and particularly on two younger children, the narrator (implied to be gay) and his friend Sashok (potentially trans), both of whom are left behind and face growing up in a hostile Russia without a mentor like Sam. Similarly, the collection of interviews and testimonies in Masha Gessen and Joseph Huff-Hannon's *Gay Propaganda: Russian Love Stories* (2014) offer a mixed view of the West: many of the interviewees compare the homophobia of Russia unfavourably with the gay-friendly West, yet they also dwell on the

---

[8] The novel has been translated into English by Marian Schwartz as *Playing a Part* (Wilke 2015). The author herself is a migrant to the West, having left Moscow in 2000 and now living in Vienna.

pain of leaving Russia and the difficulty of integrating into gay communities in the West.

By far the most famous Russian queer émigré figure is Slava Mogutin, who has since the early 1990s branched out from writing into photography and performance art in his adopted home of New York. Mogutin's often sexually explicit work celebrates the opportunities that the West offers to gay men, yet he has also proved a vocal critic of the turn towards 'consumerism and assimilation' in Western gay culture and produces transgressive art that intentionally performs 'queer insubordination and insurgency' (Mogutin, cit. Gutierrez 2017). As Vitaly Chernetsky suggests, Mogutin has managed to construct a 'new Russo-American queer identity [...] that interrogates the presuppositions of what it means to be Russian, to be American, to be gay or queer' (2017: 314). Mogutin's work, then, stands as one example of how culture might resist the binary between a homophobic Russia and a gay-friendly West, an idea that I develop further in my own readings of Tokareva and Meklina.

The Queerness of Russian Heterosexuality: Viktoriia Tokareva's 'The Violet Suit'

Where Mogutin is a radical, self-identified queer writer living in the United States, Viktoriia Tokareva belongs to an altogether more conservative milieu. Born in 1937, she gained renown in the Soviet Union for her mastery of short, psychological prose in the vein of Chekhov, but focused on women's experience. However, much of the work for which she is known today came out in the 1990s. Although her focus on recording the distinctive experience of women has led some to label her a feminist writer, she firmly rejects this label. In one interview, she calls herself a 'traditionalist', even provocatively quipping: 'What are feminists protesting against? The idea that woman is a Barbie doll, a sex toy. But that's my dream!' (Tokareva, interviewed in Kochetkova 2007). She goes on to disparage one of her translators in the West for being 'an extreme feminist' who resembles a 'Chechen militant' with a 'man's haircut and constant aggressive expression on her face' (Tokareva, interviewed in Kochetkova 2007). Here and elsewhere, Tokareva is keen to emphasize how being a woman shapes her writing, but also appears at pains to distinguish her project from Western feminism.

This clash of values between Russian and Western women is dramatized in Tokareva's 1999 story 'The Violet Suit'. The protagonist, Marina, is a Russian violinist, 37 years old, thrice divorced, and dedicated to her music, but still pining after her first love, her (male) violin teacher who emigrated to the USA. The story recounts Marina's trip to perform at a classical music festival in Paris titled 'Europe Listens', an ironic name as the story highlights miscommunication and misunderstanding between cultures. Indeed, the focus is not so much on Parisians listening to Marina's music, but on Marina's own observations about the Western mores around gender and sexuality, and the implicit or explicit comparisons with Russia. Marina becomes fascinated by Barbara, her interpreter, a strong, self-confident German woman fluent in French and Russian in addition to her native language. For Marina, Barbara is 'sure of herself, well-turned-out, dressed in an elegant violet suit: someone who has mastered life' (Tokareva 1999: 11): a strong woman, if rather less intimidating than Tokareva's own 'extreme feminist' translator. Soon, Barbara reveals she is a lesbian, and the story hinges on the complex relationship that develops between the two women, which comprises a mutual fascination and affection, as well as lust (at least on Barbara's part) and fierce rivalry (at least on Marina's part).

Tokareva sets herself up as a travel writer, revealing the mysteries of the West – while also commenting on Russia – to a largely mainstream readership who, in the 1990s, may not have had the opportunity to travel to the West, or exposure to avant-garde journals like *Babylon* [Vavilon] and *Risk* that printed queer material in that period. For contemporary Western readers, the story provides an eye-opening experience precisely because we are *not* the intended audience. It allows us to see ourselves from an outsider's point of view, while also allowing us to see how the West generally, and its queer citizens in particular, are used to imagine Russian national identity.

Marina's initial impressions of lesbians will strike many readers as condescending and naïve. 'Lesbianism', she posits, 'is a condition that comes from a bad experience with a man' (Tokareva 1999: 14). She sees lesbianism as an escapist choice that Western women make because 'they are afraid to get burnt again', distinguishing them from Russians who willingly suffer in relationships with men, 'ready to get burnt constantly' (Tokareva 1999: 14). Here, it becomes evident that Tokareva's story is not primarily an ethnographic investigation of Western lesbianism; rather, she uses lesbianism as a foil for exploring – and defending – a certain kind of Russian female heterosexuality. Tokareva is building here on a well-known national myth, dating back at least to the nineteenth century, of self-sacrifice and martyrdom as an inherent national trait of Russians, especially Russian women (Heldt 1987; Rancour-Laferriere 1995: 144–58). The story thus exploits what Kevin Moss (2017) refers to as Occidentalism in contemporary Russian homophobic discourse, that is, a simplified negative view of the West as part of a set of binary oppositions that pits a traditional, spiritual Russia against a materialistic and decadent West in thrall to new ideas.

Yet Tokareva's depiction of lesbianism is not entirely negative. As Marina grows more familiar with Barbara, she becomes more understanding of her sexuality. One passage depicts Marina in the shower, contemplating Barbara's sexuality: 'the fact that there was a lesbian waiting for her downstairs didn't worry her. But it did influence the way she thought about her own body. And how she thought about her spirit [dukh]. At the end of the day, she had a choice. It was possible for her not to depend so humiliatingly on a man' (Tokareva 1999: 18). The text here creates the potential for a feminist – and queer – alternative future for Marina that would allow an escape from the narrative of female martyrdom. At this point, we see how IR theorist Cynthia Weber's idea that states are metaphorically gendered and have sexualized interactions with one another is helpful for understanding Tokareva's story. If we take Marina as a personification of Russia – as Tokareva invites us to – then the broader geopolitical reading would be that Russia holds the potential to escape from its status as martyr among nations by following the Western model.

Barbara's violet suit, which gives the story its title, becomes a symbol of Marina's potential emancipation. Marina wants a similar suit for herself and, eventually, failing to find one in the shops, asks Barbara for hers. When Barbara refuses, Marina, realizing that Barbara has a crush on her, offers to sleep with her in exchange for the suit. During the encounter that follows, Tokareva allows Marina a fleeting moment of sexual pleasure, as she feels desire well up inside her body in response to Barbara's kisses. However, Marina is quickly repulsed and jumps out of bed. Here Tokareva not only interrupts the narrative pleasure of her readers – she denies us the possibility of a steamy scene of lesbian sex – but she also attempts to cut off the possibility of a trans-national understanding between the two women. Or, if we read the sexual encounter in metaphorical, geopolitical terms, Tokareva is insisting that Russia has refused to prostitute herself to the West, even if such an interaction should bring pleasure. This sexual metaphor proves especially resonant in the context of the late 1990s, a moment when Russians were becoming increasingly disillusioned with Western-style capitalism after the economic crisis of 1998.

A follow-up conversation between Marina and Barbara crystallizes Tokareva's critique of the West and her view of Russianness:

> 'Then why wouldn't you give me the violet suit?' asked Marina.
> 'I didn't want you to exploit my feelings,' snapped Barbara.
> Marina remembered how her violin teacher had exploited her feelings. And she, his. And that had brought HAPPINESS. And because of that she had become a REAL musician. (Tokareva 1999: 42; emphasis in the original)

Tokareva's essentialist view sees Western relationships, as exemplified by lesbianism, as inherently egalitarian, yet she sees this quality as negative, because this model of relationships does not allow for the kind of suffering and tragedy in love that she sees as necessary for happiness, and indeed for artistic creativity. A generous reader might credit Tokareva here for her critique of the atomization and individualization of Western society, although her insistence on mapping these qualities on to a particular sexual identity is problematic. Nor should we not lose sight here of the ethical problems in the formulation above: arguably, Tokareva covertly justifies suffering and even exploitation by insisting they alone generate happiness and create the possibility of art.

Intriguingly, Tokareva here performs a reversal of a long tradition of depicting homosexuality as tragic and artistically inspiring, one that marks gay and lesbian literature such as Radclyffe Hall's iconic lesbian novel *The Well of Loneliness* (1928). For Tokareva, it is rather Russian heterosexuality that appears tragic, perhaps even queer, in a Europe that has normalized lesbian relations. Where Russian heterosexual love is full of passion and tragedy, lesbianism appears clean, democratic, and refined. 'Lesbos has existed for millennia', Marina reflects, 'Cleanliness inside and out, refinement, female breasts, little napkins, cosmetics, no microbes, or disease, and certainly no deathly AIDS' (Tokareva 1999: 41). Although the reference to AIDS suggests a contrast between lesbianism and male gay relations, the real distinction in the story is between lesbianism and Russian heterosexuality, which is passionate, penetrative, and destructive. Marina reflects on the passion and pain of her own 'major, great love', her 'many mistakes and her hopes' (Tokareva 1999: 42). If we translate the story into metaphorical terms, seeing Marina as a metonym for Russia as a whole, Tokareva is both contributing to – and correcting – a long-standing gendered Russian imaginary of the nation as a particular kind of woman. For Fedor Dostoevskii in 1880, Pushkin's Tat'iana personified Russia's qualities: a woman who put her commitment to marital fidelity above her own happiness, contrasted with the flighty heterosexual dandy Onegin.[9] Tokareva, writing over a century later, keeps the image of Russia as female martyr, but Marina is a stranger – dare we say queerer? – kind of woman than Pushkin's Tat'iana. Such a depiction of Russianness jibes with Ellen Rutten's discussion of how Russians self-identify as 'imperfect-but-real' in Chapter 15 of the present volume. Thrice-divorced, passionately irrational,

---

[9] In Dostoevskii's famous 'Pushkin Speech' of 1880, he celebrated Pushkin's Tat'iana from *Evgenii Onegin* as 'the apotheosis of Russian womanhood' (Dostoevsky 1994: 1285). Dostoevskii lauded Tat'iana as a martyr willing to sacrifice her own happiness as the key to the novel, as she refuses Onegin and promises to stay faithful to her husband forever at the novel's conclusion.

and devoted above all to creativity, Marina provides a radical alternative to the 'rational', 'clean' love of lesbians in western Europe.

'The Violet Suit', like Kuzmin's *Wings*, centres around the possibility of transnational communication and homosexuality. For Kuzmin, perfection can be attained in both aesthetic and sexual terms: Shtrup teaches Vanya to read the Greek classics in the original, to recognize his homosexuality, and to fall in love with him. At the end of the story, Shtrup notes that Vania is growing metaphorical wings, an image that gives the novella its title. By contrast, Tokareva's story depicts transnational communication breaking down, both figuratively and literally. Barbara is an able linguist, but she fails where Shtrup succeeded: she cannot persuade Marina to renounce her sexuality, nor her Russian world view. Barbara cries when she sees Marina off at the airport and, as Tokareva describes it, Marina in response 'hug[s] her, her moonish girl from another planet [svoiu inoplanetianku, lunnuiu devushku]' (Tokareva 1999: 43).[10] Ultimately, for Tokareva, the role of the transnational writer is not to build bridges but to expose an unbridgeable cultural gap. In figurative, geopolitical terms, the implication is that Russia and the West are alien cultures, a damning indictment of Russia at the end of the 1990s, a decade when Russia had tried to liberalize and Westernize, and a portent of things to come in the years to follow.

Exposing the Exposers: Margarita Meklina's 'Mr Esposito'

Unlike the mainstream Tokareva, Margarita Meklina (b. 1975) began her career publishing in avant-garde and queer journals such as *Babylon* and *Mitia's Journal* [Mitin zhurnal]. 'Every artist simply has to be queer in the soul', quipped Meklina in a 2011 interview (az.gay.ru 2011) and her writing frequently features queer characters and same-sex encounters. However, her work not only unsettles categories of gender and sexuality but also challenges static conceptions of national identity in a transnational age. She draws here on biographical experience: born in Leningrad in 1975, she emigrated to the USA in 1994 before moving to Ireland in 2015. Meklina's short stories often bring a defamiliarizing outsider's gaze to American society, a feature that she shares with fellow Russian-American émigré Vladimir Nabokov. She has also inherited from Nabokov, as well as Jorge Luis Borges – an important forerunner for both writers – a taste for narrative play and for self-reflexive writing.

Queer, transnational, and self-reflexive elements come together in her story 'Mr Esposito' [Mister Esposito, 2008]. The narrator-protagonist, Mr

---

[10] The reference to the moon here may echo Rozanov's categorization of homosexuals as 'People of the Moonlight' (see note 7 above).

Nil'skii, is a Russian immigrant to the USA working as the company librarian for Zellerman, Inc., a high-profile American legal firm. In a pastiche of a thriller, the text reveals that his job includes not only a librarian's conventional duties but also collecting compromising information about individuals for the firm to use against them. At one point, he borrows the pseudonym Mr Esposito, seemingly a fitting title for one whose job involves the exposure of others. The plot revolves around one of Nil'skii's assignments: he is charged with digging up dirt on one Tamara Raval, a trans woman who was formerly known as Truman, a playful choice of name on Meklina's part, not only because its bearer, a trans woman, parodies the idea of a 'true man' but because it also evokes the gay American writer Truman Capote (1924–84). Nil'skii has been hired by Tamara's employers, who have discovered her secret and hope that he can find a pretext to fire her legally. The voyeuristic narrator is titillated by the prospect of uncovering Tamara's backstory, describing his investigator's role in strikingly sexualized terms. A photograph reveals Tamara as a 'typical American Barbie': a blonde in a 'sequined, tight-fitting top' and 'shapely, shaved legs in sheer tights' (Meklina 2008: 84). Esposito envisages writing a 'captivating, fat book' that maps Truman's transition to Tamara with photographs: a little boy playing with women's make-up; a 'strapping soldier' in the US Army; a 'long-haired woman in short shorts' (Meklina 2008: 89). Even after Tamara is fired, Nil'skii continues his investigation out of personal interest and eventually tries to contact her, hoping that she will supply a fitting ending for his book.

Meklina thus sets up the reader to expect a riveting narrative and, in Borgesian style, manages to evoke several different genres of fiction within a short story. First, the reader is led to expect a miniature version of the trans biography, a *Bildungsroman* in the vein of the published life stories of famous trans figures such as Christine Jorgenson or Jan Morris. Second, Meklina evokes the detective genre, creating a narrator-investigator who pieces together details of the exciting – and possibly tragic – life of the mysterious beauty Tamara Raval before the reader's eyes. In this regard, Nil'skii sees himself in the role of the aforementioned Truman Capote, most famous for *In Cold Blood* (1966), a non-fiction book influential in the development of 'true crime' writing that explores two killers' minds. Indeed, Nil'skii seems to promise a sensationalist ethnographic account in the same vein as Tokareva's story. However, the power of Meklina's work lies in the fact that she deliberately thwarts all these expectations, and, in doing so, interrupts the reader's pleasure and leads us to question the ethics behind these genres of writing and their power over readers.

Thus the story concludes not with the revelation of Tamara's innermost secrets, but with Esposito himself being exposed. Instead of getting his 'ending',

Nil'skii unexpectedly becomes the subject of Tamara's own investigation, after she discovers that he played a role in her sacking. The final paragraph of the story reveals that Nil'skii, who had set himself up as a 'handsome, introverted intellectual' (Meklina 2008: 81) who casually name-drops queer French intellectuals such as Barthes and Foucault, is in fact a lonely being tortured about his own sexuality. His usually bombastic, Nabokovian style of prose switches to sombre, confessional tones in the final paragraph as he admits that he leads a dual life. 'Despite all the bravado and the Barthes, I still haven't managed to sort out my own private life', he admits (Meklina 2008: 98), before explaining that he remains closeted to his family in Russia. Indeed, his only sexual pleasure comes in the form of clandestine encounters with an old school friend, now a married man in Volgograd. Moreover, when he occasionally takes on editorial work for Russian-language publications, he postures as a homophobe who refuses to print any gay-themed material. Nil'skii, then, maintains an unreconciled double transnational existence: he is both a closeted homophobic editor in Russia and an aspiring gay writer in the USA.

'Mr Esposito' thus becomes a tale of *two* transformations: Tamara's gender crossing and Nil'skii's attempt to reinvent himself as an American. Perhaps defying expectations, Meklina makes Tamara's crossing of genders appear more successful than the narrator's transnational crossing. During the narrator's hunt for *kompromat* (compromising material) on Tamara, he is disappointed to find that her qualifications are real and that reports from her previous employers are glowing. She has an active dating life and is open about her past, engaging in trans activism. By contrast, Nil'skii, who adopted the trappings of a Western intellectual – the language, the mannerisms, the clothes – is nevertheless still haunted by his own Russian background, and himself terrified of the possibility of exposure. Nil'skii is terrified by the potential shame of two revelations: on the one hand, he fears homophobic Russians discovering his gay life in the USA and, on the other, he hates the idea of liberal Americans uncovering his status as a closeted homophobe in Russia, as that would show that he had not fully 'transitioned' to an American identity with the right politically correct views on gender and sexuality. Meklina thus gives the lie to two recurring myths about identity: (a) the transphobic idea that trans people always remain *really* the gender assigned at birth; and (b) the liberal American dream of the 'melting pot', that is, that any immigrant to the USA can become fully American if s/he wishes to. Meklina's story reveals one of the fundamental contradictions at the heart of Western liberal identity politics: how the fetishization of the notion of the individual and the insistence that one can define one's own identity clash with the reification of essentialized identity categories, whether based on national identity, gender, or sexuality.

For Meklina, narrative is not an ethically neutral tool: Nil'skii's idea of penning a captivating biography based on Tamara's life story is suspect and exploitative, not only because of his own shady involvement in getting her fired but also because the genre of biography, by its nature, positions the subject as Truman-become-Tamara, not Tamara in her own right. Although Meklina's text is focalized through Nil'skii – that is, she presents the story through his eyes – she uses the Nabokovian trick of covertly inviting her reader to counterfocalize, that is, to imagine events from Tamara's perspective.[11] Moreover, the unsavoury Nil'skii's willingness to position himself as working within a line of queer post-structuralist French theorists – Foucault and Barthes – might serve as a reminder to contemporary academics working on gender and sexuality that we, too, have an ethical responsibility not to exploit the people who provide the subject of our writing. Or, in Bakhtinian terms, we might critique Nil'skii for his urge to 'finalize' [zavershit'] Tamara in narrative terms, by completing her life story in the form of a bestseller, whereas Meklina's story refuses to give away Tamara's story, allowing her to remain 'unfinalized'.[12] Furthermore, Meklina's pairing of the two transformations implies another uncomfortable truth: Nil'skii's attempted reinvention of himself as a progressive American comes as the price of his marginalization of Tamara, first by providing the information to get her fired, and then by trying to make her the subject of a bestselling book.

To develop the comparison with 'The Violet Suit', one might add that while Tokareva's text constructs a version of Russian heterosexuality by imagining an Occidentalized queer Other, Meklina's story suggests that this process of Othering is still the price needed to gain citizenship even in the supposedly progressive West. Read thus, 'Mr Esposito' can be seen as a contribution to recent debates around sexual citizenship and homonationalism in the West. Theorists of sexual citizenship have pointed out that, even in an era when the West proclaims itself liberal and inclusive on matters of gender and sexuality, this inclusivity often extends only to those individuals who behave in accordance with social and cultural norms, such as middle-class, monogamous white gay men in the context of the contemporary USA, while

---

[11] In Chapter 7 of this volume, Marijeta Bozovic calls Nabokov a 'counter-focalizer extraordinaire' (138), taking *Lolita* as the paradigm case where the reader must look beyond Humbert's dazzling prose to understand the plight of Lolita.

[12] In his later work, Mikhail Bakhtin came to see 'unfinalizability' as a virtue in art: avoiding the urge to finalize meant a writer could create a literature that was open to, and in dialogue with, the world, with complex characters who interacted and responded to the world as if they were living beings. For an extended discussion of the concept, see Morson and Emerson (1990: 89–96).

continuing to marginalize others (Richardson 2017). Where Nil'skii attempts to use guile to integrate into this part of the American mainstream, Tamara is economically disenfranchised – losing her job – and, paradoxically, she goes from being a 'Truman' (true man) to a 'Tamara', not only a woman but one with a Slavic name, seemingly ethnically Othered.

In both Russia and the West, contemporary political discourse and the media paint a picture of a gay-friendly West fighting against a traditionalist Russia. This chapter has suggested ways in which literary texts have created and reinforced this divide, but, more importantly, it also demonstrates how imaginative literature reveals the limitations of this paradigm. Queer transnational encounters do not always take the form of enlightened Westerners liberating – or seducing – their Russian counterparts; rather, the Russian subject can resist, or even discover their own kind of queer agency that subverts the Western narrative (as in the case of Tokareva's Marina), or, indeed, the homosexual Russian who becomes a good gay citizen of the West may end up oppressing another minority in his quest for acceptance (as with Meklina's Nil'skii). Reading these two texts together, we become conscious not merely of the malleability of gender, sexuality, and nationality, but also the power that writers wield when they depict these identities, a power Tokareva showcases in 'The Violet Suit' and Meklina deconstructs in 'Mr Esposito'. Moreover, we also become aware of the ethical stakes of reading; as Western readers, we ourselves are involved in an intimate queer transnational encounter both with the writer of the texts and with the characters within. There is an imperative here not to rush to judgement, not to finalize, but to be open to the queer, radical, transformative experience that literature can provide when we set aside our assumptions about what we expect to find there.

Works Cited

az.gay.ru. 2011. *Margarita Meklina*: *Kazhdyi khudozhnik v dushe prosto obiazan byt' kvirom* <http://az.gay.ru/articles/news/meklina_2011_11.html> [accessed 25 August 2017].

Baer, Brian. 2009. *Other Russias: Homosexuality and the Crisis of Post-Soviet Identity* (New York: Palgrave Macmillan).

——. 2014. 'Russian Gay and Lesbian Literature' in E. L. McCallum and Mikko Tuhkanen (eds), *The Cambridge History of Gay and Lesbian Literature* (Cambridge: Cambridge University Press), 421–37.

Baker, Catherine. 2017. 'The "Gay Olympics"? The Eurovision Song Contest and the Politics of LGBT/European Belonging', *European Journal of International Relations*, 23(1): 97–121.

Baldwin, James. 1990. *Giovanni's Room* (London: Penguin).

Bartenev, Dmitri. 2017. 'LGBT Rights in Russia and European Human Rights Standards' in Lauri Mälksoo and Wolfgang Benedek (eds), *Russia and the European Court of Human Rights* (Cambridge: Cambridge University Press), 326–52.

Bershtein, Evgenii. 2011. 'An Englishman in the Russian Bathhouse: Kuzmin's *Wings* and the Russian Tradition of Homoerotic Writing' in Lada Panova and Sarah Pratt (eds), *Mikhail Kuzmin: A Miscellany. Kuzmin mnogogrannyi: Sbornik statei i materialov* (Bloomington, IN: Slavica), 75–87.

Burgin, Diana. 1998. 'Laid Out in Lavender. Perceptions of Lesbian Love in Russian Literature and Criticism of the Silver Age, 1893–1917' in Jane T. Costlow, Stephanie Sandler, and Judith Vowles (eds), *Sexuality and the Body in Russian Culture* (Stanford, CA: Stanford University Press), 177–203.

Capote, Truman. 1966. *In Cold Blood: A True Account of a Multiple Murder and its Consequences* (London: Penguin).

Chantsev, Aleksandr. 2007. '"Otnoshenie k strasti" (lesbiiskaia literatura: ot subkul'tury – k kul'ture)', *Novoe literaturnoe obozrenie*, 6 (88) <https://magazines.gorky.media/nlo/2007/6/otnoshenie-k-strasti.html> [accessed 12 October 2019].

Chernetsky, Vitaly. 2007. *Mapping Postcommunist Cultures: Russia and Ukraine in the Context of Globalization* (Montreal: McGill-Queen's University Press).

——. 2017. 'Literary Translation, Queer Discourses and Cultural Transformation: Mogutin Translating/Translating Mogutin' in Brian James Baer and Susanna Witt (eds), *Translation in Russian Contexts: Culture, Politics, Identity* (New York: Routledge), 306–20.

Dostoevsky, Fyodor. 1994. *A Writer's Diary Volume 2: 1877–1881*, trans. Kenneth Lantz (Evanston, IL: Northwestern University Press).

Dowling, Linda. 1994. *Hellenism and Homosexuality in Victorian Oxford* (Ithaca, NY: Cornell University Press).

Edinborg, Emil. 2017. *Politics of Visibility and Belonging: From Russia's 'Homosexual Propaganda' Laws to the Ukrainian War* (Abingdon: Routledge).

Gessen, Masha, and Joseph Huff-Hannon (eds). 2014. *Gay Propaganda: Russian Love Stories*, trans. Bela Shaevich, Andrei Borodin, Dmitry Karelsky, and Svetlana Solodovnik (New York: OR Books).

Giffney, Noreen, and Michael O'Rourke (eds). 2007. *The Ashgate Research Companion to Queer Theory* (Farnham: Ashgate).

Gutierrez, Benjamin. 2017. 'Slava Mogutin: "I Transgress, Therefore I Am"', *Document Journal*, 1 August <https://www.documentjournal.com/2017/08/slava-mogutin-i-transgress-therefore-i-am/> [accessed 12 October 2019].

Hall, Radclyffe. 1928. *The Well of Loneliness* (London: Jonathan Cape).

Halperin, David M. 1995. *Saint Foucault: Towards a Gay Hagiography* (Oxford: Oxford University Press).

Hannerz, Ulf. 1996. *Transnational Connections: Cultures, People, Places* (London: Routledge).

Healey, Dan. 1999. 'Moscow' in David Higgs (ed.), *Queer Sites: Gay Urban Histories since 1600* (London: Routledge), 38–60.

——. 2018. *Russian Homophobia from Stalin to Sochi* (London: Bloomsbury Academic).

Heldt, Barbara. 1987. *Terrible Perfection: Woman and Russian Literature* (Bloomington, IN: Indiana University Press).

Karlinsky, Simon. 1976. 'Russia's Gay Literature and History', *Gay Sunshine*, 29/30: 1–7.

——. 1989. 'Russia's Gay Literature and Culture: The Impact of the October Revolution' in Martin Bauml Duberman, Martha Vicinus, and George Chauncey, Jr. (eds), *Hidden from History: Reclaiming the Gay & Lesbian Past* (New York: New American Library), 347–64.

Kochetkova, Natal'ia. 2007. 'Pisatel' Viktoriia Tokareva: "Chekhov byl genii, a ia tak – poguliat' vyshla"', *Izvestiia*, 20 November <http://iz.ru/news/330858> [accessed 23 August 2017].

Kovaleva, Svetlana. 2006. *Protestnye vystupleniia. Mai 2006 g.* <http://www.sova-center.ru/democracy/publications/2006/06/d8605/> [accessed 15 August 2017].

Kuzmin, M. A. 1984. *Proza. I: Pervaia kniga rasskazov* (Berkeley, CA: Berkeley Slavic Specialties).

Malmstad, John, and Nikolay Bogomolov. 1999. *Mikhail Kuzmin: A Life in Art* (Cambridge, MA: Harvard University Press).

Meklina, Margarita. 2008. 'Mister Esposito' in Vladimir Kirsanov (ed.), *Russkaia gei-proza 2008 goda* (Moscow: Kvir), 79–98.

Morris, Jan. 1974. *Conundrum* (London: Faber).

Morson, Gary Saul, and Caryl Emerson. 1990. *Mikhail Bakhtin: Creation of a Prosaics* (Stanford, CA: Stanford University Press).

Moss, Kevin (ed.). 1996. *Out of the Blue: Russia's Hidden Gay Literature* (San Francisco, CA: Gay Sunshine Press).

——. 2017. 'Russia as the Savior of European Civilization: Gender and the Geopolitics of Traditional Values' in Roman Kuhar and David Paternotte (eds), *Anti-Gender Campaigns in Europe: Mobilizing against Equality* (Lanham, MD: Rowman & Littlefield), 195–214.

Puar, Jasbir K. 2007. *Terrorist Assemblages: Homonationalism in Queer Times* (Durham, NC: Duke University Press).

Rancour-Laferriere, Daniel. 1995. *The Slave Soul of Russia: Moral Masochism and the Cult of Suffering* (New York: New York University Press).

Richardson, Diane. 2017. 'Rethinking Sexual Citizenship', *Sociology*, 51(2): 208–24.

Richter-Montpetit, Melanie. 2018. 'Everything You Always Wanted to Know about Sex (in IR) but were Afraid to Ask: The "Queer Turn" in International Relations', *Millennium: Journal of International Studies*, 46(2): 220–40.

Rossiiskaia Federatsiia. 2013. 'Federal'nyi zakon ot 29.06.2013 g. № 135-f3' <http://kremlin.ru/acts/bank/37386/> [accessed 15 August 2018].

Rozanov, V. V. 1913. *Liudi lunnago sveta: metafizika khristianstva* (St Petersburg: T-va A.S. Suvorina – Novoe Vremia).

Selvadurai, Shyam. 2013. *The Hungry Ghosts* (Toronto: Doubleday Canada).

Sykes, Heather. 2017. 'Decolonizing Sporting Homonationalisms: From Complicity to Solidarity' in Heather Sykes (ed.), *The Sexual and Gender Politics of Sport Mega-Events: Roving Colonialism* (Abingdon: Routledge), 153–75.

Tokareva, Viktoriia. 1999. *Lilovyi kostium* (Moscow: Izdatel'stvo AST).

Vermin, Yelo. 2006. 'Zelenye kholmy Uel'sa' <http://gay.ru/art/literature/amateur/gv/15/gv15_3.html> [accessed 10 August 2018].

Vil'ke, Dar'ia. 2013. *Shutovskoi kolpak* (Moscow: Samokat).

Weber, Cynthia. 1999. *Faking It: U.S. Hegemony in a 'Post-Phallic' Era* (Minneapolis, MN: University of Minnesota Press).

Wilke, Daria [Vil'ke, Dar'ia]. 2015. *Playing a Part*, trans. Marian Schwartz (New York: Arthur A. Levine Books).

14

The Russian Novel of Ideas
in Southern Africa

Jeanne-Marie Jackson

Roberto Schwarz, writing about the Brazilian novel, captures nineteenth-century Russia's salience as a literary template for the postcolonial world. 'The social reasons for this comparison [with South America] are clear', he suggests. 'In Russia, too, modernization [...] would clash with serfdom or its vestiges – a clash many felt as a national shame, although it gave others the standard by which to measure the madness of the individualism and progressomania that the Occident imposed and imposes on the world' (Schwarz 1980: 47). Schwarz here refers to the well-documented collision of western European post-Enlightenment ideals – individualism, secularism, progress – with the more abject Russian realities as the country confronted modernity in the second half of the nineteenth century. This collision was dramatized particularly acutely in the novel of ideas, a genre that dominated Russian letters between the 1840s and the 1880s, exploring some of the new philosophies entering Russia at that time, the psychology that underlay them, and the possible consequences for both the individual and society, if these ideas were realized.[1] Schwarz suggests that, while the nineteenth-century Russian novel

---

[1] On the development of the Russian novel of ideas from its beginnings with Aleksandr Gertsen in the 1840s to its apotheosis with Fedor Dostoevskii, Lev Tolstoi, and Ivan Turgenev in the 1860s to the 1880s, see Rzhevsky (1983) and Walicki (1979: 309–48). The Russian novel of ideas may be programmatic, extolling a particular philosophy and imagining how it would work in practice, as is the case with Nikolai Chernyshevskii's *What Is to Be Done?* [Chto delat', 1863]. However, as Morson notes, as practised by Dostoevskii, Tolstoi, and Turgenev, the Russian novel of ideas can also be read, in fact, as 'anti-ideological and anti-philosophical' (2010: 149) insofar as its masterplot involves a hero becoming disillusioned with a philosophy or ideology as s/he comes to understand its real-world consequences.

once appeared exceptional from a western European standpoint, its confrontation with progress and modernity could in fact be seen as a departure point for understanding the literatures of the global 'periphery'.[2]

In invoking questions of individualism and progress as they may or may not be transposable between one part of the world and another, Schwarz also points towards some fundamental *differences* within the Russian novel of ideas as a genre. While both Tolstoi and Dostoevskii explore a core problem of how the individual can find meaning in the secular, modernizing world of the mid- to late nineteenth century, they approach the question in markedly different ways. This chapter argues that both Dostoevskii and Tolstoi provided inspiration and material for two contemporary southern African novelists, Imraan Coovadia and Tendai Huchu, who have modelled parts of their own work on key moments from their oeuvres. The South African Coovadia looks to Tolstoi's *The Death of Ivan Il'ich* [Smert' Ivana Il'icha, 1886] in his *Tales of the Metric System* (2014), whereas Huchu – born in Zimbabwe and now resident in Scotland – channels the character of Kirillov from Dostoevskii's *Demons* [Besy, 1871–72] in *The Maestro, The Magistrate, and The Mathematician* (2014). In both cases, the nineteenth-century Russian problem of God is replaced by the twenty-first-century problem of globality as the overarching framework within which individual freedom is explored. For Tolstoi and Dostoevskii, the key question is how the individual can maintain faith in God and find meaning in an increasingly godless world. For Coovadia and Huchu, the individual struggles to find meaning in a globalized world, one where freedom is stymied by the logic and realities of global capitalism, a question that emerges as no less metaphysical than that posed by the Russian novelists.

Tolstoi and/or Dostoevskii

In their collective resonance for successive generations of writers and critics, Tolstoi and Dostoevskii obviously have much in common; so much so that they have at times even been fused into the hybrid 'Tolstoevskii'. It is important, therefore, both to establish a baseline for their joint significance and to sketch the broad strokes of their technical and ideological differentiation. If the philosophical bottom line for both Tolstoi and Dostoevskii (at least in their later works) is that freedom must be fundamentally bound to

---

[2] As Vera Tolz notes in Chapter 1 of the present volume, the Russian Slavophiles began describing Western influence in Russia as a form of cultural and intellectual colonization as early as the 1840s; Tolz notes parallels between their work and that of postcolonial thinkers of the late twentieth century.

and by a faith in Christian redemption, then Coovadia and Huchu represent individual freedom as intelligible only within a globalized structure of political and economic relations. Where Tolstoi's Ivan Il'ich and Dostoevskii's Kirillov each in their own way demonstrate the possibility of salvation through individual conscience, Coovadia's and Huchu's characters have no such option. Dostoevskii's and Tolstoi's characters are depicted as free to choose whether or not they follow God, but globality – construed here as the determination of individual experience by many distant and external factors – precludes the act of choice.

A restless grappling with Christianity marks the clearest convergence between Tolstoi and Dostoevskii *vis-à-vis* their more secular European influ-ences and contemporaries. As George Steiner writes, paraphrasing the Russian intellectuals Vissarion Belinskii and Nikolai Berdiaev, 'The Russian mind was, literally, God-haunted' (1996: 43).[3] Russia faced the West with a formative ambivalence: Europe exerts inescapable cultural, economic, and intellectual influence but, as John Burt Foster Jr. points out, it also '[takes] shape as the indiscriminate blow of an axe or the crushing momentum of a railroad car' (2013: 17), as progress without moral anchor. It is on this point – a conflict-ingly outsider self-imaginary – that nineteenth-century Russia offers a bridge to postcolonial African literature. Just as debates raged between Slavophiles and Westernizers in Dostoevskii's era, African writers leading up to and after independence from white colonial rule (attained in the Anglophone world between 1957 and, for South Africa, the belated date of 1994) interrogate the line between foreign and native, Eurocentrism and indigeneity, and nation-alist versus cosmopolitan visions of their countries' futures.

As I have written elsewhere (Jackson 2015), nineteenth-century Russian literature comes to world prominence through its own tangled reckoning with being 'outside', 'behind', and/or sceptical of European modernization. Foster thus sees a clear resonance between Russian classics, viewed as 'a first, rather easy step in moving beyond the West to create a truly global canon', and later literary groupings from elsewhere that likewise serve as a 'metonym for the world as a whole' (2013: 151). Indeed, Foster suggests 'Tolstoy may even be seen as a forerunner to contemporary African writers' such as Chinua Achebe and Wole Soyinka, who similarly 'gained admission to the Western literary system' (2013: 151) through ambiguity within and ambiva-lence in relation to it. While Foster makes this point in reference to the clearly

---

[3] There is a voluminous literature on nineteenth-century Russian religious thought, to which I cannot begin to do justice here. See, foundationally, Berdiaev (1935); Hamburg and Poole (2010) on religion and philosophy; Frede (2011) on the rise of atheism; and on eschatology and literature in particular, Bethea (1989).

'postcolonial' African writers whose international careers flourished in the post-independence era of the 1960s and '70s, African literature has, arguably, since then assumed a still more prominent place at the vanguard of world literature. As the anthropologists John and Jean Comaroff have famously written, the African continent in general may now afford the most 'privileged insight into the workings of the world at large', as its writers and intellectuals force us to reckon with the 'epistemic scaffolding' that supports long-standing European notions of progress (2012: 1). In other words, Africa today gives the lie to Western universalisms much as Russia did in the nineteenth century.

The Russia of Tolstoi and Dostoevskii, then, offers a prototype for realist literary traditions that are both limit case and Other to a falsely universalizing European canon. These writers' difficulty in reconciling Western ideals with Russian realities also yields, in part, the explosive hybridity of the Russian novel of ideas as a genre: its philosophical elements have often been observed to fit awkwardly into the novel as a form, even as they eventually define it. Henry James notoriously captured this critical sentiment in his description of *War and Peace* as a 'loose, baggy monste[r]' (1908: x). The generalized 'massiveness' (Steiner 1996: 12) of both Tolstoi's and Dostoevskii's novels, furthermore, is typically understood as a direct result of the precarious historical position they occupy. As Dmitrii Merezhkovskii put it, the famous 'accursed questions' of nineteenth-century Russian intellectual life were at once profoundly philosophical and politically immediate. They marked, for him, a painful intersection of European (and especially Herderian) theories of nationhood with the unique legacies of Russian serfdom and Orthodoxy (Merezhkovsky 1902: 250).

Tolstoi and Dostoevskii diverge in how they perform this conjunction of faith, reason, and radical political energies; and this divergence has in turn bred a critical genealogy of its own. Most famously, of course, Isaiah Berlin applied Archilochus's distinction between intellectual 'foxes' and 'hedgehogs', suggesting Tolstoi as an example of a fox wishing to be a hedgehog and Dostoevskii as a quintessential example of the latter. Tolstoi, that is, was a writer fundamentally concerned with the observable multiplicity of historical experience even as he strove to embrace salvation. He is a narrative technician who pieces together 'the sum of empirically discoverable data' that 'held the key to the mystery of why what happened, happened as it did and not otherwise' and '[threw] light on the fundamental ethical problems which obsessed him' (Berlin 1993: 13). In contrast, Dostoevskii sought to advance 'a single, universal message' (Berlin 1993: 4) through his characters' turning away from tormented delusions of secular will to embrace openness to Christian redemption (such as Raskol'nikov at the end of *Crime and Punishment*). As Berlin himself acknowledges, this distinction between the two men is in many ways reductive. It nonetheless offers a compelling means of pivoting from the philosophical problem of individual choice – what Berlin sums up as the nineteenth-century questions of 'What is to be done? How should one live? Why are we here? What must we be and do?' (1993: 13) – to these writers' hallmark narrative techniques as they are reanimated by the contemporary African novelists at the centre of this chapter's second half.

Tolstoi's *The Death of Ivan Il'ich* and Dostoevskii's *Demons* thus serve as microcosms for a larger and broadly consistent disparity in archetypally 'Tolstoian' and 'Dostoevskian' visions of the novel. In Merezhkovskii's famous assessment, Tolstoi's mode of description moves 'from the seen to the unseen, from the external to the internal, from the bodily to the spiritual, or at any rate to the emotional' (Merezhkovsky 1902: 169), as his 'religion and metaphysics enter into the delineation by [a] single trait', for example, a character's 'roundness' or characteristic quiver of the lips. In contrast, Dostoevskii moves from the inside out, from a character's psychology to his physical description (Merezhkovsky 1902: 244). If Tolstoi is a novelist who mainly manipulates bodies, then Dostoevskii is a novelist who mainly interrogates minds and souls.

In more technical terms, this contrast between 'external' monumentalism and 'internal' reckoning is most often attributed to narrative voice and, more specifically, to these writers' degree of narrative variation. Mikhail Bakhtin famously distinguished Tolstoian monologism from Dostoevskii's dialogism. For Bakhtin, Dostoevskii's heroes operate in a dialogic universe, seemingly having freedom to invent themselves using their own discourse; by contrast, the world of Tolstoi's fiction is described as a 'monologic' one where 'a second autonomous voice (alongside the author's voice) does not appear' (Bakhtin 1984: 56). Indeed, Tolstoi's externality seems somehow to proceed from on high, which is to say that his fine-grained descriptions of physical traits and tropes are unified by an almost unwaveringly consistent narratorial voice. Or, as John Bayley memorably described it, 'When crisis or alienation comes to one of Tolstoi's characters it comes from outside, like a thief reconnoitering into an orderly house' (1988: 43). It is illustrative here that *The Death of Ivan Il'ich* begins with a discussion of its eponymous character's corpse. Even the grammar with which Ivan's death is put forward bespeaks his passivity in relation to the narrator. The opening passage moves quickly from his colleagues reading about his death in a newspaper to the Tolstoian omniscient narrator's explanation that 'His post had been kept open for him' (Tolstoy 1967: 247) while he was ill. Ivan is thus identified only by his bureaucratic role in life, which in turn is set up as the sentence subject – *the post* remained open. The novella continues to cultivate a sense that Ivan is acted on, rather than a psychological actor himself, all the way through to its circling back to be present for the moment of his death. Tolstoi, describing his hero's reaction to fumbling end-of-life medical care, writes: 'Ivan Ilych knows quite well and definitely that all this is nonsense and pure deception', yet he 'submits to it all as he used to submit to the speeches of the lawyers [in his government career], though he knew very well that they were all lying and why they were lying' (Tolstoy 1967: 289).

There is, then, a sense of tired inevitability to the entire work, accentuated by the matter-of-fact evenness of Tolstoi's descriptive style. His rendering of Berlin's 'empirically discoverable data' entails a heightened focus on the visual dimensions of life-and-death affairs, as Merezhkovskii and Bayley point out: Tolstoi urges us to speculate on the emptiness of Ivan's life choices as a free man by comprehensively setting the stage of his home, rather than through deep-diving into these choices' psychic ramifications. As a case in point, we read that one of his former colleagues, Petr Ivanovich, 'upon entering the room' of Ivan's funeral:

> began crossing himself and made a slight movement resembling a bow. At the same time, as far as the motion of his head and arm allowed, he surveyed the room. Two young men – apparently nephews, one of whom was a high-school pupil – were leaving the room, crossing themselves as they did so. An old woman was standing motionless, and a lady with strangely arched eyebrows was saying something to her in a whisper. A vigorous, resolute Church Reader, in a frock-coat, was reading something in a loud voice with an expression that precluded any contradiction. The butler's assistant, Gerasim, stepping lightly in front of Peter Ivanovich, was strewing something on the floor. Noticing this, Peter Ivanovich was immediately aware of a faint odour of a decomposing body. (Tolstoy 1967: 249)

The ultimate purposelessness and hypocrisy of Ivan's bourgeois, bureaucratic existence is conveyed through a tedious stockpiling of observed detail. That Ivan is employed until his death by Russia's newly reformed legal system is also cause to read from the part to the whole; that is, from his position as a materially aspirational cog of the bloated, modernizing state to a questioning of the ethos of secular modernization writ large.

For the most part, then, Ivan and his ilk are carried along by the tides of social change. Like many of Tolstoi's most memorable characters, he thus becomes emblematic of Western individualism's deficiencies. The nervous, self-effacing character of Aleksei Kirillov from Dostoevskii's 1872 novel *Demons* is in this sense an ideal point of contrast with Ivan: he represents a feverishly active reckoning with the outer limits of individual freedom.

As part of a provincial salon of nihilists based loosely on Dostoevskii's time among the radical Petrashevskii Circle in the late 1840s, Kirillov determines to end his own life as the ultimate act of self-will, to prove that man is his own master, has power over life and death, and that God is unnecessary. Berdiaev suggests in his 1931 essay 'On Suicide' (Berdiaev 2002) that Kirillov as the self-professed man-god 'has to be the opposite in everything to the God-man' (that is, Christ). Berdiaev admits there is a certain nobility and asceticism in Kirillov's act of martyrdom yet, paradoxically, Kirillov's attempt to prove human freedom in fact demonstrates the opposite, that is, human attempts to achieve freedom without God merely culminate in death. By contrast, Berdiaev suggests, Jesus's crucifixion, which appears to be born of compulsion rather than freedom, in fact culminates in the resurrection, granting humankind the possibility of eternal life and salvation.

The narrative presentation through which Kirillov comes to his suicidal decision could not be more different from Tolstoi's reliance on replete, measured series of visual observations. Where Tolstoi, as above, alternates largely between descriptions of characters and, in turn, the characters' own pointed descriptions of their thoughts and surroundings, *Demons* relies on elusive dialogue. One pivotal philosophical exchange between Kirillov and *Demons*' anti-hero Nikolai Stavrogin in Part Two, Chapter Five of the novel occludes all but the most basic authorial set-up and description before heatedly continuing for roughly five pages. 'Man is unhappy because he doesn't know he's happy', Kirillov declaims amid speculation on the nature of allegory, goodness, and time. 'It's everything, everything! Whoever learns will at once immediately become happy, that same moment' (Dostoevsky 1994: 238). This narrative strategy typifies the more direct channel that Dostoevskii provides to his characters' minds. Tolstoi's Ivan Il'ich embodies a point with broad historical and philosophical significance – namely, that a meaningless life can only be redeemed by choosing a meaningful death. Kirillov and his interlocutors, though, actively debate what a meaningful life or death might be.

A brief return to Merezhkovskii brings this first half of the chapter full circle: while Tolstoi and Dostoevskii, he reminds us, evince significant methodological conflict, they share a common and distinctive goal of ushering an ever-more debased modernity towards Christian redemption. 'In the first place the art of both is in communion with religion', he writes, 'but that not of the present, but the future' (Merezhkovskii 1902: 302). It is on this point, too, that figures as different as Ivan and Kirillov converge: both possess the capacity to *individually* reveal the truth of God's salvation and thus give the novels in which they appear a strong sense of direction. In Ivan's case, this occurs through the positive example of his deathbed revelation – 'In place of death there was light' (Tolstoy 1967: 302) – and in Kirillov's, inversely, through the negative example of his choice to commit suicide. For both men, it is ultimately possible to make an individual choice that rejects the moral bankruptcy of 'freedom' and 'progress' as western European delusions: God offers them (and Russia) a way out.

Coovadia and/or Huchu

In the year 2014, two southern African writers published novels of which key sections are modelled on the two Russian characters – Ivan and Kirillov – that I have described above.[4] Coovadia's *Tales of the Metric System* makes use of fine-grained, stylistically consistent physical observation (including of a key character's corpse), whereas Huchu's *The Maestro, the Magistrate, and the Mathematician* displays wide stylistic variation across various character psychologies (including one who explicitly identifies with Dostoevskii's Kirillov). The two texts are united, however, by experimentation with disjointed and transnational plot structures which betray a hard-earned fatalism about southern Africa's political future because any source of individual agency is now structurally elusive. From Huchu's position in the Scotland-based Zimbabwean diaspora and Coovadia's in Cape Town, South Africa, we are presented with non-linear, chronologically confusing accounts of how individual lives come to naught. Tolstoi's and Dostoevskii's protagonists reveal God, in their deaths, as a *departure* from the notions of secular progress by which they live. In Coovadia's and Huchu's novels, the disorienting effects of globalization mean that both life *and* death are denied the possibility of meaningful choice. By 'globalization', I am referring here not simply to the increased economic, political, and cultural integration in the world at a macroscopic level, bringing opportunity to some and increased inequality to others (Robertson and White 2016). More importantly for our purposes, I refer to the associated transformation in an individual's sense of self, whereby one becomes conscious of existing within a global system of exchange and hierarchy, even though one may have little meaningful contact with others in that system (Robertson and White 2016: 60–61). What both Huchu and Coovadia borrow from the Russian novel of ideas as a genre allows them to confront this aspect of globalization, and yet both ultimately have to modify the genre in order to take account of contemporary realities.

---

[4] Huchu's references to *Demons* are explicit, and Coovadia's intended reference to *The Death of Ivan Il'ich* has been confirmed in my personal correspondence with the author.

Tales of the Metric System plays out across ten different plots divided into sections headed by references to their period or setting ('School Time', 'Soviet Embassy'), significant object ('The Pass', 'Vuvuzela'), or central event ('Truth and Reconciliation'). These sections, each of which appears only once, are arranged in non-chronological order and cover time frames from 1970, when the metric system was introduced in South Africa, to 1999, which saw the close of the post-apartheid Truth and Reconciliation Commission, to 2010, the year South Africa hosted the football World Cup. By coupling a disjointed plot structure with a mix of fictional and historical South African events (many of which are likely to be opaque to readers outside the country), Coovadia suggests the unavoidability of refracting national affairs through global structures of influence and causation. In this way, the 'freedom' of his characters to forge new narratives, either for themselves as individuals or indeed for South Africa as a nation, is curtailed by the very form of the book, which consists of a series of intentionally disordered storylines.

The section of the novel inspired by *The Death of Ivan Il'ich* takes place in 2003 and is titled 'Sparks': a reference to its eponymous main character Sparks Mokoena, whom we first meet dying in a hospital bed. Employed for decades as the South African president's 'fixer', Sparks's fictional death is based on that of a historical figure, President Thabo Mbeki's spokesperson Parks Mankahlana, who died in 2000. Mankahlana, like Sparks, died as a result of Mbeki's infamously disastrous public health policies, which denied HIV to be the cause of AIDS and, under the banner of African resistance to Western co-optation, refused to provide South Africans with access to antiretroviral medications. Like the moaning, disenchanted civil servant Ivan Il'ich, Sparks's dying body becomes a focal point for exploring broad tensions surrounding South Africa's 'new order' under Mbeki; that is, its post-apartheid emergence into a global economy through widespread reliance on international aid and development schemes. Coovadia's 'Sparks' section opens almost identically to Tolstoi's novella: Sparks, we are told, 'was making his mark just by lying there' on his deathbed, before the narrative transitions to a brief life history. Also, just like Ivan, the indifferent Sparks is disingenuously fussed over by his materialistic wife, who 'had such horror to see the thin body in the metal bed' (Coovadia 2014: 295), and their teenage daughter.

Coovadia's homage to Tolstoi extends to the realm of style; indeed, *Tales of the Metric System* is likewise unified mainly by his unwavering penchant for laconic observations on the physical world. One other example invites still further comparison with *The Death of Ivan Il'ich* in its emphasis on a corpse's metaphorical significance, as well as its smells. The most prominent description of Ivan's body in Tolstoi's novella begins, 'The dead man lay, as dead men always lie, in a specially heavy way, his rigid limbs sunk in the soft cushions of the coffin, with the head forever bowed on the pillow', and later continues, 'The expression on the face said that what was necessary had been accomplished, and accomplished rightly. Besides this there was in that expression a reproach and a warning to the living' (Tolstoy 1967: 250). In Coovadia's corresponding description of Sparks's corpse, we read that, 'In the bed a body lay calmly, making no demands, creating no complaints. One hand lay stiff across the stomach while the teeth were lengthening under thin lips. Under the sheet was a white-wine smell, as if the cork had been pulled under [his nurse's] nose' (2014: 293). Unlike the figure who ushers Ivan towards his deathbed revelation of God, though – a quintessentially hale and hearty young Russian peasant named Gerasim – Sparks's nurse here is fully implicated in the bankrupt moral economy that has condemned him to die. The nurse, Esther, then goes through Sparks's drawers, cupboards, and even hospital gown pockets in search of things to steal. In contrast to Gerasim's tenderness, she 'had looked at [Sparks], when [he was] alive and too feverish to respond, with a certain hatred' (Coovadia 2014: 294). Not coincidentally, Esther is also one of the few characters to connect different plot lines in the novel: she is elsewhere part of a crowd who wrongly accuses an innocent man of theft and burns him to death.

My point here is not that Esther is directly related to the denial of Sparks's treatment for HIV/AIDS by his employer (the president), but that the 'globalized' form that *Tales of the Metric System* auditions – that is, its horizontal connections across disparate times and places instead of anything like a linear, unfolding plot – is engineered to moot alternative structures for deriving meaning from life (such as Gerasim's, for Tolstoi). Ivan's cause of death is an ambiguous pain in his side, which begins following a fall while he is hanging new curtains that represent his materialism and bourgeois upward mobility. In other words, Tolstoi implies that Ivan is a victim of his own making, and it is fitting, therefore, that he is also able to enact his own redemption at the moment of his death. Sparks, on the other hand, is a victim of state powers that in some measure serve as a microcosm for the conflictual, reactionary dynamics of globalization; he is embedded in the book's meaning-granting frame from start to finish, not locked outside of it, as Ivan is until the moment of his death.[5] Both Tolstoi and Coovadia question the relation between 'free individuals' and their often-damning historical situation, but Coovadia's cipher has no last-minute release from the latter in the form of a turn to God. Indeed, where Ivan sees light when he departs the world,

[5] Mbeki's views on HIV/AIDS were part of a larger ideological and policy vision called 'the African Renaissance', a rejection of Western imperial dominance over African cultures and economies. See, for example, Ajulu (2001).

Coovadia lingers with Sparks's corpse as the dead man's spirit hovers over his body, observing only himself (2014: 290–94).

In *The Maestro, the Magistrate, and the Mathematician* – a novel about Zimbabwean diasporic experience in Edinburgh, Scotland – Huchu weds a similarly 'global', non-linear, transnational, and disjointed plot structure to a greater degree of stylistic variation. Like *Demons*, when providing readers with access to his characters' minds, Huchu's novel relies mainly on a combination of dialogue and free indirect speech (speech that is reported in the third person, but aligned with the consciousness, language, and perspective of the character). The book is structured as three alternating storylines that take place over a roughly ten-month span, each of which could in theory be read as an individual narrative. It begins with the Magistrate, a judge from Zimbabwe displaced because he has fallen out of favour with Robert Mugabe's regime; moves next to the Mathematician, a twenty-something PhD student named Farai; and finally introduces the Maestro, a contemplative loner employed stacking shelves at a supermarket. Each of the plot lines is marked by its own narrative voice and, in some cases, typographical distinction. The Maestro's, for example, lacks paragraph breaks to reflect his run-on style of thinking, while the Mathematician's includes symbols such as up-arrows to describe rising prices in Farai's stocks, and numbers to represent digital time to the exact second, such as '06:01:23' (Huchu 2014: 15).

It is in the Maestro's character, though, that *Demons* comes explicitly to the fore, and where his entrapment within a global denial of agency diverges from Kirillov's resolve to choose suicide and, ultimately, confirm Dostoevskii's belief that God is necessary. Overwhelmed and nearly soul-deadened by the sheer range of goods on display at the supermarket where he works, the Maestro lives by himself in a small, dishevelled flat. There he reads 'Kafka, Sartre, Dostoevsky, Nietzsche', and Boethius, compulsively ruminating on 'an incomprehensible Nothing' over which 'religions had to be formed' (Huchu 2014: 43). His free indirect narrative style, itself reminiscent of Dostoevskii, grows increasingly febrile as he moves deeper into intellectual solitude, on the other side of the widest possible chasm between his public and private lives. Likening himself, at one point, to Kirillov, the Maestro similarly ponders the relation of free will to divine power: 'How could a human being do anything other than what God already knew he was going to do? And if God did not know the future then God was not omnipotent' (Huchu 2014: 213). Unlike Kirillov, however, such contemplation is always closely linked to a literary rather than metaphysical point of reference. 'Did this moment exist before he'd read [Jon] McGregor', the Maestro asks himself, 'or had it always been there? And if it had, then why hadn't he noticed it before? Perhaps, he thought, it did not exist and only came to be after I read the book' (Huchu 2014: 42).[6]

The Maestro's heady musing also stands in stark contrast to the two other plot lines in the novel, in which the Magistrate and the Mathematician move steadily away from their respective intellectual modalities towards some variety of social integration. By contrast, it is in the Maestro's sections that we find a contemporary parallel to the Russian novel of ideas in his wrestling with philosophy. The sections devoted to the Magistrate dwell on Shona culture (the Shona being the Zimbabwean ethnocultural group to which Huchu belongs), while the Mathematician's sections provide a view of the social life of twenty-somethings in contemporary Edinburgh. The Maestro is therefore also the most socially isolated of the bunch. This applies not just to his life as it is depicted, but to both the genre (novel of ideas) and epistemology (literature) through which Huchu chooses to render him. Both the Magistrate and the Mathematician are recognizable male Zimbabwean satirical 'types': the first, the stern man of learning, is horrified at men being present for childbirth; the second, a young Afropolitan, likes clubbing and sex, insisting, 'A man must allow a maximum of 4 weeks between sexual intercourse' (Huchu 2014: 15). By contrast, the Maestro lives in his mind among abstract concerns.

Huchu's 'novel of ideas' is thus encased within an inescapable buffer of literary reference that prohibits his characters accessing more fundamental truths. And where Dostoevskii's Kirillov is goaded into his suicide by two fellow nihilists named Stavrogin and Petr Stepanovich, Huchu's *would-be* Kirillov is constantly disrupted – by his mundane job, by his mobile phone, and by the alternating structure of the novel in which he appears – in a way that indicates that his quest for meaning is at odds with the vast, amoral, and directionless domain of global consumer choice. 'He switched the TV on', Huchu writes, 'flicking through many channels and failing to find anything worth watching. There was an overwhelming choice, even avoiding the temptation of Playboy, Babestation, and the late night adult entertainment channels' (2014: 44). Ironically, the Maestro *does* end up killing himself, but in contrast with Kirillov's intellectual determination, it is almost accidental, suggesting a parody of the Dostoevskian novel. Malnourished and alienated within his thoughts, the Maestro freezes to death when he lies down in the snow to await the one friend whom he has decided he loves. Instead of his notional will climaxing in a suicidal gunshot off-stage as it does in *Demons*,

---

[6] The reference here is to the British novelist Jon McGregor (b. 1976), famous for his use of experimental narrative and restrained lyricism to depict everyday life. The book in question is McGregor's first novel, *If Nobody Speaks of Remarkable Things* (2002).

Huchu's man of mind simply dwindles into non-existence, while readers are ushered swiftly towards another one of the plot lines about transnational politics (2014: 221). The Maestro's life is not made more meaningful by death, as it turns out that he lacks the capacity to represent a more general Zimbabwean or migrant condition. Huchu, at the last moment, reveals him to be a white man, a member of an extreme minority and virtually a social pariah. In thwarting the reader's expectations about the Maestro's identity, the novel ends with a narrative disjuncture instead of a culmination.

The Maestro, the Magistrate, and the Mathematician thus falls prey to the same paradox as *Tales of the Metric System*: a world in which national affairs are necessarily enmeshed in global economic networks (whether via HIV drugs, supermarket goods, endless television channels, or transcontinental politics) is a world in which individuals have more choice – at least as capitalism defines it – but less freedom than ever before. The characters in Coovadia's and Huchu's novels represent African confrontations with global problems, but the all-consuming and frenetic nature of their novels' designs denies them the agency to move towards an alternative framework of meaning. This point is not new, but Coovadia's and Huchu's explicit channelling and reworking of the nineteenth-century Russian novel of ideas introduces a provocative contrast between lives that do and do not have the capacity to reveal Christianity as a saving grace. For both Tolstoi and Dostoevskii, 'choice' is made valuable only by the final presence of God. By the time this God makes his way, via literary influence, to a globalized southern Africa more than a century later, he is but one more reference point in the losing game of aimless hyper-connection. As a result, the afterlives of the nineteenth-century Russian novel in recent southern African fiction suggest some key broader challenges for doing transcultural literary work amidst what has been called the global turn in the humanities. While globalism may seem to offer more possibilities for the novel, its maximalist structure also limits what writers can imagine through individual lives. A comparison of Tolstoi and Dostoevskii with their postcolonial African successors thus looks away from progress and towards more nuanced exploration of what sorts of meaning different contexts allow.

Works Cited

Ajulu, Rok. 2001. 'Thabo Mbeki's African Renaissance in a Globalising World Economy: The Struggle for the Soul of the Continent', *Review of African Political Economy*, 28(87): 27–42.

Bakhtin, Mikhail. 1984. *Problems of Dostoevsky's Poetics*, trans. and ed. Caryl Emerson (Minneapolis, MN: University of Minnesota Press).

Bayley, John. 1988. *Tolstoy and the Novel* (Chicago, IL: University of Chicago Press).

Berdiaev, Nikolai. 1935. *Freedom and the Spirit*, trans. Oliver Fielding Clarke (London: Centenary Press).

——. 2002. 'On Suicide', trans. Fr. S. Janos <http://www.berdyaev.com/berdiaev/berd_lib/1931_27.html> [accessed 26 August 2018].

Berlin, Isaiah. 1993. *The Hedgehog and the Fox* (Chicago, IL: Elephant Paperbacks).

Bethea, David M. 1989. *The Shape of Apocalypse in Modern Fiction* (Princeton, NJ: Princeton University Press).

Comaroff, Jean, and John Comaroff. 2012. *Theory from the South: Or, How Euro-America Is Evolving toward Africa* (London: Routledge).

Coovadia, Imraan. 2014. *Tales of the Metric System* (Cape Town: Umuzi).

Dostoevsky, Fyodor. 1994. *Demons* (New York: Vintage).

Foster, John Burt Jr. 2013. *Transnational Tolstoy: Between the West and the World* (London: Bloomsbury).

Frede, Victoria. 2011. *Doubt, Atheism, and the Nineteenth-Century Russian Intelligentsia* (Madison, WI: University of Wisconsin Press).

Hamburg, G. M., and Randall A. Poole (eds). 2010. *A History of Russian Philosophy 1830–1930: Faith, Reason, and the Defense of Human Dignity* (Cambridge: Cambridge University Press).

Huchu, Tendai. 2014. *The Maestro, the Magistrate, and the Mathematician* (Athens, OH: Ohio University Press).

Jackson, Jeanne-Marie. 2015. *South African Literature's Russian Soul: Narrative Forms of Global Isolation* (London: Bloomsbury).

James, Henry. 1908. *The Tragic Muse*, Vol. 1 (New York: Charles Scribner's Sons).

McGregor, Jon. 2002. *If Nobody Speaks of Remarkable Things* (London: Bloomsbury).

Merezhkovsky, Dmitry Sergeyevich. 1902. *Tolstoi as Man and Artist with an Essay on Dostoievski* (New York: G. P. Putnam's Sons).

Morson, Gary Saul. 2010. 'Tradition and Counter-Tradition: The Radical Intelligentsia and Classical Russian Literature' in William Leatherbarrow and Derek Offord (eds), *A History of Russian Thought* (Cambridge: Cambridge University Press), 141–68.

Robertson, Roland, and Kathleen E. White. 2007. 'What Is Globalization?' in George Ritzer (ed.), *The Blackwell Companion to Globalization* (Chichester: Wiley-Blackwell), 54–66.

Rzhevsky, Nicholas. 1983. *Russian Literature and Ideology: Herzen, Dostoevsky, Leontiev, Tolstoy, Fadeyev* (Urbana, IL: University of Illinois Press).

Schwarz, Roberto. 1980. 'Misplaced Ideas: Literature and Society in Late Nineteenth-Century Brazil', *Comparative Civilizations Review*, 5(5): 33–51.

Steiner, George. 1996. *Tolstoy or Dostoevsky: An Essay in Contrast* (New Haven, CT: Yale University Press).

Tolstoy, Leo. 1967. 'The Death of Ivan Ilych' in *Great Short Works of Leo Tolstoy*, trans. Louise and Aylmer Maude (New York: Harper & Row), 245–302.

Walicki, Andrzej. 1979. *A History of Russian Thought from the Enlightenment to Marxism*, trans. Hilda Andrews-Rusiecka (Stanford, CA: Stanford University Press).

15

'Russian' Imperfections?
A Plea for Transcultural Readings of
Aesthetic Trends

Ellen Rutten

How does one study an aesthetic practice which surfaces across multiple world localities? In this chapter, I examine this question by unravelling a trend to aestheticize or celebrate imperfection. I use Russophone examples to underline the importance of a *transcultural* reading of aesthetic practices. In the analysis that follows, I promote 'transcultural thickenings' – a concept that media theorists Nick Couldry and Andreas Hepp (2009) use to unpack translocal meaning-making processes. According to Couldry and Hepp, to fully understand cultural developments we must unravel the different regional, national, social, and other communicative 'thickenings' or layers that feed them. To give an example: to correctly interpret the actions of Russian activist collective Pussy Riot, we need to reckon with the Russian philosophical and literary trends that inspired the collective, but we should also take into account its status as a player on the global art market, and as representative of an urban elite whose world view is cosmopolitan rather than locally oriented.

In this chapter, I use Couldry and Hepp's 'transcultural thickenings' as a tool to read and study aesthetic developments. The ensuing transcultural analysis defies both universalist and strictly nation-bound aesthetic analysis; instead, it promotes a transnational, multi-layered approach to the study of aesthetic objects.

I would like to thank Andy Byford, Connor Doak, Stephen Hutchings, Natalia Il'ina, Irina Kaspe, Barbara Roggeveen, Natalia Samutina, Dorine Schellens, and Vera Zvereva for their helpful input into the analysis in this chapter.

Aesthetics of Imperfection

We start *in medias res,* with seven cultural objects and comments on them by their makers and users:

1. The profile of Moscow-based dater Itskhak (2017) on loveplanet.ru / '[it] is our imperfection which makes us unique'.

2. Australian photographer Alex Cearns's photos of impaired animals / disabilities as 'perfect imperfection[s]', which 'make all creatures precious and unique' (Bratskeir 2015).

3. Dutch designer Maarten Baas's handmade Clay furniture / 'functional imperfection' as token of 'organic' uniqueness (Iconic Dutch n.d.).

4. American-based scholar Linda Badley's (2011: 90) study of Lars Von Trier / an 'aesthetic of [...] imperfection' in his films.

5. Art theoretician Boris Groys (2010: 138–39) on the work of photographer Boris Mikhailov / the 'eroticism of imperfection' of the collapsed Soviet experiment.

6. Texas-based professor Brené Brown's bestseller *The Gifts of Imperfection* / by accepting 'our imperfections', 'we discover the infinite power of our light' (2010: 137, 6).

7. A *Chronicle of Higher Education* essay on teaching by Cairo-based scholar Maha Bali (2017) / a 'pedagogy of imperfection' as route to 'authenticity or humanness'.

These seven examples are representative of a much wider array of similar claims. They stem from different world regions, varying creative fields, and various text genres. But they have important things in common, too.

One: all focus on that which is not 'perfect' – the 'quality or state' of being

- 'entirely without fault or defect', 'satisfying all requirements', 'corresponding to an ideal standard or abstract concept'; or
- 'pure, total', 'lacking in no essential detail' ('Perfect' n.d.)[1]

The objects in the list defy this flawless state. They – or, put more precisely, their makers and consumers – advance a logic of deformation, decay, or deviation from social norms.

---

[1] In this definition summary, I omitted obsolete (e.g. 'mature') and specialist (e.g. 'legally valid') meanings of the term.

Two: all *praise* imperfection. In each of the abovementioned claims, the non-perfected acts as a hallmark for something good – aesthetic satisfaction, for instance, authenticity, or well-being. In some cases, the perfect-imperfect dichotomy flipflops altogether, as when Cearns calls disabilities 'perfect imperfections'.

The many makers and consumers who laud imperfection respond to social transitions – ecological crises, for instance, or digitization. They are not born as fans of the non-polished: their fascination for the imperfect is an attempt to cope with a reality in drastic social flux. This attempt is, as a rule, an attempt of the privileged. Buyers of Baas's wonky looking chairs (at $2,500 apiece), for instance, can also afford picture-perfect furniture.

Imperfection and Aesthetic Theory

This chapter focuses neither on the present-day interest in imperfection as such, nor on its ethical pitfalls. Rather, my enquiry is the methodological question with which I opened this chapter. How does one study an aesthetic trend which resonates not only across various social domains and historical periods but also across various world localities? The habit of fetishizing imperfection surfaces in social fields ranging from design to psychology; it boasts a long and lush history and it resonates across different world regions.

Existing analyses helpfully map the diachronicity, transdisciplinarity, and transregionality of various cults of imperfection (Ramakers 2002: 158–72; Nemoianu 2006). However, their authors tend to juxtapose isolated disciplines, periods, and/or world regions without problematizing this comparison. This chapter does problematize – or, put less negatively, theoretically reflect upon – the act of comparing.

More pointedly, I critically interrogate the *transcultural* travels of today's imperfection cult. In the analysis that follows, I devote special attention to 'Russian' examples – and in doing so, I exchange a classic 'Russian studies' perspective (which foregrounds national traditions) for scholarship of the transnational. In recent decades, scholars have promoted 'transnational' (Robinson 2004), 'hypercultural' (Han 2005), 'transcultural' (Kimmich and Schahadat 2002), and other prisms for analysing linguistic and cultural practices. In this chapter, I build on that last domain – that of transcultural theorizing, which exchanges definitions of 'cultures as closed systems' for a focus on interactivity, and Eurocentrist bias for 'subaltern' (more diverse and non-hegemonic, that is) perspectives (König 2016).

Transcultural, transnational, and hypercultural studies offer diverse but methodologically related prisms. Rather than nationally defined developments, all examine *cultural transfers* and acts of *entangling*. Scholars have coined these terms to underline three things:

1. when cultural processes move across different regional contexts, these moves are not static acts, in which local trend A moves wholesale and unchanged to locality B;

2. instead, transcultural processes tend to be fluid and multi- rather than one-directional;

3. the borders between these contexts are always porous and in transition.

(Espagne 1999; Conrad and Randeria 2002)

Thinking about cultural transfer and entangling can help us to refine our understanding of aesthetic processes that resonate across various regional settings. How do these processes work? In this chapter, I explore the question by juxtaposing 'Russian' with 'non-Russian' examples of the trend to celebrate imperfect looks. What does a 'Russian' aesthetics of imperfection look like? And can we speak of such an aesthetics in the first place? As my case study will demonstrate, theories of the transcultural offer helpful methodological tools to answer questions like these.

Two Discourses on Imperfection

I start by comparing two claims by native Russians from the list with which we started: Itskhak's self-description and Groys's characterization of Mikhailov. At first sight, they represent two very different discourses on imperfection. Itskhak celebrates imperfect selves in an online dating profile; Groys ponders an aesthetics of imperfection in photography.

The contrast between these two takes on the imperfect is self-evident. My choice to nevertheless insist on their parallels is driven by a broader interdisciplinary aim (Klein 1999). This analysis was conducted within the confines of 'Sublime Imperfections', a research project that synthesizes existing thinking into an integrative theory of imperfection (Rutten 2015). 'Sublime Imperfections' favours rigorous interdisciplinarity over disciplinary specialization in order to point at broader patterns, and to ask: Why and how do we valorize the imperfect across different disciplinary and discursive domains, ranging from genetics to art, and from cultural theorizing to product ads? With this interdisciplinary agenda in mind, my analysis confronts domains that seem very different at first sight.

'Imperfection Makes Us Unique': Itskhak

We start with the first domain: that of online dating. Itskhak, a user of loveplanet.ru, presents himself, in English,[2] as a 40-year-old higher-educated Muscovite and 'native speaker' of Russian, with 'grey eyes', tattoos, 'average income', and 'some extra pounds', who wants to meet women 'aged 28 to 45' (Itskhak 2017). He switches to Russian to share information about his favourite music (music app Meloman), book (Sartre's 1938 novel *Nausea*), and food ('medium steak'). On his Russophone profile blog, he shares short thoughts and citations by a variety of writers and thinkers, including Arthur Schopenhauer, Persian poet Omar Khayyam, and Japanese writer Haruki Murakami.

Between 2005 and 2017, loveplanet.ru attracted roughly 21.5 million users (Loveplanet 2017). The site targets Russia-based and Russophone daters but offers five language options, and many users (such as Itskhak) mix languages.

Itskhak promotes the imperfect on multiple levels. Apart from explicitly claiming that 'our imperfection [...] makes us unique', he approves of character traits that deviate from 'good' dating practice. For example, in response to the site's question, 'What would you be able to forgive?', he writes 'Cheating? Yes!' (Itskhak 2017). His writing style oozes a similar tolerance of norm deviation. This man with higher education, knowledge of at least two languages, and a love of Sartre and Schopenhauer refuses to use online tools to correct his multiple typos, punctuation errors, and English glitches.

Itskhak is not the only imperfection aficionado on Loveplanet. Moscow-based Mariya (n.d.) writes, in Russian: 'I am not without defects, but only because I am alive and real'. Alina (n.d.) claims (in Russian, too) that 'imperfection is beautiful, madness is genius'.[3]

On other dating websites with native Russian users, similar rhetoric surfaces. A case in point is the near-exclusively Russophone mamba.ru – a site that, with roughly 31 million users (Mamba 2017), is yet more popular than loveplanet.ru. In 2011, 49-year-old Mamba user Gulya shared, in Russian, the poem 'I Am Created Out of Caresses and Tears ...' [Ia sozdana iz laski i slez], an anonymous verse in circulation on the Russian internet:

> I am a mixture of scream and smile,
> Of correct decisions and mistakes ...

---

[2] During my initial research in 2017, Itskhak's profile appeared in English when I accessed the site, but by July 2018, it had been auto-translated into Dutch (my native language). The Russian statements were not translated.

[3] By the time this chapter was completed, this post had been deleted. The archived link is https://loveplanet.ru/page/alinaevstign/.

> A blend of pain and bliss,
> I am the perfect imperfection.
> Beautiful as the morning dew,
> But mean and dangerous as the moon. (Gulya 2011)

As this fragment illustrates, the poem's verses are built around a series of oxymorons, including the collapsed perfect-imperfect dichotomy that also structures Cearns's animal photos.

Gulya, Mariya, and Itskhak share their takes on the non-polished in Russian – but analogous statements circulate among Russian users of Anglophone-only dating sites. The internationally oriented dating site russian-cupid.com, for instance, attracts a smaller audience than Loveplanet or Mamba (Russiancupid 2017); but this modest site boasts more pleas for imperfection than the others together. 'Perfection is boring', writes 32-year-old Evgeniya (n.d.) from Novosibirsk: 'The real beauty lies in imperfections'. 24-year-old Elena (n.d.) from Krasnoyarsk exclaims, in the wobbly English that thrives on the site: 'Not trying to be perfect – just flaws make us extraordinary person-ality!' Inessa (45) from Vologda (n.d.), Marina (33) from Arkhangel'sk (n.d.), and Stella (47) from Stavropol' (n.d.), are less exuberant, but all do employ a rhetoric of imperfection to underscore that, in this world of hacks and hyperpolished looks, *they*, at least, are no deceivers. 'Everybody makes a good commercial of himself through this virtual world', so Stella (n.d.) muses. 'I am not perfect [...] If [...] you are true and honest, please be mine'.

'The Eroticism of Imperfection': Groys

Itskhak's claims may mirror similar statements by online Russophone daters, but they also overlap with discussions of imperfection in a different cultural scene: that of art criticism.

Boris Groys is a world-leading contemporary art expert. He was born in 1947 in Berlin; migrated with his family to Leningrad (today St Petersburg), where he grew up and started his career; moved back to Germany, where he held several academic positions; and currently acts as Professor of Russian and Slavic Studies at New York University. Groys publishes on art and media theory in German, English, and Russian.

'The Eroticism of Imperfection' first appeared in English, and later in Russian, in the 'visual daily' *Art1* (Groys 2010, 2014).[4] In this essay, Groys

---

[4] The publication says that Andrei Fomenko translated the text 'from German'; whether the English version built on a German original was unclear when this chapter was written.

Fig. 14.1. Boris Mikhailov, 'Superimposition',
from the series *Yesterday's Sandwich* (1966).
Reproduced with permission of Boris Mikhailov.

examines the work of Boris Mikhailov. An internationally renowned photographer who gained fame in late-Soviet nonconformist circles, Mikhailov is known for his unglamorous photos of everyday life in Soviet and post-Soviet space (see Fig. 14.1).

Groys asks readers not to confuse Mikhailov's unpolished aesthetics with a broader photographic interest in dismantling staged realities. Many photographers, so he explains, (hyper-)stylize models to criticize 'the technical perfection with which someone today can don an artificial mask capable of completely obscuring his real face' (2010: 138). But Mikhailov does something else. Firstly, his photos comment not on technological flawlessness but on 'the total collective simulation called the Soviet Union' (Groys 2010: 139). Secondly, rather than using hyperbolic enlargement, 'Mikhailov thematizes the imperfect, unsuccessful, and miserably failed *mise-en-scène* – a badly made, defective mask that only heightens the embarrassment of showing the unprotected face' (Groys 2010: 138–39).

Groys spots a downright 'eroticism of imperfection' in Mikhailov's work, particularly in his portraits of fragile bodies of the socially marginalized

(2010: 143). After all, as Groys winks at Leonard Cohen,[5] it is 'when cracks start to show in the body's *mise-en-scène*, that this body becomes truly appealing, erotic, and seductive in Mikhailov's eyes' (Groys 2010: 143).

Other Anglophone and Russophone critics of Mikhailov – theoreticians, curators, art journalists – similarly frame imperfection as a gateway to aesthetic satisfaction, albeit without the erotic dimension that Groys underlines.[6] Photo critic Jeffrey Ladd (n.d.) sees the 'unprecious, imperfect, torn' prints of Soviet everyday life in Mikhailov's book *Diary* (2015) as odes to 'the imperfection, the error, and the corrosion of ideology' which remove 'the artificial "mask of beauty" on the region'. Online debaters of 'imperfection' as 'modus of the real in photography' link Mikhailov's popularity to a 'celebration of the anti-aesthetic/imperfection' that reacts to 'the impending demise of the photograph' (cited in Stiegler 2012).

These and other Anglophone critics evoke the term 'imperfection' to explain that Mikhailov's work offers a valuable aesthetic response to digitization or to (post-)Soviet reality – or, in some cases, to both at the same time. So do Russian critics in Anglophone reviews. Helen Petrovsky (2012), for instance, claims that Mikhailov foregrounds 'the energies of the private, inherently subversive' in Soviet history – energies that 'are on the side of the imperfect and the incomplete'. In Russian-language reviews, the non-perfected is also presented as an aesthetic drive in Mikhailov's work, but Russophone critics tend to avoid the *word* 'imperfection' [nesovershenstvo].[7] Instead, they employ terms like 'mud, obscenities' [griaz', nepristoinosti] (Rappoport 2002); 'cruelty' and 'pain' [zhest, bol'] (Kisina 2011); and 'abandonment', 'disrespectability', or 'poor quality' [broshennost', nerespektabel'nost', plokhoe kachestvo] (Mikhailov 2014). Only Mikhailov himself points at the 'bodily imperfection' [telesnoe nesovershenstvo] of his characters. He situates their physical flaws within a late-Soviet, nonconformist cult of the 'antihero', which allowed artists to 'demonstrate who they were without fear' (Mikhailov 2012b).

---

[5] Leonard Cohen famously claims in his song 'Anthem' (1992) that 'There is a crack in everything, that's how the light gets in'.

[6] I selected Anglophone and Russophone reviews through online searches for, respectively, 'imperfection "Boris Mikhailov"' and, in Cyrillic, 'nesovershenstvo "Boris Mikhailov"'. I did so aware of the pitfalls of digital search tools (see Pariser 2011), and I omitted the modest but not irrelevant body of Ukrainophone Mikhailov-devoted criticism.

[7] In May 2017, an online search for 'imperfection "Boris Mikhailov"' in Russian generated a wealth of links, but apart from the *Afisha* self-portrait, none were devoted to the photographer.

With the Mikhailov reviews we have trudged far from the happy-go-lucky 'perfect imperfections' of our daters. What the daters and critics share, however, is an insistence on imperfection as a route to something valuable, whether that be realness, physical appeal, or unmediated self-expression.

Itskhak and Groys: 'Russian' Imperfections?

What happens when we examine how the trend to celebrate imperfection resonates in different world localities? The 'Itskhak' and 'Groys/Mikhailov' cases tell us two things about this question.

1. Neither Itskhak and Groys, nor their takes on imperfection, are self-evidently Russian

Itskhak and Groys are less self-evidently 'Russian' research subjects than they may seem. Itskhak is a Russophone Muscovite, but his cultural horizon is far from rigidly Russian. As we saw, he mixes Russian with English writing, and in his self-description he mentions a diverse set of cultural objects from equally diverse local settings: he simultaneously enjoys Russian music app Meloman, French writing, Persian poetry, German philosophy, and steak.

Groys's and Mikhailov's cultural horizons are even less confined to Russian state borders. Groys has Russian roots but spent much of his life outside Russia. He points to his Jewish ancestry as formative to his writing (Lovink 2000); and he often uses Russian case studies to theorize global art history. In unpacking Mikhailov's aesthetics, he swiftly switches from American contemporary art through Soviet visual culture to Nazi-era cinema (Groys 2010: 138–39).

The subject of Groys's essay is an equally 'international man', as Mikhailov calls himself (2012a). Mikhailov has Russian family bonds; his native language is Russian; and curators, Groys included, locate his work within Russian art history (Groys 2010; Nikitsch and Winzen 2004). He was born in Kharkiv, however, in Ukraine; he lives there and in Berlin; and in discussing his own work, he refers to American superhero Rambo as freely as he does to Soviet-era artists (Mikhailov 2012b).

It is, in short, clear that the critics and daters have a special bond with Russia; but to what extent they are 'Russian' is harder to say. It is equally hard to assess to what extent their interest in imperfection is informed by local and non-local cultural practices. This interest is defined at least by the following, part nationally and part otherwise defined practices and beliefs:

– Soviet Russia's 'perfectionist belief system' (Haas 2005: 174). The perfection-driven Soviet ideology sparked a late-Soviet fetishization of unpolished, homemade, repair aesthetics in art/product design (Gerasimova and Chuikina 2009; Komaromi 2004). As we saw in the Mikhailov reviews, his work aligns itself with this aesthetic trend, which has local roots, but it also blends in with a transnational interest in punk and DIY in the 1970s and 1980s.

– A historical habit among writers and artists to valorize imperfection as inherent to the act of aestheticization, and to frame 'imperfections' and 'ugliness' as 'contribut[ing] to the harmony of the universe' which goes back at least to ancient Rome (Eco 2007: 30) (and which interconnects both with a historical interest in 'deliberately imperfect pictures' in documentary photography (Marien 2006: 343) and, in Russia, with the late-Soviet repair/ imperfection cults). As art professionals, Mikhailov's critics know this habit well. It informs Itskhak's self-description, too. In *Nausea*, his favourite book, Sartre admits that our very 'existence is an imperfection' (1964: 101).

– Stereotypical representations of Russia as a nation that is more imperfect than others – and that prides itself on that capacity. Negative assessments of aesthetic perfection have flourished in Orthodox theology (Hutchings 1997). Nineteenth-century intellectuals promoted an 'anti-aesthetic' of the Russian countryside 'that made a virtue of its would-be deficiency', as part of a nation-building discourse in which Russia was 'h[e]ld up as a countermodel' to a bourgeois and inauthentic West (Ely 2002: 23, 7). The classic Russian novel thrives on a logic of failure (Brouwer 2003) and, to cite Slavist Gary Saul Morson, on an 'anti-aesthetic', too; in Morson's words, Russian prose authors present 'aesthetic detachment' and 'the aesthetic experience' as 'immoral' (Morson 1978: 480, 467). And in post-Soviet discourses, '"imperfections"' are 'co-opted as positively valued aspects of national character' (Pesmen 2000: 280) – by Eurasian thinkers, for instance, who oppose Russia to a perfect-but-inauthentic West (Dugin 2014: 45, 122). The cliché of Russia as a proudly imperfect-but-real nation echoes in the daters' language. Remember how Mariya assures Anglophone daters: 'I am not without defects, but only because I am alive and real'.

– And, finally, a global interest in imperfections and glitches in design, art, photography, and film in response to digitization and mediatization.[8] Groys's definition of an artistic 'eroticism of imperfection' blends in with this interest, as his reference to parodic hyperstylization in contemporary photography illustrates (2010: 138).

---

[8] On creative counter-responses to Photoshop, spellcheckers, and other technologies that allow us to perfect everyday life, see Ramakers (2002: 158–72); Badley (2011); Rutten (2015).

2. Imperfection-is-good talk is quite popular in English, popular in English statements by Russian native speakers, but only moderately popular in Russian

It is, in short, reductive to harshly disentangle the regionally, nationally, and transnationally defined cultural practices that feed both cases. Yet more reductive would be a Russian-only reading of the language that the critics and daters use to conceptualize imperfection. As we saw, Russian and English intermingle in both cases. Several Anglophone commentators of Mikhailov's work (including native Russian critics in Anglophone reviews) employ the term 'imperfection' to explain their interest in his photographs; by contrast, Russophone critics who cater to Russian audiences rarely employ the word 'imperfection' – although they do use semantically related words to foreground Mikhailov's love for the non-polished.

The dating sites point in a similar direction. On the relatively small-scale Anglophone Russiancupid (1.5 million users), five users praise imperfection, as opposed to four for the much bulkier Russophone Loveplanet and Mamba together (42.5 million users in total). These numbers tell us that only nine out of the total of 44 million native Russian users of the three sites promote themselves by embracing their 'imperfections'.

The picture tilts somewhat if we take a closer look at the poem used by Gulya, whose lyrical ego calls herself 'the perfect imperfection'. This poem is only cited once on 'our' dating sites, but it circulates actively in self- and profile descriptions on other dating sites, amateur poetry pages, and fan fiction communities. On 17 July 2017, an online search for its Russian title generated 4,250 hits. If we look yet closer at the (to the logic that we explore, seminal) oxymoron 'perfect imperfection', however, we again see a strong contrast between Russian and English. On the same 17 July, this phrase generated 415,000 Google hits in English, as opposed to 12,300 for its Russian equivalent. Even if one factors in differences in language size and digital penetration, this outcome suggests that the phrase is tangibly less popular in Russian.

That positive readings of the term 'imperfection' are more popular in English than Russian: that same conclusion implies a look at Anglophone dating sites. More than one Western dating site uses imperfection-is-good rhetoric in marketing slogans. By July 2017, a total of five used the motto 'Love Your Imperfections' (Belle Harmonie 2017; Brecht 2017; Lexa 2017; Match 2017; Meetic 2017); one even asked users to 'tweet their imperfections' with the hashtag #loveyourimperfections (Match 2015). We find no equivalents for these slogans among popular Russian online dating companies.[9]

---

[9] For overviews of popular Russophone dating sites, I used Sears-Collins (n.d.) and the sites mentioned on the 'Saity znakomstv' (Russian for 'dating sites') lemma on Wikipedia on 17 July 2017.

The Russophone critics, dating site marketeers, and daters all use the term 'imperfection' substantially less often than their Anglophone counterparts. There are at least two reasons for this difference in selected vocabularies.

The first reason is the popularity of imperfection rhetoric in Anglophone marketing. In framing imperfections as hallmarks of authenticity and uniqueness, the daters and critics tune into a trend among Anglophone PR professionals and commercial publishers. These eagerly present imperfections and blemishes as hallmarks of authenticity or, in self-help merchandise, as tokens of human uniqueness (De Hooge 2017; Brown 2010; Zazzle 2017). This trend occurs across different world localities, but its lingua franca (in slogans, hashtags, etc.) is English.

There is a second, more fundamental reason why the word 'imperfection' circulates less prominently among the Russophone critics and daters. This reason has everything to do with that word's idiosyncratic semantics in Russian. The noun/adjective pair 'nesovershenstvo/nesovershennyi' appear as first translations of 'imperfection/imperfect' in dictionaries (see, for instance, *Novyi bol'shoi anglo-russkii slovar'* 1993), and emerge as positive values in Russian from the eighteenth century onwards (*Slovar' russkogo* 2005). But Google Translate currently offers *defektnost'* (literally 'defectivity') as the first translation for 'imperfection'. English-Russian dictionaries give alternative translations for the English adjective 'perfect' in expressions like 'a perfect day' [chudnyi (literally 'marvellous') den'!] or 'perfect bliss' [polnoe (literally 'total') blazhenstvo] (*Novyi bol'shoi anglo-russkii slovar'* 1993). In Russian, in short, those qualities and states that 'imperfect/ion' covers in English are rendered with a wider range of nouns and adjectives. This is another reason why the Russophone critics and daters use that word less frequently than their Anglophone peers.

A Transcultural Reading

The analysis of the two different discussions teaches us two things:

1. It would be incorrect to read either case by drawing exclusively on local Russian developments, as traditional Russian-studies readings often have, as we can never fully disentangle the locally, nationally, and transnationally defined practices that feed both;

2. In both dating and art-critical discourses, positive assessments of imperfection are moderately popular in Russian, and substantially more popular in English.

Both findings nuance claims that circulate in recent Western and Western-oriented aesthetic analyses. Their authors argue that we are witnessing a worldwide postmodern preoccupation with the non-perfected (Nemoianu 2006) or a universal 'fetishization of nostalgic imperfection' in contemporary art and media (Menkman 2011). In truth, as we have seen, the extent to which makers and consumers turn to imperfection to digest a reality in transition varies across different world localities; and across these localities, the interest in imperfection adopts part overlapping, part diverging guises.

To understand the nuances of the imperfection cult's local variabilities, it helps to return to transcultural theorizing. Media theorists Nick Couldry and Andreas Hepp make a plea for exchanging nation-oriented studies of cultural practices for 'a more complex' transcultural horizon, which recognizes that these practices are 'not "placed" at a defined locality but rearticulated through disembedded communicative processes', while still being related to a greater or lesser number of localities within or beyond particular national or regional boundaries' (2009: 32).

Rather than nation states, Couldry and Hepp use the concept of 'cultural thickenings' – 'translocal processes of the articulation of meaning' – as unit of comparison (2009: 32). They believe that in any cultural development, different (regional, national, local, but also social, generational, etc.) communicative layers or 'thickenings' are at play. These different thickenings are relevant, but they are difficult to unsnarl, as they continuously overlap and interact.

Without excluding the state as a comparative unit (cultural thickenings *can* overlap with national boundaries), Hepp and Couldry's concept of cultural thickenings provides a geographically layered methodological and analytical framework. Our two cases demonstrate how fine-grained and mutually interdependent this framework can be. Relevant cultural thickenings to both cases include, to varying extents and in complex interweavings, the shared traditions and beliefs of:

- urban elites (whose outlines differ little between, say, Moscow and Chicago) (for most daters and critics);

- a cosmopolitan, higher-educated middle class (ditto);

- a transnational community of art theorists, curators, and journalists (for the critics);

- the equally transnational public of active social media users (for the online daters);

as well as the nationally defined societies of

- the late Soviet Union and post-Soviet Russia (for the daters and some critics);

– (the Jewish-Soviet migrant community in) post-war Germany (for Groys); and

– (the intellectual elite of) the twenty-first-century United States (for some critics).

All these different, and mutually interlinking, territorial and social layers impact on the writings of the critics and the daters. An analysis of that writing hardly benefits from confining itself to one specific layer – that of Groys's 'Russian' or 'scholarly' roots, for instance. By contrast, transcultural theorizing reckons with the various interacting territorial and temporal spheres across which different cultural actors move.

Transnational theorizing helps us to understand not only who Groys and Itskhak are, but also what they *think* – and what they think about the non-polished, in particular. After all, the statements on imperfection by the daters and critics are unimaginable outside the transnationally, nationally, and regionally defined 'thickenings' that (without using the term 'cultural thickening' proper) I summed up earlier, from late-Soviet cults of repair to the interest in glitches in contemporary art and film.

Conclusion

Let us return to my opening question: how do we analyse an aesthetic trend which surfaces not only across multiple social domains and historical eras but also across various world localities? This chapter has presented an exercise in enlisting and clustering 'cultural thickenings' as a possible answer to that methodological question. My analysis has shunned both universalist and rigidly nation-driven readings of positive assessments of imperfection. It has demonstrated that we witness neither a uniquely 'Russian' nor a homogeneously global fascination with imperfection.

What this chapter offers instead is a transcultural reading of imperfection-lauding claims by daters and critics. As we have seen, in Russophone discourse, the trend to laud imperfection feeds on a rich menu of social, cultural, religious, and linguistic practices and beliefs. By studying this menu, I want to promote the value of the 'transcultural lens' in aesthetic theorizing. Theories of the transcultural can help us to unpack the various practices and beliefs – the 'cultural thickenings' – that inform aesthetic trends. As the preceding pages have illustrated, the lens of the transcultural sharpens our gaze by showing us, first, how aesthetic trends change over time and, second, how they sometimes do, and sometimes do not overlap with the borders of one nation state.

Works Cited

Alina. n.d. Dating profile at Loveplanet.ru <https://loveplanet.ru/page/alinaevstign/> [deleted when accessed on 15 June 2017].

Badley, Linda. 2011. *Lars von Trier* (Champaign, IL: University of Illinois Press).

Bali, Maha. 2017. 'Pedagogy of Imperfection', *The Chronicle of Higher Education*, 13 January <http://www.chronicle.com/blogs/profhacker/pedagogy-of-imperfection/63435> [accessed 24 August 2018].

Belle Harmonie. 2017. 'Acceptez-vous comme vous êtes!' *Twitter*, 8 July <https://twitter.com/Belleharmonie06/status/883633654135738368> [accessed 24 August 2018].

Bratskeir, Kate. 2015. 'These Photos Show Why "Perfectly Imperfect" Animals Are Worthy of Homes, Too', *Huffington Post*, 8 November <http://www.huffingtonpost.com/entry/photo-series-captures-the-beauty-of-24-perfectly-imperfect-animals_us_55c8ee82e4b0f73b20ba26f1> [accessed 24 August 2018].

Brecht, Katharina. 2017. 'Lovescout24 setzt "Love Your Imperfections" Kampagne fort', *Horizont*, 28 June <http://www.horizont.net/marketing/nachrichten/Dating-Portal-Lovescout24-setzt-Love-your-imperfections-Kampagne-fort-159169> [accessed 24 August 2018].

Brouwer, Sander. 2003. 'The Bridegroom Who Did Not Come: Social and Amorous Unproductivity from Pushkin to the Silver Age' in J. Andrew and R. Reid (eds), *Two Hundred Years of Pushkin*', Vol. 1, *'Pushkin's Secret': Russian Writers Reread and Rewrite Pushkin* (Amsterdam: Rodopi), 49–65.

Brown, Brené. 2010. *The Gifts of Imperfection: Let Go of Who You Think You're Supposed to Be and Embrace Who You Are* (Center City, MN: Hazelden).

Conrad, Sebastian, and Shalini Randeria (eds). 2002. *Jenseits des Eurozentrismus. Postkoloniale Perspektiven in den Geschichts- und Kulturwissenschaften* (Frankfurt: Campus).

Couldry, Nick, and Andreas Hepp. 2009. 'What Should Comparative Media Research Be Comparing? Towards a Transcultural Approach to "Media Cultures"' in D. K. Thussu (ed.), *Internationalizing Media Studies* (London: Routledge), 33–48.

De Hooge, Ilona. 2017. 'Voedselverspilling verminderen door de promotie van imperfecte voedselproducten?' *Stichting Wetenschappelijk Onderzoek Commerciële Communicatie*, 17 January <https://www.swocc.nl/kennisbank-item/voedselverspilling-verminderen-door-de-promotie-van-imperfecte-voedselproducten/> [accessed 24 August 2018].

Dugin, Alexander. 2014. *Eurasian Mission: An Introduction to Neo-Eurasianism* (Eemnes, Netherlands: Arktos).

Eco, Umberto. 2007. *On Ugliness* (Milan: Rizzolli).

Elena. n.d. Dating profile at Russiancupid.com <https://www.russiancupid.com/en/profile/showProfile/ID/1664087> [accessed 24 August 2018].

Ely, Christopher. 2002. *This Meager Nature: Landscape and National Identity in Imperialist Russia* (DeKalb, IL: Northern Illinois University Press).

Espagne, Michel. 1999. *Les transferts culturels franco-allemands* (Paris: PUF).

Evgeniya. n.d. Dating profile at Russiancupid.com <https://www.russiancupid.com/en/profile/showProfile/ID/3956055> [accessed 24 August 2018].

Gerasimova, Ekaterina, and Sof'ia Chuikina. 2009. 'The Repair Society', *Russian Studies in History*, 48(1): 58–74.

Groys, Boris. 2010. *History Becomes Form: Moscow Conceptualism* (Cambridge, MA: MIT Press).

——. 2014. 'Erotika nesovershennogo', *Art1*, 27 January <http://art1.ru/2014/01/27/erotika-nesovershennogo-30364> [accessed 24 August 2018].

Gulya. 2011. 'Ia sozdana …', mamba.ru, 18 October <https://www.mamba.ru/ru/diary/guz645> [accessed 24 August 2018].

Haas, Marc L. 2005. *The Ideological Origins of Great Power Politics, 1789–1989* (Ithaca, NY: Cornell University Press).

Han, Byung-Chul. 2005. *Hyperkulturalität. Kultur und Globalisierung* (Berlin: Merve).

Hutchings, Stephen. 1997. *Russian Modernism: The Transfiguration of the Everyday* (Cambridge: Cambridge University Press).

Iconic Dutch. n.d. 'Maarten Baas', Iconic Dutch <http://iconicdutch.com/uk/designers/maarten-baas> [accessed 24 August 2018].

Inessa. n.d. Dating profile at Russiancupid.com <https://www.russiancupid.com/en/profile/showProfile/ID/1488819> [accessed 24 August 2018].

Itskhak. 2017. Dating profile at Loveplanet.ru <http://loveplanet.ru/page/kucherjvyi/> [accessed 24 August 2018].

Kimmich, Dorothee, and Schamma Schahadat. 2002. *Kulturen in Bewegung. Beiträge zur Theorie und Praxis der Transkulturalität* (Bielefeld: Transcript).

Kisina, Iuliia. 2011. 'Amoral'nyi kodeks Borisa Mikhailova', *Radio Svoboda*, 25 May <https://www.svoboda.org/a/24205471.html> [accessed 24 August 2018].

Klein, Julie. 1999. *Interdisciplinarity: History, Theory, and Practice* (Detroit, MI: Wayne State University Press).

Komaromi, Ann. 2004. 'The Material Existence of Soviet Samizdat', *Slavic Review*, 63(3): 597–618.

König, Daniel. 2016. 'The Transcultural Approach within a Disciplinary Framework: An Introduction', *Transcultural Studies*, 2 <https://heiup.uni-heidelberg.de/journals/index.php/transcultural/article/view/23642/17366> [accessed 24 August 2018].

Ladd, Jeffrey. n.d. 'Boris Mikhailov. *Diary*. Walther König', *1000 Words* <http://www.1000wordsmag.com/boris-mikhailov/> [accessed 24 August 2018].

Lexa. 2017. Lexa.nl homepage <http://lexa.nl> [accessed 20 December 2017].

Loveplanet. 2017. Loveplanet.ru homepage <http://loveplanet.ru> [accessed 20 December 2018].

Lovink, Geert. 2000. 'Interview with Boris Groys, German Art Critic and Media Theoretician', *Nettime.org* <https://nettime.org/Lists-Archives/nettime-l-0010/msg00036.html> [accessed 24 August 2018].

Mamba. 2017. Mamba.ru homepage <http://mamba.ru> [accessed 20 December 2017].

Marien, Mary Warner. 2006. *Photography: A Cultural History* (London: Laurence Kind).

Marina. n.d. Dating profile at Russiancupid.com <https://www.russiancupid.com/en/profile/showProfile/ID/161971> [accessed 24 August 2018].

Mariya. n.d. Dating profile at Loveplanet.ru <https://loveplanet.ru/page/100002 332381d486/> [accessed 24 August 2018].

Match. 2015. 'Do You #Loveyourimperfections?', *Match.com* <https://uk.match.com/pages/advice/our-campaigns/love-your-imperfections-2015/do-you-loveyourimperfections> [accessed 24 August 2018].

——. 2017. Match.com homepage <https://uk.match.com> [accessed 20 December 2017].

Meetic. 2017. Meetic.fr homepage <https://meetic.fr> [accessed 20 December 2017].

Menkman, Rosa. 2011. *The Glitch Moment(um)* (Amsterdam: Institute of Network Cultures) <https://networkcultures.org/_uploads/NN%234_RosaMenkman.pdf> [accessed 24 August 2018].

Mikhailov, Boris. 2012a. 'Ia shukaiu sii podiv', interview with Dmitro Desiaterik. *Den'*, 18 January <https://day.kyiv.ua/uk/article/den-ukrayini/boris-mihaylov-ya-shukayu-sviy-podiv> [accessed 24 August 2018].

——. 2012b. 'Luchshie fotografy strany: Boris Mikhailov. Avtoportret', *Afisha*, 9 July <https://daily.afisha.ru/archive/gorod/archive/best-photo-boris-mihajlov/> [accessed 24 August 2018].

——. 2014. 'Geroizatsiia ubiistva – eto plokhaia fotografiia', *Kommersant*, 6 June <https://www.kommersant.ru/doc/2482016> [accessed 24 August 2018].

Morson, Gary Saul. 1978. 'The Reader as Voyeur: Tolstoi and the Poetics of Didactic Fiction', *Canadian-American Slavic Studies*, 12 (Winter): 465–80.

Nemoianu, Virgil. 2006. *The Triumph of Imperfection: The Silver Age of Sociocultural Moderation in Early 19th Century Europe* (Columbia, SC: University of South Carolina Press).

Nikitisch, Georgij, and Matthias Winzen. 2004. *Na kurort! Russische Kunst heute* (Cologne: Wienan).

Novyi bol'shoi anglo-russkii slovar' (Moscow: Russkii iazyk, 1993).

Pariser, Eli. 2011. *The Filter Bubble: What the Internet Is Hiding from You* (London: Penguin).

'Perfect' in *Merriam-Webster Dictionary* <https://www.merriam-webster.com/dictionary/perfect> [accessed 24 August 2018].

Pesmen, Dale. 2000. *Russia and Soul: An Exploration* (Ithaca, NY: Cornell University Press).

Petrovsky, Helen. 2012. 'Boris Mikhailov: A New Metaphysician', *American Suburb X*, 6 April. <http://www.americansuburbx.com/2012/04/boris-mikhailov-boris-mikhailov-new.html> [accessed 24 August 2018].

Ramakers, Renny. 2002. *Less + More: Droog Design in Context* (Rotterdam: Nai Publishers).

Rappoport, Aleksandr. 2002. 'Chelovek bez opredelennogo mesta', *Khudozhestvennyi zhurnal*, 42 <http://xz.gif.ru/numbers/42/bez-mesta/> [accessed 24 August 2018].

Robinson, William. 2004. *A Theory of Global Capitalism: Production, Class, and State in a Transnational World* (Baltimore, MD: Johns Hopkins University Press).

Russiancupid. 2017. Russiancupid.com homepage <http://russiancupid.com> [accessed 20 December 2018].

Rutten, Ellen. 2015. 'Sublime Imperfections', research project description <http://sublimeimperfections.org/about-si/> [accessed 24 August 2018].

Sartre, Jean-Paul. 1964. *Nausea* (New York: New Directions).

Sears-Collins, Addison. n.d. 'The 4 Best Online Dating Sites in Russia', *Visahunter* <http://www.visahunter.com/articles/the-best-online-dating-sites-in-russia/> [accessed 24 August 2018].

Slovar' russkogo iazyka XVIII veka. Vypusk 15. Nepochatyi-oblomat'sia. 2005 (St Petersburg: Nauka).

Stella. n.d. Dating profile at Russiancupid.com <https://www.russiancupid.com/en/profile/showProfile/ID/255623> [accessed 24 August 2018].

Stiegler, Bernd. 2012. '1. Imperfection', *Still Searching...*, 11 January <https://www.fotomuseum.ch/en/explore/still-searching/articles/26907_imperfection> [accessed 24 August 2018].

Zazzle. 2017. 'Perfect Imperfection T-Shirts' <https://www.zazzle.nl/perfect+imperfection+tshirts> [accessed 20 December 2017].

Part IV

Russia Going Global

16

Beyond a World with One Master

The Rhetorical Dimensions
of Putin's 'Sovereign Internet'

Michael Gorham

> What exactly is a unipolar world? No matter how you embellish
> it, in the end it means just one thing in practice: a single power
> centre, a single centre of decision-making. It's a world with one
> master, one sovereign. And in the end, it's fatal not only for
> those located within the framework of the system, but also for
> the sovereign himself, because it destroys him from the inside.
> Vladimir Putin, Munich, 2007

Vladimir Putin's speech at the 2007 global security summit in Munich marked
a turning point in his positioning of Russia in the global community. On the
heels of his recently announced domestic policy of 'sovereign democracy',
Putin made it clear that Russia would no longer be content with operating
under what he perceived to be a de facto unipolar world order dominated
by a single master or sovereign (the United States).[1] It would take another
four years to germinate, but the notion of sovereignty emerged in its most
potent form in connection to the rapid spread of the internet and new media
technologies (henceforth referred to as information and communication
technologies, or ICTs) which, by virtue of their American-dominated history
and fundamentally transnational architecture, as well as their growing role in
Russian politics, had become a key battleground for symbolic authority both
domestically and globally.

---

[1] Putin's chief ideologist at the time, Vladislav Surkov, is widely attributed with
coming up with the concept as a means of providing Putin's presidency with an
ideological underpinning (Surkov 2006).

After briefly exploring the early history of attitudes towards the internet in general and the Russian-language internet, or 'Runet', in particular, this chapter traces the emergence of Putin-era sovereignty-oriented rhetoric on the internet as a means of better understanding both the underlying rationale for ICT-related actions and policies, and broader visions of Russia's place in an increasingly networked, transnational world. Particularly since the start of Putin's third presidential term in 2012, the notion of sovereignty has assumed a central position in Kremlin pronouncements and policies on ICTs, tending to manifest itself in one or a combination of three dominant forms: purist calls for the protection of the Russian population, particularly its children, from pernicious social influences; statist concerns for centralized control to ensure national security; and more neoliberal, democratic declarations of the importance of 'normalizing' global internet policy in the name of transparency, free markets, and multinational oversight.

All three of these overarching official discourses point to an inherent suspicion of ICTs as a foreign import from an increasingly unfriendly global sovereign – a suspicion that dates back to the very early days of the internet's appearance on Russian soil, when it was, in fact, largely populated by tech-savvy intellectuals and Russian expatriates. But this earlier collective identification defined a community united not so much by national affiliation as by socio-economic and cultural affinities – a transnational community of practice united by higher education, technological expertise, and a more global orientation towards the world. The community also shared a romantic idealism common among early adopters which viewed the internet as an open, borderless space of free expression, outside of all regulatory purview (Konradova & Schmidt 2014). Swift access to the broadest possible range of content trumped regulation and profit. LiveJournal, the American-born platform that sparked the social networking boom in Russia, marked the advent of the lengthy, text-heavy blog post, accompanied by comment sections which, while often marked by boorish bad manners, invited the frank, open exchange of information and ideas commonly associated with democratic and civil society. Most importantly for the present discussion, this early community also tended to be made up of well-educated, opposition-minded citizens who served as something of a virtual backbone for the Russian protest movements of 2011–12 (Gusejnov 2014; Gorham 2014a: 166–91).

It is really in response to the emergence of this so-called 'creative class' of web-savvy and democratic-minded professionals as a coherent alternative voice in public debate – as well as the broader public dissatisfaction it reflected – that we see, particularly with the onset of Putin's third presidential term in the spring of 2012, a concerted effort to contain and rhetorically reshape the Runet from a transnational, politically active community of practice to a combination of culturally dubious and politically subversive outsiders in need of regulation and control, and innocent, vulnerable, and patriotic citizens in need of protection. Exactly how this tension is articulated – be it in terms of purification, containment, or sovereignization – depends on factors both national and geopolitical that are the focus of attention in this chapter.

National Identity and the Discourse of Purification

The earliest expressions of alarm over the detrimental impact of the internet often zeroed in on language, as the most palpable reflection of a (mostly younger) generation run morally amok. This discourse on language emerged largely from a purist sentiment endemic to any national culture, but arguably more pronounced in Russia, which viewed verbal innovations spawned by electronically mediated communication as a form of linguistic perversion and cultural contamination (Gorham 2016).[2] Voices of moral authority were as likely to emanate from educational and religious institutions as they were from institutions of state. Teachers bemoaned the negative impact of internet-borne 'scumbag language' [iazyk padonkov], a combination of orthographically experimental and substandard language widely believed to degrade the standard communication practices of impressionable youth (Parfeneva 2009). Leaders of the Orthodox Church lamented the 'alarming' state of the Russian language online (Russkaia Pravoslavnaia Tserkov' 2009). Pro-Kremlin intellectuals dismissed the internet as a 'garbage dump' controlled by the US State Department (Tsentral'noe televidenie, NTV 2012). At a roundtable on vulgarity on the internet, Duma deputy Elena Mizulina warned, 'One shouldn't be surprised that young people flood their real life with all the aggression and obscene language that they learn online' (Nabatov 2013). Sociologists provided academic backing for such sentiments, producing reports describing the detrimental impact of the internet on the 'mentality' of Russian youth (Laboratoriia Kryshtanovskaia 2013).

This sort of purist discourse provided the rhetorical support for some of the earliest internet-related legislation, such as the 2012 amendments to the law 'On the Protection of Children from Information Harmful to their Health and Development', which led, among other things, to the creation of a 'blacklist' of sites deemed guilty of containing pernicious content (Rossiiskaia gazeta 2012). In her defence of the bill, co-sponsor Mizulina infamously dismissed opponents of the law as advocates from the 'paedophile lobby' (Dobrokhotov, Lashuk, & Belodedov 2012). With the loose interpretation of

---

[2] The examples that follow receive more detailed attention in Gorham (2016).

the 'extremism' clause later built into the law, 'pernicious' ended up including everything from Halloween costumes to opposition-minded websites.[3]

Leading the charge for purifying the internet on behalf of the vulnerable was the non-governmental organization the Safe Internet League [Liga bezopasnogo interneta (LBI)], whose board chairman, Konstantin Malofeev (also known as 'the Orthodox oligarch') had close ties to presidential advisor and former Minister of Communications, Igor' Shchegolev (Telegina 2015). In addition to fielding legions of volunteer 'cyber-patrols' [kiberdruzhinniki] to monitor the internet for illegal content, the League also designed and produced one of the first commercial filtering mechanisms for search engines, marketing it as a means of ensuring parents and users across Russia that they and their children would have access only to a 'clean internet' (Gorham 2016). In October 2012, the organization struck an agreement with the governor of the Kostroma Oblast' to not only connect new internet users to the 'clean internet' option but to do so as the default option. As the LBI Executive Director, Denis Davydov explained, 'If someone wants to look at pornography, scenes of violence and cruelty, then he says that he wants to turn off the "clean internet" and is warned that, in such a case the contents of web pages may be harmful [vredno] and that the user assumes all risks' (Zykov 2013).[4]

National Security and the Discourse of Internet Sovereignty

In the aftermath of political unrest in 2011–12, and then Russia's annexation of Crimea and incursion into south-eastern Ukraine in the spring of 2014, the discourse on purification was eclipsed by concerns over sovereignty and border protection. The two discourses actually converged in comments by Davydov during a televised primetime debate over the internet's threat to society, in which he likened the virtual space to polluted, shark-infested waters:

> Let's go back to the source. Who built the Internet? It was the Americans who created it. Imagine a pool, just a pool, that we all swim in. This pool belongs to the Americans and they let either crocodiles

---

[3] According to one September 2014 report, 'The number of criminal cases opened on extremism charges in Russia has doubled during 2014, and the Internet is responsible for most of the growth, as more political activity, campaigning, and recruiting happen online, and law enforcement becomes more web-savvy' (Lokot 2014).

[4] After substantial protest, the 'clean internet' was offered as an option, rather than the default setting, to users when the service went live in January of 2013 (Sochnev & Kolomiichuk 2013).

in, or sharks, or they dump sewage there. And we ask, 'What can we do? It's our society that's that way, see, it's a sewer, there's scum there'. Maybe that's why it's worth building our own pool next to it, that would be connected to the American pool, from which only clear water would flow. (Pervyi kanal 2014)

The aforementioned sociological study, which blamed declining literacy on excessive online communication, likewise singled out social networks as a space particularly detrimental to political stability, noting that 'a multitude of social networks have appeared, which bring together oppositionists, fanatics, volunteers, etc., which represent a certain threat to society, since they possess considerable human resources and the ability to mobilize supporters quickly' (Laboratoriia Kryshtanovskaia 2013). Underlying both views is a suspect attitude to 'society' [obshchestvo] and 'communities' [soobshchestva], which become naturally polluted and/or pose direct threats to the state if left to their own devices. Be it members of the political opposition, football hooligans, or even volunteers, web-based networking undermined the privileged authority, or sovereignty, of the state to govern, maintain order, offer basic protection to society, and provide for its needs.

It was in the name of 'the protection of society' that Duma deputies Andrei Lugovoi and Irina Iarovaia defended their December 2013 amendments to the law 'On Information, Information Technologies, and the Protection of Information' – the so-called 'Lugovoi law' – which granted the state the extrajudicial right to block access to websites 'disseminating calls for mass unrest and [containing] other extremist information' (Rossiiskaia gazeta 2013). Thanks to the changes, Lugovoi argued, 'a real, working mechanism [was] being created for the defence of society from illegal information disseminated on the internet, calling [citizens] to mass unrest, and to the execution of extremist and terrorist acts that sow religious and national discord' (Gosudarstvennaia Duma 2013). In the face of protests over the law's potential for political abuse due to the vague nature of the terms at its centre, Lugovoi, a former security agent suspected of serving Alexander Litvinenko the polonium-laced tea that killed him, invoked 'common decency' in his defence: 'in a decent society and under decent authority the concept of "extremism", "terrorism", "mass unrest", "inciting national discord" are always understood as they should be understood' (Gosudarstvennaia Duma 2013). In a matter of months, the law provided the impetus for the closure of three opposition-run news sites – Grani.ru, Ezhednevnyi Zhurnal, and kasparov.ru – as well as the blog of Russia's most effective oppositional politician, Aleksei Naval'nyi, due to the fact that, as Roskomnadzor, the directive from the oversight and enforcement agency for mass media and information technologies, put it,

'The sites listed contain[ed] calls to illegal acts and the participation in mass events conducted in violation with established order' (Federal'naia sluzhba po nadzoru v sfere sviazi, informatsionnykh tekhnologii i massovykh kommuni-katsii 2014).

The post-Crimea raft of legislation also tended to take a different strategic approach to the internet problem: rather than devising ways of allowing the state to regulate content, the new laws and policies focused more on controlling the handling and archiving of that content, as well as the very architecture of the Runet in ways designed to guarantee the stability and security of the sovereign state and its law-abiding citizens. A package of 'anti-terrorism' laws proposed in January 2014 set limits on anonymous online payments and donations, and required internet providers and site owners to store all information about, and posts by, users of their resources for up to six months (Rothrock 2014). The so-called 'law on bloggers' passed later that spring extended rules meant for media outlets for bloggers with more than 3,000 followers, thereby holding them responsible for inaccurate, defamatory, or obscene content in both posts and comments (Rossiiskaia gazeta 2014). The summer and autumn of 2014 saw the passage of the law 'On Personal Data' that required all companies doing business on Runet to store user data on servers located inside the Russian Federation (Sivkova 2014).

The new wave of laws reflected a wartime mentality that saw the Runet as space over which Russia should have sovereign rights, but which was vulnerable to foreign and enemy manipulation at a time when Russia was in the midst of an 'information war'. United Russia Deputy Evgenii Fedorov defended a proposal to expedite the enactment of 'On Personal Data' by declaring the internet 'a direct weapon of "orange" intervention', and labelling foreign internet companies 'fifth columnists' who used data about Russians stored on foreign soil against them. LDPR deputy and co-sponsor Iaroslav Nilov justified it by pointing to a 'global information war' that was currently in its 'aggressive phase', thus making the regulation critical to Russia's 'national security interests' (Sivkova 2014).

A term that had been used sparingly in the 1990s and early 2000s, and primarily to describe battles between warring oligarchs through their media empires, the notion of an 'information war' had become geopolitically marked by the late 2000s.[5] First in reference to the Georgian media in 2008, then

---

[5] By way of example of the earlier usage: 'in 1997 a controlling package of the holding's stocks was sold at auction, an act which gave rise to an "information war" between the two oligarch groups [gruppirovki]' (Veletminskii 2005). The term actually dates back to American Cold War military policy and, today, is invoked loosely by both sides of revived tensions between Russia and the West.

the Ukrainian media in 2014, and most recently the Western media of the sanctions era, the notion signified with few exceptions an act of media-based aggression (often in the form of misinformation) brought upon Russia by a foreign adversary – as in the following warning appearing on the pages of the official government newspaper, *Rossiiskaia gazeta*, in 2016: 'When our enemies [nedrugi] are coming down hard on us with fierce anti-Russian campaigns or information wars, they are seeking not only to weaken our international positions, but also to bring chaos upon the consciousness of Russians [and] undermine the spirit and unity of the people' (Mironov 2016).

Putin's Internet World

Once one understands the degree to which, in the official eyes of Putin's Russia, the internet functions as a weapon for both internal (fifth column) and external belligerence and aggression controlled by a single, unipolar hegemon, then the focus on sovereignty and the need to defend it becomes more comprehensible. As with the notion of 'information warfare', more specific concerns for internet sovereignty do not figure prominently in official public discourse – or in Putin's public speeches for that matter – until the beginning of his third presidential term in 2012. The shift is particularly marked due to the fact that Dmitrii Medvedev, during his presidency from 2008 to 2012, embraced ICTs as a mechanism for fostering civil society and making Russia competitive in the global arena (Gorham 2012, 2014b).[6] One of Putin's first explicit statements on the internet – that it consisted of 50% pornography – clearly invoked the purist orientation (Prezident Rossii 2010). Internet sovereignty took on sharper definition in the wake of Western sanctions and the Ukraine conflict. By the spring of 2014, Putin was openly declaring the internet 'a speciality project of the CIA' (Vesti.ru 2014), and government agencies conducted joint exercises designed to test the vulnerability of Runet to external attack. The Ministry of Communications announced the results of such exercises in the sober tones of a nation on the brink of war:

> During the exercises a general evaluation was conducted of the state
> of security and stability of the functioning of the national segment of
> the network, of the degree of urgency of its connectivity to the global
> infrastructure; potential vulnerabilities were evaluated; [and] the level

---

[6] On top of his own well-known activities on social networks, Medvedev regularly hosted marathon meetings with tech leaders from Russia and abroad to plot out paths for growth and innovation. See Prezident Rossii (2011a, 2011b).

of preparedness for joint work among industry organizations, communications providers, and situational centres of federal organs of the executive branch was determined in the event of a negative targeted incident. (Minkomsviaz' 2014b)

As a result of these training exercises, the issue of internet security and, more specifically, closing off the Russian-language internet from the global internet, topped the agenda of an October 2014 Security Council meeting. In his publicized remarks at the meeting, Putin placed the issue squarely in a frame of national security, declaring that 'the reliable functioning of information systems [...] had exceptional meaning for the country's military preparedness, for the stable development of the economy and social sphere, for the defence of Russia's sovereignty in the broadest sense of the word'. Careful to deny the possibility of 'putting the web under total control [or] nationalizing the internet [ogosudarstvlivat' internet]', Putin nevertheless insisted that the state was 'obligated to defend its citizens' (Prezident Rossii 2014).

The increased importance of internet sovereignty is stark when one compares the two iterations of the 'Doctrine of Information Security of the Russian Federation' that have been produced during the Putin era – the first in 2000 and the second in 2016. The first, which came out in Putin's first year in office at a time when social networks were nonexistent and internet usage was generally low, barely mentions the notion of sovereignty. When it does, it places it on an equal footing with 'the constitutional rights and freedoms of [...] citizens' and 'the development of equal and mutually beneficial international collaboration' (Nezavisimaia gazeta 2000). The 2016 Doctrine, by contrast, mentions 'sovereignty' on nine separate occasions, and mostly in the context of something that is subject to 'undermining' [podryv suvereniteta], a term that appears four times; in need of protection [zashchita suvereniteta – appears three times]; or the object of harm [nanesenie ushcherba suverenitetu] (Rossiiskaia gazeta 2016).

Runet Architecture: Nationalizing the Transnational

In light of the constant flow of information about propaganda on the state-controlled international news channel, RT, and Russia-backed social media-based meddling in the 2016 US presidential elections, it is highly ironic that, as with the notion of 'information warfare', the need for internet sovereignty has been framed by the Putin administration as a necessary defensive move in reaction to belligerent enemies threatening the stability and integrity of Russia's rightful digital sphere of influence. As Putin put it in his remarks at the October 2014 Security Council meeting, although the information age has brought considerable benefits,

> one must take into consideration the considerable risks and threats [...] as well. We see how certain countries try to use their dominant position in the global information space to achieve their military-political goals, as well as their economic ones. They are actively using information systems as instruments of so-called 'soft power' to achieve their interests. (Prezident Rossii 2014)

Once ICTs became a central national security and sovereignty concern, the need to secure the very structure, or architecture, of the Runet became paramount. Not long after Putin's CIA claim, the newspaper *Kommersant* reported on a plan involving a tiered system of internet access that would limit the reach of local and regional networks and provide access to global networks and services only at the highest, national, level, where traffic could be better monitored and controlled (Novyi et al. 2014). In March 2015, Minister of Communications Nikolai Nikiforov delivered what was widely billed as a 'speech on the "sovereignty" of the Russian internet', in which he laid the groundwork for many of the legislative and structurally related initiatives that have followed (Magai 2015). He proposed bringing under state control four key companies responsible for some aspect of the Runet framework, including those controlling Russia's internet exchange points (where major internet providers exchange traffic) and the coordination centre responsible for the administration of top-level domains on Runet. He proposed forbidding commercial companies from using communication lines that crossed national borders. He proposed creating a domestic backup system of root servers, all of which are located outside the Russian Federation, either in western Europe or the United States. And he proposed creating a complete backup copy of the systems critical to operating Runet without interruption. A year later, in December 2016, the Ministry of Communications submitted draft amendments to the law 'On Communications' [O sviazi] proposing the creation of internet exchange points on Russian soil, controlled by Russia, and through which internet service providers would be required to route their Russia-based clients. The goal, according to a report on the policy as announced by the Ministry, was to reduce the amount of Runet traffic travelling outside Russian boundaries from 99% (the estimated figure in 2014) down to 1% by the year 2020 (Kantyshev & Golitsyna 2016). In justifying the move, German Klimenko, special internet advisor to the president, argued that it was 'important that electronic mail, telegraph, telephones, and social networks in Russia continue to work. Critical infrastructure, including a copy of the domain zone, must be located on our territory, so no one can turn it off' (Bondarev 2017).[7]

Despite Putin's assurances to participants in a media forum sponsored by the All-Russian People's Front (ONF) in April 2017 that, 'for now, the restrictions [on the internet] are sufficient' (Pervyi kanal 2017), the steady flow of draft laws and initiatives promoting internet sovereignty shows no sign of letting up. Concurrent to this chapter's drafting, multiple initiatives aimed at weaning Russian users off of their dependence on foreign technology have emerged. One followed up on the 2015 law creating a 'registry' of software secured and approved by the FSB, with a stipulation that all software and mobile apps seeking inclusion would need to be compatible with a new, state-certified operating system ('Sailfish'), in addition to American-made systems such as iOS and Android (Belokopytova 2017). Another involved the creation of a 'closed internet' for official state use (called 'RSNet') and the development of a secure, Russian-designed messaging service for the same purpose (Zykov 2017).

Most recently, in December 2018 Duma deputies introduced draft legislation to 'ensure the security and stability of the functioning of the internet on the territory of the Russian Federation', which quickly became known by parties across the political spectrum as the 'sovereign internet' law (Zakonoproekt No. 608767–7 2018). A more ambitious revival of the idea first floated by Nikiforov in 2015, the legislation essentially called for the creation of a nationalized network in which local internet service providers would be required to use only exchange points located within Russia. Here a new, Runet-specific domain name system would be created to isolate (and ostensibly protect) Russian sites from external exchanges. The flow of information to and from the global internet could then be monitored by security agencies and, in extreme situations, controlled by the regulatory agency Roskomnadzor (Jee 2019). Putin directly invoked the discourse of sovereignty (with regard to US cyber-espionage) when defending the plan at a Kremlin meeting with executives, noting: 'The more sovereignty we have, including in the digital field, the better' (Khrennikov & Kravchenko 2019). Despite the enormous cost (25 billion roubles for the implementation of the system, and another 134 billion roubles of direct and indirect costs in annual maintenance (c-news 2019)), concerns over the negative impact on a concurrent push to expand Russia's digital economy (Tishina 2019) and scepticism as to whether the entire project would even work as planned (Malkova 2019; Infox.ru 2019),

---

[7] Critics argue that this very centralization of traffic would actually make Runet *more* not less vulnerable to attacks, offering an easier target than the more dispersed and redundant set up that currently exists (Kantyshev & Ser'gina 2017; c-news 2018).

the law sailed through the lower branch of parliament in its first reading in February 2019, and was fast-tracked for passage and signing into law later that spring.

Global Multipolarity and the Discourse of Democratic Values

The general shift from monitoring content to more ambitious attempts to bring the very architecture of the internet and new media technologies under sovereign control may also be seen in Russian initiatives in the international arena. While completely in line with domestic initiatives, the language used by Russian authorities to express their positions relies far less on metaphors of stability and external threat than on the language of liberal democracy – transparency, international cooperation, and multipolarity in a time of heightened globalism. While an in-depth look at Russia's ongoing protests at the US Treasury Department's oversight of the International non-profit Cooperation for Assigned Names and Numbers, or ICANN (Prezident Rossii 2014), a closer look at an extended interview with Putin's primary communications advisor, Shchegolev, sheds some light on the rhetorical foundations of the position. Here, as often seen in the language of Foreign Minister Sergei Lavrov (and Putin himself, for that matter), Shchegolev stakes a claim for Russia's position in the international mainstream by invoking existing precedent by countries affiliated with the West. When defending Russia's push towards internet sovereignty, Shchegolev notes how 'the concept of digital sovereignty is cropping up more frequently in the official documents of many countries' and goes on to cite France in particular (Annenkov 2014). The discourse of democracy and democratic values come to the fore: 'As a democratic state, we observe freedom of the press [and] the right of citizens to receive and distribute information' (Annenkov 2014). Not unlike Western European governments, he also points disparagingly to monopolistic tendencies on the part of US corporate giants, Google, Facebook, and Twitter, when spelling out the consequences of their failure to comply with Russian law:

> Simply convincing them in conversation doesn't work. Complete blockage is too radical a measure. If, as one of the measures, we declare it possible and expedient to slow down traffic, then perhaps that would throw cold water on the global giants, who in various ways aim to abuse their monopolistic status in our market and delay compliance with the decisions of Russian authorities. (Annenkov 2014)

Addressing the oversight issue head-on at an October 2014 meeting of the International Telecommunications Union in Seoul, Nikiforov called for the establishment of 'international norms and rules', declaring that, 'on the platform of the UN, we must propose an evolution of relations on the internet, in which states return to themselves their sovereignty' (Minkomsviaz' Rossii 2014a). Six months later, a cooperative agreement on cybersecurity between Russia and China echoed the same norm-based justification for internet sovereignty, demanding (in somewhat convoluted bureaucratese) that 'state sovereignty and the international norms and principles that emanate from state sovereignty extend to the behaviour of states in the framework of activity tied to the use of information and communication technologies, and the jurisdiction of states over the information infrastructure on their territory' (Pravitel'stvo Rossii 2015).[8]

Selective Sovereignty and Transnationalism

Rhetorically, then, we see a variety of strategies for articulating the need for a more state-controlled, sovereign internet on the domestic front, while at the same time embracing the essentially transnational nature of the internet in the global arena. While one can trace a shift from largely purist to statist or sovereign discourse to the onset of Putin's third term, the two have coexisted, and even shared conceptual space, with the language of democracy and free market regularly sprinkled throughout. Rather than ideological confusion or cognitive dissonance, the hybrid nature of Russian state rhetoric on ICTs more readily reflects an opportunistic pragmatism, grounded in a recognition of the push and pull of competing audiences, as well as strategic goals and interests. Purist protests of the contamination of external linguistic and cultural influences tend to arise in contexts where national identity is perceived to be the main threat. More statist regulatory acts and pronouncements gain in linguistic capital when the stability and integrity of the sovereign state itself is at the centre of concern. And the language of democratic and free market principles tends to come to the fore when there is a high premium on confirming Russia's membership in a broader global community.

In fact, the hybridity of discourses on the internet itself is not unique to Russia, developing countries and markets, or authoritarian regimes. Rather, it is emblematic of the multifarious functions that new media play in nearly all twenty-first-century wired societies. One need merely recall American debates over 'cyber bullying', 'NSA spying', and 'net neutrality' to find a comparable range in vocabularies in the American context. And the level of rhetorical

---

[8] LBI Executive Director Davydov was more direct in his characterization of the import of the agreement, calling it the 'first nail in the coffin of American hegemony [...] over the management of the internet' (Tsar'grad TV 2016).

expediency is comparable, too. As eager as they are to invoke ICANN, Edward Snowden, and NSA wire-tapping as examples of American 'double standards', Russian officials remain silent or equivocate when it comes to documented examples of Russian-backed trolling, hacking, and fake news both at home and abroad. Where the linguistic landscapes reveal national particularities is in the specific keywords that enjoy enhanced political capital and provide rhetorical grounds for implementing concrete policies regarding both content and architecture. In the United States, where the history of ICTs makes it hard to get nationalistic or statist, free speech and free market discourses tend to dominate, although more recent debates of uncivil discourse and fake news have enhanced the linguistic capital of 'cyber pessimists'. A year into Putin's fourth term, the dominant discourse in Russia has become that of security and sovereignty, powered by the impression that Russia is under siege by antagonistic forces, some internal (fifth columnist), but mostly external. The Medvedev presidency demonstrated that the Russian verbal landscape is perfectly open, if not receptive, to alternative, more transnational discourses with regard to ICTs. And time, demographics, and economic development certainly favour a more open approach in the long term. In the short term, it may be a question of how much 'sovereignty' Russian society and the technology itself can withstand, before – to paraphrase Putin in Munich – it destroys the sovereign from within.

Works Cited

Annenkov, Andrei. 2014. 'Igor' Shchegolev: "Ucheniia podtverdili nedostatochnuiu ustoichivost' Runeta pri nedruzhestvennykh 'tselenapravelennykh deistviiakh"', *Ekspertnyi tsentr elektronnogo gosudarstva*, 17 October <http://d-russia.ru/ucheniya-podtverdili-nedostatochnuyu-ustojchivost-runeta-pri-nedruzhest-vennyx-celenapravlennyx-dejstviyax.html> [accessed 28 May 2017].

Belokopytova, Vasilisa. 2017. 'Bez versii dlia Sailfish – ne otechestvennoe', *Izvestiia*, 26 April <http://izvestia.ru/news/691793> [accessed 29 May 2017].

Bondarev, Denis. 2017. 'Minkomsviazi predlozhilo uzhestochit' trebovaniia k operatoram sviazi', *RBK*, 12 January <http://www.rbc.ru/technology_and_media/12/01/2017/587652c89a794745a5b74256> [accessed 29 May 2017].

c-news. 2018. '"Suverennyi Runet" oboidets'a biudzhetu v 130 mlrd. rub. v god', 25 December <http://www.cnews.ru/news/top/2018-12-25_eksperty_pri_pravitelstve_avtonomiya_runeta> [accessed 29 March 2019].

Dobrokhotov, Roman, Nikita Lashuk, and Margarita Belodedova. 2012. 'Elena Mizulina: "Vikipediia – prikrytie pedofil'skogo lobbi"', *Slon*, 10 July <http://slon.ru/russia/elena_mizulina_vikipediya_prikrytie_pedofilskogo_lobbi-809860.xhtml> [accessed 2 June 2017].

Federal'naia sluzhba po nadzoru v sfere sviazi, informatsionnykh tekhnologii i massovykh kommunikatsii (Roskomnadzor). 2014. 'Ogranichen dostup k riadu internet-resursov, rasprostraniavshikh prizyvy k nesanktsionirovannym massovym meropriatiiam', 13 March <http://rkn.gov.ru/news/rsoc/news24447.ht> [accessed 28 May 2017].

Gorham, Michael S. 2012. 'Medvedev's New Media Gambit: The Language of Power in 140 Characters or Less' in Per-Arne Bodin, Stefan Hedlund, and Elena Namli (eds), *Power and Legitimacy: Challenges from Russia* (London: Routledge), 199–219.

——. 2014a. *After Newspeak: Language Culture and Politics in Russia from Gorbachev to Putin* (Ithaca, NY: Cornell University Press).

——. 2014b. 'Politicians Online: Prospects and Perils of "Direct Internet Democracy"' in Michael S. Gorham, Ingunn Lunde, and Martin Paulsen (eds), *Digital Russia: The Language, Culture, and Politics of New Media Communication* (London: Routledge Press), 233–50.

——. 2016. 'O "padonkakh" i "kiberdruzhinnikakh": Virtual'nye istochniki porchi iazyka' in E. G. Lapina-Kratasyuk, O. V. Moroz, and E. G. Nim (eds), *Nastroika iazyka: Upravlenie kommunikatsiiami na postsovetskom prostranstve* (Moscow: NLO Press), 240–58.

Gosudarstvennaia Duma. 2013. 'Stenogrammy obsuzhdeniia zakonoproekta No 380323-6', 20 December <http://api.duma.gov.ru/api/transcript/380323-6> [accessed 28 May 2017].

Gusejnov, Gasan. 2014. 'Divided by a Common Web: Some Characteristics of the Russian Blogosphere' in Michael S. Gorham, Ingunn Lunde, and Martin Paulsen (eds), *Digital Russia: The Language, Culture, and Politics of New Media Communication* (London: Routledge Press), 57–104.

Infox.ru. 2019. '"Khaos i nerazberikha": Chem obernets'a zakon o suverennom internete', 18 March <https://www.infox.ru/news/283/social/rupolitics/214375-haos-i-nerazberiha-cem-obernetsa-zakon-o-suverennom-internete> [accessed 29 March 2019].

Jee, Charlotte. 2019. 'Russia Wants to Cut Itself off from the Global Internet. Here's What that Really Means', *MIT Technology Review*, 21 March <https://www.technologyreview.com/s/613138/russia-wants-to-cut-itself-off-from-the-global-internet-heres-what-that-really-means/> [accessed 29 March 2019].

Kantyshev, Pavel, and Anastasiia Golitsyna. 2016. 'Runet budet polnost'iu obosoblen k 2020 godu', *Vedomosti*, 13 May <https://www.vedomosti.ru/technology/articles/2016/05/13/640856-runet-obosoblen> [accessed 29 May 2017].

Kantyshev, Pavel, and Elizaveta Ser'gina. 2017. 'Minekonomrazvitiia snimet rezervnuiu kopiiu runeta', *Vedomosti*, 13 January <https://www.vedomosti.ru/technology/articles/2017/01/13/672826-minekonomrazvitiya-rezervnuyu-kopiyu> [accessed 29 May 2017].

Khrennikov, Ilya, and Stepan Kravchenko. 2019. 'Putin Wants His Own Internet', *Bloomberg*, 4 March <https://www.bloomberg.com/news/articles/2019-03-05/vladimir-putin-wants-his-own-internet> [accessed 29 March 2019].

Konradova, Natalya, and Henrike Schmidt. 2014. 'From the Utopia of Autonomy to a Political Battlefield: Towards a History of the "Russian Internet"' in Michael S. Gorham, Ingunn Lunde, and Martin Paulsen (eds), *Digital Russia: The Language, Culture, and Politics of New Media Communication* (London: Routledge Press), 34–44.

Laboratoriia Kryshtanovskaia. 2013. 'Mental'nost' rossiiskoi molodezhi: politicheskie orientiry i kumiry', *Gefter*, 18 April <http://webcache.googleusercontent.com/search?q=cache:http://gefter.ru/archive/8369> [accessed 27 May 2017].

Lokot, Tetyana. 2014. 'The Internet Helps Double Russia's Number of Extremism Cases', *Global Voices*, 17 September <https://globalvoices.org/2014/09/17/russia-extremism-internet-ukraine-criminal/> [accessed 28 May 2017].

Magai, Marina. 2015. 'Minkomsviazi predlozhit usilit' goskontrol' nad Runetom', *RBK*, 26 March <http://www.rbc.ru/technology_and_media/26/03/2015/551419309a7947aa840a5742> [accessed 29 May 2017].

Malkova, Irina. 2019. 'Pravitel'stvo predupredili o sboe vsei sistemy sviazi v Rossii iz-za zakona Lugovogo i Klishas', *The Bell*, 11 January <https://thebell.io/pravitelstvo-predupredili-o-sboe-vsej-sistemy-svyazi-v-rossii-iz-za-zakona-lugovogo-i-klishasa/> [accessed 29 March 2019].

Minkomsviaz' Rossii. 2014a. 'Glava Minkomsviazi Rossii zaiavil o neobkhodimosti priniatiia mezhdunarodnoi konventsii po upravleniiu infrastrukturoi interneta', 20 October <http://minsvyaz.ru/ru/events/31863/> [accessed 29 May 2017].

——. 2014b. 'Minkomsviaz', FSB i Minoborony proveli ucheniia po zashchite rossiiskogo segmenta internet', 28 July <http://minsvyaz.ru/ru/events/31441> [accessed 28 May 2017].

Mironov, Sergei. 2016. 'Nuzhna li gosudarstvennaia ideologiia? Nuzhna!', *Rossiiskaia gazeta*, 13 December.

Nabatov, Aleksandr. 2013. 'Elena Mizulina: "Nyneshniaia molodezh" putaet svobodu i vsedozvolennost'', *Argumenty i fakty Omsk*, 9 September <http://www.omsk.aif.ru/society/society_details/114945> [accessed 3 October 2013].

Nezavisimaia gazeta. 2000. 'Doktrina informatsionnoi bezopasnosti Rossiiskoi Federatsii' 15 September <http://www.ng.ru/politics/2000-09-15/0_infodoctrine.html> [accessed 28 May 2017].

Novyi, Vladislav, Anna Balashova, Denis Skorobogat'ko, and Roman Rozhkov. 2014. 'Domen – i tochka', *Kommersant*, 29 April <http://www.kommersant.ru/doc/2462760> [accessed 1 June 2017].

Parfeneva, Tat'iana. 2009. 'Vkus Slova', *Uchitel'skaia gazeta*, 15 December <https://dlib.eastview.com/browse/doc/21060094> [accessed 2 June 2017 via East View Information Services].

Pervyi kanal. 2014. 'Vremia pokazhet. Vypusk ot 03.10.2014', 3 October <http://www.1tv.ru/shows/vremya-pokazhet/vypuski/vremya-pokazhet-vypusk-ot-03-10-2014> [accessed 28 May 2017].

——. 2017. 'Vladimir Putin otvetil na voprosy uchastnikov mediaforuma ONF v Sankt-Peterburge', 3 April <https://www.1tv.ru/news/2017-04-03/322765-vladimir_putin_otvetil_na_voprosy_uchastnikov_mediaforuma_onf_v_sankt_peterburge> [accessed 29 May 2017].

Pravitel'stvo Rossii. 2015. 'O podpisanii Soglasheniia mezhdu Pravitel'stvom Rossiiskoi Federatsii i Pravitel'stvom Kitaiskoi Narodnoi Respubliki o sotrudnichestve v oblasti obespecheniia mezhdunarodnoi informatsionnoi bezopasnosti', 30 April <http://government.ru/media/files/5AMAccs7mSlXg bff1Ua785WwMWcABDJw.pdf> [accessed 29 May 2017].

Prezident Rossii. 2010. 'Stenograficheskii otchet o zasedanii Gosudarstvennogo soveta po voprosam razvitiia politicheskoi sistemy strany', 22 January <http://kremlin.ru/events/president/transcripts/6693> [accessed 1 June 2017].

——. 2011a. 'Vstrecha s mezhdunarodnymi i rossiiskimi ekspertami v oblasti mediainnovatsii', 23 June <http://kremlin.ru/events/president/news/11679> [accessed 1 June 2017].

——. 2011b. 'Vstrecha s predstaviteliami internet-soobshchestva', 29 April <http://kremlin.ru/events/president/news/11115> [accessed 1 June 2017].

——. 2014. 'Zasedanie Soveta Besopasnosti', 1 October <http://kremlin.ru/transcripts/46709> [accessed 28 May 2017].

Putin, Vladimir. 2007. 'Vystuplenie i diskussiia na miunkhenskoi konferentsii po voprosam politiki besopasnosti', *Kremlin.ru*, 10 February <http://www.kremlin.ru/events/president/transcripts/24034> [accessed 26 May 2017].

Rossiiskaia gazeta. 2012. 'Federal'nyi zakon ot 28 iulia 2012 g. N 139–F3 "O vnesenii izmenenii v Federal'nyi zakon 'O zashchite detei ot informatsii, prichiniaiushchei vred ikh zdorov'iu i razvitiiu' i otdel'nye zakonodatel'nye akty Rossiiskoi Federatsii"', 30 July <https://rg.ru/2012/07/30/zakon-dok.html> [accessed 31 May 2017].

——. 2013. 'Federal'nyi zakon ot 28 dekabria 2013 g. N 398–F3 "O vnesenii izmenenii v Federal'nyi zakon 'Ob informatsii, informatsioinnykh tekhnologiiakh i o zashchite informatsii"', 30 December <https://rg.ru/2013/12/30/extrem-site-dok.html> [accessed 31 May 2017].

——. 2014. 'Federal'nyi zakon ot 5 maia 2014 g. N 97–F3 "O vnesenii izmenii v Federal'nyi zakon 'Ob informatsii, informatsionnykh tekhnologiiakh i o zashchite informatsii' i otdel'nye zakonodatel'nye akty Rossiiskoi Federatsii po voprosam uporiadocheniia obmena informatsiei s ispol'zovaniem informatsionno-telekommunikatsionnykh setei"', 7 May <https://rg.ru/2014/05/07/informtech-dok.html> [accessed 28 May 2017].

——. 2016. 'Doktrina informatsionnoi bezopasnosti Rossiiskoi Federatsii', 6 December <https://rg.ru/2016/12/06/doktrina-infobezobasnost-site-dok.html> [accessed 23 August 2018].

Rothrock, Kevin. 2014. 'Russia's Parliament Prepares New "Anti-Terrorist" Laws for Internet', *Global Voices*, 16 January <https://advox.globalvoices.org/2014/01/16/russias-parliament-prepares-new-anti-terrorist-laws-for-internet-censorship-putin/> [accessed 31 May 2017].

Russkaia Pravoslavnaia Tserkov'. 2009. 'Vystuplenie mitropolita Klimenta na zasedanii "Internet-obshchenie: kul'turnaia revoliutsiia ili kul'turnaia degradatsiia" v Obshchestvennoi palate RF', 25 March <http://www.patriarchia.ru/db/text/597095.html> [accessed 2 June 2017].

Sivkova, Alena. 2014. 'Personal'nye dannye grazhdan obiazhut khranit' v Rossii s 1 ianvaria 2015 g.', *Izvestiia*, 1 September <http://izvestia.ru/news/575983> [accessed 28 May 2017].

Sochnev, Aleksei, and Daniil Kolomiichuk. 2013. '"Chistyi internet" okazalsia belym i pushistym', *PublicPost* (*Radio Ekho Moskvy*), 1 February <http://echo.msk.ru/blog/publicpost/1002660-echo/> [accessed 31 May 2017].

Surkov, Viacheslav. 2006. 'Suverenitet – eto politicheskii sinonim konkurentosposobnosti' in N. V. Garadzha (ed.), *Suverenitet: Sbornik* (Moscow: Izdatel'stvo 'Evropa'), 43–79.

Telegina, Natal'ia. 2015. 'Put' Malofeeva: ot detskogo pitaniia k sponsorstvu Donbassa i proshchennym $500 mln', *Republic*, 12 May <https://republic.ru/posts/50662> [accessed 28 May 2018].

Tishina, Iuliia. 2019. 'Operatory zadumalis' o veshchnom', *Kommersant*, 21 March <https://www.kommersant.ru/doc/3917500> [accessed 29 March 2019].

Tsar'grad TV. 2016. 'Suverennyi internet (Russkii otvet)', 28 April <https://www.youtube.com/watch?v=OsnY0l7sphQ> [accessed 29 May 2017].

Tsentral'noe televidenie, NTV. 2012. 'Stanislav Govorukhin ob internete', 20 February <https://www.youtube.com/watch?feature=player_embedded&v=AbQC0H_rY6> [accessed 27 May 2017].

Veletminskii, Igor'. 2005. 'Sviaz'invest poidet na torg', *Rossiiskaia gazeta*, 29 September.

Vesti.ru. 2014. 'Putin: Internet voznik kak proekt TsRU, tak i razvivaetsia', 24 April <http://www.vesti.ru/doc.html?id=1512663> [accessed 1 June 2017].

Zakonoproekt No. 608767-7. 2018. 'O vnesenii izmenenii v nekotorye zakonodatel'nye akty Rossiiskoi Federatsii (v chasti obespecheniia bezopasnogo i ustoichivogo funktsionirovaniia seti "Internet" na territorii Rossiiskoi Federatsii)', *Sistema obespecheniia zakonodatel'noi deiatel'nosti* <http://sozd.duma.gov.ru/bill/608767-7> [accessed 29 March 2019].

Zykov, Vladimir. 2013. 'Bortsy s pedofilami zapuskaiut "chistyi internet"', *Izvestiia*, 30 January <http://izvestia.ru/news/543946> [accessed 28 May 2017].

——. 2017. 'V zakrytom gosinternete poiavitsia messendzher', *Izvestiia*, 5 April <http://izvestia.ru/news/675914> [accessed 29 May 2017].

17

RT and the Digital Revolution

Reframing Russia for a Mediatized World

Stephen Hutchings

Introduction: A New Warrior Is Born

Russia's primary international broadcaster, RT, thrives on the notoriety it has gained as one of the key weapons in Vladimir Putin's purported 'disinformation arsenal'. This is in part connected to the channel's emergence at the intersection of the communications revolution which coincided with the end of the Soviet Union and the subsequent reconfiguration of the geopolitical landscape. Among the ramifications of this convergence for RT's place in the post-Cold War media 'ecology' (the assemblage of relationships between media forms, publics, and actors at any given time) is a carefully cultivated disregard for established Western journalistic conventions. To adapt the title of one of its flagship television shows, RT has constructed an entire, iconoclastic ethos around its efforts to 'Break the Set' of mainstream global news reporting, simultaneously earning itself pariah status throughout the Western media. My chapter aims to tease out the full implications of this phenomenon by examining how RT repurposes programme genres or types with familiar, transnational currency to fit its audience strategies and institutional culture. In particular, I examine the role played in this process by its intuitive grasp of

I would like to thank Andy Byford and Connor Doak for their astute and thorough commentary on earlier drafts of the chapter. Some of the second section overlaps with material in my chapter 'Projecting Russia on the Global Stage: International Broadcasting and "Recursive Nationhood"', which appeared in Sarah Hudspith and Vlad Strukov (eds), *Russian Culture in the Era of Globalization* (Abingdon: Routledge, 2018). The context and conceptual framework for this material differ from those of the present analysis.

the potentials and limitations of the multiple new interactive media platforms facilitated by digital technology. I also, however, highlight the contradictions and dissonances created by RT's immersion in the decentred, unanchored meanings of the online world regarding both its external image as a unidirectional tool of state propaganda and its own ability to maintain active agency on behalf of its Kremlin sponsors.

RT's apparent shift in function from nuanced tool of soft power to aggressive weapon of 'information war' is linked to a tension between its nation-projecting function and its reliance on allegiances born of an increasingly transnational, networked media environment. The central argument of this chapter is that RT fails to overcome this contradiction, yet uses it to engage in a disruptive re-evaluation of established news values over which, however, it cannot exert full control. The chapter therefore illustrates what we mean in this volume's Introduction when we say that the term 'Russian' refers to a geopolitical constellation which is inherently trans- and multinational. It is important, however, first to understand the background to RT's seemingly Phoenix-like rise from the ashes of the Soviet propaganda machine.

From the beginning of the Soviet period, Lenin's Bolshevik government stressed the significance of mass communication (Winek 2009: 100). In 1929, the Soviet Union became the first nation to recognize the importance of international broadcasting when it established Radio Moscow with French-, English-, and German-language services. The challenge posed to Western powers by Radio Moscow was met with major investment in radio stations whose purpose was to 'tell the truth' about the Communist world: Radio Liberty, Radio Free Europe, Voice of America, and the BBC Russian Service. A milestone in radio's history was the development of the transistor in 1947. Pocket-size transistor radios brought mobility of access, increased choice, and a personalized listening environment permitting broadcasters to speak directly to the private Soviet citizen (Lovell 2015: 204). The Cold War history of Radio Moscow and its Western counterparts demonstrates that the capacity to engage in instant, transnational communication represented a double-edged sword for totalitarian states: the price to pay for its worldwide propaganda potential is that this capacity could be exploited by hostile powers.

Similar dilemmas affect latter-day authoritarian states in regard to the communicative potential of the online world whose advent in 1991 (Bryant 2011) coincided with that of post-Communist Russia. One year earlier, Joseph Nye's celebrated essay on 'soft power' (the exertion of influence through attraction rather than force) marked a turn in Western foreign policy towards more subtle forms of persuasion (1990). International broadcasting now acquired new importance. BBC World News, CNN, and Al Jazeera, which all began broadcasting in the 1990s, embraced digitization's potential to offer states enhanced access to transnational audiences. However, as Castells (2000) establishes, the digital revolution also encouraged the growth of online publics whose transnational networking mechanisms operate 'horizontally', evading the involvement of states (a Facebook group with postings from different countries is just one example of such networking). This tension shapes my discussion of RT.

RT was launched as Russia Today in 2005 by Russia's former state news agency, RIA Novosti. According to its young editor-in-chief, Margarita Simonian, its mission was to adopt a 'professional format' akin to the BBC that would 'reflect Russia's opinion of the world' and present a 'more balanced picture' of Russia (Sputnik News 2005). This first phase of RT's development was part of a wider drive to improve Russia's public image following President Medvedev's interest in adapting Nye's concept of soft power to the Russian context, whilst drawing on Soviet practices that amounted to a form of soft power *avant la lettre*. Exploiting the new communications environment, RT initially began broadcasting via cable networks in English, but subsequently launched sister channels in Arabic, Spanish, and French; a documentary channel; and different versions of its English-language output targeting the USA and the UK more specifically. The channel has an extensive online presence through websites in English, Russian, German, and French, and a YouTube version which claims to be 'the most watched news channel' on this platform. It maintains an active Twitter account, as do its journalists.

Having drawn worldwide attention for its pro-Russian coverage of the 2008 South Ossetian war, in 2009 Russia Today rebranded itself as RT, a gesture seen by critics as an attempt to hide its propaganda motives. In 2010 it unveiled a campaign around the slogan 'Question More', which it adopted to reposition itself in its second phase as the preferred channel for those hostile to the US's hegemonic hold on global agendas, and the associated 'biases' of the West's 'mainstream media'. It has, since 2009, presented itself as the figurehead of a geopolitical movement whose purpose is to dismantle the post-Cold War 'unipolar world'.

The third phase of RT's evolution was precipitated in part by the Kremlin's heightened fear of Western efforts to foment opposition to the Putin regime in connection with the mass protests sparked by the 2012 presidential election. The formal commencement of this phase – in December 2013 – was marked by Simonian's appointment to the post of editor-in-chief of the new Russia Today [Rossiia Segodnia] news agency, created by executive order of President Putin in an effort to tighten state control of Russian media outlets and to align Russia's international and domestic news output more closely. RT was soon to become the focus of Western opprobrium for its leading role in Russia's purported state-led 'information war' against Western democracy, which intensified during the 2014 Ukraine crisis. The extent to which RT's broadcasting and social media activities conformed to this characterization is a moot point (the relationship between the pariah image imposed on RT by its adversaries and its own behaviour as a media actor forms an inter-active dynamic); what is clear is that some of its activities during the Ukraine crisis were coordinated with those of Russian's intelligence agencies in an unprecedented way (RT's website was, for example, the outlet of choice for the publication of controversial leaked telephone conversations between Ukrainian and US officials). RT was also undoubtedly involved in dissemi-nating disinformation denying Russia's covert military intervention in Eastern Ukraine. However, there is a strong tendency in Western public discourse mistakenly to assume that RT and the Russian intelligence apparatus invar-iably operate hand in glove. When Russian cyber hackers, trolls, and bots were accused of interfering in the 2016 US presidential election, RT was namechecked alongside them in a report by the US Office of the Director of National Intelligence (ODNI 2017) which concluded that Putin had ordered the election interference campaign. Embarrassingly, the evidence adduced to demonstrate RT's involvement was taken from television broadcasts dating to 2009, well before the idea of Donald Trump as president was anything other than a characteristically ludicrous plot line for an old *The Simpsons* episode broadcast in early 2000 and entitled 'Bart to the Future'.

The boundaries between the three phases are not hard and fast and there is a good deal of overlap between them. Simonian's initial aspiration to create a respectable channel akin to the BBC was reflected in RT's adoption of trans-national programme genres typical of established news channels. These have endured throughout RT's existence. Hourly news bulletins are interspersed with documentaries (many deploying the tools of investigative journalism), talk shows, panel discussions, business briefings, and political satire. RT's flagship remains the discussion show *CrossTalk*. Each edition features guests from different countries expressing a range of views on global news stories. The signature music is accompanied by multiple voices speaking simultane-ously, in imitation of open debate. The intonation of the anchors, the design of the studios, and the frequent commercial breaks are sufficiently reassuring to attract international audiences familiar with this style of presentation.

However, whilst RT's news agendas track the same major events as their 'mainstream' rivals, the angle it adopts is consistently anti-American. Coverage of the Syrian conflict dwells on atrocities against Syrian citizens committed by US-backed anti-Assad rebels, whom the channel refuses to differentiate from ISIS terrorists; Western reports of Assad's savage attacks on Syrian cities outside his control are ignored or undermined.

The pitch that RT honed in phase two, but which was present in incipient form in phase one and has persisted into phase three, is that it offers insights into 'inconvenient' stories that the 'mainstream media' overlook. It de-emphasizes its affiliation to the Russian perspective, presenting itself as the voice of a transnational anti-imperialist movement. Its eschewal of journalistic principles of balance and impartiality and its embrace of conspiracy theory derives from the same anti-imperialist context: the 'truth' is a conspiracy of the powerful to be uncovered by 'experts' rather than an equilibrium achieved by balancing different viewpoints. The 'tag lines' of some of RT's flagship shows are revealing (*Truthseeker*: 'Seek truth from facts'; *The Big Picture*: 'What's actually going on in the world'). RT is adept at securing the services of prominent figures at the political margins: Julian Assange, founder of the Wikileaks movement, was given his own show, as was maverick left-wing British politician George Galloway and Alex Salmond, ex-leader of the SNP whose Scottish nationalist platform found favour with RT during the 2014 independence referendum. One of its most successful US-based shows, *Breaking the Set*, was hosted by Abby Martin, a veteran of the Occupy anti-capitalist movement.

The title of Martin's show embodies RT's claim to iconoclasm which it has in part cultivated on the model of right-wing outlets in the USA such as Fox News (Hutchings et al. 2015). Like Fox, it disdains mainstream news agendas and discards broadcasting conventions requiring anchors to serve as impartial facilitators, according them the right to intervene with their own, passionately held views. (It is no accident that 'mainstream media', or MSM, as it is consistently referred to by its opponents, is now a frequent target of the ire of President Trump.) This iconoclastic ethos is consistent with the irreverent style characteristic of social media platforms and of outlets such as Fox and Breitbart News, but alien to the formal registers dominating traditional broadcasting. Much of this irreverence is spontaneous: the careless 'laughing off' of technical glitches; the frequent use of the vernacular idiom (terms like 'bullshit' are bandied around repeatedly in *CrossTalk*).

New Platforms, New Values

As a child of the digital revolution, RT immerses itself in the social media world, deploying its resources, idioms, and values to modulate, reinvigorate, and reinforce the messages of the channel's broadcast and website content. During its television coverage of the 2014 Sochi Winter Olympics, its social media editor, Ivor Crotty, delivered two reports on declining Twitter interest in political controversies besetting the hosts, using them to authenticate the RT narrative of a hostile, out-of-touch Western media. The deserved reputation that RT, the broadcaster, has acquired as a crude ideological blunderbuss belies its uncannily intuitive grasp of the puzzling ambiguities of meaning that often surround online activity. One example is the incident during the Sochi Olympics, widely reported in the Western press, which saw members of the punk group Pussy Riot brutally whipped by uniformed Cossacks, renowned for their zealous commitment to Putin's 'traditional values' agenda, for performing an anti-Putin song. Less widely acknowledged is the fact that it was an RT crew that had captured the incident on film, having received prior notice that the event was to occur. RT immediately uploaded the video to its website, confounding many of its viewers. Comments on the numerous YouTube videos of the event included, 'Why would they do this?', 'I am confused!', and, 'I think it is strange that RT, Russia's semi-official news TV source would actually show this. Why would they go out of their way to do that?' Some speculated that RT approved of the whipping: 'RT is airing this because they think it's a good thing'. Others expressed outrage and incomprehension: 'Horrific: Pussy Riot whipped, pepper sprayed, thrown to the ground by Cossacks in Sochi. Why is RT airing this? No idea'. Also to be found was praise for RT's 'balanced' approach: 'RT is pro-Russian but they are not delusionally pro-Russian. That's why I like them, I can expect more real news from RT than any other MSM network' (YouTube 2014). The RT website retained a still from the video in which the Cossacks are seen whipping the women, but under the headline 'Pussy Riot in Sochi Performance Fail' (a tongue-in-cheek reference to the #SochiFails hashtag initiated mischievously to track the problems, technical, political, economic, and sporting, besetting the Sochi Games organizers). It thus simultaneously subverted the anti-Kremlin #SochiFails hashtag and hedged its bets over the ultra-conservative motivations of the Cossacks (RT 2014).

The hedging approach was epitomized in a dramatic, if short-lived, scandal that arose later in 2014 when, at the end of one of her shows, Abby Martin issued an extraordinary, and ostensibly sincere, on-air protest against Russia's imperialistic annexation of Crimea – a dramatic, carefully prepared statement to camera which concluded with Martin's affirmation of her editorial independence. The incident went viral and was featured widely in the Western press (briefly making the BBC headlines). RT issued an instant rejection of Martin's protest, with Simonian herself pointing out that this American journalist knew nothing of Ukraine, and sarcastically offering her an educative stint reporting from Crimea (Martin politely, but equally sarcastically, declined). RT's reaction to the Martin scandal represents a complex attempt to exploit the uncertain meanings generated by new platforms. The fact that it immediately followed widespread criticism on Twitter from Western journalists who accused Simonian of running a propaganda outlet complicates, without altogether undermining, the authenticity of the protest which was successfully exploited by RT to disrupt the mainstream narrative portraying it as a Kremlin mouthpiece; Simonian frequently cited the incident as evidence that RT accords its journalists free speech. Its careful staging – Martin's eloquent, visually choreographed protest can only have happened with the full participation of her production team – eluded most Western broadcasters who focused solely on the words of Martin's 'brave insurrection'. However, Martin's actions subsequently precipitated an unambiguously authentic, and unanticipated, on-air resignation by RT newsreader Liz Wahl, disillusioned with what she saw as the channel's 'whitewashing' of Russian aggression in Ukraine. Reversing the sequence of cross-platform activity relating to the Martin incident, Wahl's protest was addressed through an intensive Twitter campaign by RT journalists 'exposing' the resignation as a US intelligence provocation.

There was a different response to a later, equally unanticipated, YouTube video made by an independent Australian comedy collective and consisting of comical 'rap' accounts of the Ukraine crisis, satirically dubbed Putin's 'Paramilitary Games'. Because it also targeted hypocritical 'mainstream media' attacks on the Kremlin's repression of free speech by including a scene featuring Martin's 'protest', RT uploaded it to its website, enabling it to bolster its efforts to link Sochi and Ukraine via a single narrative, and reinforce Martin's own implicit refutation of the notion that RT suppresses independent thought.

RT frequently uses YouTube – arguably its primary mode of communication. Its YouTube channel has nearly 1.5 million subscribers, with monthly views of its videos approximating 10.5 million (Livshen, Nelson, & Orttung 2015). It has adapted well to the medium's specificities; YouTube videos are cast into the spatially borderless realm of the web, but also limited by the platform's 'here today, gone tomorrow' temporality. RT works with the grain of an online world in which, rather than being 'broadcast' from a centre to a periphery, meaning develops in decentred, fragmented nodes. It monitors social media themes and aligns itself with the tones and discourses favoured by new platforms. But it also actively deploys social media tools to promote RT's agenda. Simonian exploits Twitter skilfully, blending informal daily trivia with personalized proselytizing. There is, however, little use of social media in co-production (audience participation) contexts. This would contradict RT's revelatory ethos according to which 'experts' uncover 'truths' hidden by shady, hegemonic forces.

Notwithstanding what Nick Couldry and Andreas Hepp (2017) call 'the continuing lure' of a mythical 'mediated centre', the radical disruption of centre-periphery structures has severely restricted the power of states to shape meaning within a political environment which is increasingly 'media-tized' – a term that designates the way in which global media flows have penetrated the very substance of politics (as well as other areas of daily life, including personal relationships). One consequence of this phenomenon is a transformation in the nature and function of large-scale state-media collaborations including royal weddings, historical anniversaries, sporting events, and so on – what Dayan and Katz (1992) first dubbed 'media events'. The stabilizing, nation-building myths and rituals for which such occasions were traditionally ideal vehicles are increasingly exposed to and challenged by alternative narratives, discourses, and voices of diverse, often transna-tional, origin. Moreover, the creative 'event-ness' of the multiplatform act of mediation is now prone to displace that of the historical or ceremonial occasion being marked.

A case in point is RT's highly impressive multimedia project to celebrate the hundredth anniversary of the 1917 revolution, of which the centre-piece was a full-scale Twitter re-enactment of the whole of the year 1917. It included over 90 Twitter accounts set up in the names of historical figures such as Lenin, Trotskii, Stalin, and the tsar. Also featured were tweets – often humorous and expressed in self-consciously anachronistic, contemporary Twitter jargon – by fictional characters whom ordinary users imagined participating in what amounted simultaneously to a carnivalesque dethroning of the sanctified heroes and epic temporality of the revolution, and a problematizing of the 'documented fact/fictional invention' distinction that has become such an article of faith within the contemporary 'quality news' industry. Meanwhile, the bold gesture of handing 'control' of the project to the #1917Live 'crowd' of ordinary Twitter users transposed the drama of revolution from the historical events of 1917 to the mediatized celebration marking their anniversary in 2017.

Capitalizing on the cultural capital that the 1917 revolution enjoys within progressive, leftist movements across the globe, RT effectively sidelined the domestic Russian media narrative depicting the event as Russia's tragic descent into needless chaos and bloodshed. It also exploited the gradually unfolding, quotidian temporality of the #1917Live project as a means of adapting to, and ultimately neutralizing, hostile efforts to draw it into the arena of the 'information war', and of weaving the meaning of the Bolsheviks' audacious act of revolt into the protective fabric surrounding the project itself. Over the course of 2017, for example, the British embassy took strong exception to the Twitter account set up in its name as part of the #1917Live project's efforts to recreate the key actors in the lead-up to the allied inter-vention in Russia following the Bolsheviks' seizure of power. With the assistance of none other than Julian Assange, a former RT presenter, the project team managed at once to pour scorn on the embassy's poe-faced, legalistic indignation and to insinuate that its reaction was motivated by fears of what its archives might reveal about the history of Western interference in Russia's affairs. On 3 September 2017, Assange tweeted: 'UK government gets Twitter to suspend RT account showing what the FCO was saying in 1917 about Russian revolution' (Assange 2017).

As its discarding of the Kremlin's approved, negative line on the significance of the 1917 revolution attests, however, RT's approach hardly facilitates a grand public diplomacy strategy in which Russia's key soft power tool captures national audiences with a Russian 'strategic narrative' (Miskimmon et al. 2013). Critics correctly identify this failure, highlighting the channel's relatively low audience ratings: it has rarely exceeded the 500,000 mark in reports issued by the UK's main ratings agency (BARB 2017), as compared with the several million scored by broadcasters like Sky and the BBC. However, quite apart from ignoring the channel's far more impressive YouTube showings and ability to work within a decentred, mediatized environment, such observations overlook its appeal to small, subnational constituencies with anti-establishment leanings networked across national boundaries: right-wing extremists attracted by Putin's conservative hostility to liberal democracy; left-wing global activists who share Russian antipathy towards the USA; environmentalists; ethnic minority diaspora in the West alienated by the xenophobia of their host communities. These constituencies cannot coalesce into a coherent whole, nor do their values always coincide with those of the Russian state. But RT's appeal to them, however partial and transient, with a broad-brush narrative opposing US-style liberal democracy and promulgating 'traditional values', demonstrates the channel's capacity to assimilate to a media landscape in which, accelerated by global connectivity, Cold War geopolitical and ideological boundaries are being reconfigured.

The fact that the narrative RT projects is internally ambivalent reflects its recognition of the modes of viewing prevailing across its younger audiences. Rather than pledging loyalty to one channel, they use new technology to sample many outlets. In this context, RT's 'Question More' ethos comes to the fore. Its multiplatform dissemination of contradictory narratives and unverifiable rumours rather than uniform 'state propaganda' lines are, as Pomerantsev (2014) argues, designed to sew confusion, working with the impulses of contemporary news audiences immersed in online gaming cultures which require players to complete game narratives actively to 'piece together' scattered, ambivalent facts as coherent news stories. For example, in March 2018, during the Salisbury nerve agent scandal, RT aired a far-fetched *Worlds Apart* broadcast suggesting that double agent Sergei Skripal' and his daughter were poisoned by the British intelligence services rather than the Russian state.

At the same time, it gave prominence to semi-humorous theories suggesting that the pair were suffering the ill effects of narcotics abuse.

Post-truth and the Transformed Media Ecology

RT represents an extreme version of global developments. Globalization is changing what it means to 'project' a nation within an 'international' arena. In the context of mass population movement, the creation of multiple diasporas, and the emergence of competing forms of allegiance (religious, cultural, ethnic), it is increasingly difficult to determine the borders and identity of the nation to be projected. Those same phenomena constrain the power of political elites to decide who articulates patriotic narratives, and whose version of patriotism to prioritize (Strukov 2016). Extreme voices from the margins must now be accommodated, even by authoritarian regimes which face familiar anti-immigration pressures from below, yet also from an intellectual class steeped in global discourses. This creates sharp tensions, as illustrated by RT's ambivalent coverage of the ultra-conservative Cossack beating of Pussy Riot.

International broadcasters provide the media personalities responsible for shaping nation projection. Regardless of the loyalty these personalities display, narratives of nation undergo further mediation at this level. Two recent examples from RT's output include (a) the bold gesture of choosing an openly gay British presenter to front the channel's coverage of the Sochi Olympics (at a time when Russia was under scrutiny for repressing LGBT rights); and (b) RT's multimedia #1917Live project, launched under the stewardship of RT's Irish social media editor, Ivor Crotty, despite the Kremlin's efforts to ignore the occasion (RT 2017).

Finally, new technologies afford national political elites multiple channels of remediation (the adaptation of content produced by one medium for reproduction by another). This, however, reduces control over audience reception. Web 2.0 networking and interactivity modes transform the transaction between 'mediator (projector)' and 'mediated (projected) to' as audiences become actively involved in shaping and changing the meanings of news events. When the Liz Wahl on-air resignation scandal broke, RT's efforts to control the 'message' of the story by using social media to reinforce the aspersions on Wahl's motivations that it cast in its subsequent news broadcasts led to a vicious Twitter war in which the channel then had to rebut negative commentary coordinated by neoconservative forces influenced by Cold War thinking (Hutchings et al. 2015).

State actors like RT, however, operate in a complex global ecology in which Cold War bipolarity has been replaced by a multipolar landscape characterized by interacting transnational news cultures and audiences, and by conflicting spheres of influence which disrupt journalistic value systems and challenge the very meaning of 'news'. 'Rogue' broadcasters are more than passive vessels for transnational currents as US Secretary of State John Kerry recognized when targeting RT's semi-militarized campaign on behalf of a repressive Russian state and describing the channel as the Kremlin's 'propaganda bullhorn' (LoGiurato 2014). The defensive posture Simonian adopted in response betrayed professional values quite different from those adhered to by Western journalists:

> Every [...] single hour the guys who work for us are told, 'You are liars, you are no journalists, you are the Kremlin propaganda mouthpiece. You've sold yourselves to the Russians' [...] I can see very clearly why I continue to work for a channel that stands alone, showing everybody the other side of the story. It's my country. I have no choice. (Simonian 2014)

In embracing patriotic partiality over scrupulous neutrality, RT views its mission as identical to that of its rivals, embracing a relativism reminiscent of the Marxist-Leninist media theories that drove Radio Moscow's output. As Simonian puts it:

> Information-propaganda weapons are deployed by all those who have the opportunity. There are many examples [...] Strictly speaking this is how the success of CNN began; it became precisely such a weapon. (Simonian 2013)

Far from languishing at the margins, such attitudes now penetrate the global media ecology. Together with pseudo-cosmopolitan trends like Assange's Wikileaks movement, they influence audiences wary of 'mainstream media' agendas. Approaches to nation projection must explain a blurring of boundaries between news, information, propaganda, and public diplomacy. Governments reacting to Russia's disruptive presence on the international stage now recognize that they are embroiled in a multidirectional 'information war' (Halliday 2014). It forms part of the broader 'post-truth' environment facilitated by new technology that, as Viner (2016) suggests, has corrupted news reporting across the globe.

Respectable broadcasters like the BBC respond by vigorously defending traditional journalistic standards. Yet, as the BBC acknowledges, impartiality is an elastic concept. This is partly because of the rise of anti-establishment populism and the recognition that impartiality is measured in relation to shared consensus (BBC Trust 2013); ignoring consensus could compromise impartiality, even when that consensus seems skewed. The BBC's recent difficulties over its perceived under-representation of the 'negative consequences' of mass immigration is an example. Another tension arises from the BBC World Service's parallel commitment to 'sustain civil society' by facilitating a 'global conversation'. As it discovered when hosting a debate among ordinary Russian citizens on the eve of the Sochi Olympics, it is one thing to give them a voice in shaping broadcasting output and another for them to reflect the pluralism that is impartiality's lifeblood when exposed to polarizing rhetoric from monopoly state broadcasters (Hutchings et al. 2015). Marie Gillespie (2013) identifies similar tensions in her analysis of an experiment in which BBC Arabic co-created a political debate television series with citizen producers.

More recently, the BBC World Service has expanded its Russian-language broadcasts in response to Russia's 'democratic deficit' (BBC 2015). This is part of a wider Western reaction to Russia's international disinformation campaign, of which RT is the primary tool. The BBC is thus drawn into an information war fought largely on Russia's terms, a strategy which further complicates its commitment to impartiality.

The information war belongs to a broader, transnational development. A combination of the communications revolution, the post-1991 reconfiguration of geopolitical forces, and the crisis of trust precipitated by the 2008 financial crash is changing the very meaning of 'news'. The rise of the 'post-truth' phenomenon belongs to this context. The term is an umbrella for related meanings that should be separated out, and in all of which RT has a stake. As recent events in the USA demonstrate, however, RT does not enjoy a monopoly. 'Post-truth' is used to denote the 'truth of affect' that appeals to grass-roots populists ('what is true is what feels true'). This accounts for the influence of conspiracy theory throughout anti-establishment politics of both left and right – an influence that RT embraces (Yablokov 2015). It is also employed in the context of the individualized news consumption fostered by big data targeting tools: the replacement of public news agendas by personal feeds allowing people to select what appeals to them. This, in turn, is linked to the 'echo chamber' effect in which exchanging opinions becomes the sharing of similar views presented as 'debate' (Krasodomski-Jones 2015); programmes like *CrossTalk* involve up to four guest commentators reinforcing one another's anti-US sentiments, with a token dissenting voice. Again, the Russian channel's strategy of targeting discrete communities at the margins of Western societies, as well as its unorthodox presentation style, accords with this development, and with the principle that all news is driven by ideological interests.

'Fake news' represents a version of 'post-truth' with a direct connection to the blatant disinformation of which RT regularly stands accused. The currency of fake news within grass-roots anti-establishment politics emerged out of the 2008 financial crisis, which shook the entire political process and the credibility of establishment institutions and 'mainstream media'. Actors like the influential right-wing US outlet Breitbart News have also embraced this crisis, disseminating rumours and, often, deliberate falsehoods. The phenomenon reached a crescendo in the lead-up to the 2016 US presidential election, when unsubstantiated stories about Hillary Clinton's alleged 'criminality' were rife. RT was prominent in giving credence to these myths. Before then, it had followed domestic Russian outlets in reporting unfounded rumours that the Malaysia Airlines passenger flight (MH17) shot down over Ukraine, almost certainly by pro-Russian separatists mistaking it for a Ukrainian fighter, had in fact been destroyed by Ukrainian forces thinking it was Putin's presidential plane.

To temper the moral panic surrounding RT, however, we should categorize types of 'fake news' based on the intentions of the source and the purveyor, the attitude of the receiver, and the mode of dissemination (Hutchings 2017). A news story can be deliberately intended as 'fake', whether cynically to deceive or as satirical mockery of gullible audiences. Alternatively, news can be purveyed in good faith as 'true' but interpreted as false by its recipients (many conspiracy theories fit this category). Moreover, in a post-truth world, the propensity to believe fake news may depend less on its source and more on the identity of the disseminator. Considerable credence was given in the West to far-fetched, unverifiable stories promoted in established media outlets, including the BBC, about Trump's purported sexual misdemeanours in Moscow. Had they been disseminated by the likes of RT (whose role in this instant, ironically, was to subject them to the cold light of rational analysis), it is likely that they would have been dismissed as irresponsible 'conspiracy theories'.

Fake news stories can be 'double-voiced' (i.e. intended to mislead one audience but not another, or to deceive and not deceive the same audience on different levels). Putin's widely reported blatant denials of the fact that the 'Little Green Men' who signalled Russia's annexation of Crimea were Russian military personnel were, on the one hand, intended to hoodwink Western media audiences into believing that they were Crimean self-defence forces. On the other hand, the denials were so shameless (the president claimed that the military equipment the soldiers were carrying could be 'bought in shops') as to indicate that Putin knew that they would not be believed. Instead, he claimed for them a 'higher' truth (that of Russia's right to defend its geopolitical interests, and of the fact that Crimea 'belongs' to Russia anyway) to which domestic audiences who supported the annexation would be receptive.

RT's playfully disreputable approach to news means that it is at ease with such double-voicedness, as we saw with Abby Martin's anti-imperial protest, her subsequent 'castigation' by Margarita Simonian, and her 'rebuttal' of the castigation.

This double-voicedness is in turn closely linked to RT's affinities with a form of (self)-satirical discourse that emerged in late-Soviet Russia and has persisted into the post-Soviet period. Known as *stiob*, it is defined by Alexei Yurchak as requiring 'such a degree of overidentification with the object, person, or idea at which [it] was directed that it was often impossible to tell whether it was a form of sincere support, subtle ridicule, or a peculiar mixture of the two' (Yurchak 2006: 250). RT's puzzling PR stunt at once exposing, endorsing, and making light of the Cossacks' 'punishment' of Pussy Riot readily submits to this account. What is critical to understand, however, is that the contradictory readings generated by the stunt reflect an interplay of (a) sympathy with the Cossacks on the part of conservative Russian patriots; (b) alignment with Western horror at their behaviour; and (c) a discursive position ridiculing both reactions. Rather than occurring as the result of a linear strategy of obfuscation, or even fakery, on RT's part, the *stiob* effect thus represents the point of intersection of a nexus of intra-national and transnational flows of ideological meaning within which the broadcaster enjoys only limited agency.

Moreover, in a global media environment characterized by ever-expanding transnational flows, obfuscation in the form of 'fake news' becomes detached from its empirical definition and free to circulate that environment as a rhetorical trope available for incorporation in polemics. Trump resorted to it to dismiss speculations about links between his election campaign and the Kremlin, even levelling the allegation against reputable broadcasters like CNN. It is now a regular theme of his press conferences and Twitter output. A cross-national organization called 'Stop Fake' has been set up to counter Russian fake news about Ukraine. Meanwhile, on 15 March 2017, RT itself launched 'FakeCheck' – an 'interactive, multimedia project' to monitor 'the fake news distributed in mass volume by the mainstream media'. This is more than an example of the cynical 'mimesis' strategy that van Herpen (2016) associates with Soviet propaganda, which, he claims, regularly appropriated Western critiques of Soviet behaviour and applied them, in reverse, to Western policies. It exploits Fake News's currency as an anchorless global meme which acquires new semiotic momentum from each stage in a perpetual, recursive 'doubling back' process in which it is hurled as an insult back and forth across boundaries national, cultural, and ideological. It also illustrates the breakdown in trust eroding Western political culture that did not apply during the Cold War period.

We live in a topsy-turvy world in which a democratically elected American president suspected of collusion with the Kremlin joins Russia's primary instrument of international propaganda in accusing respectable media outlets (a favoured target of the right-wing organizations behind Trump's rise to power) of peddling disinformation. RT's approach to news thus belongs to developments which extend well beyond Russian state borders, and which have transformed the transnational media landscape.

What our analysis in this chapter shows, then, is that familiar, Cold-War inflected accounts of RT as the linear instrument of a single-minded state propaganda machine are both simplistic and misleading. They fail to reflect fissures within the Russian state apparatus and issues affecting the inner coherence of RT itself, including sharp cultural differences between its non-Russian staff and their Russian counterparts. They ignore both the significant modification and tailoring of style and substance that state narratives must undergo for transmission to the heterogeneous transnational audience constituencies which RT targets, and the disorienting geopolitical reconfigurations which invalidate reductive Cold War paradigms pitting 'Western democracy' against 'Russian totalitarianism'. They downplay RT's ability to work creatively to exploit the undecidable, decentred meanings that abound in a digital media ecology criss-crossed by transnational flows, but also the limitations that these flows place on RT's own agency.

The central argument this chapter has advanced, however, is *not* one about the tensions and opportunities that arise when a 'tool' intended to promote national interests is 'deployed' in a transnational environment. Crystallizing in the concluding discussions of *stiob* and fake news, it rather posits that the deeply mediatized environment in which RT is immersed places its national and transnational dimensions in a relationship of mutual dependency and of a recursive 'doubling back' (of national assertions upon transnational mediations, and vice versa). This process ultimately erodes the distinction between national and transnational. As a consequence, both RT's pariah status within Western public discourse and the audacious counter-discourses it embraces in response, are the structural 'effects' of a dynamic but impersonal process over which state actors exert minimal control, yet of which, in RT's case, they sometimes demonstrate an acute, self-reflexive awareness. An illustration of RT's capacity to project that self-awareness as part of its mercurial, ever-shifting brand image is the scandal-seeking poster campaign it unleashed on the London Underground and elsewhere in 2017, featuring humorously provocative slogans such as 'Beware! A "propaganda bullhorn" is at work here' and 'Missed a train? Lost a vote? Blame it on us!'[1]

---

[1] For more detail on the controversy generated by these posters, see Elgot (2017).

An exploration of the implications of the argument for approaches to future relations between the Russian state and its adversaries lies beyond this chapter's scope. The need to undertake it is no less urgent for that.

Works Cited

Assange, Julian. 2017. 'UK Government Gets Twitter ...', 3 September, tweet @JulianAssange <https://twitter.com/JulianAssange/status/904251492122681348> [accessed 3 September 2017].

BBC. 2015. 'BBC World Service Gets Funding Boost from Government', 23 November <http://www.bbc.co.uk/news/entertainment-arts-34902244> [accessed 15 May 2017].

BBC Trust. 2013. 'A BBC Trust Review of the Breadth of Opinion Reflected in the BBC's Output' <http://downloads.bbc.co.uk/bbctrust/assets/files/pdf/our_work/breadth_opinion/breadth_opinion.pdf> [accessed 15 May 2017].

Broadcasters Audience Research Board (BARB). 2017. 'Quarterly Reach Report, Q3' <www.barb.co.uk/wp-content/uploads/2017/11/BARB-Quarterly-Reach-Report-Quarter-3-2017-weeks-2554-2566.pdf> [accessed 23 February 2018].

Bryant, Martin. 2011. '20 Years Ago Today, the World Wide Web Opened to the Public', *The Insider*, 6 August <https://thenextweb.com/insider/2011/08/06/20-years-ago-today-the-world-wide-web-opened-to-the-public/#.tnw_JSQtukH2> [accessed 2 May 2017].

Castells, Manuel. 2000. *The Rise of the Network Society* (Oxford: Blackwell).

Couldry, Nick, and Andreas Hepp. 2017. 'The Continuing Lure of the Mediated Centre in Times of Deep Mediatization: Media Events and its Enduring Legacy', *Media Culture and Society*, 40(1): 114–17.

Dayan, Daniel, and Elihu Katz. 1992. *Media Events: The Live Broadcasting of History* (Cambridge, MA: Harvard University Press).

Elgot, Jessica. 2017. 'RT Spent £310,000 on London Transport Ads, TfL Figures Suggest', *Guardian*, 14 December <https://www.theguardian.com/uk-news/2017/dec/14/rt-london-transport-ads-tfl-transport-for-london> [accessed 24 April 2019].

Gillespie, Marie. 2013. 'BBC Arabic, Social Media and Citizen Production: An Experiment in Digital Democracy before the Arab Spring', *Theory, Culture & Society*, 30(4): 92–130.

Halliday, Josh. 2014. 'BBC World Service Fears Losing Information War as Russia Today Ramps up Pressure', *Guardian*, 21 December <https://www.theguardian.com/media/2014/dec/21/bbc-world-service-information-war-russia-today> [accessed 15 April 2017].

Hutchings, Stephen. 2017. 'Fake News and "Post-Truth": Some Preliminary Notes', *Russian Journal of Communication*, 9(2) <http://dx.doi.org/10.1080/19409419.2017.1323178> [accessed 15 May 2017].

Hutchings, Stephen, Marie Gillespie, Ilya Yablokov, Ilia Lvov, and Alexander Voss. 2015. 'Staging the Sochi Winter Olympics 2014 on Russia Today and BBC World News: From Soft Power to Geopolitical Crisis', *Participations*, 12(1): 630–58.

Krasodomski-Jones, Alex. 2015. *Talking to Ourselves? Political Debate Online and the Echo Chamber Effect* <https://www.demos.co.uk/wp-content/uploads/2017/02/Echo-Chambers-final-version.pdf> [accessed 15 May 2017].

Livshen, Anthony, Elizabeth Nelson, and Robert Orttung. 2015. 'How Russia Today Is Using YouTube', *The Washington Post*, 23 March <https://www.washingtonpost.com/news/monkey-cage/wp/2015/03/23/how-russia-today-is-using-youtube/?utm_term=.e4e10260c439> [accessed 23 February 2018].

LoGiurato, Brett. 2014. 'RT Is Very Upset with John Kerry for Blasting them as "Putin's Propaganda Bullhorn"', *Business Insider*, 26 April <http://www.businessinsider.com/john-kerry-rt-propaganda-bullhorn-russia-today-2014-4?IR=T> [accessed 26 August 2016].

Lovell, Stephen. 2015. *Russia in the Microphone Age: A History of Soviet Radio, 1919–1970* (Oxford: Oxford University Press).

Miskimmon, Alister, Ben O'Loughhlin, and Laura Roselle. 2013. *Strategic Narratives: Communication Power and the New World Order* (Abingdon: Routledge).

Nye, Joseph. 1990. *Bound to Lead: The Changing Nature of American Power* (New York: Basic Books).

Office of the Director of National Intelligence (ODNI). 2017. 'Background to "Assessing Russian Activities and Intentions in Recent US Elections": The Analytic Process and Cyber Incident', 6 January <https://www.dni.gov/files/documents/ICA_2017_01.pdf> [accessed 2 May 2017].

Pomerantsev, Peter. 2014. *Nothing Is True and Everything Is Possible: The Surreal Heart of the New Russia* (New York: PublicAffairs).

RT. 2014. 'Pussy Riot in Sochi Performance Fail', 19 February <https://www.rt.com/news/pussy-riot-sochi-cossacks-748/> [accessed 12 February 2018].

——. 2017. 'Join the Revolution! #1917LIVE Launches Interactive Website, Storms Twitter', 27 February <https://www.rt.com/news/378740-rt-project-revolution-1917/> [accessed 15 May 2017].

Simonian, Margarita. 2013. 'Smertel'noe Oruzhie v Efire', *Rossiiskaia gazeta*, 7 July <http://www.rg.ru/2013/07/03/simonian.html> [accessed 10 June 2014].

——. 2014. 'About Abby Martin, Liz Wahl and Media Wars', *RT*, 6 March <http://rt.com/op-edge/about-liz-wahl-media-wars-126/> [accessed 6 September 2014].

Sputnik News. 2005. 'RIA Novosti Launches a TV Channel, Russia Today', 7 June <https://sptnkne.ws/eq6C> [accessed 2 May 2017].

Strukov, Vlad. 2016. 'Digital Conservatism: Framing Patriotism in the Era of Global Journalism' in Mikhail Suslov and Mark Bassin (eds), *Eurasia 2.0: Russian Geopolitics in the Age of New Media* (Lanham, MD: Lexington), 185–209.

Van Herpen, Marcel. 2016. *Putin's Propaganda Machine: Soft Power and Russian Foreign Policy* (New York: Rowman and Littlefield).

Viner, Katharine. 2016. 'How Technology Disrupted the Truth', *Guardian*, 12 July <https://www.theguardian.com/media/2016/jul/12/how-technology-disrupted-the-truth> [accessed 28 August 2016].

Winek, Mark. 2009. 'Radio as a Tool of the State: Radio Moscow and the Early Cold War', *Comparative Humanities Review*, 3: 98–113.

Yablokov, Ilya. 2015. 'Conspiracy Theories as a Russian Public Diplomacy Tool: The Case of *Russia Today* (*RT*)', *Politics*, 35(3–4): 301–15.

YouTube. 2014. 'Pussy Riot Whipped by Cossacks Patrolling Sochi Winter Olympics' <https://www.youtube.com/watch?v=eiw0fw_sJOk> [accessed 22 February 2018].

Yurchak, Alexei. 2006. *Everything Was Forever Until it Was No More: The Last Soviet Generation* (Princeton, NJ: Princeton University Press).

18

Meduza

A Russo-centric Digital Media Outlet
in a Transnational Setting

Vlad Strukov

Introduction

The Russian Federation (hereafter, the RF) has been an active participant in the global information exchange facilitated by the rise of digital media technologies in the twenty-first century. Thus far, research on Russian media has tended to focus especially on disruptive activity, including hacking and trolling, piracy and illegal data sharing (e.g. Strukov 2011), or else on the top-down organization of information flows, surveillance, propaganda, and political interference, as stemming from the interests of the Russian state (e.g. Oates 2006). Needless to say, the veritable explosion of Russian-language digital communications during the 2000s and 2010s has turned this field into a focus of extensive study from a wide variety of perspectives – technological (e.g, Nikkarila & Ristolainen 2017), sociological (e.g. Lonkila & Gladarev 2008), linguistic (e.g. Gorham, Lunde, & Paulsen 2014), and, of course, political (e.g. Oates 2013). This wave of interest has also included the study of the many different Russian digital media outlets from the perspective of media and communication studies (Hutchings et al. 2015; Kuntsman 2010). However, it is becoming increasingly difficult to define what precisely makes Russian digital media 'Russian', and how exactly one should conceptualize what these media do as 'Russian media' (i.e. precisely who they are produced by; to whom they appeal; and what political, social, or cultural stances they project).

The aim of this chapter is to explore this broader problem of defining and analysing 'Russian' media in the digital age by focusing on the example of Meduza – a successful digital media outlet set up in 2014 by journalists from the RF, with a base in Riga, Latvia. This chapter will be the first attempt to conceptualize the work of the outlet in a transnational setting. Meduza began as mainly a news aggregator but evolved rapidly into one of the leading Russophone news portals, providing extensive analytical reports about social, political, and cultural life in the RF and the wider world to audiences living both in and outside of the country. Its revenue is not based on subscriptions, but advertising, and it is therefore freely available to all users. Mixing news with lifestyle advice, Meduza models itself on *The New York Times*, a Western liberal media outlet, not Fox, the *Daily Telegraph*, or similar conservative networks available in the RF online. Meduza's audience is mixed in terms of age, socioeconomic status, citizenship, and residence, but it generally consists of well-educated and technologically savvy individuals who share an interest in current affairs, social trends, and 'edgy' cultural phenomena. Meduza uses a range of formats and platforms for information distribution, including a website, social media, messengers, and apps. It employs the most up-to-date models of information presentation and circulation, such as succinct evening releases of major stories on messengers. Its emphasis on flexible formats, cross-channel communication, and immediate response to demand for the consumption of information in any place and at any time situates it at the cutting edge of global digital media developments.

Meduza positions itself as unbound by geography, nation state borders, or even language, but as strategically embedded in the global system of capital, labour, and information flows. Yet, despite its global reach, cosmopolitan style, and growing influence in parts of the world where there are larger populations of Russophones, Meduza can hardly be described as an 'international' or even 'global' media outlet as such. It appeals first and foremost to Russian-speakers (to be understood as a group defined not by ethnicity or nationhood but by the commonality of language and sociocultural experience) and its proper environment is the Russian-language internet, known as the Runet.[1] Furthermore, the dominant focus of Meduza's interest is Russia-related politics, society, technology, and culture, even if it consistently places these in the wider context of international news and global trends. At the same time, though, Meduza is not one of Russia's 'national' media outlets, either on the basis of its editorial base or owing to its journalistic positioning. But nor is it a 'diasporic' outlet or an outlet 'in exile' (i.e. defined principally by its position on the other side of Russian sovereign borders). Even if its offices are in Riga,

---

[1] In addition to publishing news in the Russian language, Meduza releases some materials in English for Anglophone users interested in Russian politics. This provision is limited, however, due to the considerable costs of translating from Russian into English.

Meduza is certainly not catering in any special way for Latvian Russophones; nor is it, like, say, Snob.ru, targeting privileged 'global Russians' (Ryazanova-Clarke 2014). Arguably the most accurate way in which Meduza's position can be conceptualized is as a *transnational* media outlet. What is crucial to Meduza's transnationalism is that it has a discernible vector; the way it channels the production, dissemination, and consumption of information around Russian society, politics, technology, and culture makes Meduza's transnationalism 'Russo-centric'.

The remainder of the chapter is devoted to an elaboration of just what Russo-centric transnationalism means. The discussion that follows is the outcome of research carried out between 2014 and 2018 and is based on an analysis of Meduza's publications and on data gathered from around 50 semi-structured interviews with journalists and producers affiliated to a variety of Russophone digital media outlets, including Meduza's chief editors. I begin my argument by sketching out some of the historical background relevant to Meduza's emergence in the mid-2010s. In particular, I focus on the growing tension between the transnationalism inherent in the Runet and the drive towards the 'sovereignization' of the internet which became the policy of the RF government in the 2010s (see Gorham in this volume). I then describe the specific political and financial circumstances that resulted in the founding of Meduza and analyse its positioning in relation to other key Russophone digital media outlets, highlighting that this positioning is governed more by the logic of professional than of political differentiation. Finally, I account for Meduza's transnational Russo-centrism by expounding on the ambiguities underpinning the outlet's strategic combination of the advantages of digital 'deterritorialization' with its role as 'trendsetter' in a specific society and also across different societies. I conclude the chapter by suggesting that, while the story of Meduza cannot be understood without viewing it as part of the history of the Runet and without situating it in the politics of the RF in the twenty-first century (especially the politics of media), the distinctiveness of Meduza's position lies in it being simultaneously and in an intertwined way 'Russian' and 'global'.

The Runet and the Russian Internet

The arrival of digital technologies in the RF coincided with the end of the Cold War and the country's entry into the global space of transnational commerce, communication, and cultural exchange. This included an unprecedented surge in cross-border mobility, leading during the 1990s–2000s to the global expansion of an increasingly digitally networked transnational community of Russophones. Unlike earlier waves of emigration from the

Russian Empire and the USSR, the post-Soviet Russian-speaking diaspora was made up of individuals who, for the most part, emigrated for economic and professional reasons and who did not therefore find themselves in political exile, but continued to maintain extensive links with Russia – personal, professional, economic, and cultural. Crucial to these links has been the proliferation of computer technologies, above all the internet and eventually social media; the latter has resulted in the creation of one of the most vibrant and influential global digital networks – the Runet (e.g. Alexanyan 2009; Etling et al. 2010).

The Runet must be distinguished from 'the Russian internet' (Schmidt, Teubener, & Konradova 2006). Both concepts are fluid and regularly overlap, but they are not congruent and can be in tension. Runet refers to the digital communication network in the Russian language irrespective of the global location of those in the network; it is a fundamentally transnational entity which transgresses nation state borders to form a global digital realm of communication in the Russian language. The Russian internet, by contrast, refers to digital networks with a physical base on the territory of the RF, and these do not, in fact, have to be in the Russian language. For instance, while a Russian-language blog authored by someone based in Athens belongs to the Runet, a person blogging in Tatar from Kazan is doing so on the Russian internet. However, it is problematic to try and situate a specific digital communication as belonging only to the Runet or to the Russian internet, especially since communications regularly straddle both.[2]

Historically, the Runet and the Russian internet arose together and remain dynamically entwined. In fact, the same media and technical elites living and working transnationally between the RF, the USA, Israel, and other countries have led the way in the building of both the Runet and the Russian internet (Schmidt et al. 2006). An exemplary figure in this respect was Anton Nosik (1966–2017), who was born in the USSR but emigrated to Israel in the early 1990s and there worked as a blogger in online Russophone media. In 1997 he moved back to Moscow, where he took charge of several international IT start-ups and served as editor of a number of influential online media, including Lenta.ru. During the 2000s, Lenta.ru became one of the most successful Russian-language online news aggregators, often challenging the political stance and professional standards of Russian media majors. Furthermore, Nosik's personal blog on the social networking service LiveJournal became one of the most popular blogs on the Runet, making a

---

[2] VPN and other technologies enabling deterritorialized use of the internet make the technological and geopolitical distinction between the Runet and the Russian internet even more problematic.

significant impact on the Russian blogosphere through its innovative style of communication (Strukov 2009). LiveJournal itself, however, while especially popular among Russophone users, including many in the diaspora, was established in the late 1990s by US entrepreneurs based in California. In 2007, though, in a move of strategic 'nationalization' of Runet communications, the Russian company SUP Media, of which Nosik was one of the executives, purchased and relocated LiveJournal's base to the RF (Strukov 2009).

For much of this period, the Russian government was in response mode with respect to developments in the digital realm, leaving the Runet to grow relatively spontaneously through the entrepreneurial activity of a transnational tech-savvy elite (Strukov 2009). By the 2010s, however, the Russian authorities had come to realize the political significance not simply of the internet and social media as such (this had been evident for some time) but of the need to assume control over digital communications, with a view to subordinating them to their power as much as possible. The impetus for this was initially largely protective as the Russian government became increasingly alarmed by the vulnerabilities that the rise in digital communications was creating for the state even on its own territory. In consequence, especially after the rise of the anti-government protest movement from 2011–12, the Russian authorities began introducing new laws with the aim of bringing the internet into the orbit of the sovereign control of the Russian state (for more detail, see Gorham in this volume). In other words, the government now looked to construct the Russian internet precisely as an entity separate from the Runet, and this specifically with a view to undermining the latter's transnational character.

For example, in 2016, a law was introduced which required companies collecting and processing the personal data of Russian nationals to ensure that servers storing that data be physically located on the territory of the RF.[3] This law appears, on the one hand, to be protecting the interests of Russian citizens and companies by increasing online safety and regulating data mining carried out by transnational corporations with a base outside the RF, such as Facebook. On the other hand, however, this law also gives greater powers to Russian security forces, providing them with direct access to the data of Russian citizens stored on these servers. The question from the perspective of the Russian authorities is not whether there should be digital surveillance of Russian citizens' digital communications – such surveillance is widespread (Soldatov & Borogan 2015) – but of who should be conducting

---

[3] This is the so-called 'Iarovaia law', which includes a pair of Russian federal bills, 374-FZ and 375-FZ, passed in 2016.

it. The users of Russian social networking services, such as, for example, Vkontakte, have been visible to Russian security forces for some time; but what about the Russian users of, for instance, Facebook, which is registered in California? And, indeed, since the ratcheting up of tensions between the RF and the West in the mid-2010s, the mass gathering and political use of the data of digital media users *transnationally* has come to be seen as a major means to conduct cyber warfare, something that most states, whether authoritarian or democratic, are now actively seeking to protect themselves against (e.g. Deibert & Rohozinski 2010).

The introduction of the above law was accompanied by heated discussions in the RF about privacy, the rights and responsibilities of companies and individuals, the configurations of national and international security, and the role of the state in regulating the digital economy (see e.g. Meduza 2016; Dmitriev & Borzenko 2018). These debates were not dissimilar to those taking place in the West at roughly the same time (for example, those surrounding the Leveson Inquiry in the UK, which investigated phone hacking carried out by Rupert Murdoch's *News of the World*; see Brock 2012). However, while some countries have responded to digital uncertainties by introducing firewalls (e.g. China and Iran) or paywalls (e.g. Portugal and the USA), the RF has instead opted for a semi-open structure which provides the Kremlin with opportunities to manipulate information flows to its own benefit as a way of ensuring the hegemony of its agenda on the relevant networks (Strukov 2016). The Russian internet is, in fact, a poorly regulated but closely monitored realm of communication in which the authorities have legal tools to intervene when it becomes necessary to impose control, mostly through censoring exemplary individuals or diverting flows on the internet away from social movements critical of the government. However, while both surveillance and legal powers allow the Russian government to control key sections of the Russian internet, this is not, of course, the case with the Runet more broadly. *And yet*, the Runet and the Russian internet are not so easy to disaggregate; indeed, the RF government's strategy to 'sovereignize' the Russian internet and the various tactics that it deploys for this purpose are impacting on the structures of the Runet as well. One of the outcomes has, in fact, been precisely the emergence of media outlets such as Meduza, the character and positioning of which is shaped to a significant degree by the above shifts in the politics of the digital media within the RF itself.

The Emergence of Meduza: National Politics and Transnational Capital

So how did Meduza come about? Towards the end of 2013, Russian billionaire Aleksandr Mamut gained control over Lenta.ru through his holding SUP Media – the same company through which Nosik had earlier transferred LiveJournal from the USA to the RF.[4] On 12 March 2014, Mamut sacked Galina Timchenko from her position as director of Lenta.ru, a post that she had held since 2004. This happened directly after Lenta.ru received an official warning from Roskomnadzor (the Federal Service of Supervision in the Sphere of Telecom, Information Technologies, and Mass Communications, the official body responsible for regulating the media in the RF) because it had published materials that referred to an interview by one of the leaders of Right Sector, an ultranationalist Ukrainian political organization.[5] This was all happening at a time when tensions in the relationship between the RF and Ukraine were surging in the context of the annexation of Crimea in February 2014: Timchenko's sacking occurred two days before the controversial referendum in which the residents of Crimea voted to join the RF as a federal subject.

Gleb Pavlovskii (b. 1951), one of the pioneers of the Runet, decried Timchenko's dismissal as a dangerous attack on the freedom of the press in the RF (Makeeva 2014). Pavlovskii's statement is revealing; he was not only a former political dissident from the late Soviet era, but also one of the people who, during the late 1990s–early 2000s, connected the rapidly growing field of digital media to the practice of controversial politics in the RF. In 1995 he became one of the founders of the so-called Foundation for Effective Politics [Fond effektivnoi politiki, hereafter FEP], an organization responsible for generating and supporting numerous Russian political digital media outlets in the decade that followed. The FEP helped El'tsin get re-elected in 1996, at a time when his ratings were at a historical low. The FEP also contributed to his succession by Putin in 1999–2000 and supported Putin's own re-election in 2004, often using dubious communication tools. For Pavlovskii, who styles himself a 'political technologist',[6] censoring cutting-edge digital media outlets, as was done to Lenta.ru through the summary sacking of its

---

[4] Mamut made his wealth in large part during the 1990s as a lawyer and investor with close connections with the Russian political and financial elite, including El'tsin and Berezovskii. He developed a strong interest in digital media in the 2000s and became one of the founders of SUP Media in 2006 and its principle owner in 2012.

[5] See Lenta.ru's own account of these events (Lenta.ru 2014).

[6] See Pavlovskii's webpage on the Echo of Moscow website, where he describes himself as a 'political technologist' (Ekho Moskvy n.d.)

long-standing and highly respected chief editor, was a form of state censorship. Yet Pavlovskii himself was responsible for constructing the environment in which such actions were now possible. Timchenko's sacking was the start of a debate about what constitutes quality journalism outside the framework of political affiliation, sponsorship, and so on. And, indeed, Pavlovskii clearly recognized that Timchenko's dismissal marked the emergence of an entirely new relationship between communication technologies, capital, and political power in the RF. In this new configuration some entrepreneurial 'political technologists', like Pavlovskii, had fallen out of favour and Russian oligarch capital was now being deployed as part of the government's strategy of imposing greater control over the internet.

In any event, in protest at Timchenko's dismissal, a group of her fellow journalists resigned from Lenta.ru and in October 2014 joined her to launch a new media outlet – namely, Meduza. For a long time, it was not known who provided the financial backing for Meduza (logistical and professional backing was provided by Timchenko's former colleagues, such as Nosik); however, in 2016 it emerged that this was none other than the former oligarch turned enemy of Putin, Mikhail Khodorkovskii (Zhegulev 2016). Khodorkovskii had come to prominence in the 1990s as the owner of the massive oil company Yukos and was at that time considered the richest man in the RF. In the early 2000s he developed political ambitions and attempted to use his capital to challenge Putin. In 2003, however, he was arrested on charges of embezzlement and then jailed in 2005. At the end of 2013, shortly before Meduza appeared, Khodorkovskii was pardoned by Putin and released from prison, upon which he swiftly left the RF to take up residency in Switzerland.

Some may be inclined to consider Khodorkovskii's support for Meduza as evidence that the latter is simply another weapon in the arsenal of the so-called 'oppositional oligarchs' who are waging war on the Kremlin from abroad (Esch & Sandberg 2018). However, this is a limited interpretation that misrepresents the distinctiveness of Meduza as a media outlet. Firstly, while Meduza is certainly critical of the Kremlin, it is nothing like Khodorkovskii's actual project of opposition to Putin's regime, Open Russia (https://openrussia. org/), which has all the characteristics of a dissident outlet with an explicit political goal, namely, regime change in the RF. Secondly, Khodorkovskii is not the only oligarch supporting Meduza. Dmitrii Zimin, founder of the major Russian telecommunications company Beeline, is another of Meduza's financial backers. While Zimin resides in London, his company is fully embedded in the economy of the RF and he is hardly an 'oppositional oligarch'. Rather, his support for Meduza is part of his family's philanthropic support for the Russian arts and sciences more generally (Zimin Foundation 2016). Finally, Meduza's own developmental strategy is to extricate itself over time from its reliance on handouts from oligarchs, whatever their agenda, and to become economically independent. It is, for example, working especially hard to increase its advertising revenues,[7] and it is also developing other types of economically viable activities, such as its summer school of journalism (Meduza 2018).

The summer school is not simply a revenue generator, but also part of Meduza's ambition to develop a new generation of journalists with a particular set of high professional standards. This aim is especially important to Meduza's positioning as a media outlet more generally. In order to understand the latter, it is useful to situate Meduza in relation to other media outlets, especially those that operate transnationally. Here I distinguish three main political positions: (a) outlets that support the Kremlin (this is the position of the majority of Russian news media, including, prominently, those targeting audiences outside the RF, such as RT or Sputnik; see also Hutchings in this volume); (b) outlets that directly attack the Kremlin, predominantly from abroad, and lobby actively for regime change (the aforementioned Open Russia); and finally (c) those critical of the Kremlin, especially of its political authoritarianism and illiberal social policies (such as, for example, the 'anti-gay propaganda law'), but that are not involved in political mobilization as such. This last group includes outlets such as TV Rain [Dozhd'], *Vedomosti*, Fontanka.ru, *Kommersant*, and a number of regional media outlets, including the Voronezh-based newspaper and internet portal Mine! [Moe!].

What distinguishes members of this latter group, and it also applies to Meduza, is arguably not so much their political agenda per se, but their positioning within the professional field of journalism. To put it slightly differently, their critical stance in relation to what goes on in the RF politically, socially, and otherwise is first and foremost a *professional* rather than a political position. While they differ in terms of funding model and ownership, editorial focus and style, all the outlets listed under (c) above share the professional objective to provide what they understand to be balanced, unbiased, and unprejudiced information about the RF and the world to users who value 'quality journalism'. In this regard, they distinguish themselves professionally from outlets that serve principally as political tools (whether their agenda is

---

[7] In digital media, the flow of information is inseparable from the flow of capital. An analysis of advertisements placed on Meduza's website can, for example, serve as a general indication of where Meduza is positioned in terms of capital flows. The latter shows that Meduza is attracting a very wide range of national and multinational corporations, all of which are simultaneously 'global' and 'Russian' – from McDonald's to Sberbank (Russia's state-backed bank, which also branches in other countries).

pro- or anti-regime), but also, and possibly even more so, from the lowbrow mass outlets and sensationalist social media influencers who thrive on the dissemination of scandalous, and frequently false, information, purely to attract attention (e.g. Djafarova & Trofimenko 2018).

However, Meduza is to some degree distinctive in that it pitches its own opposition to false, biased, and prejudiced information not only in the context of the RF itself, but also as a response to the *global* crisis of quality journalism (Alexander, Breese, & Luengo 2016). Meduza was one of the first media outlets in the world to introduce the fact-check icon as an indication that the information presented in a news report had been verified by Meduza itself or else to indicate that a piece of information comes from a trusted source but still requires further investigation. The purpose of using this icon is, of course, not simply to establish the facts as such but, much more importantly, to build trust in the information that Meduza provides, since this trust is the outlet's key selling point. Meduza's rapid ascent to the position of one of the leading media outlets on the Runet owes a great deal to the crisis of trust in media based in the RF. And essential to Meduza's success in this context is that it positions itself as part of a much wider – international – digital communication realm, and that it takes as its professional model Western liberally oriented quality journalism, while at the same time focusing its reporting on the RF. In other words, it assumes the position of a 'globalized' digital media outlet, yet one whose influence is directed first and foremost towards Russian society, no matter whether it is confined to the RF or stretches across other nation states. However, what is crucial about Meduza's positioning here is that it entails a resistance to the segregation of digital communications on the internet between digital communications that are 'inside' the sovereign Russian space and those which appear to come from 'outside' this space.

Where Is Meduza? On Transnational Russo-centrism

When it was announced that Timchenko was to base her new project in Latvia, many commentators described the future Meduza as a 'media outlet in exile', thereby endowing its journalists with the image of dissident émigrés from earlier times forced to flee their homeland in order to continue to speak truth to power. In reality, though, the move to Riga, as a physical location, was only part of a much broader countermove to the 'sovereignization' of digital communication in the RF outlined above. The ultimate objective of this countermove was to reclaim the Runet as originally conceived (i.e. not subject to Russian state control); or, more specifically, to develop a position in the Runet that would be resistant to 'sovereignization' while, crucially, still continuing to be an active part of the digital realm of the RF. What was necessary for this to be achieved was not for the new media outlet to *move territory* but rather for it to re-establish itself as *deterritorialized*, something that communication on the Runet was expected to be by definition. And, indeed, despite the fact that Meduza's editorial base is in Riga, as a *digital* entity Meduza is not Latvia-based. Like many similar outlets, Meduza uses a country code top-level domain (https://meduza.io/). However, this code (.io) is neither Russian (.ru) nor Latvian (.lv); it indicates the property of the offshore British Indian Ocean Territory. Key here is that, irrespective of the physical location of its offices, Meduza in digital terms remains for both legal and financial purposes outside of the direct regulatory jurisdiction of either the RF or the European Union (EU).[8]

Furthermore, while there are many good reasons and clear advantages to Meduza's offices being located physically in Riga, this location is not in itself critical to the project that Meduza embodies as a digital media outlet. At the time of writing (summer of 2018), Meduza's headquarters occupy one floor of an old apartment block in the centre of the Latvian capital. Latvia is one of the three former Baltic republics of the USSR which in 2004 became member states of both the EU and NATO (Mole 2012). It has a population of about 2 million people, of whom around a quarter belong to the minority that define themselves as Russian. The proportion of Russian speakers, though, is considerably higher, reaching close to 50 per cent of the country's population. In fact, Latvia is a dynamically multilingual space where, moreover, a host of different types of Russianness are articulated and performed. One must distinguish between the Russian-speaking minority dating back to Soviet and even earlier times, which would not necessarily be 'ethnically Russian', the more recent expats from the RF and Russophones immigrating from other parts of the former Soviet Union, and, finally, a significant portion of Russian-speaking 'ethnic' Latvians and many with a mixed heritage.[9] Riga is therefore a space that is nationally Latvian, governed by Western transnational political, economic, and military structures, but, due to Latvia's extensive historical links with Russia, also a site of a large and vibrant, as well as ethno-nationally

---

[8] The ambiguity of Meduza's position *vis-à-vis* regulatory (inter)national frameworks became apparent in 2018, when it was embroiled in a sexual harassment scandal. Allegations brought against the editor-in-chief by another member of staff meant that the case had to be investigated. However, it was not clear if Russian, Latvian, or British law was to be employed. In the end Meduza carried out its own investigation, thus bypassing other frameworks.

[9] In my own analysis I resist ideologically charged terms such as 'ethnicity', hence the inverted commas here.

complex Russophone social and cultural scene (e.g. see Platt 2013a, 2013b, 2015, 2018).

There is therefore much in this location, situated at the crux of shifting imperial borderlands, that fits Meduza's 'deterritorialized' self-image. Yet, in truth, *as a media outlet* Meduza is not embedded all that strongly in this distinctive locality. Meduza's editors have, in fact, been criticized for failing to engage more with it, both in terms of the types of news and reports that their outlet carries, and in the way that it as an organization links up with the local communities. For example, in the interview that I carried out with Timchenko in the summer of 2017, she admitted that, despite the fact that, in accordance with EU employment law, she regularly placed job advertisements locally, she had not hired a single Latvian citizen. In fact, a lot of Meduza's technical production, such as web design, is carried out by individuals who are still based in the RF.

Meduza's journalists and editors are not in any meaningful way living in 'exile' from the RF but continue to hold Russian citizenship and are active in the RF's professional media network, often taking part in events on the territory of the RF, including events supported by Russian officialdom. For example, in June 2016, the editor of Meduza's lifestyle section, Il'ia Krasil'shchik, took part in a media forum in Voronezh (an event observed by the author), which was organized with the personal support of the Putin-appointed governor of the region, Aleksei Gordeev. Furthermore, when participating in these and similar events in the RF, Meduza's editors and journalists generally feel free to openly criticize the Russian authorities from their professional perspective. For example, in July 2017, Timchenko took part in a public discussion at the State Hermitage Museum in St Petersburg (an event observed by the author), where she was scathing in her condemnation of the Kremlin's media regulation policies and more generally critical of the regime's authoritarian approach to freedom of speech in the country.

Yet more important than the way in which Meduza's journalists themselves perform on the territory of the RF is the way in which Meduza as a media outlet positions itself in relation to Russian society as such. Here Meduza seeks to develop a distinctive position between and across 'the global' and 'the Russian' that is simultaneously *both* global *and* Russian. For instance, Meduza regularly follows the participation of RF citizens in global cultural and other events. In doing so, however, it does not simply celebrate Russian achievements on the world stage but looks to provide an informed and often quite critical approach to these global events themselves. It does so in a way that is not a critique of 'Western' practices from a 'Russian' perspective; rather, Meduza treats Russian participation in global developments as part of these global developments themselves. One example of this would be Meduza's coverage of the Cannes International film festival: while undoubtedly applauding the success of Russian films at Cannes, Meduza accompanied this with a critical account of the wider context of the global film market, including Russian film producers' place in it (see Dolin 2018).

In other words, Meduza is to some extent assuming a position of supra- or a-national professionalism, rooted in the idea of global standards of quality journalism and associated with its 'deterritorialized' image. However, this is just one half of the equation. Equally important is Meduza's aspiration actively to influence social discourse – specifically discourses of Russophone media, and here primarily (though of course not exclusively) discourses prevalent in the society of the RF itself. In this context, Meduza is keen to be perceived as a 'trendsetter', a leader of progressive change, especially in terms of seeking to inspire the adoption of more liberal attitudes and discourses that come from the wider, global context.

One example of Meduza's progressivist credentials is its ardent support of Ali Feruz (aka Khudoberdi Nurmatov), an Uzbekistani journalist who had worked for the Russian oppositional newspaper *Novaia gazeta* but overstayed his visa permit in the RF and was about to be deported when he applied for political asylum in the RF on grounds that, as a homosexual, he would be persecuted in Uzbekistan. The Russian court declined Feruz's application and ordered him to return to Uzbekistan, after which he successfully applied for asylum in Germany instead. Meduza covered this fellow journalist's ordeals at length, situating them in the context of a wider coverage of discrimination of both asylum seekers and the LGBTQ+ community, in the RF and globally (see, e.g. Gaisina 2017).

One of the 'trends' that Meduza sought to initiate in this context was the dropping of what in Russian is the fairly common use of the term *gomoseksualist*, which, through the suffix '-ist' suggests that homosexuality is a form of lifestyle rooted in moral and aesthetic choice. What Meduza argued for was to establish the term *gomoseksual*, which implies that homosexuality is a specific subjectivity, as normative within Russophone media discourse on homosexuality.[10] Crucial to observe here, though, is that while Meduza's campaign touched on general social attitudes in the RF, the specific area in which

---

[10] Meduza has published a number of items on the subject and has, in fact, been successful to an extent: for example, when reporting about the release of the CIA's secret reports about Hitler's sexuality, the Mamut-owned media.ru used the word *gomoseksual*, not *gomoseskualist* (see Novosti mail.ru 2018). This usage remains inconsistent, though. In *Other Russias*, Brian James Baer (2009: 37) claims that the term *gomoseksual* comes from Russian medical discourse and *gomoseksualist* from legal discourse. See also Chapter 6 in Baer (2016).

Meduza sought to make a difference was the media itself. In other words, yet again, Meduza's most important target of influence is its own professional domain – its institutions and discourses, standards and freedoms.

Conclusions

Meduza's case reveals that Russian media entrepreneurs have been able to launch a successful initiative which is, thus far, circumventing the RF's state-led attempts to 'nationalize' digital networks through its strategy of 'sovereignization'. By setting up offices in another country, by using deterritorialized forms of operation, such as registration in offshore territories, and by relying on the transient, transnational nature of both digital communication networks and global capital flows, Meduza has been able to produce and deliver news to a Russophone audience that is not automatically united by or dependent on the geographical, social, political, and legal context of any given nation state. By deploying a wide range of formats and platforms, Meduza has built its own community of users. This community is not characterized by its geographical location or its allegiance and sense of belonging to a given state, society, or nation as such. Rather, it builds on its members' shared experience of the twenty-first-century global fluidity of spaces and subjectivities, culture, and, above all, information. It also emerges from their need for a certain anchor in this fluidity. Meduza sets itself the mission of providing that anchor in the form of globally determined professional standards of digital media communication associated with 'quality journalism'.

At the same time, Meduza maintains a crucial link to media in the RF, not simply because it still relies on the RF for crucial parts of its funding, workforce, and, of course, audience but because, even while evading 'nationalization', it maintains direct and intimate links with the media profession in the RF. This link is also maintained because while Meduza continues to seek to shape and influence digital media communication on the internet more generally, it achieves such influence principally by positioning itself as something of a global vanguard within the Runet, a vanguard that is (a) committed to keeping the Runet at the technological and programming cutting edge of global digital media, (b) defends the Runet as a realm governed by the liberal ethos of free and open digital communication, and (c) embodies and promotes the highest professional standards in shaping and channelling this communication as a media outlet. Meduza's Russo-centricity and its transnationalism are thus not only mutually compatible, but utterly interdependent.

Works Cited

Alexander, Jeffrey C., Elizabeth Butler Breese, and María Luengo. 2016. *The Crisis of Journalism Reconsidered: Democratic Culture, Professional Codes, Digital Future* (Cambridge: Cambridge University Press).

Alexanyan, Karina. 2009. 'The RuNet: Lost in Translation', *Russian Analytical Digest*, 69 (14 December): 2–5.

Baer, Brian James. 2009. *Other Russias: Homosexuality and the Crisis of Post-Soviet Identity* (Basingstoke: Palgrave Macmillan).

——. 2016. *Translation and the Making of Modern Russian Literature* (London: Bloomsbury).

Brock, George. 2012. 'The Leveson Inquiry: There's a Bargain to Be Struck Over Media Freedom and Regulation', *Journalism*, 13(4): 519–28.

Deibert, Ronald, and Rafal Rohozinski. 2010. 'Liberation vs Control: The Future of Cyberspace', *The Journal of Democracy*, 21(4): 43–57.

Djafarova, Elmira, and Oxana Trofimenko. 2018. '"Instafamous" – Credibility and Self-Presentation of Micro-Celebrities on Social Media', *Information, Communication and Society*, 19 February <https://www.tandfonline.com/doi/pdf/10.1080/1369118X.2018.1438491?needAccess=true> [accessed 24 September 2018].

Dmitriev, Denis, and Aleksandr Borzeko. 2018. 'Iarovaia predlagaet novye bloki-rovki – za vovlechenie detei v opasnye dlia zhizni protivopravyne deistviia. Chto eto izmenit?', *Meduza*, 18 May <https://meduza.io/cards/yarovaya-predl-agaet-novye-blokirovki-za-vovlechenie-detey-v-opasnye-dlya-zhizni-protivo-pravnye-deystviya-chto-eto-izmenit> [accessed 4 November 2018].

Dolin, Anton. 2018. 'Zepret na selfi …', *Meduza*, 8 May 2018 <https://meduza.io/feature/2018/05/08/zapret-na-selfi-bolshe-zhenschin-i-rossiyan-vozvra-schenie-fon-triera> [accessed 15 October 2018].

Ekho Moskvy. n.d. 'Gleb Pavlovskii' <https://echo.msk.ru/guests/466/> [accessed 15 October 2018].

Esch, Christian, and Britta Sandberg. 2018. 'Interview with Mikhail Khodorovsky: I Believe Putin Is Capable of Change', *Der Spiegel*, 30 June <http://www.spiegel.de/international/world/mikhail-khodorkovsky-i-believe-putin-is-capable-of-change-a-1215799.html> [accessed 18 October 2018].

Etling, Bruce, Karina Alexanyan, John Kelly, Robert Farris, John Palfrey, and Urs Gasser. 2010. 'Public Discourse in the Russian Blogosphere: Mapping RuNet Politics and Mobilization'. The Berkman Center for Internet & Society at Harvard University. Berkman Center Research Publication No. 2010–11.

Gaisina, Liliia. 2017. 'Korrespondenta "Novoi gazety" Ali Feruza khotiat vydvorit' iz Rossii', *Meduza*, 2 August 2017 <https://meduza.io/feature/2017/08/02/korrespondenta-novoy-gazety-ali-feruza-hotyat-vydvorit-iz-rossii-v-znak-protesta-on-sovershil-popytku-samoubiystva> [accessed 15 October 2018].

Gorham, Michael, Ingunn Lunde, and Martin Paulsen. 2014. *Digital Russia: The Language, Culture and Politics of New Media Communication* (London: Routledge).

Hutchings, Stephen, Marie Gillespie, Ilya Yablokov, Ilia Lvov, and Alexander Voss. 2015. 'Staging the Sochi Winter Olympics 2014 on Russia Today and BBC World News: From Soft Power to Geopolitical Crisis', *Participations*, 12(1): 630–58.

Kuntsman, Adi. 2010. 'Webs of Hate in Diasporic Cyberspaces: The Gaza War in the Russian-Language Blogosphere', *Media, War and Conflict*, 3(3): 299–313.

Lenta.ru. 2014. 'Dorogim chitateliam ot dorogoi redaktsii', 12 March <https://lenta.ru/info/posts/statement/> [accessed 15 October 2018].

Lonkila, Markku, and Boris Gladarev 2008. 'Social Networks and Cellphone Use in Russia: Local Consequences of Global Communication Technology', *New Media and Society*, 10(2): 273–93.

Makeeva, Marina. 2014. 'Pochemu rastushchaia populiarnost' "Lenty.ru" stala prichinoi uvlneniia Galiny Timchenko', Telekenal dozhd', 12 March <https://tvrain.ru/teleshow/here_and_now/pochemu_rastuschaja_populjarnost_lentyru_stala_prichinoj_uvolnenija_galiny_timchenko-364871/> [accessed 4 November 2018].

Meduza. 2016. '"Paket Iarovoi" priniat. I eto ochen' plokho', 24 June <https://meduza.io/feature/2016/06/24/paket-yarovoy-prinyat-i-eto-ochen-ploho> [accessed 4 November 2018].

——. 2018. 'Ferma Tretii nabor v shkolu "Meduzy"' <https://special.meduza.io/landing/ferma/2018/> [accessed 4 November 2018].

Mole, Richard C. M. 2012. *The Baltic States from the Soviet Union to the European Union* (Abingdon: Routledge).

Nikkarila, Juha-Pekka, and Mari Ristolainen. 2017. '"RuNet 2020" – Deploying Traditional Elements of Combat Power in Cyberspace?' Paper delivered at '2017 International Conference on Military Communications and Information Systems (ICMCIS)' <https://ieeexplore.ieee.org/abstract/document/7956478/> [accessed 24 September 2018].

Novosti mail.ru. 2018. 'TsRU rassekretilo doklad o seksula'noi orientatsii Gitlera' <https://news.mail.ru/society/35073322/> [accessed 4 November 2018].

Oates, Sarah. 2006. *Television, Democracy and Elections in Russia* (London: Routledge).

——. 2013. *Revolution Stalled: The Political Limits of the Internet in the Post-Soviet Sphere* (Oxford: Oxford University Press).

Platt, Kevin M. F. 2013a. 'Eccentric Orbit: Mapping Russian Culture in the Near Abroad' in Sanna Turoma and Maxim Waldstein (eds), *Empire De/Centered: New Spatial Histories of Russia* (Aldershot: Ashgate), 271–96.

——. 2013b. 'Russian Empire of Pop: Post-Socialist Nostalgia and Soviet Retro in Latvia', *Russian Review*, 72(3): 447–69.

——. 2015. 'Lyric Cosmopolitanism in a PostSocialist Borderland', *Common Knowledge*, 21(2): 305–26.

——. 2018. 'Distance and Proximity in the Baltic "Near Abroad"' in Kevin M. F. Platt (ed.), *Global Russian Cultures* (Madison, WI: University of Wisconsin Press), 94–112.

Ryazanova-Clarke, Lara (ed.). 2014. *The Russian Language Outside the Nation* (Edinburgh: Edinburgh University Press).

Schmidt, Henrike, Katherine Teubener, and Natalia Konradova (eds). 2006. *Control + Shift: Public and Private Usages of the Russian Internet* (Norderstedt: BOD-Verlag).

Soldatov, Andrei, and Irina Borogan. 2015. *The Red Web* (Washington, DC: PublicAffairs).

Strukov, Vlad. 2009. 'Russia's Internet Media Policies: Open Space and Ideological Closure' in Birgit Beumers, Stephen Hutchings, and Natalia Rulyova (eds), *The Post-Soviet Russian Media: Conflicting Signals* (London: Routledge), 208–22.

——. 2011. 'Translated by Goblin: Global Challenge and Local Response in Post-Soviet Translations of Hollywood Films' in Brian Baer (ed.), *Contexts, Subtexts and Pretexts: Literary translation in Eastern Europe and Russia* (Amsterdam: John Benjamins), 235–48.

——. 2016. 'Digital Conservativism: Framing Patriotism in the Era of Global Journalism' in M. Suslov and M. Bassin (eds), *Eurasia 2.0: Russian Geopolitics in the Age of New Media* (Lanham, MD: Lexington), 185–208.

Zhegulev, Il'ia. 2016. 'Korporatsiia "Khodorkovskii": Chto sdelal byvshii oligarkh za dva s polovinoi goda na svobode', *Meduza*, 11 August <https://meduza.io/feature/2016/08/11/korporatsiya-hodorkovskiy> [accessed 18 October 2018].

Zimin Foundation. 2016. 'Zimin Foundation' <https://www.ziminfoundation.org/> [accessed 4 November 2018].

19

Transnational Self and Community in the Talk of Russophone Cultural Leaders in the UK

Lara Ryazanova-Clarke

With the collapse of the Soviet Union and the opening up of the borders of Russia and other former Soviet states, the world saw an emigration of Russian speakers of unprecedented scale,[1] propelling Russia to the position of the world's third largest sender of migrants by 2015 (United Nations 2015: 3). This migration of Russophones across the world was concurrent with the era of intensified globalization characterized by a radical intensification of the movement of goods, services, information, and culture, leading to fundamental transformations in the relations of people to space on the global scale. In addition to the traditional unidirectional emigration, tens of thousands headed out on 'new types of journey' (Rosello 2001: vii), including labour and business travel, study abroad, international tourism, and 'new nomadism' (Hoffman 1998; Richards 2015), not to mention 'virtual mobility', that is, crossing borders symbolically with the help of communication technology. The UK has, along with other Western countries, experienced a dramatic growth of Russian-speaking migrants and has seen a rapid development of Russophone communities and border-spanning cultural activities.

---

[1] Due to Russia's imperial history, the conflation of notions of Russians and Russian speakers has been pervasive among groups of those who discuss and even conceptualize Russophone migration: Russian elites and lawmakers, communities of migrants from the post-Soviet states and host communities in the UK. The terms accepted here are 'Russian-speaking migrants' and 'Russophones', which relates to a wider conglomerate group of various ethnic origins and who were born in the Russian Federation, the post-Soviet states, and other countries (e.g. Israel, Germany, the US, Sweden).

Contemporary scholarship has developed the concept of transnationalism to conceptualize the modern stage of migration and the associated expansion of diasporic networks. Steven Vertovec explains that transnationalism refers to 'sustained cross-border relationships, patterns of exchange', and 'a range of practices and institutions linking migrants, people and organizations in their homelands or elsewhere in a diaspora' (2009: 13). The increased connectivity emerging in the context of transnational relations creates new forms of networks and linkages (Acharya 2016), including new forms of imagining the diasporic community, identity construction, and communication (De Fina & Perrino 2013: 510; Gupta & Ferguson 1992: 9).

The view of diaspora as a bounded physical group of people cut off from their homelands has been challenged by the postmodern social constructivist perspective which understands the diaspora rather as a network of practice including engagement in various cultural, social, and political projects (Baubök & Faist 2010). From this perspective, diaspora is a dynamic triad of relationships between the diasporic community, the homeland, and the host society, and may be construed as 'an idiom, a stance, a claim' (Brubaker 2005: 12; 2017). This means that, being a type of imagined community (Anderson 1991), diaspora is in effect a discursive construct compounded by 'different ways of constructing, managing, and imagining relationships between homelands and their dispersed people' (Waldinger 2003: xvi).

According to the above perspective, identity in mobility – that is, an image of an individual migrant or migrant community – is not a fixed essence or a predetermined, or pre-linguistic characteristic, but is something that is multiple and incomplete; moreover, something that is constructed, conveyed, and negotiated by various social agents. As in the case of diaspora, language and discourse are the means through which transnational identity is constructed, performed, and negotiated (Hall & Du Gay 1996; Benwell & Stokoe 2006; De Fina 2011, 2016; De Fina et al. 2006; Wodak 2012; Wodak et al. 2009; Wodak & Boukala 2015). The notion of hybridity has been developed to describe the complexity of diasporic identities, a sense of double belonging, and a hyphenated fusion of national, cultural, and linguistic features in the content of identity production (Bhabha 1994; Dervin & Risager 2015; Zhu Hua 2017).

The fluidity of contemporary Russophone migration makes it difficult to ascertain the exact number of Russophone migrants in the UK. The existing figures to date vary dramatically, ranging from 67,400 according to the Office of National Statistics 2011 Census (ONS 2013) to 427,000 cited in the 2007 International Organization for Migration data (IOM 2007), to 766,000 provided by a Moscow-based sociological company for the British

Russian-speaking magazine *Zima* (2017).[2] All sources agree though that London has by far the UK's most numerous Russian-speaking population and is the major hub of Russophone cultural activity. In the superdiverse megapolis that London has now become (Blommaert 2010; 2013a; 2013b), the Russophone community stands out with its high visibility and its assertive display of cultural activity, which includes the Maslenitsa (Shrovetide) celebrations in Trafalgar Square, Russian balls, theatres, cultural centres, and a variety of community schools focusing on language, culture, maths, ballet, and other 'Russian skills'.

Given that culture is the major point of diasporic identification (Hall 1999), this chapter explores the patterns of construction and negotiation of transnational selves and community as have emerged from the discourse of interviews given by Russophone cultural leaders and entrepreneurs – those who organize cultural events or lead institutions of the kind listed above. While having Russian as their first language, the migrants in the focus of this research are limited neither to ethnic Russians nor to migrants from the Russian Federation. Rather, this is a loose group of people of various countries of origin (not restricted to the former Soviet states) who identify with the Russian language and Russian or Russophone cultures. Cultural leaders are fundamental in fostering the community-forming projects and in articulating the community's identity narratives.

In the analysis that follows, I will address the following questions: How do Russophone diasporic cultural leaders talk about their own transnational selves and their cultural activism and how does this talk shape the imagination of the Russophone diasporic communities in the UK? What are the discursive articulations of the respondents' transnational identities – in Brubaker's words, the 'idioms', the 'claims', and the 'stances'[3] that are used by the respondents and that indicate their perceived value of and allegiance to the various sides of the diasporic triad? And, finally, to what extent does their performance of identity display complexity, hybridity, and variation? In order to address these questions, the second part of the chapter will discuss examples from interviews with three cultural leaders conducted in London in 2017.

---

[2] Darya Malyutina explains why the statistical data concerning Russian-speaking migration to the UK varies and is not fully reliable: 'The data may be incomplete and imprecise for a number of reasons: the small size of the groups studied, gaps in methodology [...] lack or difficulty of access to particular groups (for example, irregular migrants)' (2015: 33).

[3] The stance is a 'display of evaluative, affective and epistemic orientations in discourse' (Bucholtz & Hall 2010: 22).

With the arrival to British shores of many representatives of the educated, creative, and affluent social groups of Russophones, the questions of what the Russian-speaking diaspora is and who can make claims to it have become a matter of intense coverage in both the Russian media and cultural productions. Among the latter was the 28-episode television series entitled *Londongrad*, which was screened in 2015 by Russia's STS television channel. The series worked as a sensational exposition of the UK-based Russophone community for the 'homeland' audience, in which the daily life and adventures of British Russophones became a subject of elaborate fictional scrutiny. Scripted by Michael Idov, a Russian-speaking Latvian-American writer and journalist, the show itself offered a transnational perspective on this community. While Idov's vision of his characters celebrated the cosmopolitan London-dwelling Russians who manifestly have no longing for their homeland (Ryazanova-Clarke, 2019),[4] the TV channel's top brass put its own spin on the interpretation by adding to the title the slogan *znai nashikh* (lit. 'know our own')[5] (Idov 2016). This phrase containing the pronoun *nashi* ('our', pl., meaning here 'of our kin', 'kindred people') served to requalify the Russian-speaking migrants not so much as new Londoners, or hybrid 'Londongradians', but rather as compatriots who belong to and are claimed by the country they left. Moreover, the added phrase is commonly used as a boastful and supporting cry, which implies a division between the *nashi* in-group and the non-*nashi* out-group while indicating a sense of the speaker's gleeful superiority over the out-group. The altered wording allowed STS to redefine the identity of the British Russian speakers and linguistically reappropriate them. In Idov's admission, in the post-Crimean context marked by the acceleration of confrontation between Russia and the West, the purpose of the intervention in the title of the series was 'To make it seem as if the show was about the Russians triumphing over the West, as opposed to integrating into it' (Idov 2016: 35).

The story of the two perspectives on the *Londongrad* characters illustrates the mechanism of the migrants' identity construction and negotiation. Diasporic identity-making proves to be a dialectic process produced from both the homeland and the diasporic spaces. It includes the top-down mobilization of diasporic activism, which may involve governments and official

---

[4] Stephen Hutchings has argued, however, that with Idov's influence receding towards the end of the series, the show's ideological messages were reoriented towards 'unambiguously traditional values, tinged with the tones of official patriotism' (2017: 153).

[5] A more fluent, non-literal translation of this Russian phrase would be 'this is how we do it!', however this does not fully render the sense of kinship, group belonging, and the emotional bond reflected in the Russian notion of *nashi*.

institutions engaged in operations known as 'soft power', 'cultural diplomacy', and 'outreach' (Byford 2012: 717), as well as bottom-up grass-roots community activism (Vertovec 2001; Barabantseva & Sutherland 2011; De Fina & Perrino 2013). The narrative presenting the global Russophone world outside Russia as *nashi* taps into Russia's prominent official discourse of Russkii Mir (The Russian World), which intends to define the increasingly overlapping notions of Russian-speaking, Russianness, and 'compatriotism'. In recent years, the Russkii Mir discourse has shown signs of evolving into Russia's official albeit loosely defined ideology predicated on the idea that the Russophone world is a separate and unified civilization (Vojtíšková et al. 2016; Suslov 2018). The idea of who the Russian compatriots[6] are has fluctuated over time from the decentred image of the 'Russian archipelago' in the 1990s to the 2000s assertion of Russian 'spheres of interests', to the current conservative irredentist and isolationist project advancing a Russo-centric, anti-Western, and neo-imperialist vision of global Russianness controlled by the Russian state (Byford 2012; Laruelle 2015a, 2015b; Grigas 2016; Nikolko & Carment 2017; Ryazanova-Clarke 2017; Suslov 2017, 2018).

The transnational vehicles to propagate the official Russkii Mir doctrine and to mobilize the compatriots across the world around its preferred version of Russophone identity were Kremlin-controlled organizations – the Russkiy Mir Foundation, whose primary aim is to promote the Russian language abroad, and the Federal Agency for the Commonwealth of Independent States, Compatriots Living Abroad, and International Humanitarian Cooperation (Rossotrudnichestvo), set up in 2007 and 2008, respectively.[7] The same purpose is served by the 1999 Law on State Policy of the Russian Federation with regard to Compatriots Abroad, which has since then undergone five amendments, showing just how painstakingly the officially prescribed compatriot identity has been negotiated and redefined over the years. This law has cast the diasporic net widely and, in addition to those with Russian or dual citizenship, embraces as compatriots those who merely descended from the territories of the Russian Federation and those who might have in the past held Soviet citizenship. In fact, belonging to the compatriot community is ultimately determined through self-identification and is non-obligatory. However, the

---

[6] The Russian term *sootechestvennik* (compatriot) is derived from the noun *otechestvo* (fatherland) and the shifts in the post-Soviet use of the term reflect the dynamics and trajectory of the top-down 'diasporic nation-building' undertaken by the Russian Federation.

[7] The Foundation operates the annual budget of €5.12m and Rossotrudnichestvo has €40m annually, which is expected to increase to €110m by 2020 (Vojtíšková et al. 2016: 29).

more recent amendments in 2010 and 2013 add stipulations for membership, which aim at cultivating in the diaspora loyalty to the Russian Federation and political support for the current regime. Thus, Article 3.2 states that a compatriot is expected to confirm his or her status by manifestly engaging in Russian cultural activism, namely, in 'public or professional activity aiming at the maintenance of the Russian language and other indigenous languages of the Russian Federation, the promotion of the Russian culture abroad', and 'to engage in public diplomacy in support of Russia in the country of their residence'[8] (Rossiiskaia Federatsiia 2013; Ryazanova-Clarke 2017: 5). In return, the rights and privileges of the compatriots provided by the law include, for example, a simplified procedure for obtaining Russian citizenship (Art. 11.1) and assistance in voluntary resettlement to the Russian Federation (Art. 13.1).

The next section of this chapter deals, however, with the analysis of the diasporic voices which relate to a different level of identity construction – the grass-roots, bottom-up dynamics. How do Russophone cultural leaders in the UK negotiate the image of themselves and of the community that they assume to be part of, represent, and lead in the face of the above constructions of global Russianness prescribed by such a powerful external agent as the Russian state?[9] The discussion focuses on three examples of Russophone cultural leaders residing in London. Their recorded interview transcripts are analysed for their deployment of linguistic resources to talk about the elements of the diasporic triad – the homeland, the host land, and the Russophone community built around their activity, including, of course, themselves as agents of this activity. These three conversations represent a small sample of the data from 95 semi-structured interviews which I conducted across the UK in 2017–18. The analysis does not aspire to arrive at an overall typology of

---

[8] In this chapter, all translations from Russian are my own.

[9] There are many different constructions of the global Russophone world by a variety of agents, from the Russian state to individuals who see themselves as part of this world. The term 'global Russians' was reputedly first used to refer to members of Snob – an exclusive virtual 'club' (which included a printed magazine and a subscription-only social media platform) of self-proclaimed globally dispersed cosmopolitan Russian 'elites'. This project's site defined 'global Russians' as 'people who live in various countries and speak various languages but think in Russian' (*O proekte* n.d.), although, over time, this label has disappeared from the club's members' self-description (Roesen 2011: 87). A very different meaning has been attached to 'global Russians' by transnational business, which uses it for top managers and executives from the Russian Federation (Podtserob 2016). The present chapter understands 'global Russianness' as a construct that translates someone's participation in the global Russophone world into a particular way of being 'Russian' it the contemporary globalized world, bearing in mind that different agents construct this 'global Russianness' differently.

Russophone identities and community imaginaries. Rather, it aims to demonstrate how discourse, set against the context of its emergence (the speaker's biographical data, behavioural repertoire,[10] etc.), reveals the mechanisms of cultural identity production in 'a constantly shifting description of ourselves' (Barker & Galasiński 2001: 30), and to illustrate the level of uniformity or variability of such identities. The three narrative examples have nevertheless been selected for the purpose of illustrating patterns of complexity and salient trends in identity and community construction, replicated in the larger data.

Self and Community in the Russophone Diasporic Imagination

Anna

Anna[11] works at a supplementary school dealing with the Russian language and culture. She is in her fifties, grew up and went to university in parts of the Soviet Union that are now independent states (Moldavia, Ukraine), and has been living in the UK since the early 1990s, so for a substantial part of her life. While she has never lived in Russia, she speaks passionately about her role as a promoter of Russian language and culture. In her story, Anna highlights that she was a founder of several international Russophone communities' cross-European activities and organizations, set up under the aegis of the Russian Federation, and that she was an active participant in major initiatives and events organized by the Russian government targeting compatriots, such as the annual International Compatriots Forums in Russia[12] hosted by the Russkiy Mir Foundation and the EU Russian Speakers' Alliance.[13]

Anna's discourse about her involvement with many initiatives supported by the Russian government displays a strong orientation[14] towards the official

---

[10] Behavioural repertoire is 'the actual range of forms of behaviour that people display, and that makes them identifiable as members of a culture' (Blommaert & Jie 2010).

[11] All participant names have been changed.

[12] To demonstrate the indoctrination work with compatriots, the 2018 Forum was held under the slogan 'Together with Russia', and declared its objectives to 'actively involve members of Russophone diaspora in the political life in Russia and in the forthcoming Russian Presidential elections'. The programme of events included the demonstration of a Ministry of Defence-developed project which counters the 'falsification' of the history of the Second World War, see <https://www.russkiymir.ru/the-forum-together-with-russia/> [accessed 15 April 2018].

[13] An organization of Russian speaking public figures, journalists and politicians living in the EU, co-founded and led by the Latvian pro-Russian MEP (2004–2018) Tat'iana Zhdanok (<https://eursa.eu/question/> [accessed 13 November 2019]).

[14] As Jan Blommaert explains, 'Identity discourses and practices can be described

Russian compatriot doctrine. For her, Russia is a 'homeland' and a 'cultural civilization' to which she belongs, and she marks her allegiance by her deployment of key words from the Russkii Mir discourse, such as 'compatriots' [sootechestvenniki], 'cultural code' [kul'turnyi kod], and Russian 'civilization',[15] and marks her stance towards the host state by using the word 'Russophobia' [rusofobiia], also from the vocabulary of Russian officialdom, not least when alleging anti-Russian attitudes in the UK.[16] She assumes a position of someone with roots in the Soviet Union ('I am reasoning from the point of view of a person who has lived here for 26 years and who came from the Soviet Union' [ia rassuzhdaiu s tochki zreniia cheloveka, kotoryi zhivet zdes' 26 let i vyekhal iz Sovetskogo Soiuza]) and re-enacts Soviet knowledge frames, practices, and rituals as elements of cultural community-building in her school. This is indicated, for example, in the personalities to whom she attributes cultural value. Her description of the children's song competitions she organizes reveals her pride in having Sergei Zakharov, a 1970s Soviet pop icon, as the competition's judge and patron (she uses the Russian officialese word *kurator*). Anna also describes how she engages the children at her school in activities evoking Soviet practices. Seeking to preserve tradition, she introduced a rule into her school that children must address their teachers by name and patronymic. She also assumes a romantic nostalgic tone for Soviet rituals as she justifies the adoption of the celebration of the Soviet and Russian Army Day on 23 February in her school, when boys get congratulations, cards, and gifts placed on their desks. In passages (1) and (2), we see how Anna's happy memories of her own Soviet school day practices inform their re-enactment as a diasporic ritual in London:

(1)
Anna: In my childhood, I used to give presents to the boys I fancied on the 23 February, and I had the most pleasant memory, and on the 8 March [International Women's Day], they would give me presents in return … and we danced so well then.

---

as discursive orientations towards sets of features that are seen (or can be seen) as emblematic of particular identities. These features can be manifold and include artifacts, styles, forms of language, places, times, forms of art or aesthetics, ideas, and so forth' (2013: 616).

[15] According to the nationalist and statist writer and philosopher Aleksandr Prokhanov (2014), it was Vladimir Putin who plucked the term 'Russian civilization' from the narrow usage of the small circle of conservative patriotic thinkers and introduced it into the vernacular.

[16] Russian official organizations tend to respond to criticisms of Russia's international behaviour, levelled by Western states, by claiming that its cause is the anti-Russian sentiment of those states, dubbed 'Russophobia'.

(2)

Anna: I will show you a card we made for our men here for the 23 February, very amusing. One of them, F., was born here so he does not quite understand what 23 February means (laughs).
Moderator: (laughs).
A: But in any case, he was amused, they got poems from the women and attention.
M: Umm.
A: And a nice little card [otkrytochku], why not? Who said that's bad?
M: Sure, but you might do that on 14 February instead.
A: Well no, 14 February [is very personal].
M: [Valentine][17]
A: It is very personal, it is <u>different</u>[18] [drugoe], it is. Yes, it is different ... This is what each of them will give to themselves [*sic*], within a couple.
M: Mm.
A: And here they put it around on the desks for everyone ... and here one could ... one could go a bit wild [razguliat'sia].

Showing allegiance to Soviet practices as they are transplanted to and naturalized in her school ('and a nice little card – why not?'), Anna discursively produces firm national boundaries and categorizes the British as an out-group, indexing this in a number of ways: qualifying British Valentine's Day practices as 'drugoe' (different, or Other), emphasizing this word with her tone and through its repetition. In contrast, she describes the Soviet/Russian Army Day celebration using the verb 'razguliat'sia' which is given positive, folksy, and poetic connotations.

The negative stance towards the host society may be detected in other parts of Anna's narrative where she uses generalizing negative depictions of the British, saying they are hostile to Russian speakers, and associates the public mood in the UK with 'Russophobic sentiments' [rusofobskie nastroeniia].

In addition, Anna assumes a negative stance towards bilingualism and biculturalism as she explains the motivations for Russophone children to join her school community. She discusses the imperfect Russian language skills of Russophone children from the Baltic states in terms of trauma

---

[17] Following the Jefferson Transcription System used widely in the transcription of interaction data, square brackets indicate overlapping utterances.
[18] Here and in the interview excerpts that follow, the words spoken with additional emphasis are underlined.

and psychological suffering. Anna explains that integration into a different society threatens children with a loss of their language and cultural identity, something that, in her evaluation, leads ultimately to a mental health condition, which only speaking Russian can heal. In (3) she talks about her school as a 'psychological centre' [psikhologicheskii tsentr] safeguarding children from a mental institution and, in (4), of a summer camp she organizes as 'psychologically important' therapy. She self-identifies as a saviour of such children by providing them with an experience of a community united by what she construes as an innate, instinctively felt Russophone temperament and 'cultural code':

(3)
Anna: So we prevent so many children from ... ahh ... will say crudely, from the lunatic asylum probably.

(4)
Anna: Being in such a camp ... is <u>very</u> therapeutic for them ... important, very psychologically important ... because suddenly they can socialize at the level of their temperament, their cultural code regardless of being from different countries, they understand with their guts what unites them.

Anna's narrative identifies her own self and imagines a version of a Russophone community which she links to the Russian cultural practices of celebrations, popular song festivals, schooling, and camping that she fosters. As she speaks and selects from her repertoire of meanings, she constructs a diasporic imaginary which valorizes the Soviet past and transmits many contemporary meanings that dominate the official Russian discourse. The activities she endorses (the Army Day celebrations, the activities of the compatriot network) and her discursive performance display a high level of allegiance to the Russia-promoted Russkii Mir doctrine. At the same time, she complained on several occasions that despite embracing the *sootechestvenniki* movement and values, she felt abandoned by the Russian authorities and that the little funding she used to receive in support of her cultural enterprise had dwindled over time. In terms of her stance towards the host land, she depicts a chasm between 'Russianness' and 'British life' as she imagines these, seeing a flaw in cultural hybridization and integration.

However, Anna further demonstrates more complexity, admitting to her own hybrid identity. When asked whether she has any British side to her, she changes her discursive strategy and repositions herself as a Brit – a fluent English speaker, an admirer of English culture, and a provider of jobs in

London. She marks this side of her identity by unexpectedly switching from Russian to English for the chunky length of 300 words.

(5)
M: Well, you have lived here so long … don't you feel at least a little bit English or British? [a vot vse-taki, vy tak dolgo zdes' zhivete, vy ne chuvstvuete sebia niskol'ko anglichankoi, ili britankoi?]
Anna: (in Russian) Well, you know, I very much … [a vy znaete, ia ochen'] (in English) I can speak English quite well, this is umm, my favourite country in the world.
M: Umm.
A: And I studied British culture very well and British history umm … I adore this country absolutely … and when I came to this country, well, I did have an illusion that I would be, absolutely English.

In other parts of her conversation, Anna does not mix her Russian and English and this code-switching episode indicates that in her linguistic repertoire, English seems to be treated as a rigidly different, insular code suitable specifically to perform her 'Englishness'. However, even while expressing her adoration for England and its culture, Anna talks about the impossibility of being English when you have a Russian heritage, and frames her love for England as a youthful, romantic illusion. Overall, Anna's narrative demonstrates that 'Britishness' and 'Russianness' sit uneasily in her imagination, living a conflictual, fractured coexistence. Like many Russian speakers, she equates Englishness and Britishness, but the idealized image of the country she lives in is probably a reflection of Soviet-era idealizations of a nineteenth-century genteel monocultural England. This image is at odds with today's complex, multicultural Britain, which she has to reckon with, not only as a lover of quintessential English culture but also as a member of a migrant minority. Consequently, she construes superdiverse London communities as a racially compartmentalized, competitive terrain of zero-sum games, characterized by discriminatory attitudes towards Russians.

(6)
Anna: Unfortunately, from the British authorities, apart from our football club, some trifles towards our football club, we could never get any funding, ever. That is to say, hmm, to help the black community, yes, that's fine, then there is a strong Jewish diaspora in … our area, they receive good financing, but in my experience, Russian-speaking organizations struggle very much.

Boris

My second respondent, Boris (late twenties), is an executive responsible for organizing a high-profile Russian film event in London. Like Anna, Boris has never lived in Russia: he was born and spent his early childhood in Sweden and then went to an elite private school and university in the UK. He is fluent in three languages – Swedish, his first language, English, and Russian, his mother tongue (i.e. the language that his parents used with him at home). Although Boris has a day job as a business investor, he explains his commitment to Russian cultural activism drawing on his Russian identity, which he defines through his ethnicity ('I am Russian by blood', he says) and through his parents' cultural heritage, citing, for instance, his father as a collector of Russian art, including film posters. Boris's narrative positions him close to some of Russia's official organizations – he speaks about how he has collaborated with the EU Russian Speakers' Alliance as a member of its youth wing and how, as a student, he organized the Russian Economic Weeks at his university, which featured among the guests President Medvedev and Foreign Minister Lavrov. He discursively marks his allegiance to the Russian officials by telling a story of his selection to run the programme of Russian film events, focusing on the details of the names, titles, and positions of high-powered Russians and using their words for his positive self-categorization as a 'quality person':

(7)
Boris: When last year there was the literature and language cross-cultural year in England ... and in Russia, it was the year of <u>film</u>. I was approached, to be more precise, the ambassador of the Russian Federation was approached by Mikhail Shvydkoi who is ah, in culture, the adviser to the president and also works in the Foreign Ministry.
Moderator: Uh-huh.
B.: And he approached the ambassador, said if there are people who can, quality people ... so to speak, who could organize a film event.
M.: Uh-huh.
B: Uh-huh. The ambassador approached me and said would you like ... you have organized plenty of things ... would you like to take on cinema ... And at that moment, I was fully immersed in my business ... and I thought this was an interesting challenge.

These discursive tools indicate Boris's positive stance regarding official Russian soft power initiatives and operations, the components of the Russkii Mir doctrine. His stance is also manifested in the details he brings in. For example, he mentions that he endorsed the Golden Unicorn as the prize to be awarded at the film event he was responsible for, and he justifies this with the argument that a unicorn is a symbol connecting Russia and Britain. He explains that while featuring in the British crown arms, a unicorn can also be found in one of Ivan the Terrible's state seals. References to Ivan the Terrible have become popular in the current dominant Russian political discourse, which aims to rehabilitate the tyrant for contemporary political expediency. Boris here seems quite eager to facilitate the transmission of this particular flow of cultural and political semantics.

In his narrative, Boris identifies himself as a globally aware, well-connected, urbane, and cosmopolitan Russian who, being British-educated, is well integrated into British life. At some point, he says that as a product of three cultures, he 'has no identity'. But then his discourse shows that while he feels no allegiance to Sweden, he combines an emotional attachment to his imagined homeland – Russia, a place he has only visited and never lived in – with the claim that, over time, Britain has become his home. In general, Boris's orientations are, in equal measure, to Russia, the UK, and to the wider cosmopolitan world: 'I like London, I like Los Angeles, perhaps New York ... or Moscow, I would be glad to [live in] Moscow. In principle, I do not mind where I live as long as there are opportunities and work. Currently, these are in London'. In addition, his complex, or at least double, belonging is indexed by his performance of connectedness at the top level of the British and Russian states, which may be seen in his strategy of name dropping in reference to both Russian and British elites – the ambassador, Mikhail Shvydkoi, but also Prince Michael and the art auctioneer William MacDougal. Yet another strategy that Boris chooses for his discursive performance of a hybrid self is his smooth use of Russian-English code mixing. In the conversation of bi- and multilinguals, both code-switching and code-mixing strategies are usually indicative of group belonging (Auer 1998). But while in Anna's conversation the two distinct codes are presented as two different universes tearing the speaker's self apart, throughout Boris's talk, his flawless English phrases slip mid-sentence into his sophisticated Russian, arriving at a blended complexity of his linguistic repertoire.[19] For example, 'interesnyi [interesting] challenge', 'u menia bol'shaia industry programma' [I have a large industry programme], 'my ne znaem local publiku' [we do not know the local public], 'nachali [began] with a big bang', and 'my obrashchaemsia [we approach] proactively'. The deployment of these units indexes a choice of a semiotic system affected by a transnational condition and cosmopolitan lifestyle, and enables Boris to play an 'authentic', 'hyphenated', unconflicted identity. Perhaps because of

---

[19] Jan Blommaert (2013a; 2013b) argues that in the context of mobility, complexity is a more accurate frame for describing language and identity work, in contrast to codes as ontologically intact linguistic units.

this, in many contexts, Boris departs from the Russkii Mir discursive script – rather than referring to 'compatriots', he is more comfortable with the more neutral term 'diaspora', and, contrary to the Russian traditional premise of the collective, he construes the Russophone community as organized around himself, as in the following exchange.

(8)
Moderator: Do you feel yourself part of the Russian diaspora?
Boris: Of course, what would I do without it? [Konechno, kak zhe bez nee?]
M: And what makes you part of the diaspora?
B: Well, I have done a lot for it … Well, I don't know, about 30,000 attended my events.

When speaking outside the context of the events he organized, Boris is critical about the UK Russophone community, applying distancing strategies in reference to its members. The diaspora emerges from his discourse as an entity separate from himself and is emphatically negatively characterized: 'The Russian diaspora is very disorganized, very chaotic, and very passive', he says. He therefore sees his mission as organizing and educating the diaspora. However, unlike Anna, he does not target his activities solely at Russophones. The Russian film event that he organizes has elements of a traditional British red-carpet event, which involves members of the British cinema establishment and British audiences, and in this way is transcultural and hybrid, reaching out to both constituencies.

Boris's narrative clearly displays a hybrid diasporic identity and presents an example of a 'prosthetic' (Appadurai 1996: 96) homeland allegiance as he shows a high level of orientation to the Russia of his imagination, where he has never lived and whose language is not his first language. Being global and British does not prevent him, though, from internalizing and promoting aspects of the Russkii Mir imaginary, as facilitated by the Russian state.

Aleksandr

My third respondent is Aleksandr, a man in his forties, a former Muscovite and an employee of a London-based political organization which actively opposes the current Russian authorities. Aleksandr is involved in organizing hundreds of events as part of this organization's campaign programme: lectures by political and cultural figures, film screenings, and debates which are attended by thousands of Russian-speaking Londoners. While living in Russia, Aleksandr used to work for the figure who acts as this organization's principal sponsor and he then emigrated with him to Britain in 2013 in a move that he describes as 'a flight, an evacuation', emphasizing the dramatic emergency of his departure. Aleksandr positions himself in his narrative as an exile, a refugee, and he defines his migration as a 'very non-standard story', thereby separating himself from the wider migrant community. He says he did not choose the UK as his host country and is not going to return to his homeland until radical changes at the top of Russian power have occurred. His association with Britain appears to be distant – while he accepts with some hesitancy that his home is now in Britain, he uses the pronoun 'they' when referring to the host society (see (9) below) and admits that his English is not fluent and that he speaks it infrequently. He positions himself, through the story of his travels, as someone whose identity is global rather than British. His discourse displays a salient orientation to his homeland and is characterized by the semantics of lack and nonexistence. His story rescales Russia – his vision of homeland zooms into the local area of Moscow and the house where he spent his childhood, which is now reconstructed to an unrecognizable state. 'Personally, I have no nostalgia at all. What does it mean? Perhaps, I do have some warm memories of the place where I was born and grew up. It was in the centre of Moscow. It does not exist any more. Simply. It is no more', he says, stressing the sense of absence with his shortened incomplete sentences as he proceeds. A stark contrast to Anna's memories lamenting the loss of the Soviet era, Aleksandr's memories of Russia focus on the intimate as he switches register from business-like to poetic and contradicts his earlier statement by displaying a nostalgic stance: 'that house with a quiet courtyard ... and a quiet, wonderful garden full of maple leaves'.

Given the sheer volume of practices and activities in which Aleksandr's organization engages in London, it has considerable potential to promote its philosophy of liberal, democratic, and ethical values among the diaspora, and to try to mobilize and shape the UK Russophone community around them. And yet Aleksandr's discourse produces little by way of imagining a diasporic community and refuses to see British Russophones as a group he can define and relate to. While both Anna and Boris negotiated the term for the Russophone community they constructed, Anna preferring 'compatriots' and Boris 'diaspora', Aleksandr is uneasy about what label to use. This is evidenced in his hedging in (9), which stands for his torturous hesitancy and, ultimately, his inability to find a term, or a description, to define the people who attend his events. As in his narrative about his homeland, Aleksandr ends up conceding that he is attempting to define a void.

(9)
Aleksandr: Well, I have a lot ... of contacts and links ...
Moderator: Hmm.

A.: ... well ... with Russians ... loosely speaking [uslovno], Russians ...

M.: Uh well, Russians, yeah, we always say, loosely speaking.

A.: Well, yes, let's say.

M.: It's very difficult with Russian speakers ... compatriots ... diaspora too.

A.: None of these describe this category fully enough and ... from all angles.

M.: And is there any word that describes them?

A.: Hmm. I don't think so ... I actually have no single word that in any way fully ... would describe those people who could here be provisionally called Russians.

M.: Uh-uh.

A.: Well, not talking about whom the British call 'Russians' ... Look at their 'Meet the Russians' series.

M.: Yes, yes, yes (laughs).

A: (laughs) Where, to be honest, if you look ... there are no Russians ... at all.

This excerpt manifestly demonstrates that Aleksandr deploys the discursive strategies of community dismantling as opposed to the strategies of community construction (Wodak et al. 2009) that may otherwise have been expected from a cultural leader. Furthermore, in another part of his discourse, he linguistically devalues the members of the Russophone community, saying that for his organization, the audience attending its events in London is of 'least importance' [imeet piatoe znachenie].

We can, therefore, observe that the diasporic triad emerging from Aleksandr's talk is missing a community-building core. The political activity of his organization, he claims, is fully directed at the homeland and although it stages events in London, the real aim is to effect change in Russia. And British Russophones, he maintains, have little to do with that. The imaginary that Aleksandr's discourse presents is a form of political transnationalism, or 'homeland politics' (Vertovec 2009: 93). It involves mobilization for consciousness-raising and a long-term preparation for transformation in Russia, but unlike the textbook political mobilization in exile, it downplays the role of diaspora engagement in such mobilization.

Conclusion

The three narratives of UK-based Russophone cultural leaders and entrepreneurs presented in this chapter show that the patterns of self and community construction vary as all three respondents diverge in the meanings and values they ascribe to their transnational selves and to cultural activism, and to the host country, homeland, and diasporic community they imagine. In other words, these grass-roots agents discursively negotiate what transnational Russophone identity and community are, producing stances, idioms, and claims of belonging. While constructing their images of self and community, the speakers engage in a dialogue not only with other community facilitating actors like themselves but also with the Russian state's Russkii Mir doctrine.

Anna's version of Russophone transnational self has a prominent element oriented to her imagined homeland constructed from her Soviet memories, which seems to sit uneasily with the partially integrated 'British' element in her nevertheless hybrid identity. Her allegiance to the deceased Soviet Union experienced from its non-Russian peripheries conflicts with her Russia-oriented narrative and further complicates her identity imagination. She embraces the Russkii Mir discourse and the practices it promotes, and naturalizes them in the school and camp communities she oversees, but also produces a resentful litany when, despite her expressed loyalty, resources from Russia are not forthcoming for her cultural undertakings. Thus, the transnational identity Anna imagines is complex and fractured, as manifested, among other things, in her use of the discursive strategies of boundary construction, code switching, and metaphors of psychological trauma.

Boris displays an identity narrative which may be described as 'happy hybridity' (Otsuji & Pennycook 2010). It is aligned with the semantics produced by the Russian elites and at the same time is well integrated into the British middle class, his language indexing his belonging to both. He constructs the Russian side of his identity through loyalty to his imagined, prosthetic homeland and is amenable to the soft power semiotics of the Russkii Mir doctrine, which blends effortlessly with his cosmopolitan, global self. The Russophone community he imagines is generally deficient and he sees his role as improving it through cultural education and events organization. However, his cultural work does more than Russophone community-building – the Russian film events he organizes are well integrated into the contemporary British cultural scene and serve as a contact zone in London's superdiverse urban cosmopolitan environment. Boris's example thus illustrates how the 'Russianness' promoted by Russian-speaking cultural entrepreneurs may not only build a Russophone community of a specific kind but also affect, blend with, and potentially reconfigure segments of wider British society.

Aleksandr portrays himself as a political exile of a new type – well-travelled, non-nostalgic, and cosmopolitan – but also reveals a detached stance towards his host country. His cultural and political activism aims to achieve changes in his homeland, which, however, in its current state, he describes in terms of 'nonexistence'. Being in disagreement with the current Russian regime, as might be expected, he sees no relevance in the narratives of Russkii Mir and the compatriots. At the same time, he creates no diasporic imagination to counter them: he acknowledges no diasporic community that could be mobilized, struggling to define the attendees of the events he organizes.

On account of the endless time and energy that these three cultural leaders invest in promoting the Russian language and Russian culture through their respective projects, they would all, no doubt, qualify for compatriot status as per Russia's Compatriots Law. In terms of responding to the mobilizing influence exerted by the Russian official compatriot narratives, the three interviews may be placed on a scale from following those narratives closely, in the case of Anna, to their full rejection, in the case of Aleksandr, with Boris's discourse standing somewhere in the middle. However, while Anna's discourse seems to be overdetermined by the Russkii Mir doctrine and heavily layered with Russian official semiotics, on closer examination, even her narrative exposes her independent agency in adopting stances that appear to counter that doctrine (for example, taking issue with Russian compatriot organizations, or presenting herself as a job provider in Britain). Rather than falling unequivocally into the Russia-determined mould of compatriots, the three narratives, projected by individuals who position themselves and act (in different ways) as cultural leaders, demonstrate the considerable variety, complexity, and fluidity that characterize Russophone identities in the diaspora, revealing a whole set of internal conflicts, while at the same time opening up spaces for further grass-roots identity imagination.

Works Cited

Acharya, Malasree. 2016. 'Cosmopolitanism' in Noel Salazar and Kiran Jayaram (eds), *Keywords of Mobility: Critical Engagements* (New York: Berghahn Books), 33–54.

Anderson, Benedict. 1991. *Imagined Communities* (London: Verso).

Appadurai, Arjun. 1996. *Modernity at Large* (Minneapolis, MN: University of Minnesota Press).

Auer, Peter (ed.). 1998. *Code-switching in Conversation: Language, Interaction and Identity* (London: Routledge).

Barabantseva, Elena, and Claire Sutherland. 2011. 'Diaspora and Citizenship: Introduction', *Nationalism and Ethnic Politics*, 17(1): 1–13.

Barker, Chris, and Dariusz Galasiński. 2001. *Critical Studies and Discourse Analysis: A Dialogue on Language and Identity* (London: Sage).

Baubök, Rainer, and Thomas Faist (eds). 2010. *Diaspora and Transnationalism: Concepts, Theories and Methods* (Amsterdam: Amsterdam University Press).

Benwell, Bethen, and Elizabeth Stokoe. 2006. *Discourse and Identity* (Edinburgh: Edinburgh University Press).

Bhabha, Homi. 1994. *The Location of Culture* (London: Routledge).

Blommaert, Jan. 2010. *The Sociolinguistics of Globalization* (Cambridge: Cambridge University Press).

——. 2013a. *Ethnography, Superdiversity and Linguistic Landscapes: Chronicles of Complexity* (Bristol: Multilingual Matters).

——. 2013b. 'Complexity, Accent and Conviviality: Concluding Comments', *Applied Linguistics*, 34(5): 613–22.

Blommaert, Jan, and Dong Jie. 2010. *Ethnographic Fieldwork: A Beginner's Guide* (Bristol: Multilingual Matters).

Brubaker, Rogers. 2005. 'The "Diaspora" Diaspora', *Ethnic and Racial Studies*, 28(1): 1–19.

——. 2017. 'Revisiting "The 'Diaspora' Diaspora"', *Ethnic and Racial Studies* 40(9): 1556–61.

Bucholtz, Mary, and Kira Hall. 2010. 'Locating Identity in Language' in Carmen Llamas and Dominic Watt (eds), *Language and Identity* (Edinburgh: Edinburgh University Press), 18–28.

Byford, Andy. 2012. 'The Russian Diaspora in International Relations: "Compatriots" in Britain', *Europe-Asia Studies*, 64(4): 715–35.

De Fina, Anna. 2011. 'Discourse and Identity' in Teun van Dijk (ed.), *Discourse Studies: A Multidisciplinary Introduction* (Los Angeles: Sage), 263–83.

——. 2016. 'Linguistic Practices and Transnational Identities' in Sian Preece (ed.), *The Routledge Handbook of Language and Identity* (London: Routledge), 163–79.

De Fina, Anna, and Sabina Perrino. 2013. 'Transnational Identities', *Applied Linguistics*, 34(5): 509–15.

De Fina, Anna, Debora Schiffrin, and Michael Bamberg (eds). 2006. *Discourse and Identity* (Cambridge: Cambridge University Press).

Dervin, Fred, and Karen Risager (eds). 2015. *Researching Identity and Interculturality* (New York: Routledge).

Grigas, Agnia. 2016. *Beyond Crimea: The New Russian Empire* (New Haven, CT: Yale University Press).

Gupta, Akhil, and James Ferguson. 1992. 'Beyond Identity: Space, Culture and the Politics of Difference', *Cultural Anthropology*, 7(1): 6–23.

Hall, Stuart. 1999. 'Cultural Identity and Diaspora' in Nicholas Mirzoeff (ed.), *Diaspora and Visual Culture* (London: Routledge), 21–34.

Hall, Stuart, and Paul Du Gay (eds). 1996. *Questions of Cultural Identity* (London: Sage).

Hoffman, Eva. 1998. 'The New Nomads', *Yale Review*, 86(4): 43–58.

Hutchings, Stephen. 2017. 'A Home from Home: Recursive Nationhood, the 2015 STS Television Serial, *Londongrad*, and Post-Soviet *Stiob*', *Russian Journal of Communication*, 9(2): 142–57.

Idov, Michael. 2016. 'Situation Comedy: My Strange Phenomenally Successful Career as an American Screenwriter in Russia', *The New York Times Magazine*, 1 October, 30–36.

IOM (International Organization for Migration). 2007. *Russia: Mapping Exercise*, London, July 2007.

Laruelle, Marlene. 2015a. 'Russia as a "Divided Nation", from Compatriots to Crimea': A Contribution to the Discussion of Nationalism and Foreign Policy', *Problems of Post-Communism*, 62(2): 88–97.

——. 2015b. 'The Russian World: Russia's Soft Power and Geopolitical Imagination', Centre on Global Interests, May <globalinterests.org> [accessed 23 July 2017].

Malyutina, Darya. 2015. *Migrant Friendship in a Super-Diverse City: Russian Speakers and their Social Relationships in London in the 21ˢᵗ Century* (Stuttgart: Ibidem-Verlag).

Nikolko, Milana, and David Carment (eds). 2017. *Post-Soviet Migration and Diasporas* (Oxford: Palgrave Macmillan).

O proekte. Snob. n.d. <https://snob.ru/basement> [accessed 12 July 2018].

ONS (Office of National Statistics). 2011. <http://www.nomisweb.co.uk/census/2011> [accessed 23 June 2017].

Otsuji, Emi, and Alastair Pennycook. 2010. 'Metrolingualism, Fixity, Fluidity and Language in Flux', *International Journal of Multilingualism*, 7(3): 240–54.

Podtserob, Maria. 2016. 'Kto takie "global'nye russkie" i pochemu ikh zhdut rossiiskie rabotadateli', *Vedomosti*, 23 June <https://www.vedomosti.ru/management/articles/2016/06/23/646436-globalnie-russkie> [accessed 7 February 2018].

Prokhanov, Aleksandr. 2014. 'Putin vvel termin 'Russkaia tsivilizatsiia', *Russkaia narodnaia liniia*, 18 January <http://ruskline.ru/news_rl/2014/01/18/aleksandr_prohanov_putin_vvel_termin_russkaya_civilizaciya/> [accessed 28 June 2018].

Richards, Greg. 2015. 'The New Global Nomads: Youth Travel in a Globalizing World', *Tourism Recreation Research*, 40(3): 340–52.

Roesen, Tine. 2011. 'www.snob.ru: A Social Network Site for the Elite', *Digital Icons*, 6: 81–92.

Rosello, Mireille. 2001. *Postcolonial Hospitality: The Immigrant as Guest* (Stanford, CA: Stanford University Press).

Rossiiskaia Federatsiia. 2013. 'Federal'nyi Zakon "O Gusudarstvennoi politike Rossiiskoi Federatsii v otnoshenii sootechestvennikov za rubezhom"', 99-FZ <http://www.consultant.ru/document/cons_doc_LAW_23178/4733d92796950eff2201181bdbcf75ca68fa7ddc/> [accessed 12 April 2018].

Ryazanova-Clarke, Lara. 2017. 'From Commodification to Weaponization: The Russian Language as "Pride" and "Profit" in Russia's Transnational Discourses', *International Journal of Bilingual Education and Bilingualism*, 20(4): 443–56.

——. 2019. 'Londongrad as a Linguistic Imaginary: Russophone Migrants in the UK in the Work of Michael Idov and Andrei Ostalsky' in Per Arne Boudin and Mikhail Suslov (eds), *The Post-Soviet Politics of Utopia: Language, Fiction and Fantasy in Modern Russia* (London: I. B. Tauris), 235–57.

Suslov, Mikhail. 2017. *Russian World: Russia's Policy Towards its Diaspora*, IFRI, July <https://www.ifri.org/en/publications/notes-de-lifri/russieneivisions/russian-world-russias-policy-towards-its-diaspora> [accessed 23 March 2018].

——. 2018. '"Russian World" Concept: Post-Soviet Geopolitical Ideology and the Logic of "Spheres of Interest"', *Geopolitics*, 23(2): 330–353.

United Nations Department of Economic and Social Affairs. 2015. 'Trends in International Migration, 2015', *Population Facts*, 4 <http://www.un.org/en/development/desa/population/migration/publications/populationfacts/docs/MigrationPopFacts20154.pdf> [accessed 23 March 2018].

Vertovec, Steven. 2001. 'Transnationalism and Identity', *Journal of Ethnic and Migration Studies*, 27(4): 573–82.

——. 2009. *Transnationalism* (London: Routledge).

Vojtíšková, Vladislava, Vít Novotný, Hubertus Schmid-Schmidsfelden, and Kristina Potapova. 2016. *The Bear in Sheep's Clothing: Russia's Government-Funded Organisations in the EU* (Brussels: Wilfried Martens Centre for European Studies).

Waldinger, Roger. 2003. 'Foreword' in Stéphane Dufoix, *Diasporas* (Berkeley, CA: University of California Press), xi–xviii.

Wodak, Ruth. 2012. 'Language, Power and Identity', *Language Teaching*, 45(2): 215–33.

Wodak, Ruth, and Salomi Boukala. 2015. '(Supra)national Identity and Language: Rethinking National and European Migration Policies and the Linguistic Integration of Migrants', *Annual Review of Applied Linguistics*, 35: 253–73.

Wodak, Ruth, Rudolf De Cillia, Martin Reisigl, and Karen Liebhart. 2009. *The Discursive Construction of National Identity*, 2nd ed. (Edinburgh: Edinburgh University Press).

Zhu Hua. 2017. 'New Orientations to Identity in Mobility' in Suresh Canagarajah (ed.), *The Routledge Handbook of Migration and Language* (London: Routledge), 117–32.

Zima. 2017. 'Russkoiazychnye v Britanii', 30 October <https://zimamagazine.com/2017/10/russian-speaking-in-britain/> [accessed 12 November 2017].

Index